Praise for the First Edition

This is an excellent work, a worthy successor to others in Manning's "In Action" series. It is highly readable and chock-full of working code. The Lab pages are a marvelous way to explore the library, which should become an important part of every web developer's arsenal. Five stars all 'round!

—David Sills, JavaLobby, Dzone

I highly recommend the book for learning the fundamentals of jQuery and then serving as a good reference book as you leverage the power of jQuery more and more in your daily development.

—David Hayden, MVP C#, Codebetter.com

The Elements of Style *for JavaScript.*

—Joshua Heyer, Trane Inc.

For those new to jQuery, this book is a good primer that covers a range of common uses of the framework.... The examples throughout the book are relevant, and make the point effectively. The code snippets are easily distinguishable from the rest of the text, and the text is clear and easy to follow.

—Grant Palin, Blogger

It works and makes for a very readable book that you can just breeze through very quickly and pick up and retain a lot of information.

—Rich Strahl, Blogger

Thanks to the authors Bear Bibeault and Yehuda Katz and their exemplary style, this comprehensive book, or operating manual as it might be called, can be taken in a front-to-back approach to learn from scratch, or as a reference to those already dabbling in jQuery and needing verification of best practices.

—Matthew McCullough,
Denver Open Source Users Group

With its capable technical coverage, extensive use of sample code, and approachable style, jQuery in Action *is a valuable resource for any Web developer seeking to maximize the power of JavaScript, and a must-have for anyone interested in learning jQuery.*

—Michael J. Ross,
Web Developer, Slashdot Contributor

More Praise for the First Edition

jQuery in Action

Second Edition

BEAR BIBEAULT
YEHUDA KATZ

MANNING
Greenwich
(74° w. long.)

Manning Publications Co.   Development editor: Lianna Wlasiuk
180 Broad St.   Copyeditor: Andy Carroll
Suite 1323   Typesetter: Dottie Marsico
Stamford, CT 06901   Cover designer: Marija Tudor

Third, corrected printing, December 2010
ISBN 978-1-935182-32-0
Printed in the United States of America
4 5 6 7 8 9 10 – MAL – 15 14 13 12 11

brief contents

contents

list of lab pages

foreword to the first edition

It's all about simplicity. Why should web developers be forced to write long, complex, book-length pieces of code when they want to create simple pieces of interaction? There's nothing that says that complexity has to be a requirement for developing web applications.

When I first set out to create jQuery I decided that I wanted an emphasis on small, simple code that served all the practical applications that web developers deal with day to day. I was greatly pleased as I read through *jQuery in Action* to see in it an excellent manifestation of the principles of the jQuery library.

With an overwhelming emphasis on practical, real-world code presented in a terse, to-the-point format, *jQuery in Action* will serve as an ideal resource for those looking to familiarize themselves with the library.

What's pleased me the most about this book is the significant attention to detail that Bear and Yehuda have paid to the inner workings of the library. They were thorough in their investigation and dissemination of the jQuery API. It felt like nary a day went by in which I wasn't graced with an email or instant message from them asking for clarification, reporting newly discovered bugs, or recommending improvements to the library. You can be safe knowing that the resource that you have before you is one of the best thought-out and researched pieces of literature on the jQuery library.

One thing that surprised me about the contents of this book is the explicit inclusion of jQuery plugins and the tactics and theory behind jQuery plugin development. The reason why jQuery is able to stay so simple is through the use of its plugin architecture. It provides a number of documented extension points upon which plugins can add functionality. Often that functionality, while useful, is not generic enough for inclusion in jQuery itself—which is what makes the plugin architecture necessary. A few of the plugins discussed in this book, like the Forms, Dimension, and LiveQuery plugins, have seen widespread adoption and the reason is obvious: They're expertly constructed, documented, and maintained. Be sure to pay special attention to how plugins are utilized and constructed as their use is fundamental to the jQuery experience.

With resources like this book, the jQuery project is sure to continue to grow and succeed. I hope the book will end up serving you well as you begin your exploration and use of jQuery.

JOHN RESIG
CREATOR OF jQUERY

preface to the second edition

It's been two years since the first edition of *jQuery in Action* was published. Was it really necessary to update the book so soon?

Absolutely!

Compared to the steady world of server-side languages such as Java, the client-side technologies of the web move at a mighty fast clip. And jQuery isn't eating anyone's dust; rather, it's at the forefront of the rush!

The jQuery team releases a major new version of the library just about every year (lately, striving for every January), in addition to the minor updates that are made throughout the calendar year. That means that there have been numerous minor releases, and two major versions since the publication of the first edition, which was written against jQuery 1.2. And what updates jQuery 1.3 and jQuery 1.4 have been!

With each major release, the capabilities of jQuery have been extended and enhanced in significant ways. Whether it be the addition of custom events, event namespaces, function and effect queuing, or simply the large handful of really useful methods and functions that have been added, the range of capabilities that jQuery spans has increased significantly since the first edition hit the stands.

And that doesn't even consider jQuery UI! In its nascent stages two years ago, jQuery UI merited a few sections in one chapter of the first edition. Since then, jQuery UI has grown in scope and maturity and warrants a complete book part in this edition, consisting of three full chapters.

So it should come as no surprise that this second edition has made its way onto the shelves covering the advances that jQuery and jQuery UI have made over the past two years.

What's new in the second edition?

When we decided to go ahead with creating a second edition of *jQuery in Action*, I remember someone saying to me, "Should be a piece of cake. After all, you just need to make some updates to the first edition."

How wrong they were! It actually took longer to complete this second edition than to write the book in the first place. You see, we didn't want to fall into the trap of "phoning it in" by just adding updates here and there and calling it done. We wanted this second edition to be much more than a warmed over version of the first edition.

Anyone comparing the table of contents of the first and second editions of this book will note that the structure of chapters 1 through 8 hasn't changed all that much. But that's pretty much where the similarities stop.

This second edition isn't just a tepid rehash of the first edition with some extra information sprinkled here and there. Each and every paragraph in the text, and each and every line in the example code, has undergone a careful inspection. Not only have the additions and changes made to jQuery between versions 1.2 and 1.4 been taken into account, the information in the chapters and the example code have been updated to reflect current best practices regarding page scripting and the use of jQuery. After all, as a community, we've got two more years of experience writing highly interactive scripted pages using jQuery under our belts.

Every example has been examined and either updated to better show how to use jQuery 1.4 in practice, or replaced with an example that is better suited to showcasing the concepts being discussed. For example, readers of the first edition may remember the comprehensive Bamboo Grille example at the end of chapter 4 that highlighted jQuery event handling. Try as we might, we were unable to reshape that example to flaunt the newest jQuery event handling concepts, such as "live" and custom events. So it has been completely replaced with the DVD Ambassador example that serves as a better vehicle for demonstrating the advanced event-handling concepts.

The second part of the book, focusing on jQuery UI, is completely new material, covering the extensive changes that jQuery UI has undergone since the first edition was published.

We'd estimate that, counting the additions, replacements, and updates of the material presented throughout the first part of the book, as well as the completely new content of part 2, that at least 50 percent of this second edition is brand new material. The other 50 percent has undergone extensive rework to ensure that it is up to date and reflective of modern best practices.

So much for the "piece of cake"!

preface to the first edition

One of your authors is a grizzled veteran whose involvement in programming dates back to when FORTRAN was the bomb, and the other is an enthusiastic domain expert, savvy beyond his years, who's barely ever known a world without an Internet. How did two people with such disparate backgrounds come together to work on a joint project?

The answer is, obviously, *jQuery*.

The paths by which we came together over our affection for this most useful of client-side tools are as different as night and day.

I (Bear) first heard of jQuery while I was working on *Ajax in Practice*. Near the end of the creation cycle of a book is a whirlwind phase known as the *copyedit* when the chapters are reviewed for grammatical correctness and clarity (among other things) by the copyeditor and for technical correctness by the technical editor. At least for me, this is the most frenetic and stressful time in the writing of a book, and the *last* thing I want to hear is "you really should add a completely new section."

One of the chapters I contributed to *Ajax in Practice* surveys a number of Ajax-enabling client-side libraries, one of which I was already quite familiar with (Prototype) and others (the Dojo Toolkit and DWR) on which I had to come up to speed pretty quickly.

While juggling what seemed like a zillion tasks (all the while holding down a day job, running a side business, and dealing with household issues), the technical editor, Valentin Crettaz, casually drops this bomb: "So why don't you have a section on jQuery?"

"J who?" I asked.

I was promptly treated to a detailed dissertation on how wonderful this fairly new library was and how it really should be part of any modern examination of Ajax-enabling client-side libraries. I asked around a bit. "Have any of you ever heard of this jQwerty library?"

I received a large number of positive responses, all enthusiastic and all agreeing that jQuery really was the cat's pajamas. On a rainy Sunday afternoon, I spent about four hours at the jQuery site reading documentation and writing little test programs to get a feel for the jQuery way of doing things. Then I banged out the new section and sent it to the technical editor to see if I had really gotten it.

The section was given an enthusiastic thumb's up, and we went on to finally complete the *Ajax in Practice* book. (That section on jQuery eventually went on to be published in the online version of *Dr. Dobb's Journal.*)

When the dust had settled, my frenzied exposure to jQuery had planted relentless little seeds in the back of my mind. I'd liked what I'd seen during my headlong research into jQuery, and I set out to learn more. I started using jQuery in web projects. I still liked what I saw. I started replacing older code in previous projects to see how jQuery would simplify the pages. And I *really* liked what I saw.

Enthusiastic about this new discovery and wanting to share it with others, I took complete leave of my senses and submitted a proposal for *jQuery in Action* to Manning. Obviously, I must've been convincing. (As penance for causing such mayhem, I asked the technical editor who started all the trouble to also be the technical editor for *this* book. I'll bet *that* taught him!)

It's at that point that the editor, Mike Stephens, asked, "How would you like to work with Yehuda Katz on this project?"

"Yehenta who?" I asked...

Yehuda came to this project by a different route; his involvement with jQuery predates the days when it even had version numbers. After he stumbled on the Selectables Plugin, his interest in the jQuery core library was piqued. Somewhat disappointed by the (then) lack of online documentation, he scoured the wikis and established the Visual jQuery site (visualjquery.com).

Before too long, he was spearheading the push for better online documents, contributing to jQuery, and overseeing the plugin architecture and ecosystem, all while evangelizing jQuery to the Ruby community.

Then came the day when he received a call from Manning (his name having been dropped to the publisher by a friend), asking if he'd be interested in working with this Bear guy on a jQuery book...

Despite the differences in our backgrounds, experiences, and strengths, and the manner in which we came together on this project, we've formed a great team and have had a lot of fun working together. Even geographic distance (I'm in the heart of Texas, and Yehuda is on the California coast) proved no barrier. Thank goodness for email and instant messaging!

We think that the combination of our knowledge and talents brings you a strong and informative book. We hope you have as much fun reading this book as we had working on it.

We just advise you to keep saner hours.

acknowledgments

Have you ever been surprised, or even bewildered, by the seemingly endless list of names that scrolls up the screen during the ending credits of a motion picture? Do you ever wonder if it really takes that many people to make a movie?

Similarly, the number of people involved in the writing of a book would probably be a big surprise to most people. It takes a large collaborative effort on the part of many contributors with a variety of talents to bring the volume you are holding (or ebook that you are reading onscreen) to fruition.

The staff at Manning worked tirelessly with us to make sure that this book attained the level of quality that we hoped for, and we thank them for their efforts. Without them, this book would not have been possible. The "end credits" for this book include not only our publisher, Marjan Bace, and editor Mike Stephens, but also the following contributors: Lianna Wlasiuk, Karen Tegtmayer, Andy Carroll, Deepak Vohra, Barbara Mirecki, Megan Yockey, Dottie Marsico, Mary Piergies, Gabriel Dobrescu, and Steven Hong.

Enough cannot be said to thank our peer reviewers who helped mold the final form of the book, from catching simple typos to correcting errors in terminology and code and even helping to organize the chapters within the book. Each pass through a review cycle ended up vastly improving the final product. For taking the time to help review the book, we'd like to thank Tony Niemann, Scott Sauyet, Rich Freedman, Philip Hallstrom, Michael Smolyak, Marion Sturtevant, Jonas Bandi, Jay Blanchard, Nikander Bruggeman, Margriet Bruggeman, Greg Donald, Frank Wang, Curtis Miller, Christopher Haupt, Cheryl Jerozal, Charles E. Logston, Andrew Siemer, Eric

Raymond, Christian Marquardt, Robby O'Connor, Marc Gravell, Andrew Grothe, Anil Radhakrishna, Daniel Bretoi, and Massimo Perga.

Very special thanks go to Valentin Crettaz, who served as the book's technical editor. In addition to checking each and every sample of example code in multiple environments, he also offered invaluable contributions to the technical accuracy of the text, located information that was originally missing, kept abreast of rapid changes to the libraries while we were writing to make sure that the book represented an up-to-date and accurate view of jQuery and jQuery UI, and even provided the PHP versions of the examples requiring server-side code.

Bear Bibeault

For this, my fourth published tome, the cast of characters I'd like to thank has a long list of "usual suspects," including, once again, the membership and staff at javaranch.com. Without my involvement in JavaRanch, I'd never have gotten the opportunity to start writing in the first place, and so I sincerely thank Paul Wheaton and Kathy Sierra for starting the whole thing, as well as fellow staffers who gave me encouragement and support, including (but probably not limited to) Eric Pascarello, Ben Souther, Ernest Friedman-Hill, Mark Herschberg, Andrew Monkhouse, Jeanne Boyarsky, Bert Bates, Max Habibi, and Gregg Bolinger.

Thanks go out to Valentin Crettaz, not only for serving as a superb technical editor and code contributor (as noted above), but also for introducing me to jQuery in the first place.

My partner Jay, and my dogs, Little Bear and Cozmo (whose visages grace the pages of this book), get the usual warm thanks for putting up with the shadowy presence who shared their home but who rarely looked up from his MacBook Pro keyboard for all the months it took to write this book.

And finally, I'd like to thank my coauthor, Yehuda Katz, without whom this project would not have been possible, as well as John Resig and the rest of the jQuery and jQuery UI contributors.

Yehuda Katz

To start, I'd like to thank Bear Bibeault, my coauthor, for the benefit of his extensive writing experience. His talented writing and impressive abilities to navigate the hurdles of professional publishing were a tremendous part of what made this book possible.

While speaking of making things possible, it's necessary that I thank my lovely wife Leah, who put up with the long nights and working weekends for far longer than I would have felt comfortable asking. Her dedication to completing this book rivaled even my own; and, as in all things, she made the most difficult part of this project bearable. I love you, Leah.

Obviously, there would be no *jQuery in Action* without the jQuery library itself. I'd like to thank John Resig, the creator of jQuery, for changing the face of client-side development and easing the burden of web developers across the globe (believe it or not, we have sizable user groups in China, Japan, France, and many other countries). I also count him as a friend who, as a talented author himself, helped me to prepare for this tremendous undertaking.

There would be no jQuery without the incredible community of users and core team members, including Brandon Aaron and Jörn Zaefferer on the development team; Rey Bango and Karl Swedberg on the evangelism team; Paul Bakaus, who heads up jQuery UI; and Klaus Hartl and Mike Alsup, who work on the plugins team with me. This great group of programmers helped propel the jQuery framework from a tight, simple base of core operations to a world-class JavaScript library, complete with user-contributed (and modular) support for virtually any need you could have. I'm probably missing a great number of jQuery contributors; there are a lot of you guys. Suffice it to say that I would not be here without the unique community that has come up around this library, and I can't thank you enough.

Lastly, I want to thank my family, whom I don't see nearly enough since my recent move across the country. Growing up, my siblings and I shared a tight sense of camaraderie, and the faith my family members have in me has always made me imagine I can do just about anything. Mommy, Nikki, Abie, and Yaakov: thank you, and I love you.

about this book

Do more with less.

Stated plainly and simply, that is the purpose of this book: to help you learn how to do more on your web application pages with less script. Your authors, one an avid and enthusiastic user, and the other a jQuery contributor and evangelist, believe that jQuery is the best library available today to help you do just that.

This book is aimed at getting you up and running with jQuery quickly and effectively while having some fun along the way. All the APIs for the core jQuery library and its companion jQuery UI library are discussed, and each API method is presented in an easy-to-digest syntax block that describes the parameters and return values of the method. Many examples of effective use of the APIs are included; and, for those big concepts, we provide what we call Lab pages. These comprehensive and fun pages are an excellent way for you to see the nuances of the jQuery methods in action, without the need to write a slew of code yourself.

All example code and Lab pages are available for download at http://www.manning.com/jQueryinActionSecondEdition or http://www.manning.com/bibeault2.

We could go on and on with some marketing jargon telling you how great this book is, but you don't want to waste time reading that, do you? What you really want is to get into the bits and bytes up to your elbows, isn't it? Well, that's exactly the intention of this book.

What's holding you back? Read on!

Audience

This book is aimed at web developers, from novice to advanced, who want to take control of the JavaScript on their pages and produce great, interactive web applications without the need to write all the raw, browser-dependent client-side code necessary to achieve such applications from scratch.

All web developers who wish to leverage the power of jQuery to create highly interactive and usable web applications that delight rather than annoy their users will benefit from this book.

Although novice web developers may find some sections a tad involved, this should not deter them from diving into this book. We've included an appendix on essential JavaScript concepts that will help in using jQuery to its fullest potential, and such readers will find that the jQuery library itself is novice-friendly once they understand a few key concepts. And even though jQuery is friendly to novices, it makes plenty of power available to more advanced web developers.

Whether novices or veterans of web development, client-side programmers will benefit greatly from adding jQuery to their repertoire of development tools. We know that the lessons within this book will help add this knowledge to your toolbox quickly.

Roadmap

This book is organized to help you wrap your head around jQuery and jQuery UI in the quickest and most efficient manner possible. It starts with an introduction to the design philosophies on which jQuery was founded and quickly progresses to fundamental concepts that govern the jQuery API. We then take you through the various areas in which jQuery can help you write exemplary client-side code, from the handling of events all the way to making Ajax requests to the server. To top it all off, we take an extensive tour through the jQuery UI companion library.

The book is divided into two parts: the first covering the core jQuery library, and the second dealing with jQuery UI. Part 1 consists of eight chapters.

In chapter 1, we'll learn about the philosophy behind jQuery and how it adheres to modern principles such as Unobtrusive JavaScript. We examine why we might want to adopt jQuery, and we run through an overview of how it works. We delve into key concepts such as document-ready handlers, utility functions, Document Object Model (DOM) element creation, and how jQuery extensions are created.

Chapter 2 introduces us to the jQuery wrapped set—the core concept around which jQuery operates. We'll learn how this wrapped set-a collection of DOM elements that's to be operated upon—can be created by selecting elements from the page document using the rich and powerful collection of jQuery selectors. We'll see that these selectors use standard CSS notation, which makes them quite powerful even as they leverage the CSS knowledge we most likely already possess.

In chapter 3, we'll learn how to use the jQuery wrapped set to manipulate the page DOM. We'll cover changing the styling and attributes of elements, setting element content, moving elements around, creating elements from scratch, and dealing with form elements.

Chapter 4 shows us how we can use jQuery to vastly simplify the handling of events on our pages. After all, handling user events is what makes interactive web applications possible, and anyone who's had to deal with the intricacies of event handlers across the differing browser implementations will certainly appreciate the simplicity that jQuery brings to this particular area. Advanced event-handling concepts, such as event namespacing, custom event triggering and handling, and even establishing of proactive "live" handlers, are examined in detail and brought together in a comprehensive example project.

The world of animations and effects is the subject of chapter 5. We'll see how jQuery makes creating animated effects not only painless but also efficient and fun. Function queuing, for serially running effects as well as general functions, is covered in detail.

In chapter 6, we'll learn about the utility functions and flags that jQuery provides, not only for page authors, but also for those who will write extensions and plugins for jQuery.

We'll focus on writing such extensions and plugins in chapter 7. We'll see how jQuery makes it extraordinarily easy for anyone to write such extensions without intricate JavaScript or jQuery knowledge and why it makes sense to write any reusable code as a jQuery extension.

Chapter 8 concerns itself with one of the most important areas in the development of modern web applications: making Ajax requests. We'll see how jQuery makes it almost brain-dead simple to use Ajax on our pages, shielding us from all the usual pitfalls, while vastly simplifying the most common types of Ajax interactions (such as returning JSON constructs). Another comprehensive example project brings all that we've learned about jQuery into focus.

In part 2, which consists of three chapters, we'll explore jQuery's essential companion library: jQuery UI.

Chapter 9 introduces jQuery UI, and explains how to configure and obtain a customized version of the library code, as well as the visual themes used to style the elements of the UI library. The visual themes are dissected so that we can learn not only how they're constructed, but also how we can modify them to our own needs. Rounding out the chapter is a discussion of the extended effects that jQuery UI adds to the jQuery core, as well as how core methods are augmented to take advantage of those extensions.

In chapter 10, we explore the mouse interaction capabilities that jQuery UI provides. This extends from dragging and dropping to handling the sorting, selection, and resizing of elements.

Finally, chapter 11 wraps up with a thorough examination of the widget set provided by jQuery UI to extend the available set of input mechanisms we can present on our pages. This includes such simple controls as buttons through to more sophisticated controls such as date pickers, autocompleters, tabbed panes, and dialog boxes.

To top it all off, we have provided an appendix highlighting key JavaScript concepts such as function contexts and closures—essential to making the most effective use of jQuery on our pages—for readers who are unfamiliar with, or who would like a refresher on, these concepts.

Margin icons

Throughout this book, unique Lab pages are introduced to help illustrate jQuery and jQuery UI concepts. These labs pages are interactive web pages, provided with the downloaded example code, that you can run on your own local system.

 When a new Lab page is introduced, a Labs Icon (the flask icon show at left) is placed in the left margin. This makes it easy for you to find the location within the text where a lab is first described. A handy list of the Lab pages is also included right after the Table of Contents, and links to the labs are provided in the index page of the downloaded example code.

You can also access the Labs, as well as the rest of the example code, remotely by pointing your browser at http://www.bibeault.org/jqia2 or from the publisher's website at http://www.manning.com/jQueryinActionSecondEdition.

 Another margin icon you will find sprinkled throughout the book is the Exercises Icon (the triangle and pencil), which pinpoints text passages where exercises that you should work through are presented. Frequently, these exercises will be related to a particular Lab page, but sometimes they are logical extensions of other code examples described throughout the book, or simply standalone exercises that you should solve to make sure that the concepts are gelling in your mind.

Code conventions

All source code in listings or in the text is in a `fixed-width font like this` to separate it from ordinary text. Method and function names, properties, XML elements, and attributes in the text are also presented in this same font.

In some cases, the original source code has been reformatted to fit on the pages. In general, the original code was written with page-width limitations in mind, but sometimes you may find a slight formatting difference between the code in the book and that provided in the source download. In a few rare cases, where long lines could not be reformatted without changing their meaning, the book listings contain line-continuation markers.

Code annotations accompany many of the listings, highlighting important concepts. In many cases, numbered bullets link to explanations that follow in the text.

Code downloads

Source code for all the working examples in this book (along with some extras that never made it into the text) is available for download from the book's web page at http://www.manning.com/jQueryinActionSecondEdition. For the convenience of those who may not be able to run the examples locally for whatever reason, a working version of the examples is available online at http://www.bibeault.org/jqia2/.

The code examples for this book are organized into a web application, with separate sections for each chapter, ready to be easily served by a local web server such as the Apache HTTP Server. You can simply unzip the downloaded code into a folder of your choice, and make that folder the document root of the application. A launch page is set up at the application root in the index.html file.

With the exception of the examples for the Ajax chapter (chapter 8) and a handful from the jQuery UI chapters, most of the examples don't require the presence of a web server at all and can be loaded directly into a browser for execution, if you so desire. The Ajax examples require more backend interaction than Apache can deliver, so running them locally requires either setting up PHP for Apache, or running a web server capable of executing Java servlets and JavaServer Pages (JSP), such as Tomcat. Instructions for easily setting up Tomcat to use as the web server for the Ajax examples are provided in the chapter8/tomcat.pdf file.

All examples were tested in a variety of browsers that include Internet Explorer 7 and 8, Firefox 3, Safari 3 and 4, and Google Chrome.

Author Online

The purchase of *jQuery in Action, Second Edition* includes free access to a private forum run by Manning Publications where you can make comments about the book, ask technical questions, and receive help from the authors and other users. To access and subscribe to the forum, point your browser to http://www.manning. com/jQueryin-ActionSecondEdition, and click the Author Online link. This page provides information on how to get on the forum once you are registered, what kind of help is available, and the rules of conduct in the forum.

Manning's commitment to our readers is to provide a venue where a meaningful dialogue between individual readers and between readers and the authors can take place. It's not a commitment to any specific amount of participation on the part of the authors, whose contribution to the book's forum remains voluntary (and unpaid). We suggest you try asking the authors some challenging questions, lest their interest stray!

The Author Online forum and the archives of previous discussions will be accessible from the publisher's website as long as the book is in print.

about the authors

 BEAR BIBEAULT has been writing software for over three decades, starting with a Tic-Tac-Toe program written on a Control Data Cyber supercomputer via a 100-baud teletype. Because he has two degrees in Electrical Engineering, Bear should be designing antennas or something; but, since his first job with Digital Equipment Corporation, he has always been much more fascinated with programming.

Bear has also served stints with companies such as Lightbridge Inc., BMC Software, Dragon Systems, Works.com, and a handful of other companies. Bear even served in the U.S. Military teaching infantry soldiers how to blow up tanks; skills that come in handy during those daily scrum meetings. Bear is currently a Software Architect for a leading provider of cloud management software.

In addition to his day job, Bear also writes books (duh!), runs a small business that creates web applications and offers other media services (but not wedding videography, never, ever wedding videography), and helps to moderate JavaRanch.com as a "sheriff" (senior moderator). When not planted in front of a computer, Bear likes to cook big food (which accounts for his jeans size), dabble in photography and video, ride his Yamaha V-Star, and wear tropical print shirts.

He works and resides in Austin, Texas; a city he dearly loves except for the completely insane drivers.

YEHUDA KATZ has been involved in a number of open source projects over the past several years. In addition to being a core team member of the jQuery project, he is also a contributor to Merb, an alternative to Ruby on Rails (also written in Ruby).

Yehuda was born in Minnesota, grew up in New York, and now lives in sunny Santa Barbara, California. He has worked on websites for the New York Times, Allure Magazine, Architectural Digest, Yoga Journal, and other similarly high-profile clients. He has programmed professionally in a number of languages including Java, Ruby, PHP, and JavaScript.

In his copious spare time, he maintains VisualjQuery.com and helps answer questions from new jQuery users in the IRC channel and on the official jQuery mailing list.

about the cover illustration

The figure on the cover of *jQuery in Action, Second Edition* is called "The Watchman." The illustration is taken from a French travel book, *Encyclopédie des Voyages* by J. G. St. Saveur, published almost 200 years ago. Travel for pleasure was a relatively new phenomenon at the time and travel guides such as this one were popular, introducing both the tourist as well as the armchair traveler to the inhabitants of other regions of the world, as well as to the regional costumes and uniforms of French soldiers, civil servants, tradesmen, merchants, and peasants.

The diversity of the drawings in the *Encyclopédie des Voyages* speaks vividly of the uniqueness and individuality of the world's towns and provinces just 200 years ago. Isolated from each other, people spoke different dialects and languages. In the streets or in the countryside, it was easy to identify where they lived and what their trade or station in life was just by how they were speaking or what they were wearing.

Dress codes have changed since then and the diversity by region, so rich at the time, has faded away. It is now often hard to tell the inhabitant of one continent from another. Perhaps, trying to view it optimistically, we have traded a cultural and visual diversity for a more varied personal life. Or a more varied and interesting intellectual and technical life.

We at Manning celebrate the inventiveness, the initiative, and the fun of the computer business with book covers based on the rich diversity of regional life two centuries ago brought back to life by the pictures from this travel guide.

Part 1

Core jQuery

When someone hears the name jQuery, they inevitably think of the core jQuery library. But one could also argue that outside of the core, jQuery has created an entire ecosystem around itself consisting of companion libraries such as jQuery UI (the subject of the second part of this book), the official plugins (see http://plugins.jquery.com/), and the myriad unofficial plugins that people have created that can easily be found with a web search. (Googling the term "jQuery plugin" results in over 4 million entries!)

But just as the extensive market for third-party add-on products for Apple's iPod would not exist if the iPod itself did not, the core jQuery library is the heart of it all.

In the eight chapters in part 1 of this book, we'll cover the core library from stem to stern. When you finish these chapters, you'll know the jQuery library soup to nuts and be ready to tackle any web project armed with one of the most powerful client-side tools available. You'll also be prepared to use the jQuery companions, which, much like an iPod accessory, are useless without their core reason for being.

So turn the page, dig in, and get ready to learn how to make breathing life into your web applications not only easy, but fun!

Introducing jQuery

This chapter covers

- Why you should use jQuery
- What *Unobtrusive JavaScript* means
- The fundamental elements and concepts of jQuery
- Using jQuery in conjunction with other JavaScript libraries

Sneered at as a "not-very-serious" language by many web developers for much of its lifetime, JavaScript has regained its prestige in the past few years as a result of the renewed interest in highly interactive, next-generation web applications (which you might also have heard referred to as *rich internet applications* or DOM-*scripted applications*) and Ajax technologies. The language has been forced to grow up quickly as client-side developers have tossed aside cut-and-paste JavaScript for the convenience of full-featured JavaScript libraries that solve difficult cross-browser problems once and for all, and provide new and improved patterns for web development.

A relative latecomer to this world of JavaScript libraries, jQuery has taken the web development community by storm, quickly winning the support of major companies for use in mission-critical applications. Some of jQuery's prominent users include the likes of IBM, Netflix, Amazon, Dell, Best Buy, Twitter, Bank of America, and scores of other prominent companies. Microsoft has even elected to distribute jQuery with its Visual Studio tool, and Nokia uses jQuery on all its phones that include their Web Runtime component.

Those are *not* shabby credentials!

Compared with other toolkits that focus heavily on clever JavaScript techniques, jQuery aims to change the way that web developers think about creating rich functionality in their pages. Rather than spending time juggling the complexities of advanced JavaScript, designers can leverage their existing knowledge of Cascading Style Sheets (CSS), Hypertext Markup Language (HTML), Extensible Hypertext Markup Language (XHTML), and good old straightforward JavaScript to manipulate page elements directly, making rapid development a reality.

In this book, we're going to take an in-depth look at what jQuery has to offer us as developers of highly interactive web applications. Let's start by finding out exactly what jQuery brings to the web development party.

You can obtain the latest version of jQuery from the jQuery site at http://jquery.com/. Installing jQuery is as easy as placing it within your web application and using the HTML <script> tag to include it in your pages, like this:

```
<script type="text/javascript"
        src="scripts/jquery-1.4.js"></script>
```

The specific version of jQuery that the code in this book was tested against is included as part of the downloadable code examples (available at http://www.manning.com/bibeault2).

1.1   *Power in the economy of code*

If you've spent any time at all trying to add dynamic functionality to your pages, you've found that you're constantly following a pattern of selecting an element (or group of elements) and operating upon those elements in some fashion. You could be hiding or revealing the elements, adding a CSS class to them, animating them, or inspecting their attributes.

Using raw JavaScript can result in dozens of lines of code for each of these tasks, and the creators of jQuery specifically created that library to make common tasks trivial. For example, anyone who has dealt with radio groups in JavaScript knows that it's a lesson in tedium to discover which radio element of a radio group is currently checked and to obtain its value attribute. The radio group needs to be located, and the resulting array of radio elements must be inspected, one by one, to find out which element has its checked attribute set. This element's value attribute can then be obtained.

Such code might be implemented as follows:

```
var checkedValue;
var elements = document.getElementsByTagName('input');
for (var n = 0; n < elements.length; n++) {
  if (elements[n].type == 'radio' &&
      elements[n].name == 'someRadioGroup' &&
```

```
    elements[n].checked) {
  checkedValue = elements[n].value;
  }
}
```

Contrast that with how it can be done using jQuery:

```
var checkedValue = $('[name="someRadioGroup"]:checked').val();
```

Don't worry if that looks a bit cryptic right now. In short order, you'll understand how it works, and you'll be whipping out your own terse—but powerful—jQuery statements to make your pages come alive. Let's briefly examine how this powerful code snippet works.

We identify all elements that possess a `name` attribute with the value `someRadio-Group` (remember that radio groups are formed by naming all their elements using the same name), then filter that set to only those that are in `checked` state, and find the value of that element. (There will be only one such element, because the browser will only allow a single element of the radio group to be checked at a time.)

The real power in this jQuery statement comes from the *selector*, which is an expression used to identify target elements on a page. It allows us to easily locate and grab the elements that we need; in this case, the checked element in the radio group.

If you haven't downloaded the example code yet, now would be a great time to do so. It can be obtained from a link on this book's web page at http://www.manning.com/bibeault2 (don't forget the 2 at the end). Unpack the code and either navigate to the files individually, or use the nifty index page at index.html in the root of the unpacked folder hierarchy.

Load the HTML page that you find in file chapter1/radio.group.html into your browser. This page, shown in figure 1.1, uses the jQuery statement that we just examined to determine which radio button has been checked.

Even this simple example ought to convince you that jQuery is the hassle-free way to create the next generation of highly interactive web applications. But just wait until we show you how much power jQuery offers for taming your web pages as we progress through this book's chapters.

We'll soon study how to easily create the jQuery selectors that made this example so easy, but first let's examine how the inventors of jQuery think JavaScript can be most effectively used on our pages.

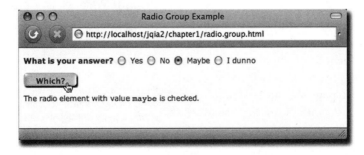

Figure 1.1   Determining which radio button is checked is easy to accomplish in one statement with jQuery!

1.2   Unobtrusive JavaScript

You may recall the bad old days before CSS, when we were forced to mix stylistic markup with the document structure markup in our HTML pages. Anyone who's been authoring pages for any amount of time surely does, most likely with less than fondness.

The addition of CSS to our web development toolkits allows us to separate stylistic information from the document structure and gives travesties like the <font> tag the well-deserved boot. Not only does the separation of style from structure make our documents easier to manage, it also gives us the versatility to completely change the stylistic rendering of a page by simply swapping out different style sheets.

Few of us would voluntarily regress back to the days of applying styles with HTML elements; yet markup such as the following is still all too common:

```
<button
  type="button"
  onclick="document.getElementById('xyz').style.color='red';">
    Click Me
</button>
```

You can easily see that the style of this button element, including the font of its caption, isn't applied via the use of the <font> tag and other deprecated style-oriented markup, but is determined by whatever CSS rules (not shown) are in effect on the page. But although this declaration doesn't mix *style* markup with structure, it does mix *behavior* with structure by including the JavaScript to be executed when the button is clicked as part of the markup of the button element via the onclick attribute (which, in this case, turns some Document Object Model (DOM) element with the id value of xyz red).

Let's examine how we might improve this situation.

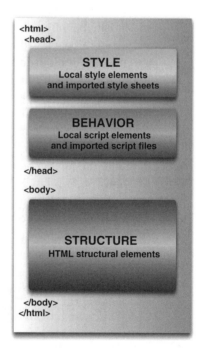

Figure 1.2   With structure, style, and behavior each neatly tucked away within a page, readability and maintainability are maximized.

1.2.1   Separating behavior from structure

For all the same reasons that it's desirable to segregate style from structure within an HTML document, it's just as beneficial (if not more so) to separate the *behavior* from the structure.

Ideally, an HTML page should be structured as shown in figure 1.2, with structure, style, *and* behavior each partitioned nicely in its own niche.

This strategy, known as *Unobtrusive JavaScript*, was brought into the limelight by the inventors of jQuery and is now embraced by every major JavaScript library, helping page authors achieve this useful separation on their pages. As the library that popularized this movement, jQuery's core is well optimized for producing Unobtrusive JavaScript quite easily. Unobtrusive JavaScript considers *any* JavaScript expressions or statements embedded in the <body> of HTML pages, either as attributes of HTML elements (such as onclick) or in script blocks placed within the body of the page, to be incorrect.

"But how can I instrument the button without the onclick attribute?" you might ask. Consider the following change to the button element:

```
<button type="button" id="testButton">Click Me</button>
```

Much simpler! But now, you'll note, the button doesn't *do* anything. We can click it all day long, and no behavior will result.

Let's fix that.

1.2.2 Segregating the script

Rather than embedding the button's behavior in its markup, we'll segregate the script by moving it to a script block in the <head> section of the page, *outside* the scope of the document body (see note below), as follows:

```
<script type="text/javascript">
  window.onload = function() {
    document.getElementById('testButton').onclick = function() {
      document.getElementById('xyz').style.color = 'red';
    };
  };
</script>
```

We place the script in the onload handler for the page to assign an inline function to the onclick attribute of the button element.

We add this script in the onload handler (as opposed to within an inline script block) because we need to make sure that the button element exists *before* we attempt to augment it. (In section 1.3.3 we'll see how jQuery provides a better place for us to put such code.)

> **NOTE** For performance reasons, script blocks can also be placed at the bottom of the document body, though modern browsers make the performance difference rather moot. The important concept is to avoid embedding behavioral elements within the structural elements.

If any of the code in this example looks odd to you (such as the concept of function literals and inline functions), fear not! The appendix to this book provides a look at the important JavaScript concepts that you'll need to use jQuery effectively. We'll also examine, in the remainder of this chapter, how jQuery makes writing this code easier and quicker and makes the code more versatile all at the same time.

Unobtrusive JavaScript, though a powerful technique to add to the clear separation of responsibilities within a web application, doesn't come without a price. You might already have noticed that it took a few more lines of script to accomplish our goal than when we placed it into the button markup. Unobtrusive JavaScript *may* increase the line count of the script that needs to be written, and it requires some discipline and the application of good coding patterns to the client-side script.

But none of that is bad; anything that persuades us to write our client-side code with the same level of care and respect usually allotted to server-side code is a good thing! But it *is* extra work—without jQuery, that is.

As mentioned earlier, the jQuery team has specifically focused jQuery on the task of making it easy and delightful for us to code our pages using Unobtrusive JavaScript techniques, without paying a hefty price in terms of effort or code bulk. We'll find that making effective use of jQuery will enable us to accomplish much more on our pages while writing *less* code.

Without further ado, let's start looking at how jQuery makes it so easy for us to add rich functionality to our pages without the expected pain.

1.3   *jQuery fundamentals*

At its core, jQuery focuses on retrieving elements from HTML pages and performing operations upon them. If you're familiar with CSS, you're already well aware of the power of selectors, which describe groups of elements by their type, attributes, or placement within the document. With jQuery, we can employ that knowledge, and that degree of power, to vastly simplify our JavaScript.

jQuery places a high priority on ensuring that code will work consistently across all major browsers; many of the more difficult JavaScript problems, such as waiting until the page is loaded before performing page operations, have been silently solved for us.

Should we find that the library needs a bit more juice, jQuery has a simple but powerful built-in method for extending its functionality via *plugins*. Many new jQuery programmers find themselves putting this versatility into practice by extending jQuery with their own plugins on their first day.

Let's start by taking a look at how we can leverage our CSS knowledge to produce powerful, yet terse, code.

1.3.1   *The jQuery wrapper*

When CSS was introduced to web technologies in order to separate design from content, a way was needed to refer to groups of page elements from external style sheets. The method developed was through the use of selectors, which concisely represent elements based upon their type, attributes, or position within the HTML document.

Those familiar with XML might be reminded of XPath as a means to select elements within an XML document. CSS selectors represent an equally powerful concept, but are tuned for use within HTML pages, are a bit more concise, and are generally considered easier to understand.

For example, the selector

```
p a
```

refers to the group of all links (<a> elements) that are nested inside a <p> element. jQuery makes use of the same selectors, supporting not only the common selectors currently used in CSS, but also some that may not yet be fully implemented by all browsers, including some of the more powerful selectors defined in CSS3.

To collect a group of elements, we pass the selector to the jQuery function using the simple syntax

```
$(selector)
```

or

```
jQuery(selector)
```

Although you may find the $() notation strange at first, most jQuery users quickly become fond of its brevity. For example, to wrap the group of links nested inside any <p> element, we can use the following:

```
$("p a")
```

The $() function (an alias for the jQuery() function) returns a special JavaScript object containing an array of the DOM elements, in the order in which they are defined within the document, that match the selector. This object possesses a large number of useful predefined methods that can act on the collected group of elements.

In programming parlance, this type of construct is termed a *wrapper* because it wraps the collected elements with extended functionality. We'll use the term *jQuery wrapper* or *wrapped set* to refer to this set of matched elements that can be operated on with the methods defined by jQuery.

Let's say that we want to hide all <div> elements that possess the class notLongFor-ThisWorld. The jQuery statement is as follows:

```
$("div.notLongForThisWorld").hide();
```

A special feature of a large number of these methods, which we often refer to as jQuery *wrapper methods*, is that when they're done with their action (like a hide operation), they return the same group of elements, ready for another action. For example, say that we want to add a new class, removed, to each of the elements in addition to hiding them. We would write

```
$("div.notLongForThisWorld").hide().addClass("removed");
```

These jQuery *chains* can continue indefinitely. It's not uncommon to find examples in the wild of jQuery chains dozens of methods long. And because each method works on all of the elements matched by the original selector, there's no need to loop over the array of elements. It's all done for us behind the scenes!

Even though the selected group of objects is represented as a highly sophisticated JavaScript object, we can pretend it's a typical array of elements, if necessary. As a result, the following two statements produce identical results:

```
$("#someElement").html("I have added some text to an element");
```
and

```
$("#someElement")[0].innerHTML =
  "I have added some text to an element";
```

Because we've used an ID selector, only one element will match the selector. The first example uses the jQuery html() method, which replaces the contents of a DOM element with some HTML markup. The second example uses jQuery to retrieve an array of elements, selects the first one using an array index of 0, and replaces the contents using an ordinary JavaScript property assignment to innerHTML.

If we wanted to achieve the same results with a selector that results in multiple matched elements, the following two fragments would produce identical results (though the latter example is not a recommended way of coding using jQuery):

```
$("div.fillMeIn")
  .html("I have added some text to a group of nodes");
```

and

```
var elements = $("div.fillMeIn");
for(var i=0;i<elements.length;i++)
  elements[i].innerHTML =
    "I have added some text to a group of nodes";
```

As things get progressively more complicated, making use of jQuery's chainability will continue to reduce the lines of code necessary to produce the results we want. Additionally, jQuery supports not only the selectors that you have already come to know and love, but also more advanced selectors—defined as part of the CSS specification—and even some custom selectors.

Here are a few examples:

Selector	Results
$("p:even")	Selects all even <p> elements
$("tr:nth-child(1)")	Selects the first row of each table
$("body > div")	Selects direct <div> children of <body>
$("a[href$= 'pdf ']")	Selects links to PDF files
$("body > div:has(a)")	Selects direct <div> children of <body>-containing links

That's powerful stuff!

You'll be able to leverage your existing knowledge of CSS to get up and running fast, and then learn about the more advanced selectors that jQuery supports. We'll be covering jQuery selectors in great detail in chapter 2, and you can find a full list on the jQuery site at http://docs.jquery.com/Selectors.

Selecting DOM elements for manipulation is a common need in web pages, but some things that we'll also need to do don't involve DOM elements at all. Let's take a brief look at what jQuery offers beyond element manipulation.

1.3.2 Utility functions

Even though wrapping elements to be operated upon is one of the most frequent uses of jQuery's $() function, that's not the only duty to which it's assigned. One of its additional duties is to serve as the *namespace prefix* for a handful of general-purpose utility functions. Because so much power is given to page authors by the jQuery wrapper created as a result of a call to $() with a selector, it's somewhat rare for most page authors to need the services provided by some of these functions. In fact, we won't be looking at the majority of these functions in detail until chapter 6 as a preparation for writing jQuery plugins. But you *will* see a few of these functions put to use in the upcoming sections, so we'll briefly introduce them here.

The notation for these functions may look odd at first. Let's take, for example, the utility function for trimming strings. A call to it could look like this:

```
var trimmed = $.trim(someString);
```

If the $. prefix looks weird to you, remember that $ is an identifier like any other in JavaScript. Writing a call to the same function using the jQuery identifier, rather than the $ alias, may look a bit less odd:

```
var trimmed = jQuery.trim(someString);
```

Here it becomes clear that the trim() function is merely namespaced by jQuery or its $ alias.

> **NOTE** Even though these elements are called the utility *functions* in jQuery documentation, it's clear that they're actually *methods* of the $() function (yes, in JavaScript, functions can have their own methods). We'll put aside this technical distinction and use the term *utility function* to describe these methods so as not to introduce terminology that conflicts with the online documentation.

We'll explore one of these utility functions that helps us to extend jQuery in section 1.3.5, and one that helps jQuery peacefully coexist with other client-side libraries in section 1.3.6. But first, let's look at another important duty that jQuery's $() function performs.

1.3.3 The document ready handler

When embracing Unobtrusive JavaScript, behavior is separated from structure, so we're performing operations on the page elements outside of the document markup that creates them. In order to achieve this, we need a way to wait until the DOM elements of the page are fully realized before those operations execute. In the radio group example, the entire body must load before the behavior can be applied.

Traditionally, the `onload` handler for the `window` instance is used for this purpose, executing statements after the entire page is fully loaded. The syntax is typically something like

```
window.onload = function() {
  // do stuff here
};
```

This causes the defined code to execute *after* the document has fully loaded. Unfortunately, the browser not only delays executing the `onload` code until after the DOM tree is created, but also waits until after all external resources are fully loaded and the page is displayed in the browser window. This includes not only resources like images, but QuickTime and Flash videos embedded in web pages, and there are more and more of them these days. As a result, visitors can experience a serious delay between the time that they first see the page and the time that the `onload` script is executed.

Even worse, if an image or other resource takes significant time to load, visitors will have to wait for the image loading to complete before the rich behaviors become available. This could make the whole Unobtrusive JavaScript proposition a non-starter for many real-life cases.

A much better approach would be to wait *only* until the document structure is fully parsed and the browser has converted the HTML into its resulting DOM tree before executing the script to apply the rich behaviors. Accomplishing this in a cross-browser manner is somewhat difficult, but jQuery provides a simple means to trigger the execution of code once the DOM tree has loaded (without waiting for external resources). The formal syntax to define such code (using our hiding example) is as follows:

```
jQuery(document).ready(function() {
  $("div.notLongForThisWorld").hide();
});
```

First, we wrap the `document` instance with the `jQuery()` function, and then we apply the `ready()` method, passing a function to be executed when the document is ready to be manipulated.

We called that the *formal syntax* for a reason; a shorthand form, used much more frequently, is as follows:

```
jQuery(function() {
  $("div.notLongForThisWorld").hide();
});
```

By passing a function to `jQuery()` or `$()`, we instruct the browser to wait until the DOM has fully loaded (but only the DOM) before executing the code. Even better, we can use this technique multiple times within the same HTML document, and the browser will execute all of the functions we specify in the order that they are declared within the page. In contrast, the window's `onload` technique allows for only a single function. This limitation can also result in hard-to-find bugs if any included third-party code uses the `onload` mechanism for its own purpose (not a best-practice approach).

That's another use of the $() function; now let's look at yet something else it can do for us.

1.3.4 Making DOM elements

As you can see by now, the authors of jQuery avoided introducing a bunch of global names into the JavaScript namespace by making the $() function (which you'll recall is merely an alias for the jQuery() function) versatile enough to perform many duties. Well, there's one more duty that we need to examine.

We can create DOM elements on the fly by passing the $() function a string that contains the HTML markup for those elements. For example, we can create a new paragraph element as follows:

```
$("<p>Hi there!</p>")
```

But creating a disembodied DOM element (or hierarchy of elements) isn't all that useful; usually the element hierarchy created by such a call is then operated on using one of jQuery's DOM manipulation functions. Let's examine the code of listing 1.1 as an example.

Listing 1.1 Creating HTML elements on the fly

```
<html>
  <head>
    <title>Follow me!</title>
    <link rel="stylesheet" type="text/css"
        href="../styles/core.css"/>
    <script type="text/javascript" src="../scripts/jquery-1.4.js">
    </script>
    <script type="text/javascript">                    ❶ Ready handler that
      $(function(){                                       creates HTML element
        $("<p>Hi there!</p>").insertAfter("#followMe");
      });
    </script>
  </head>

  <body>                                               ❷ Existing element
    <p id="followMe">Follow me!</p>                      to be followed
  </body>
</html>
```

This example establishes an existing HTML paragraph element named followMe ❷ in the document body. In the script element within the <head> section, we establish a ready handler ❶ that uses the following statement to insert a newly created paragraph into the DOM tree after the existing element:

```
$("<p>Hi there!</p>").insertAfter("#followMe");
```

The result is shown in figure 1.3.

We'll be investigating the full set of DOM manipulation functions in chapter 3, where we'll see that jQuery provides many means to manipulate the DOM to create nearly any structure that we may desire.

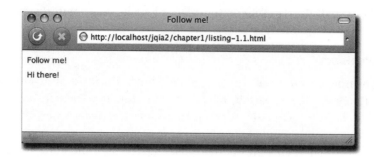

Figure 1.3 **Dynamically creating and inserting elements, usually requiring many lines of code, can be accomplished in a single line of jQuery code.**

Now that you've seen the basic syntax of jQuery, let's take a look at one of the most powerful features of the library.

1.3.5   *Extending jQuery*

The `jQuery` wrapper function provides a large number of useful methods we'll use again and again in these pages. But no library can anticipate everyone's needs. It could be argued that no library should even try to anticipate every possible need; doing so could result in a large, clunky mass of code that contains little-used features that merely serve to gum up the works!

The authors of the jQuery library recognized this concept and worked hard to identify the features that most page authors would need and included only those in the core library. Recognizing also that page authors would each have their own unique requirements, jQuery was designed to be easily extended with additional functionality.

We could write our own functions to fill in any gaps, but once we've been spoiled by the jQuery way of doing things, we'll find that doing things the old-fashioned way is beyond tedious. By extending jQuery, we can use the powerful features it provides, particularly in the area of element selection.

Let's look at a specific example: jQuery doesn't come with a predefined function to disable a group of form elements. If we're using forms throughout an application, we might find it convenient to be able to write code such as the following:

```
$("form#myForm input.special").disable();
```

Fortunately, and by design, jQuery makes it easy to extend its set of methods by extending the wrapper returned when we call `$()`. Let's take a look at the basic idiom for how that's accomplished by coding a new `disable()` function:

```
$.fn.disable = function() {
  return this.each(function() {
    if (this.disabled != null) this.disabled = true;
  });
}
```

A lot of new syntax is introduced here, but don't worry about it too much yet. It'll be old hat once you've made your way through the next few chapters; it's a basic idiom that you'll use over and over again.

First, `$.fn.disable` means that we're extending the `$` wrapper with a method named `disable`. Inside that function, the `this` keyword is the collection of wrapped DOM elements that are to be operated upon.

Then, the `each()` method of this wrapper is called to iterate over each element in the wrapped collection. We'll be exploring this and similar methods in greater detail in chapter 3. Inside of the iterator function passed to `each()`, `this` is a reference to the specific DOM element for the current iteration. Don't be confused by the fact that `this` resolves to different objects within the nested functions. After writing a few extended functions, it becomes natural to remember that `this` refers to the function context of the current function. (The appendix is also there to explain the JavaScript concept of the `this` keyword.)

For each element, we check whether the element has a `disabled` attribute, and if it does, we set it to `true`. We return the result of the `each()` method (the wrapper) so that our brand new `disable()` method will support chaining, like many of the native jQuery methods. We'll be able to write

```
$("form#myForm input.special").disable().addClass("moreSpecial");
```

From the point of view of our page code, it's as though our new `disable()` method was built into the library itself! This technique is so powerful that most new jQuery users find themselves building small extensions to jQuery almost as soon as they start to use the library.

Moreover, enterprising jQuery users have extended jQuery with sets of useful functions that are known as *plugins*. We'll be talking more about extending jQuery in this way in chapter 7.

Testing for existence

You might have seen this common idiom for testing the existence of an item:

```
if (item) {
   //do something if item exists
}
else {
   //do something if item doesn't exist
}
```

The idea here is that if the item doesn't exist, the conditional expression will evaluate to `false`.

Although this works in most circumstances, the framers of jQuery feel that it's a bit too sloppy and imprecise and recommend the more explicit test used in the `$.fn.disable` example:

```
if (item == null) ...
```

This expression will correctly test for `null` or `undefined` items.

For a full list of the various coding styles recommended by the jQuery team, visit the jQuery documentation page at http://docs.jquery.com/JQuery_Core_Style_Guidelines.

Before we dive into using jQuery to bring life to our pages, you may be wondering if we're going to be able to use jQuery with Prototype or other libraries that also use the $ shortcut. The next section reveals the answer to this question.

1.3.6   *Using jQuery with other libraries*

Even though jQuery provides a set of powerful tools that will meet most of our needs, there may be times when a page requires that multiple JavaScript libraries be employed. This situation could come about when we're transitioning an application from a previously employed library to jQuery, or we might want to use both jQuery and another library on our pages.

The jQuery team, clearly revealing their focus on meeting the needs of their user community rather than any desire to lock out other libraries, have made provisions for allowing jQuery to cohabitate with other libraries.

First, they've followed best-practice guidelines and have avoided polluting the global namespace with a slew of identifiers that might interfere not only with other libraries, but also with names we might want to use on our pages. The identifier jQuery and its alias $ are the limit of jQuery's incursion into the global namespace. Defining the utility functions that we referred to in section 1.3.2 as part of the jQuery namespace is a good example of the care taken in this regard.

Although it's unlikely that any other library would have a good reason to define a global identifier named jQuery, there's that convenient but, in this particular case, pesky $ alias. Other JavaScript libraries, most notably the Prototype library, use the $ name for their own purposes. And because the usage of the $ name in that library is key to its operation, this creates a serious conflict.

The thoughtful jQuery authors have provided a means to remove this conflict with a utility function appropriately named noConflict(). Anytime after the conflicting libraries have been loaded, a call to

```
jQuery.noConflict();
```

will revert the meaning of $ to that defined by the non-jQuery library.

We'll cover the nuances of using this utility function in chapter 7.

1.4   *Summary*

We've covered a great deal of material in this whirlwind introduction to jQuery, in preparation for diving into using jQuery to quickly and easily enable the development of next-generation web applications.

jQuery is generally useful for any page that needs to perform anything but the most trivial of JavaScript operations, but it's also strongly focused on enabling page authors to employ the concept of Unobtrusive JavaScript within their pages. With this approach, behavior is separated from structure in the same way that CSS separates style from structure, achieving better page organization and increased code versatility.

Despite the fact that jQuery introduces only two new names in the JavaScript namespace—the self-named jQuery function and its $ alias—the library provides a great deal of functionality by making that function highly versatile, adjusting the operation that it performs based upon the parameters passed to it.

As we've seen, the `jQuery()` function can be used to do the following:

- Select and wrap DOM elements to be operated upon by wrapper methods
- Serve as a namespace for global utility functions
- Create DOM elements from HTML markup
- Establish code to be executed when the DOM is ready for manipulation

jQuery behaves like a good on-page citizen not only by minimizing its incursion into the global JavaScript namespace, but also by providing an official means to reduce that minimal incursion in circumstances when a name collision might still occur—namely when another library, such as Prototype, requires use of the $ name. How's *that* for being user friendly?

In the chapters that follow, we'll explore all that jQuery has to offer us as developers of rich internet applications. We'll begin our tour in the next chapter as we learn how to use jQuery selectors to quickly and easily identify the elements that we wish to act upon.

Selecting the elements upon which to act

2

This chapter covers

- Selecting elements to be wrapped by jQuery using selectors
- Creating and placing new HTML elements in the DOM
- Manipulating the wrapped element set

In the previous chapter, we discussed the many ways that the jQuery function can be used. Its capabilities range from the selection of DOM elements to defining functions to be executed when the DOM is loaded.

In this chapter, we'll examine (in great detail) how the DOM elements to be acted upon are identified by looking at two of the most powerful and frequently used capabilities of jQuery's $() function: the selection of DOM elements via *selectors* and the creation of new DOM elements.

A good number of the capabilities required by interactive web applications are achieved by manipulating the DOM elements that make up the pages. But before they can be manipulated, they need to be identified and selected. Let's begin our detailed tour of the many ways that jQuery lets us specify which elements are to be targeted for manipulation.

2.1 Selecting elements for manipulation

The first thing we need to do when using virtually any jQuery method (frequently referred to as jQuery *wrapper methods*) is to select some document elements to act upon. Sometimes, the set of elements we want to select will be easy to describe, such as "all paragraph elements on the page." Other times, they'll require a more complex description like "all list elements that have the class `listElement`, contain a link, and are first in the list."

Fortunately, jQuery provides a robust *selector* syntax we can use to easily specify sets of elements elegantly and concisely. You probably already know a big chunk of the syntax: jQuery uses the CSS syntax you already know and love, and extends it with some custom means to perform both common and complex selections.

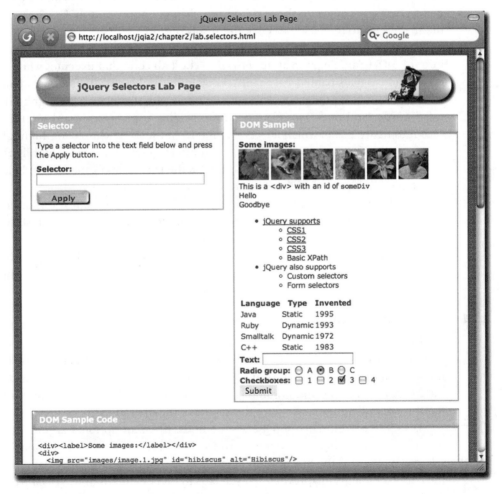

Figure 2.1 The jQuery Selectors Lab Page allows you to observe the behavior of any selector you choose in real time.

To help you learn about element selection, we've put together a jQuery Selectors Lab Page that's available within the downloadable code examples for this book (in file chapter2/lab.selectors.html). The Selectors Lab allows you to enter a jQuery selector string and see (in real time!) which DOM elements get selected. When displayed, the Lab should look as shown in figure 2.1 (if the panes don't appear correctly lined up, you may need to widen your browser window).

> **TIP** If you haven't yet downloaded the example code, you really ought to do so now—the information in this chapter will be much easier to absorb if you follow along with the Lab exercises. Visit this book's web page at http://www.manning.com/bibeault2 to find the download link.

The Selector pane at top left contains a text box and a button. To run a Lab "experiment," type a selector into the text box and click the Apply button. Go ahead and type the string li into the box, and click the Apply button.

The selector that you type (in this case li) is applied to the HTML fragment loaded into the DOM Sample pane at upper right. The Lab code that executes when Apply is clicked adds a class named wrappedElement to be applied to all matching elements. A CSS rule defined for the page causes all elements with that class to be highlighted with a red border and pink background. After clicking Apply, you should see the display shown in figure 2.2, in which all <li> elements in the DOM sample are highlighted.

Note that the <li> elements in the sample fragment have been highlighted and that the executed jQuery statement, as well as the tag names of the selected elements, have been displayed below the Selector text box.

The HTML markup used to render the DOM sample fragment is displayed in the lower pane, labeled DOM Sample Code. This should help you experiment with writing selectors targeted at the elements in this sample.

We'll talk more about using this Lab as we progress through the chapter. But first, your authors must admit that they've been blatantly over-simplifying an important concept, and that's going to be rectified now.

2.1.1 *Controlling the context*

Up to this point, we've been acting as if there were only one argument passed to jQuery's $() function, but this was just a bit of hand waving to keep things simple at the start. In fact, for the variants in which a selector or an HTML fragment is passed to the $() function, a second argument is accepted. When the first argument is a selector, this second argument denotes the *context* of the operation.

As we'll see with many of jQuery's methods, when an optional argument is omitted, a reasonable default is assumed. And so it is with the context argument. When a selector is passed as the first argument (we'll deal with passing HTML fragments later), the context defaults to applying that selector to every element in the DOM tree.

That's quite often exactly what we want, so it's a nice default. But there may be times when we want to limit our search to a subset of the entire DOM. In such cases, we

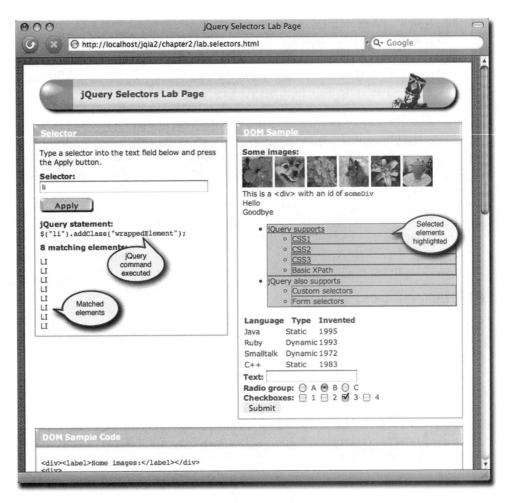

Figure 2.2 A selector value of `li` matches all `<li>` elements when applied, as shown by the displayed results.

can identify a subset of the DOM that serves as the root of the sub-tree to which the selector is applied.

The Selectors Lab offers a good example of this scenario. When that page applies the selector that you typed into the text field, the selector is applied *only* to the subset of the DOM that's loaded into the DOM Sample pane.

We can use a DOM element reference as the context, but we can also use either a string that contains a jQuery selector, or a wrapped set of DOM elements. (So yes, that means that we can pass the result of one $() invocation to another—don't let that make your head explode just yet; it's not as confusing as it may seem at first.)

When a selector or wrapped set is provided as the context, the identified elements serve as the contexts for the application of the selector. As there can be multiple such elements, this is a nice way to provide disparate sub-trees in the DOM to serve as the contexts for the selection process.

Let's take the Lab Page as an example. We'll assume that the selector string is stored in a variable conveniently named `selector`. When we apply this submitted selector, we only want to apply it to the sample DOM, which is contained within a `<div>` element with an `id` value of `sampleDOM`.

Were we to code the call to the jQuery function like this,

```
$(selector)
```

the selector would be applied to the entire DOM tree, including the form in which the selector was specified. That's not what we want. What we want is to limit the selection process to the sub-tree of the DOM rooted at the `<div>` element with the id of `sample-DOM`; so instead we write

```
$(selector,'div#sampleDOM')
```

which limits the application of the selector to the desired portion of the DOM.

OK, now that we know how to control where to apply selectors, let's see how to code them beginning with familiar territory: traditional CSS selectors.

2.1.2   *Using basic CSS selectors*

For applying styles to page elements, web developers have become familiar with a small, but powerful and very useful, group of selection expressions that work across all browsers. Those expressions can select by an element's ID, by CSS class names, by tag names, and by the hierarchy of the page elements within the DOM.

Table 2.1 provides some examples to give you a quick refresher. We can mix and match these basic selector types to identify fairly fine-grained sets of elements.

With jQuery, we can easily select elements using the CSS selectors that we're already accustomed to using. To select elements using jQuery, wrap the selector in `$()`, like this:

```
$("p a.specialClass")
```

With a few exceptions, jQuery is fully CSS3 compliant, so selecting elements this way will present no surprises; the same elements that would be selected in a style sheet by a

Table 2.1   Some simple CSS selector examples

Example	Description
a	Matches all anchor (`<a>`) elements
#specialID	Matches the element with the id value of `specialID`
.specialClass	Matches all elements with the class `specialClass`
a#specialID.specialClass	Matches the element with the id value `specialID` if it's an anchor tag and has class `specialClass`
p a.specialClass	Matches all anchor elements with the class `specialClass` that are descendants of `<p>` elements

standards-compliant browser will be selected by jQuery's selector engine. Note that jQuery does *not* depend upon the CSS implementation of the browser it's running within. Even if the browser doesn't implement a standard CSS selector correctly, jQuery will correctly select elements according to the rules of the World Wide Web Consortium (W3C) standard.

jQuery also lets us combine multiple selectors into a single expression using the comma operator. For example, to select all <div> and all <span> elements, you could do this:

```
$('div,span')
```

 For some practice, play with the Selectors Lab and run some experiments with some basic CSS selectors until you feel comfortable with them.

These basic selectors are powerful, but sometimes we'll need even finer-grained control over which elements we want to match. jQuery meets this challenge and steps up to the plate with even more advanced selectors.

2.1.3 *Using child, container, and attribute selectors*

For more advanced selectors, jQuery uses the most up-to-date generation of CSS supported by Mozilla Firefox, Internet Explorer 7 and 8, Safari, Chrome and other modern browsers. These advanced selectors allow us to select the direct children of some elements, elements that occur after other elements in the DOM, and even elements with attributes matching certain conditions.

Sometimes, we'll want to select only the direct children of a certain element. For example, we might want to select list elements directly under some list, but not list elements belonging to a sublist. Consider the following HTML fragment from the sample DOM in the Selectors Lab:

```
<ul class="myList">
  <li><a href="http://jquery.com">jQuery supports</a>
    <ul>
      <li><a href="css1">CSS1</a></li>
      <li><a href="css2">CSS2</a></li>
      <li><a href="css3">CSS3</a></li>
      <li>Basic XPath</li>
    </ul>
  </li>
  <li>jQuery also supports
    <ul>
      <li>Custom selectors</li>
      <li>Form selectors</li>
    </ul>
  </li>
</ul>
```

Suppose that we wanted to select the link to the remote jQuery site, but not the links to various local pages describing the different CSS specifications. Using basic CSS selectors, we might try something like `ul.myList li a`. Unfortunately, that selector would grab all links because they all descend from a list element.

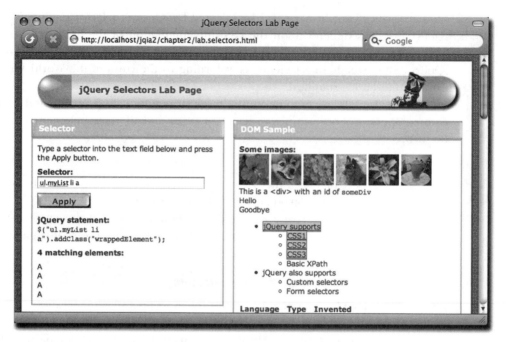

Figure 2.3   All anchor tags that are descendants, at any depth, of an <li> element are selected by ul.myList li a.

You can verify this by entering the selector ul.myList li a into the Selectors Lab and clicking Apply. The results will be as shown in figure 2.3.

A more advanced approach is to use *child selectors*, in which a parent and its *direct* child are separated by the right angle bracket character (>), as in

```
p > a
```

This selector matches only links that are *direct* children of a <p> element. If a link were further embedded, say within a <span> within the <p>, that link would not be selected.

Going back to our example, consider a selector such as

```
ul.myList > li > a
```

This selector selects only links that are direct children of list elements, which are in turn direct children of <ul> elements that have the class myList. The links contained in the sublists are excluded because the <ul> elements serving as the parent of the sublists' <li> elements don't have the class myList, as shown in the Lab results in figure 2.4.

Attribute selectors are also extremely powerful. Say that we want to attach a special behavior only to links that point to locations outside your site. Let's take another look at that portion of the Lab example that we previously examined:

```
<li><a href="http://jquery.com">jQuery supports</a>
    <ul>
      <li><a href="css1">CSS1</a></li>
```

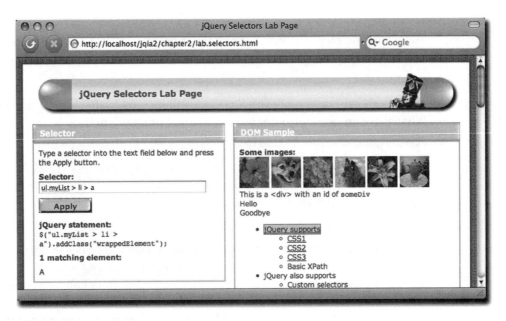

Figure 2.4 With the selector `ul.myList > li > a`, only the direct children of parent nodes are matched.

```
      <li><a href="css2">CSS2</a></li>
      <li><a href="css3">CSS3</a></li>
      <li>Basic XPath</li>
   </ul>
</li>
```

What makes the link pointing to an external site unique is the `http://` at the beginning of the string value for the link's `href` attribute. We could select links that have an `href` value starting with `http://` with the following selector:

```
a[href^='http://']
```

This matches all links with an `href` value beginning with the exact string `http://`. The caret character (`^`) is used to specify that the match is to occur at the beginning of a value. As this is the same character used by most regular expression processors to signify matching at the beginning of a candidate string, it should be easy to remember.

Visit the Lab page again (from which the previous HTML fragment was lifted), type `a[href^='http://']` into the text box, and click Apply. Note how only the jQuery link is highlighted.

There are other ways to use attribute selectors. To match an element that possesses a specific attribute, regardless of its value, we can use

```
form[method]
```

This matches any `<form>` element that has an explicit `method` attribute.

To match a specific attribute value, we use something like

```
input[type='text']
```

This selector matches all input elements with a type of text.

We've already seen the "match attribute at beginning" selector in action. Here's another:

```
div[title^='my']
```

This selects all <div> elements with a title attribute whose value begins with my.

What about an "attribute ends with" selector? Coming right up:

```
a[href$='.pdf']
```

This is a useful selector for locating all links that reference PDF files.

And here's a selector for locating elements whose attributes contain arbitrary strings anywhere in the attribute value:

```
a[href*='jquery.com']
```

As we'd expect, this selector matches all <a> elements that reference the jQuery site.

Table 2.2 shows the basic CSS selectors that we can use with jQuery.

With all this knowledge in hand, head over to the Selectors Lab page, and spend some more time running experiments using selectors of various types from table 2.2. Try to make some targeted selections like the <span> elements containing the text *Hello* and *Goodbye* (hint: you'll need to use a combination of selectors to get the job done).

As if the power of the selectors that we've discussed so far isn't enough, there are some more options that offer an even finer ability to slice and dice the page.

Table 2.2 The basic CSS selectors supported by jQuery

Selector	Description
*	Matches any element.
E	Matches all elements with tag name E.
E F	Matches all elements with tag name F that are descendants of E.
E>F	Matches all elements with tag name F that are direct children of E.
E+F	Matches all elements with tag name F that are immediately preceded by sibling E.
E~F	Matches all elements with tag name F preceded by any sibling E.
E.C	Matches all elements with tag name E with class name C. Omitting E is the same as *.C.
E#I	Matches all elements with tag name E with the id of I. Omitting E is the same as *#I.
E[A]	Matches all elements with tag name E that have attribute A of any value.
E[A=V]	Matches all elements with tag name E that have attribute A whose value is exactly V.
E[A^=V]	Matches all elements with tag name E that have attribute A whose value starts with V.
E[A$=V]	Matches all elements with tag name E that have attribute A whose value ends with V.
E[A!=V]	Matches all elements with tag name E that have attribute A whose value doesn't match the value V, or that lack attribute A completely.
E[A*=V]	Matches all elements with tag name E that have attribute A whose value contains V.

2.1.4   *Selecting by position*

Sometimes, we'll need to select elements by their position on the page or in relation to other elements. We might want to select the first link on the page, or every other paragraph, or the last list item of each list. jQuery supports mechanisms for achieving these specific selections.

For example, consider

```
a:first
```

This format of selector matches the first <a> element on the page.

What about picking every other element?

```
p:odd
```

This selector matches every odd paragraph element. As we might expect, we can also specify that evenly ordered elements be selected with

```
p:even
```

Another form,

```
ul li:last-child
```

chooses the last child of parent elements. In this example, the last <li> child of each <ul> element is matched.

There are a whole slew of these selectors, some defined by CSS, others specific to jQuery, and they can provide surprisingly elegant solutions to sometimes tough problems. The CSS specification refers to these types of selectors as *pseudo-classes*, but jQuery has adopted the crisper term *filters*, because each of these selectors filter a base selector. These filter selectors are easy to spot, as they all begin with the colon (:) character. And remember, if you omit any base selector, it defaults to *.

See table 2.3 for a list of these positional filters (which the jQuery documentation terms the *basic* and *child* filters).

Table 2.3   The positional filter selectors supported by jQuery

Selector	Description
:first	Matches the first match within the context. li a:first returns the first link that's a descendant of a list item.
:last	Matches the last match within the context. li a:last returns the last link that's a descendant of a list item.
:first-child	Matches the first child element within the context. li:first-child returns the first list item of each list.
:last-child	Matches the last child element within the context. li:last-child returns the last list item of each list.
:only-child	Returns all elements that have no siblings.

Table 2.3 The positional filter selectors supported by jQuery *(continued)*

Selector	Description
`:nth-child(n)`	Matches the *n*th child element within the context. `li:nth-child(2)` returns the second list item of each list.
`:nth-child(even|odd)`	Matches even or odd children within the context. `li:nth-child(even)` returns the even list items of each list.
`:nth-child(Xn+Y)`	Matches the *n*th child element computed by the supplied formula. If `Y` is 0, it may be omitted. `li:nth-child(3n)` returns every third list item, whereas `li:nth-child(5n+1)` returns the item after every fifth element.
`:even`	Matches even elements within the context. `li:even` returns every even list item.
`:odd`	Matches odd elements within the context. `li:odd` returns every odd list item.
`:eq(n)`	Matches the *n*th matching element.
`:gt(n)`	Matches matching elements after and excluding the *n*th matching element.
`:lt(n)`	Matches matching elements before and excluding the *n*th matching element.

There is one quick gotcha (isn't there always?). The `:nth-child` filter starts counting from 1 (for CSS compatibility), whereas the other selectors start counting from 0 (following the more common programming convention). This becomes second nature with practice, but it may be a bit confusing at first.

Let's dig in some more.

Consider the following table from the Lab's sample DOM. It contains a list of programming languages and some basic information about them:

```
<table id="languages">
  <thead>
    <tr>
      <th>Language</th>
      <th>Type</th>
      <th>Invented</th>
    </tr>
  </thead>
  <tbody>
    <tr>
      <td>Java</td>
      <td>Static</td>
      <td>1995</td>
    </tr>
    <tr>
      <td>Ruby</td>
      <td>Dynamic</td>
      <td>1993</td>
```

```
      </tr>
      <tr>
        <td>Smalltalk</td>
        <td>Dynamic</td>
        <td>1972</td>
      </tr>
      <tr>
        <td>C++</td>
        <td>Static</td>
        <td>1983</td>
      </tr>
    </tbody>
</table>
```

Let's say that we wanted to get all of the table cells that contain the names of programming languages. Because they're all the first cells in their rows, we could use

```
table#languages td:first-child
```

We could also easily use

```
table#languages td:nth-child(1)
```

but the first syntax would be considered pithier and more elegant.

To grab the language type cells, we'd change the selector to use :nth-child(2), and for the year they were invented, we'd use :nth-child(3) or :last-child. If we wanted the absolute last table cell (the one containing the text 1983), we'd use td:last. Also, whereas td:eq(2) returns the cell containing the text 1995, td:nth-child(2) returns all of the cells giving programming language types. Again, remember that :eq is zero-based, but :nth-child is one-based.

 Before we move on, head back over to the Selectors Lab and try selecting entries two and four from the list. Then, try to find three different ways to select the cell containing the text *1972* in the table. Also, try and get a feel for the difference between the :nth-child type of filters and the absolute position selectors.

Even though the CSS selectors we've examined so far are incredibly powerful, let's discuss ways of squeezing even more power out of jQuery's selectors.

2.1.5 *Using CSS and custom jQuery filter selectors*

The CSS selectors that we've seen so far give us a great deal of power and flexibility to match the desired DOM elements, but there are even more selectors that give us further ability to filter the selections.

As an example, we might want to match all checkboxes that are in checked state. You might be tempted to try something along these lines:

```
$('input[type=checkbox][checked]')
```

But trying to match by attribute will only check the *initial* state of the control as specified in the HTML markup. What we really want to check is the real-time state of the controls. CSS offers a pseudo-class, :checked, that matches elements that are in a checked state. For example, whereas the input selector selects all <input> elements, the `input:checked` selector narrows the search to only `<input>` elements that are checked.

As if that wasn't enough, jQuery provides a whole handful of powerful custom filter selectors, not specified by CSS, that make identifying target elements even easier. For example, the custom `:checkbox` selector identifies all check box elements. Combining these custom selectors can be powerful; consider `:checkbox:checked` or `:radio:checked`.

As we discussed earlier, jQuery supports the CSS filter selectors and also defines a number of custom selectors. They're described in table 2.4.

Table 2.4   The CSS and custom jQuery filter selectors

Selector	Description	In CSS?
`:animated`	Selects only elements that are currently under animated control. Chapter 5 will cover animations and effects.	
`:button`	Selects only button elements (`input[type=submit]`, `input[type=reset]`, `input[type=button]`, or `button`).	
`:checkbox`	Selects only checkbox elements (`input[type=checkbox]`).	
`:checked`	Selects only checkboxes or radio elements in checked state.	✓
`:contains(food)`	Selects only elements containing the text `food`.	
`:disabled`	Selects only elements in disabled state.	✓
`:enabled`	Selects only elements in enabled state.	✓
`:file`	Selects only file input elements (`input[type=file]`).	
`:has(selector)`	Selects only elements that contain at least one element that matches the specified selector.	
`:header`	Selects only elements that are headers; for example, `<h1>` through `<h6>` elements.	
`:hidden`	Selects only elements that are hidden.	
`:image`	Selects only image input elements (`input[type=image]`).	
`:input`	Selects only form elements (`input`, `select`, `textarea`, `button`).	
`:not(selector)`	Negates the specified selector.	✓
`:parent`	Selects only elements that have children (including text), but not empty elements.	
`:password`	Selects only password elements (`input[type=password]`).	
`:radio`	Selects only radio elements (`input[type=radio]`).	
`:reset`	Selects only reset buttons (`input[type=reset]` or `button[type=reset]`).	

Table 2.4   The CSS and custom jQuery filter selectors *(continued)*

Selector	Description	In CSS?
`:selected`	Selects only `<option>` elements that are in selected state.	
`:submit`	Selects only submit buttons (`button[type=submit]` or `input[type=submit]`).	
`:text`	Selects only text elements (`input[type=text]`).	
`:visible`	Selects only elements that are visible.	

Many of these CSS and custom jQuery filter selectors are form-related, allowing us to specify, rather elegantly, a specific element type or state. We can combine selector filters too. For example, if we want to select only enabled and checked checkboxes, we could use

`:checkbox:checked:enabled`

 Try out as many of these filters as you like in the Selectors Lab until you feel that you have a good grasp on their operation.

These filters are an immensely useful addition to the set of selectors at our disposal, but what about the *inverse* of these filters?

USING THE :NOT FILTER

If we want to negate a selector, let's say to match any input element that's *not* a checkbox, we can use the `:not` filter.

For example, to select non-checkbox `<input>` elements, you could use

`input:not(:checkbox)`

But be careful! It's easy to go astray and get some unexpected results!

For example, let's say that we wanted to select all images except for those whose `src` attribute contained the text "dog". We might quickly concoct the following selector:

`$(':not(img[src*="dog"])')`

But if we used this selector, we'd find that not only did we get all the image elements that don't reference "dog" in their `src`, we'd also get every element in the DOM that isn't an image element!

Whoops! Remember that when a base selector is omitted, it defaults to *, so our errant selector actually reads as "fetch all elements that aren't images that reference 'dog' in their `src` attributes." What we really intended was "fetch all image elements that don't reference 'dog' in their `src` attributes," which would be expressed like this:

`$('img:not([src*="dog"])')`

 Again, use the Lab page to conduct experiments until you're comfortable with how to use the `:not` filter to invert selections.

jQuery also adds a custom filter that helps when making selections using parent-child relationships.

WARNING   If you're still using jQuery 1.2, be aware that filter selectors such as `:not()` and `:has()` can only accept other filter selectors. They can't be passed selectors that contain element expressions. This restriction was lifted in jQuery 1.3.

USING THE :HAS FILTER

As we saw earlier, CSS defines a useful selector for selecting elements that are descendants of particular parents. For example, this selector,

```
div span
```

would select all `<span>` elements that are descendants of `<div>` elements.

But what if we wanted the opposite? What if we wanted to select all `<div>` elements that contained `<span>` elements?

That's the job of the `:has()` filter. Consider this selector,

```
div:has(span)
```

which selects the `<div>` ancestor elements, as opposed to the `<span>` descendant elements.

This can be a powerful mechanism when we get to the point where we want to select elements that represent complex constructs. For example, let's say that we want to find which table row contains a particular image element that can be uniquely identified using its `src` attribute. We might use a selector such as this,

```
$('tr:has(img[src$="puppy.png"])')
```

which would return any table row element containing the identified image anywhere in its descendant hierarchy.

You can be sure that this, along with the other jQuery filters, will play a large part in the code we examine going forward.

As we've seen, jQuery offers a large toolset with which to select existing elements on a page for manipulation via the jQuery methods, which we'll begin to examine in chapter 3. But before we look at the manipulation methods, let's look at how to use the `$()` function to create *new* HTML elements.

2.2   *Generating new HTML*

Sometimes, we'll want to generate new fragments of HTML to insert into the page. Such dynamic elements could be as simple as extra text we want to display under certain conditions, or something as complicated as creating a table of database results we've obtained from a server.

With jQuery, creating dynamic elements is a simple matter, because, as we saw in chapter 1, the `$()` function can create elements from HTML strings in addition to selecting existing page elements. Consider this line:

```
$("<div>Hello</div>")
```

This expression creates a new `<div>` element ready to be added to the page. Any jQuery methods that we could run on wrapped element sets of existing elements can be run on the newly created fragment. This may not seem impressive on first glance, but when we throw event handlers, Ajax, and effects into the mix (as we will in the upcoming chapters), you'll see that it could come in mighty handy.

Note that if we want to create an empty <div> element, we can get away with this shortcut:

```
$("<div>")
```

This is identical to $("<div></div>") and $("<div/>"), though it is recommended that you use well-formed markup and include the opening and closing tags for any element types that can contain other elements.

It's almost embarrassingly easy to create such simple HTML elements, and thanks to the chainability of jQuery methods, creating more complex elements isn't much harder. We can apply any jQuery method to the wrapped set containing the newly created element. For example, we can apply styles to the element with the css() method. We could also create attributes on the element with the attr() method, but jQuery provides an even better means to do so.

We can pass a second parameter to the element-creating $() method that specifies the attributes and their values. This parameter takes the form of a JavaScript object whose properties serve as the name and value of the attributes to be applied to the element.

Let's say that we want to create an image element complete with multiple attributes, some styling, and let's make it clickable to boot! Take a look at the code in listing 2.1.

Listing 2.1 Dynamically creating a full-featured `<img>` element

```
$('<img>',                          ⊲ ❶ Creates the basic <img> element
  {
    src: 'images/little.bear.png',        ⊲ ┐
    alt: 'Little Bear',                   ❷ Assigns various attributes
    title:'I woof in your general direction', ┘
    click: function(){                    ⊲ ┐ Establishes click
      alert($(this).attr('title'));       ❸ handler
    }
  })
  .css({                            ⊲ ❹ Styles the image
    cursor: 'pointer',
    border: '1px solid black',
    padding: '12px 12px 20px 12px',
    backgroundColor: 'white'
  })                                    ❺ Attaches the element
  .appendTo('body');                    ⊲ ┘ to the document
```

The single jQuery statement in listing 2.1 creates the basic <img> element ❶, gives it important attributes, such as its source, alternate text, and flyout title ❷, styles it to look like a printed photograph ❹, and attaches it to the DOM tree ❺.

We also threw a bit of a curve ball at you here. We used the attribute object to establish an event handler that issues an alert (garnered from the image's title) when the image is clicked ❸.

jQuery not only lets us specify attributes in the attribute parameter; we can also establish handlers for all the event types (which we'll be exploring in depth in chapter 4), as well as supply values for handful of jQuery methods whose purpose is to set various facets of the element. We haven't examined these methods yet, but we can set values for the following methods (which we'll mostly discuss in the next chapter): val, css, html, text, data, width, height, and offset.

So, in listing 2.1 we could omit the call to the chained css() method, replacing it with the following property in the attribute parameter:

```
css: {
  cursor: 'pointer',
  border: '1px solid black',
  padding: '12px 12px 20px 12px',
  backgroundColor: 'white'
}
```

Regardless of how we arrange the code, that's a pretty hefty statement—which we spread across multiple lines, and with logical indentation, for readability—but it also does a heck of a lot. Such statements aren't uncommon in jQuery-enabled pages, and if you find it a bit overwhelming, don't worry, we'll be covering every method used in this statement over the next few chapters. Writing such compound statements will be second nature before much longer.

Figure 2.5 shows the result of this code, both when the page is first loaded (2.5a), and after the image has been clicked upon (2.5b).

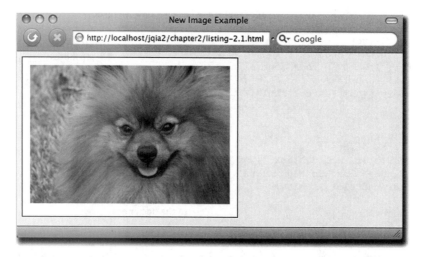

Figure 2.5a Creating complex elements on the fly, including this image, which generates an alert when it's clicked upon, is easy as pie.

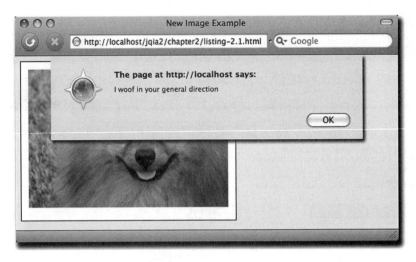

Figure 2.5b   The dynaimcally-generated image possesses all expected styles and attributes, including the mouse click behavior of issuing an alert

The full code for this example can be found in the book's project code at chapter2/ listing-2.1.html.

Up until now, we've applied wrapper methods to the entire wrapped set as created by the jQuery function when we pass a selector to it. But there may be times when we want to further manipulate that set before acting upon it.

2.3   *Managing the wrapped element set*

Once we've got a set of wrapped elements, whether identified from existing DOM elements with selectors, or created as new elements using HTML snippets (or a combination of both), we're ready to manipulate those elements using the powerful set of jQuery methods. We'll start looking at those methods in the next chapter, but what if we want to further refine the set of elements wrapped by the jQuery function? In this section, we'll explore the many ways that we can refine, extend, or subset the set of wrapped elements that we wish to operate upon.

In order to help you in this endeavor, we've included another Lab in the downloadable project code for this chapter: the jQuery Operations Lab Page (chapter2/ lab.operations.html). This page, which looks a lot like the Selectors Lab we employed earlier in this chapter, is shown in figure 2.6.

This new Lab page not only looks like the Selectors Lab, it also operates in a similar fashion. Except in *this* Lab, rather than typing a selector, we can type in any *complete* jQuery operation that results in a wrapped set. The operation is executed in the context of the DOM Sample, and, as with the Selectors Lab, the results are displayed.

In a sense, the jQuery Operations Lab is a more general case of the Selectors Lab. Where the latter only allowed us to enter a single selector, the jQuery Operations Lab allows us to enter any expression that results in a jQuery wrapped set. Because of the

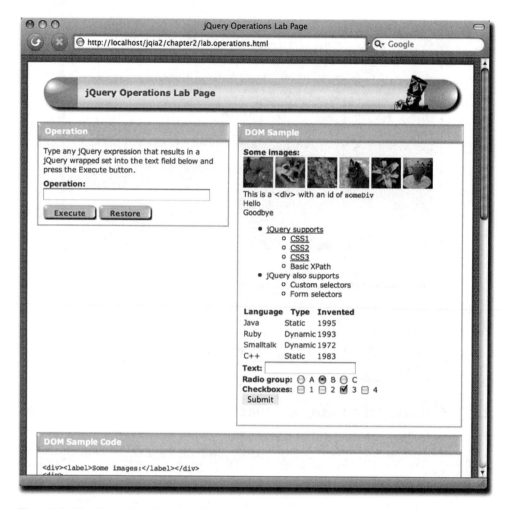

Figure 2.6 The jQuery Operations Lab Page lets us compose wrapped sets in real time to help us see how wrapped sets can be created and managed.

way jQuery chaining works, this expression can also include wrapper methods, making this a powerful Lab for examining the operations of jQuery.

Be aware that you need to enter *valid* syntax, as well as expressions that result in a jQuery wrapped set. Otherwise, you're going to be faced with a handful of unhelpful JavaScript errors.

To get a feel for the Lab, display it in your browser and enter this text into the Operation field:

```
$('img').hide()
```

Then click the Execute button.

This operation is executed within the context of the DOM Sample, and you'll see how the images disappear from the sample. After any operation, you can restore the DOM Sample to its original condition by clicking the Restore button.

We'll see this new Lab in action as we work our way through the sections that follow, and you might even find it helpful in later chapters to test various jQuery operations.

2.3.1 Determining the size of a wrapped set

We mentioned before that the set of jQuery wrapped elements acts a lot like an array. This mimicry includes a `length` property, just like JavaScript arrays, that contains the number of wrapped elements.

Should we wish to use a method rather than a property, jQuery also defines the `size()` method, which returns the same information.

Consider the following statement:

```
$('#someDiv')
    .html('There are '+$('a').size()+' link(s) on this page.');
```

The jQuery expression embedded in the statement matches all elements of type `<a>` and returns the number of matched elements using the `size()` method. This is used to construct a text string, which is set as the content of an element with `id` of `someDiv` using the `html()` method (which we'll see in the next chapter).

The formal syntax of the `size()` method is as follows:

Method syntax: size

size()
Returns the count of elements in the wrapped set.

Parameters
  none

Returns
The element count.

OK, so now we know how many elements we have. What if we want to access them directly?

2.3.2 Obtaining elements from a wrapped set

Usually, once we have a wrapped set of elements, we'll use jQuery methods to perform some sort of operation upon them as a whole; for example, hiding them all with the `hide()` method. But there may be times when we want to get our grubby little hands on a direct reference to an element or elements to perform raw JavaScript operations upon them.

Let's look at some of the ways that jQuery allows us to do just that.

FETCHING ELEMENTS BY INDEX

Because jQuery allows us to treat the wrapped set as a JavaScript array, we can use simple array indexing to obtain any element in the wrapped list by position. For example, to obtain the first element in the set of all <img> elements with an `alt` attribute on the page, we could write

```
var imgElement = $('img[alt]')[0]
```

If you prefer to use a method rather than array indexing, jQuery defines the `get()` method for that purpose:

Method syntax: get

get(index)
Obtains one or all of the matched elements in the wrapped set. If no parameter is specified, all elements in the wrapped set are returned in a JavaScript array. If an `index` parameter is provided, the indexed element is returned.

Parameters
    index   (Number) The index of the single element to return. If omitted, the entire set is returned in an array.

Returns
A DOM element or an array of DOM elements.

The fragment

```
var imgElement = $('img[alt]').get(0)
```

is equivalent to the previous example that used array indexing.

The `get()` method will also accept a negative index value as a parameter. In this case, it fetches the element relative to the end of the wrapped set. For example `.get(-1)` will retrieve the last element in the wrapped set, `.get(-2)` the second to last, and so on.

In addition to obtaining a single element, `get()` can also return an array.

Although the `toArray()` method (discussed in the next section) is the preferred way to obtain a JavaScript array of the elements within a wrapped set, the `get()` method can also be used to obtain a plain JavaScript array of all the wrapped elements.

This method of obtaining an array is provided for backward compatibility with previous versions of jQuery.

The `get()` method returns a DOM element, but sometimes we'll want a wrapped set containing a specific element rather than the element itself. It would look really weird to write something like this:

```
$($('p').get(23))
```

So jQuery provides the `eq()` method, that mimics the action of the `:eq` selector filter:

Method syntax: eq

`eq(index)`

Obtains the indexed element in the wrapped set and returns a new wrapped set containing just that element.

Parameters

index   (Number) The index of the single element to return. As with `get()`, a negative index can be specified to index from the end of the set.

Returns

A wrapped set containing one or zero elements.

Obtaining the first element of a wrapped set is such a common operation that there's a convenience method that makes it even easier: the `first()` method.

Method syntax: first

`first()`

Obtains the first element in the wrapped set and returns a new wrapped set containing just that element. If the original set is empty, so is the returned set.

Parameters

Returns

A wrapped set containing one or zero elements.

As you might expect, there's a corresponding method to obtain the last element in a wrapped set as well.

Method syntax: last

`last()`

Obtains the last element in the wrapped set and returns a new wrapped set containing just that element. If the original set is empty, so is the returned set.

Parameters

Returns

A wrapped set containing one or zero elements.

Now let's examine the preferred method of obtaining an array of wrapped elements.

FETCHING ALL THE ELEMENTS AS AN ARRAY

If we wish to obtain all of the elements in a wrapped set as a JavaScript array of DOM elements, jQuery provides the `toArray()` method:

Method syntax: toArray

`toArray()`
Returns the elements in the wrapped set as an array of DOM elements.

Parameters
  none
Returns

A JavaScript array of the DOM elements within the wrapped set.

Consider this example:

```
var allLabeledButtons = $('label+button').toArray();
```

This statement collects all the `<button>` elements on the page that are immediately preceded by `<label>` elements into a jQuery wrapper, and then creates a JavaScript array of those elements to assign to the `allLabeledButtons` variable.

FINDING THE INDEX OF AN ELEMENT

While `get()` finds an element given an index, we can use an inverse operation, `index()`, to find the index of a particular element in the wrapped set. The syntax of the `index()` method is as follows:

Method syntax: index

`index(element)`
Finds the passed element in the wrapped set and returns its ordinal index within the set, or finds the ordinal index of the first element of the wrapped set within its siblings. If the element isn't found, the value -1 is returned.

Parameters
  element   (Element|Selector) A reference to the element whose ordinal value is to be determined, or a selector that identifies the element. If omitted, the first element of the wrapped set is located within its list of siblings.
Returns

The ordinal value of the passed element within the wrapped set or its siblings, or -1 if not found.

Let's say that for some reason we want to know the ordinal index of an image with the id of `findMe` within the entire set of images in a page. We can obtain this value with this statement:

```
var n = $('img').index($('img#findMe')[0]);
```

We can also shorten this:

```
var n = $('img').index('img#findMe');
```

The index() method can also be used to find the index of an element within its parent (that is, among its siblings). For example,

```
var n = $('img').index();
```

This will set n to the ordinal index of the first <img> element within its parent.

Now, rather than obtaining *direct* references to elements or their indexes, how would we go about adjusting the set of elements that are wrapped?

2.3.3 *Slicing and dicing a wrapped element set*

Once you have a wrapped element set, you may want to augment that set by adding to it or by reducing the set to a subset of the originally matched elements. jQuery offers a large collection of methods to manage the set of wrapped elements. First, let's look at adding elements to a wrapped set.

ADDING MORE ELEMENTS TO A WRAPPED SET

We may often find ourselves wanting to add more elements to an existing wrapped set. This capability is most useful when we want to add more elements after applying some method to the original set. Remember, jQuery chaining makes it possible to perform an enormous amount of work in a single statement.

We'll look at some concrete examples of such situations in a moment, but first, let's start with a simpler scenario. Let's say that we want to match all <img> elements that have either an alt or a title attribute. The powerful jQuery selectors allow us to express this as a single selector, such as

```
$('img[alt],img[title]')
```

But to illustrate the operation of the add() method, we could match the same set of elements with

```
$('img[alt]').add('img[title]')
```

Using the add() method in this fashion allows us to chain a bunch of selectors together, creating a union of the elements that satisfy either of the selectors.

Methods such as add() are also significant (and more flexible than aggregate selectors) within jQuery method chains because they don't augment the original wrapped set, but create a *new* wrapped set with the result. We'll see in just a bit how this can be extremely useful in conjunction with methods such as end() (which we'll examine in section 2.3.6) that can be used to "back out" operations that augment original wrapped sets.

This is the syntax of the add() method:

Method syntax: add

add(expression,context)

Creates a copy of the wrapped set and adds elements, specified by the `expression` parameter, to the new set. The expression can be a selector, an HTML fragment, a DOM element, or an array of DOM elements.

Parameters

expression   (Selector|Element|Array) Specifies what is to be added to the matched set. This parameter can be a jQuery selector, in which case any matched elements are added to the set. If the parameter is an HTML fragment, the appropriate elements are created and added to the set. If it is a DOM element or an array of DOM elements, they're added to the set.

context   (Selector|Element|Array|jQuery) Specifies a context to limit the search for elements that match the first parameter. This is the same context that can be passed to the `jQuery()` function. See section 2.1.1 for a description of this parameter.

Returns

A copy of the original wrapped set with the additional elements.

 Bring up the jQuery Operations Lab page in your browser, and enter this expression:

```
$('img[alt]').add('img[title]')
```

Then click the Execute button. This will execute the jQuery operation and result in the selection of all images with either an `alt` or `title` attribute.

Inspecting the HTML source for the DOM Sample reveals that all the images depicting flowers have an `alt` attribute, the puppy images have a `title` attribute, and the coffee pot image has neither. Therefore, we should expect that all images but the coffee pot will become part of the wrapped set. Figure 2.7 shows a screen capture of the results.

We can see that five of the six images (all but the coffee pot) were added to the wrapped set. The red outline may be a bit hard to see in the print version of this book with grayscale figures, but if you have downloaded the project (which you should have) and are using it to follow along (which you should be), it's very evident.

Now let's take a look at a more realistic use of the add() method. Let's say that we want to apply a thick border to all <img> elements that have an `alt` attribute, and then apply a level of transparency to all <img> elements that have either an `alt` or `title` attribute. The comma operator (,) of CSS selectors won't help us with this one because we want to apply an operation to a wrapped set and *then* add more elements to it before applying another operation. We could easily accomplish this with multiple statements, but it would be more efficient and elegant to use the power of jQuery chaining to accomplish the task in a single expression, such as this:

```
$('img[alt]')
  .addClass('thickBorder')
  .add('img[title]')
  .addClass('seeThrough')
```

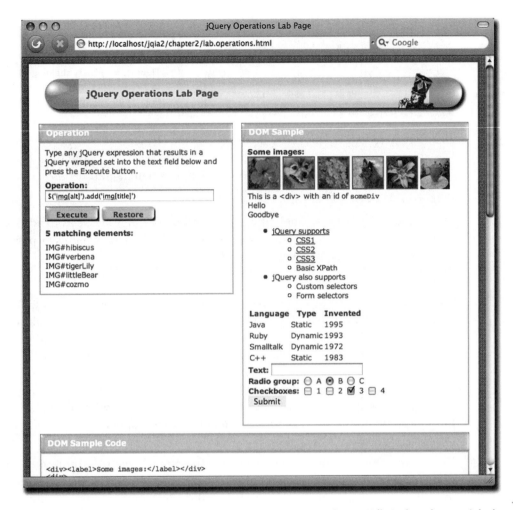

Figure 2.7 The expected image elements, those with an `alt` or `title` attribute, have been matched by the jQuery expression.

In this statement, we create a wrapped set of all `<img>` elements that have an `alt` attribute, apply a predefined class that applies a thick border, add the `<img>` elements that have a `title` attribute, and finally apply a class that establishes a level of transparency to the newly augmented set.

Enter this statement into the jQuery Operations Lab (which has predefined the referenced classes), and view the results as shown in figure 2.8.

In these results, we can see that the flower images (those with `alt`) have thick borders, and all images but the coffee pot (the only one with neither an `alt` nor a `title`) are faded as a result of applying an opacity rule.

The `add()` method can also be used to add elements to an existing wrapped set, given direct references to those elements. Passing an element reference, or an array of

Figure 2.8   jQuery chaining allows us to perform complex operations in a single statement, as seen in these results.

element references, to the add() method adds the elements to the wrapped set. If we had an element reference in a variable named someElement, it could be added to the set of all images containing an alt property with this statement:

```
$('img[alt]').add(someElement)
```

As if that wasn't flexible enough, the add() method not only allows us to add existing elements to the wrapped set, but we can also use it to add new elements by passing it a string containing HTML markup. Consider

```
$('p').add('<div>Hi there!</div>')
```

This fragment creates a wrapped set of all <p> elements in the document, and then creates a new <div>, and adds it to the wrapped set. Note that doing so only adds the new element to the wrapped set; no action has been taken in this statement to add the new element to the DOM. We might then use the jQuery appendTo() method (patience, we'll be talking about such methods soon enough) to append the elements we selected, as well as the newly created HTML, to some part of the DOM.

Augmenting the wrapped set with add() is easy and powerful, but now let's look at the jQuery methods that let us *remove* elements from a wrapped set.

HONING THE CONTENTS OF A WRAPPED SET

We saw that it's a simple matter to augment wrapped sets from multiple selectors chained together with the add() method. It's also possible to chain selectors together to form an *except* relationship by employing the not() method. This is similar to the :not filter selector we discussed earlier, but it can be employed in a similar fashion to the add() method to remove elements from the wrapped set anywhere within a jQuery chain of methods.

Let's say that we want to select all <img> elements in a page that sport a title attribute *except* for those that contain the text "puppy" in the title attribute value. We could come up with a single selector that expresses this condition (namely img[title]:not([title*=puppy])), but for the sake of illustration, let's pretend that we forgot about the :not filter. By using the not() method, which removes any elements from a wrapped set that match the passed selector expression, we can express an *except* type of relationship. To perform the described match, we can write

```
$('img[title]').not('[title*=puppy]')
```

Type this expression into the jQuery Operations Lab Page, and execute it. You'll see that only the tan puppy image has the highlight applied. The black puppy, which is

included in the original wrapped set because it possesses a `title` attribute, is removed by the `not()` invocation because its `title` contains the text "puppy".

Method syntax: not

`not(expression)`

Creates a copy of the wrapped set and removes elements from the new set that match criteria specified by the value of the `expression` parameter.

Parameters

`expression`	(Selector|Element|Array|Function) Specifies which items are to be removed. If the parameter is a jQuery selector, any matching elements are removed. If an element reference or array of elements is passed, those elements are removed from the set.
	If a function is passed, the function is invoked for each item in the wrapped set (with `this` set to the item), and returning `true` from the invocation causes the item to be removed from the wrapped set.

Returns

A copy of the original wrapped set without the removed elements.

The `not()` method can be used to remove individual elements from the wrapped set by passing a reference to an element or an array of element references. The latter is interesting and powerful because, remember, any jQuery wrapped set can be used as an array of element references.

When maximum flexibility is needed, a function can be passed to `not()`, and a determination of whether to keep or remove the element can be made on an element-by-element basis. Consider this example:

```
$('img').not(function(){ return !$(this).hasClass('keepMe'); })
```

This expression will select all `<img>` elements and then remove any that don't have the class "keepMe".

This method allows us to filter the wrapped set in ways that are difficult or impossible to express with a selector expression by resorting to programmatic filtering of the wrapped set items.

For those times when the test applied within the function passed to `not()` seems to be the opposite of what we want to express, `not()` has an inverse method, `filter()`, that works in a similar fashion, except that it removes elements when the function returns `false`.

For example, let's say that we want to create a wrapped set of all `<td>` elements that contain a numeric value. As powerful as the jQuery selector expressions are, such a requirement is impossible to express using them. For such situations, the `filter()` method can be employed, as follows:

```
$('td').filter(function(){return this.innerHTML.match(/^\d+$/)})
```

This jQuery expression creates a wrapped set of all `<td>` elements and then invokes the function passed to the `filter()` method for each, with the current matched elements as the this value for the invocation. The function uses a regular expression to determine whether the element content matches the described pattern (a sequence of one or more digits), returning false if not. Elements whose filter function invocation returns false aren't included in the returned wrapped set.

Method syntax: filter

filter(expression)

Creates a copy of the wrapped set and removes elements from the new set that don't match criteria specified by the value of the expression parameter.

Parameters

expression	(Selector|Element|Array|Function) Specifies which items are to be removed.
	If the parameter is a jQuery selector, any elements that don't match are removed.
	If an element reference or array of elements is passed, all but those elements are removed from the set.
	If a function is passed, the function is invoked for each element in the wrapped set (with this referencing the element), and returning false from the invocation causes the element to be removed from the wrapped set.

Returns

A copy of the original wrapped set without the filtered elements.

 Again, bring up the jQuery Operations Lab, type the previous expression in, and execute it. You'll see that the table cells for the "Invented" column are the only <td> elements that end up being selected.

The filter() method can also be used with a passed selector expression. When used in this manner, it operates in the inverse manner than the corresponding not() method, removing any elements that don't match the passed selector. This isn't a super-powerful method, as it's usually easier to use a more restrictive selector in the first place, but it can be useful within a chain of jQuery methods. Consider, for example,

```
$('img')
  .addClass('seeThrough')
  .filter('[title*=dog]')
  .addClass('thickBorder')
```

This chained statement selects all images, applies the seeThrough class to them, and then reduces the set to only those image elements whose title attribute contains the string dog before applying another class named thickBorder. The result is that all the images end up semi-transparent, but only the tan dog gets the thick border treatment.

The not() and filter() methods give us powerful means to adjust a set of wrapped elements on the fly, based on just about any criteria concerning the wrapped elements. But we can also subset the wrapped set, based on the *position* of the elements within the set. Let's look at those methods next.

OBTAINING SUBSETS OF A WRAPPED SET

Sometimes you may wish to obtain a subset of a wrapped set based upon the position of the elements within the set. jQuery provides a `slice()` method to do that. This method creates and returns a new set from any contiguous portion, or a slice, of an original wrapped set.

Method syntax: slice

`slice(begin,end)`

Creates and returns a new wrapped set containing a contiguous portion of the matched set.

Parameters

`begin`	(Number) The zero-based position of the first element to be included in the returned slice.
`end`	(Number) The optional zero-based index of the first element not to be included in the returned slice, or one position beyond the last element to be included. If omitted, the slice extends to the end of the set.

Returns

The newly created wrapped set.

If we want to obtain a wrapped set that contains a single element from another set, based on its position in the original set, we can employ the `slice()` method, passing the zero-based position of the element within the wrapped set.

For example, to obtain the third element, we could write

```
$('*').slice(2,3);
```

This statement selects all elements on the page and then generates a new set containing the third element in the matched set.

Note that this is different from `$('*').get(2)`, which returns the third *element* in the wrapped set, not a wrapped set containing the element.

Therefore, a statement such as

```
$('*').slice(0,4);
```

selects all elements on the page and then creates a set containing the first four elements.

To grab elements from the end of the wrapped set, the statement

```
$('*').slice(4);
```

matches all elements on the page and then returns a set containing all but the first four elements.

Another method we can use to obtain a subset of a wrapped set is the `has()` method. Like the `:has` filter, this method tests the children of the wrapped elements, using this check to choose the elements to become part of the subset.

Method syntax: has

has(test)

Creates and returns a new wrapped set containing only elements from the original wrapped set that contain descendents that match the passed `test` expression.

Parameters

test   (Selector|Element) A selector to be applied to all descendents of the wrapped elements, or an element to be tested. Only elements possessing an element that matches the selector, or the passed element, are included in the returned wrapped set.

Returns

The resulting wrapped set.

For example, consider this line:

```
$('div').has('img[alt]')
```

This expression will create a wrapped set of all <div> elements, and then create and return a second set that contains only those <div> elements that contain at least one descendent <img> element that possess an `alt` attribute.

TRANSLATING ELEMENTS OF A WRAPPED SET

We'll often want to perform transformations on the elements of a wrapped set. For example, what if we wanted to collect all the id values of the wrapped elements, or perhaps collect the values of a wrapped set of form elements in order to create a query string from them? The map() method comes in mighty handy for such occasions.

Method syntax: map

map(callback)

Invokes the callback function for each element in the wrapped set, and collects the returned values into a jQuery object instance.

Parameters

callback   (Function) A callback function that's invoked for each element in the wrapped set. Two parameters are passed to this function: the zero-based index of the element within the set, and the element itself. The element is also established as the function context (the `this` keyword).

Returns

The wrapped set of translated values.

For example, the following code will collect all the id values of all <div> elements on the page into a JavaScript array:

```
var allIds = $('div').map(function(){
  return (this.id==undefined) ? null : this.id;
}).get();
```

If any invocation of the callback function returns `null`, no corresponding entry is made in the returned set.

TRAVERSING A WRAPPED SET'S ELEMENTS

The map() method is useful for iterating over the elements of a wrapped set in order to collect values or translate the elements in some other way, but we'll have many occasions where we'll want to iterate over the elements for more general purposes. For these occasions, the jQuery each() method is invaluable.

Method syntax: each

each(iterator)
Traverses all elements in the matched set, invoking the passed iterator function for each.

Parameters

iterator   (Function) A function called for each element in the matched set. Two parameters are passed to this function: the zero-based index of the element within the set, and the element itself. The element is also established as the function context (the this reference).

Returns

The wrapped set.

An example of using this method could be to easily set a property value onto all elements in a matched set. For example, consider this:

```
$('img').each(function(n){
   this.alt='This is image['+n+'] with an id of '+this.id;
});
```

This statement will invoke the passed function for each image element on the page, modifying its alt property using the order of the element and its id value.

As a convenience, the each() method will also iterate over arrays of JavaScript objects and even individual objects (not that the latter has a lot of utility). Consider this example:

```
$([1,2,3]).each(function(){ alert(this); });
```

This statement will invoke the iterator function for each element of the array that's passed to $(), with the individual array items passed to the function as this.

And we're not done yet! jQuery also gives us the ability to obtain subsets of a wrapped set based on the *relationship* of the wrapped items to other elements in the DOM. Let's see how.

2.3.4 *Getting wrapped sets using relationships*

jQuery allows us to get new wrapped sets from an existing set, based on the hierarchical relationships of the wrapped elements to the other elements within the HTML DOM.

Table 2.5 shows these methods and their descriptions. Most of these methods accept an optional selector expression that can be used to choose the elements to be collected into the new set. If no such selector parameter is passed, all eligible elements are selected.

All of the methods in table 2.5, with the exception of contents() and offset-Parent() accept a parameter containing a selector string that can be used to filter the results.

Table 2.5   Methods for obtaining a new wrapped set based on relationships to other HTML DOM elements

Method	Description
children([selector])	Returns a wrapped set consisting of all unique children of the wrapped elements.
closest([selector])	Returns a wrapped set containing the single nearest ancestor that matches the passed expression, if any.
contents()	Returns a wrapped set of the contents of the elements, which may include text nodes, in the wrapped set. (This is frequently used to obtain the contents of <iframe> elements.)
next([selector])	Returns a wrapped set consisting of all unique next siblings of the wrapped elements.
nextAll([selector])	Returns a wrapped set containing all the following siblings of the wrapped elements.
nextUntil([selector])	Returns a wrapped set of all the following siblings of the elements of the wrapped elements until, but not including, the element matched by the selector. If no matches are made to the selector, or if the selector is omitted, all following siblings are selected.
offsetParent()	Returns a wrapped set containing the closest relatively or absolutely positioned parent of the first element in the wrapped set.
parent([selector])	Returns a wrapped set consisting of the unique direct parents of all wrapped elements.
parents([selector])	Returns a wrapped set consisting of the unique ancestors of all wrapped elements. This includes the direct parents as well as the remaining ancestors all the way up to, but not including, the document root.
parentsUntil([selector])	Returns a wrapped set of all ancestors of the elements of the wrapped elements up until, but not including, the element matched by the selector. If no matches are made to the selector, or if the selector is omitted, all ancestors are selected.
prev([selector])	Returns a wrapped set consisting of all unique previous siblings of the wrapped elements.
prevAll([selector])	Returns a wrapped set containing all the previous siblings of the wrapped elements.
prevUntil([selector])	Returns a wrapped set of all preceding siblings of the elements of the wrapped elements until, but not including, the element matched by the selector. If no matches are made to the selector, or if the selector is omitted, all previous siblings are selected.
siblings([selector])	Returns a wrapped set consisting of all unique siblings of the wrapped elements.

Consider a situation where a button's event handler (which we'll be exploring in great detail in chapter 4) is triggered with the button element referenced by the this keyword within the handler. Further, let's say that we want to find the <div> block within which the button is defined. The closest() method makes it a breeze:

```
$(this).closest('div')
```

But this would only find the most immediate ancestor <div>; what if the <div> we seek is higher in the ancestor tree? No problem. We can refine the selector we pass to closest() to discriminate which elements are selected:

```
$(this).closest('div.myButtonContainer')
```

Now the ancestor <div> with the class myButtonContainer will be selected.

The remainder of these methods work in a similar fashion. Take, for example, a situation in which we want to find a sibling button with a particular title attribute:

```
$(this).siblings('button[title="Close"]')
```

These methods give us a large degree of freedom to select elements from the DOM based on their relationships to the other DOM elements. But we're still not done. Let's see how jQuery deals further with wrapped sets.

2.3.5 *Even more ways to use a wrapped set*

As if all that were not enough, there are still a few more tricks that jQuery has up its sleeve to let us refine our collections of wrapped objects.

The find() method lets us search through the *descendants* of the elements in a wrapped set and returns a new set that contains all elements that match a passed selector expression. For example, given a wrapped set in variable wrappedSet, we can get another wrapped set of all citations (<cite> elements) within paragraphs that are descendants of elements in the original wrapped set:

```
wrappedSet.find('p cite')
```

Like many other jQuery wrapper methods, the find() method's power comes when it's used within a jQuery chain of operations.

Method syntax: find

find(selector)

Returns a new wrapped set containing all elements that are descendants of the elements of the original set that match the passed selector expression.

Parameters

selector   (String) A jQuery selector that elements must match to become part of the returned set.

Returns

The newly created wrapped set.

This method becomes very handy when we need to constrain a search for descendant elements in the middle of a jQuery method chain, where we can't employ any other context or constraining mechanism.

The last method that we'll examine in this section is one that allows us to test a wrapped set to see if it contains at least one element that matches a given selector expression. The `is()` method returns `true` if at least one element matches the selector, and `false` if not. For example,

```
var hasImage = $('*').is('img');
```

This statement sets the value of the `hasImage` variable to `true` if the current DOM has an image element.

Method syntax: is

`is(selector)`

Determines if any element in the wrapped set matches the passed selector expression.

Parameters

selector   (String) The selector expression to test against the elements of the wrapped set.

Returns

true if at least one element matches the passed selector; `false` if not.

This is a highly optimized and fast operation within jQuery and can be used without hesitation in areas where performance is of high concern.

2.3.6 *Managing jQuery chains*

We've made a big deal about the ability to chain jQuery wrapper methods together to perform a lot of activity in a single statement, and we'll continue to do so, because it *is* a big deal. This chaining ability not only allows us to write powerful operations in a concise manner, but it also improves efficiency because wrapped sets don't have to be recomputed in order to apply multiple methods to them.

Depending upon the methods used in a method chain, multiple wrapped sets may be generated. For example, using the `clone()` method (which we'll explore in detail in chapter 3) generates a new wrapped set, which creates copies of the elements in the first set. If, once a new wrapped set was generated, we had no way to reference the original set, our ability to construct versatile jQuery method chains would be severely curtailed.

Consider the following statement:

```
$('img').filter('[title]').hide();
```

Two wrapped sets are generated within this statement: the original wrapped set of all the <img> elements in the DOM, and a second wrapped set consisting of only those wrapped elements which also possess `title` attributes. (Yes, we could have done this with a single selector, but bear with us for illustration of the concept. Imagine that we do something important in the chain before the call to `filter()`.)

But what if we subsequently want to apply a method, such as adding a class name, to the original wrapped set *after* it's been filtered? We can't tack it onto the end of the existing chain; that would affect the titled images, not the original wrapped set of images.

jQuery provides for this need with the `end()` method. This method, when used within a jQuery chain, will "back up" to a previous wrapped set and return it as its value so that subsequent operations will apply to that previous set.

Consider

```
$('img').filter('[title]').hide().end().addClass('anImage');
```

The `filter()` method returns the set of titled images, but by calling `end()` we back up to the previous wrapped set (the original set of all images), which gets operated on by the `addClass()` method. Without the intervening `end()` method, `addClass()` would have operated on the set of clones.

Method syntax: end

end()

Used within a chain of jQuery methods to back up the current wrapped set to a previously returned set.

Parameters

   none

Returns

The previous wrapped set.

It might help to think of the wrapped sets generated during a jQuery method chain as being held on a stack. When `end()` is called, the top-most (most recent) wrapped set is popped from the stack, leaving the previous wrapped set exposed for subsequent methods to operate upon.

Another handy jQuery method that modifies the wrapped set "stack" is `andSelf()`, which merges the two topmost sets on the stack into a single wrapped set.

Method syntax: andSelf

andSelf()

Merges the two previous wrapped sets in a method chain.

Parameters

   none

Returns

The merged wrapped set.

Consider

```
$('div')
  .addClass('a')
  .find('img')
  .addClass('b')
  .andSelf()
  .addClass('c');
```

This statement selects all <div> elements, adds class a to them, creates a new wrapped set consisting of all <img> elements that are descendants of those <div> elements, applies class b to them, creates a third wrapped set that's a merger of the <div> elements and their descendant <img> elements, and applies class c to them.

Whew! At the end of it all, the <div> elements end up with classes a and c, whereas the images that are descendants of those elements are given classes b and c.

We can see that jQuery provides the means to manage wrapper sets for just about any type of operations that we want to perform upon them.

2.4   *Summary*

This chapter focused on creating and adjusting sets of elements (referred in this chapter and beyond as the *wrapped set*) via the many means that jQuery provides for identifying elements on an HTML page.

jQuery provides a versatile and powerful set of *selectors*, patterned after the selectors of CSS, for identifying elements within a page document in a concise but powerful syntax. These selectors include the CSS3 syntax currently supported by most modern browsers.

The creation and augmentation of wrapped sets using HTML fragments to create new elements on the fly is another important feature that jQuery provides. These orphaned elements can be manipulated, along with any other elements in the wrapped set, and eventually attached to parts of the page document.

A robust set of methods to adjust the wrapped set in order to refine the contents of the set, either immediately after creation, or midway through a set of chained methods, is available. Applying filtering criteria to an already existing set can also easily create new wrapped sets.

All in all, jQuery offers a lot of tools to make sure that you can easily and accurately identify the page elements we wish to manipulate.

In this chapter, we covered a lot of ground without really *doing* anything to the DOM elements of the page. But now that we know how to select the elements that we want to operate upon, we're ready to start adding life to our pages with the power of the jQuery DOM manipulation methods.

Bringing pages to life
with jQuery

3

This chapter covers

- Getting and setting element attributes
- Storing custom data on elements
- Manipulating element class names
- Setting the contents of DOM elements
- Storing and retrieving custom data on elements
- Getting and setting form element values
- Modifying the DOM tree by adding, moving, or replacing elements

Remember those days (luckily, now fading into memory) when fledgling page authors would try to add pizzazz to their pages with counterproductive abominations such as marquees, blinking text, loud background patterns (that inevitably interfered with the readability of the page text), annoying animated GIFs, and, perhaps worst of all, unsolicited background sounds that would play upon page load (and only served to test how fast a user could close down the browser)?

We've come a long way since then. Today's savvy web developers and designers know better, and use the power given to them by DOM scripting (what us old-timers might once have called Dynamic HTML, or DHTML) to *enhance* a user's web experience, rather than showcase annoying tricks.

Whether it's to incrementally reveal content, create input controls beyond the basic set provided by HTML, or give users the ability to tune pages to their own liking, DOM manipulation has allowed many a web developer to amaze (not annoy) their users.

On an almost daily basis, many of us come across web pages that do something that makes us say, "Hey! I didn't know you could do that!" And being the commensurate professionals that we are (not to mention being insatiably curious about such things), we immediately start looking at the source code to find out *how* they did it.

But rather than having to code up all that script ourselves, we'll find that jQuery provides a robust set of tools to manipulate the DOM, making those types of "Wow!" pages possible with a surprisingly small amount of code. Whereas the previous chapter introduced us to the many ways jQuery lets us select DOM elements into a wrapped set, this chapter puts the power of jQuery to work performing operations on those elements to bring life and that elusive "Wow!" factor to our pages.

3.1   *Working with element properties and attributes*

Some of the most basic components we can manipulate, when it comes to DOM elements, are the properties and attributes assigned to those elements. These properties and attributes are initially assigned to the JavaScript object instances that represent the DOM elements as a result of parsing their HTML markup, and they can be changed dynamically under script control.

Let's make sure that we have our terminology and concepts straight.

Properties are intrinsic to JavaScript objects, and each has a name and a value. The dynamic nature of JavaScript allows us to create properties on JavaScript objects under script control. (The Appendix goes into great detail on this concept if you're new to JavaScript.)

Attributes aren't a native JavaScript concept, but one that only applies to DOM elements. Attributes represent the values that are specified on the markup of DOM elements.

Consider the following HTML markup for an image element:

```
<img id="myImage" src="image.gif" alt="An image" class="someClass"
    title="This is an image"/>
```

In this element's markup, the tag name is `img`, and the markup for `id`, `src`, `alt`, `class`, and `title` represents the element's attributes, each of which consists of a name and a value. This element markup is read and interpreted by the browser to create the JavaScript object instance that represents this element in the DOM. The attributes are gathered into a list, and this list is stored as a property named, reasonably enough, `attributes` on the DOM element instance. In addition to storing the attributes in this list, the object is given a number of properties, including some that represent the attributes of the element's markup.

As such, the attribute values are reflected not only in the `attributes` list, but also in a handful of properties.

Figure 3.1 shows a simplified overview of this process.

There remains an active connection between the attribute values stored in the `attributes` list, and the corresponding properties. Changing an attribute value results in a change in the corresponding property value and vice versa. Even so, the values may not always be identical. For example, setting the `src` attribute of the image element to `image.gif` will result in the `src` property being set to the full absolute URL of the image.

For the most part, the name of a JavaScript property matches that of any corresponding attribute, but there are some cases where they differ. For example, the `class` attribute in this example is represented by the `className` property.

jQuery gives us the means to easily manipulate an element's attributes and gives us access to the element instance so that we can also change its properties. Which of these we choose to manipulate depends on what we want to do and how we want to do it.

Let's start by looking at getting and setting element properties.

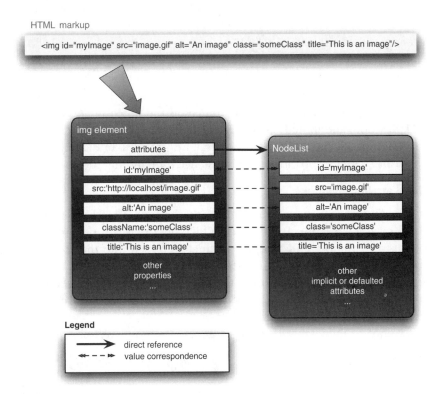

Figure 3.1   HTML markup is translated into DOM elements, including the attributes of the tag and properties created from them. The browser creates a correspondence between the attributes and properties of the elements.

3.1.1   *Manipulating element properties*

jQuery doesn't possess a specific method to obtain or modify the properties of elements. Rather, we use the native JavaScript notation to access the properties and their values. The trick is in getting to the element references in the first place.

But it's not really tricky at all, as it turns out. As we saw in the previous chapter, jQuery gives us a number of ways to access the individual elements of the wrapped set. Some of these are

- Using array indexing on the wrapped set, as in `$(whatever)[n]`
- Using the `get()` method, which returns either an individual element by index, or `toArray()`, which returns an array of the entire set of elements
- Using the `each()` or `map()` methods, where the individual elements are made available in the callback functions
- Using the `eq()` method or `:eq()` filter
- Via callback functions to some methods (like `not()` and `filter()`, for example) that set elements as the function context of the callback

As an example of using the `each()` method, we could use the following code to set the `id` property of every element in the DOM to a name composed of the element's tag name and position within the DOM:

```
$('*').each(function(n){
  this.id = this.tagName + n;
});
```

In this example, we obtain element references as the function context (`this`) of the callback function, and directly assign values to their `id` properties.

Dealing with attributes is a little less straightforward than dealing with properties in JavaScript, so jQuery provides more assistance for handling them. Let's look at how.

3.1.2   *Fetching attribute values*

As we'll find is true with many jQuery methods, the `attr()` method can be used either as a read or as a write operation. When jQuery methods can perform such bilateral operations, the number and types of parameters passed into the method determine which variant of the method is executed.

As one of these bilateral methods, the `attr()` method can be used to either fetch the value of an attribute from the first element in the matched set, or to set attribute values onto all matched elements.

The syntax for the fetch variant of the `attr()` method is as follows:

Method syntax: attr

attr(name)
Obtains the value assigned to the specified attribute for the first element in the matched set.

Parameters
  name   (String) The name of the attribute whose value is to be fetched.

Returns
The value of the attribute for the first matched element. The value `undefined` is returned if the matched set is empty or the attribute doesn't exist on the first element.

Even though we usually think of element attributes as those predefined by HTML, we can use `attr()` with custom attributes set through JavaScript or HTML markup. To illustrate this, let's amend the `<img>` element of our previous example with a custom markup attribute (highlighted in bold):

```
<img id="myImage" src="image.gif" alt="An image" class="someClass"
     title="This is an image" data-custom="some value"/>
```

Note that we've added a custom attribute, unimaginatively named `data-custom`, to the element. We can retrieve that attribute's value, as if it were any of the standard attributes, with

```
$("#myImage").attr("data-custom")
```

Attribute names aren't case sensitive in HTML. Regardless of how an attribute such as `title` is declared in the markup, we can access (or set, as we shall see) attributes using any variants of case: `Title`, `TITLE`, `TiTlE`, and any other combinations are all equivalent. In XHTML, even though attribute names must be lowercase in the markup, we can retrieve them using any case variant.

At this point you may be asking, "Why deal with attributes at all when accessing the properties is so easy (as seen in the previous section)?"

The answer to that question is that the jQuery `attr()` method is much more than a wrapper around the JavaScript `getAttribute()` and `setAttribute()` methods. In addition to allowing access to the set of element attributes, jQuery provides access to some commonly used properties that, traditionally, have been a thorn in the side of page authors everywhere due to their browser dependency.

> **Custom attributes and HTML**
>
> Under HTML 4, using a nonstandard attribute name such as `data-custom`, although a common sleight-of-hand trick, will cause your markup to be considered invalid, and it will fail formal validation testing. Proceed with caution if validation matters to you.
>
> HTML 5, on the other hand, formally recognizes and allows for such custom attributes, as long as the custom attribute name is prefixed with the string `data-`. Any attributes following this naming convention will be considered valid according to HTML 5's rules; those that don't will continue to be considered invalid. (For details, see the W3C's specification for HTML 5: http://www.w3.org/TR/html5/dom.html#attr-data.)
>
> In anticipation of HTML 5, we've adopted the `data-` prefix in our example.

This set of normalized-access names is shown in table 3.1.

Table 3.1   jQuery `attr()` normalized-access names

jQuery normalized name	DOM name
`cellspacing`	`cellSpacing`
`class`	`className`
`colspan`	`colSpan`
`cssFloat`	`styleFloat` for IE, `cssFloat` for others

Table 3.1   jQuery `attr()` normalized-access names *(continued)*

jQuery normalized name	DOM name
float	styleFloat for IE, cssFloat for others
for	htmlFor
frameborder	frameBorder
maxlength	maxLength
readonly	readOnly
rowspan	rowSpan
styleFloat	styleFloat for IE, cssFloat for others
tabindex	tabIndex
usemap	useMap

In addition to these helpful shortcuts, the set variant of `attr()` has some of its own handy features. Let's take a look.

3.1.3   *Setting attribute values*

There are two ways to set attributes onto elements in the wrapped set with jQuery. Let's start with the most straightforward, which allows us to set a single attribute at a time (for all elements in the wrapped set). Its syntax is as follows:

Method syntax: attr

`attr(name,value)`

Sets the named attribute to the passed value for all elements in the wrapped set.

Parameters

name   (String) The name of the attribute to be set.

value   (Any|Function) Specifies the value of the attribute. This can be any JavaScript
         expression that results in a value, or it can be a function. The function is invoked for
         each wrapped element, passing the index of the element and the current value of
         the named attribute. The return value of the function becomes the attribute value.

Returns

The wrapped set.

This variant of `attr()`, which may at first seem simple, is actually rather sophisticated in its operation.

In its most basic form, when the `value` parameter is any JavaScript expression that results in a value (including an array), the computed value of the expression is set as the attribute value.

Things get more interesting when the `value` parameter is a function reference. In such cases, the function is invoked for *each* element in the wrapped set, with the return value of the function used as the attribute value. When the function is invoked, it's passed two parameters: one that contains the zero-based index of the element within the wrapped set, and one that contains the current value of the named attribute. Additionally, the element is established as the function context (`this`) for the function invocation, allowing the function to tune its processing for each specific element—the main power of using functions in this way.

Consider the following statement:

```
$('*').attr('title',function(index,previousValue) {
  return previousValue + ' I am element ' + index +
       ' and my name is ' + (this.id || 'unset');
});
```

This method will run through all elements on the page, modifying the title attribute of each element by appending a string (composed using the index of the element within the DOM and the id attribute of each specific element) to the previous value.

We'd use this means of specifying the attribute value whenever that value is dependent upon other aspects of the element, when we need the orginal value to compute the new value, or whenever we have other reasons to set the values individually.

The second set variant of attr() allows us to conveniently specify multiple attributes at a time.

Method syntax: attr

attr(attributes)
Uses the properties and values specified by the passed object to set corresponding attributes onto all elements of the matched set.

Parameters

attributes   (Object) An object whose properties are copied as attributes to all elements in the wrapped set.

Returns
The wrapped set.

This format is a quick and easy way to set multiple attributes onto all the elements of a wrapped set. The passed parameter can be any object reference, commonly an object literal, whose properties specify the names and values of the attributes to be set. Consider this:

```
$('input').attr(
  { value: '', title: 'Please enter a value' }
);
```

This statement sets the value of all <input> elements to the empty string, and sets the title to the string Please enter a value.

Note that if any property value in the object passed as the value parameter is a function reference, it operates similarly to the previous format of attr(); the function is invoked for each individual element in the matched set.

> **WARNING** Internet Explorer won't allow the name or type attributes of <input> elements to be changed. If you want to change the name or type of <input> elements in Internet Explorer, you must replace the element with a new element possessing the desired name or type. This also applies to the value attribute of file and password types of <input> elements.

Now that we know how to get and set attributes, what about getting rid of them?

3.1.4   Removing attributes

In order to remove attributes from DOM elements, jQuery provides the `removeAttr()` method. Its syntax is as follows:

Method syntax: removeAttr

`removeAttr(name)`
Removes the specified attribute from every matched element.

Parameters
name   (String) The name of the attribute to be removed.

Returns
The wrapped set.

Note that removing an attribute doesn't remove any corresponding property from the JavaScript DOM element, though it may cause its value to change. For example, removing a `readonly` attribute from an element would cause the value of the element's `readOnly` property to flip from `true` to `false`, but the property itself isn't removed from the element.

Now let's look at some examples of how we might use this knowledge on our pages.

3.1.5   Fun with attributes

Let's see how these methods can be used to fiddle with the element attributes in various ways.

EXAMPLE #1—FORCING LINKS TO OPEN IN A NEW WINDOW

Let's say that we want to make all links on our site that point to external domains open in new windows. This is fairly trivial if we're in total control of the entire markup and can add a `target` attribute, as shown:

```
<a href="http://external.com" target="_blank">Some External Site</a>
```

That's all well and good, but what if we're not in control of the markup? We could be running a content management system or a wiki, where end users will be able to add content, and we can't rely on them to add the `target="_blank"` to all external links. First, let's try and determine what we want: we want all links whose `href` attribute begins with `http://` to open in a new window (which we've determined can be done by setting the `target` attribute to _blank).

Well, we can use the techniques we've learned in this section to do this concisely, as follows:

```
$("a[href^='http://']").attr("target","_blank");
```

First, we select all links with an `href` attribute starting with `http://` (which indicates that the reference is external). Then, we set their `target` attribute to _blank. Mission accomplished with a single line of jQuery code!

EXAMPLE #2—SOLVING THE DREADED DOUBLE-SUBMIT PROBLEM

Another excellent use for jQuery's attribute functionality is helping to solve a long-standing issue with web applications (rich and otherwise): the Dreaded Double-Submit Problem. This is a common dilemma for web applications when the latency of form submissions, sometimes several seconds or longer, gives users an opportunity to press the submit button multiple times, causing all manner of grief for the server-side code.

For the client side of the solution (the server-side code should still be written in a paranoid fashion), we'll hook into the form's `submit` event and disable the submit button after its first press. That way, users won't get the opportunity to click the submit button more than once and will get a visual indication (assuming that disabled buttons appear so in their browser) that the form is in the process of being submitted. Don't worry about the details of event handling in the following example (we'll get more than enough of that in chapter 4), but concentrate on the use of the `attr()` method:

```
$("form").submit(function() {
  $(":submit",this).attr("disabled", "disabled");
});
```

Within the body of the event handler, we grab all submit buttons that are inside our form with the `:submit` selector and modify the `disabled` attribute to the value `"disabled"` (the official W3C-recommended setting for the attribute). Note that when building the matched set, we provide a context value (the second parameter) of `this`. As we'll find out when we dive into event handling in chapter 4, the `this` pointer always refers to the page element for which the event was triggered while operating inside event handlers; in this case, the form instance.

When is "enabled" not enabling?

Don't be fooled into thinking that you can substitute the value `enabled` for `disabled` as follows:

```
$(whatever).attr("disabled","enabled");
```

and expect the element to become enabled. This code will *still* disable the element!

According to W3C rules, it's the *presence* of the `disabled` attribute, not its value, that places the element in disabled state. So it really doesn't matter what the value is; if the `disabled` attribute is present, the element is disabled.

So, to re-enable the element, we'd either remove the attribute or use a convenience that jQuery provides for us: if we provide the Boolean values `true` or `false` as the attribute value (*not* the strings "true" or "false"), jQuery will do the right thing under the covers, removing the attribute for `false`, and adding it for `true`.

WARNING Disabling the submit button(s) in this way doesn't relieve the server-side code from its responsibility to guard against double submission or to perform any other types of validation. Adding this type of feature to the client code makes things nicer for the end user and helps prevent the double-submit problem under normal circumstances. It doesn't protect against attacks or other hacking attempts, and server-side code must continue to be on its guard.

Element attributes and properties are useful concepts for data as defined by HTML and the W3C, but in the course of page authoring, we frequently need to store our own custom data. Let's see what jQuery can do for us on that front.

3.1.6   *Storing custom data on elements*

Let's just come right out and say it: global variables suck.

Except for the infrequent, truly global values, it's hard to imagine a worse place to store information that we'll need while defining and implementing the complex behavior of our pages. Not only do we run into scope issues, they also don't scale well when we have multiple operations occurring simultaneously (menus opening and closing, Ajax requests firing, animations executing, and so on).

The functional nature of JavaScript can help mitigate this through the use of closures, but closures can only take us so far and aren't appropriate for every situation.

Because our page behaviors are so element-focused, it makes sense to make use of the elements themselves as storage scopes. Again, the nature of JavaScript, with its ability to dynamically create custom properties on objects, can help us out here. But we must proceed with caution. Being that DOM elements are represented by JavaScript object instances, they, like all other object instances, can be extended with custom properties of our own choosing. But there be dragons there!

These custom properties, so-called *expandos*, aren't without risk. Particularly, it can be easy to create circular references that can lead to serious memory leaks. In traditional web applications, where the DOM is dropped frequently as new pages are loaded, memory leaks may not be as big of an issue. But for us, as authors of highly interactive web applications, employing lots of script on pages that may hang around for quite some time, memory leaks can be a huge problem.

jQuery comes to our rescue by providing a means to tack data onto any DOM element that we choose, in a controlled fashion, without relying upon potentially problematic expandos. We can place any arbitrary JavaScript value, even arrays and objects, onto DOM elements by use of the cleverly named `data()` method. This is the syntax:

Method syntax: data

`data(name,value)`
Adds the passed value to the jQuery-managed data store for all wrapped elements.

Parameters
`name`   (String) The name of the data to be stored.
`value`   (Object|Function) The value to be stored. If a function, the function is invoked for each wrapped element, passing that element as the function context. The function's returned value is used as the data value.

Returns
The wrapped set.

Data that's write-only isn't particularly useful, so a means to retrieve the named data must be available. It should be no surprise that the data() method is once again used. Here is the syntax for retrieving data using the data() method:

Method syntax: data

data(name)
Retrieves any previously stored data with the specified name on the first element of the wrapped set.

Parameters
name   (String) The name of the data to be retrieved.

Returns
The retrieved data, or undefined if not found.

In the interests of proper memory management, jQuery also provides the remove-Data() method as a way to dump any data that may no longer be necessary:

Method syntax: removeData

removeData(name)
Removes any previously stored data with the specified name on all elements of the wrapped set.

Parameters
name   (String) The name of the data to be removed.

Returns
The wrapped set.

Note that it's not necessary to remove data "by hand" when removing an element from the DOM with jQuery methods. jQuery will smartly handle that for us.

The capability to tack data onto DOM elements is one that we'll see exploited to our advantage in many of the examples in upcoming chapters, but for those who have run into the usual headaches that global variables can cause, it's easy to see how storing data in-context within the element hierarchy opens up a whole new world of possibilities. In essence, the DOM tree has become a complete "namespace" hierarchy for us to employ; we're no longer limited to a single global space.

We mentioned the className property much earlier in this section as an example of a case where markup attribute names differ from property names; but, truth be told, class names are a bit special in other respects as well, and are handled as such by jQuery. The next section will describe a better way to deal with class names than by directly accessing the className property or using the attr() method.

3.2 Changing element styling

If we want to change the styling of an element, we have two options. We can add or remove a class, causing any existing style sheets to restyle the element based on its new classes. Or we can operate on the DOM element itself, applying styles directly.

Let's look at how jQuery makes it simple to make changes to an element's style via classes.

3.2.1   *Adding and removing class names*

The class attribute of DOM elements is unique in its format and semantics and is crucially important to the creation of interactive interfaces. The addition of class names to and removal of class names from an element are the primary means by which their stylistic rendering can be modified dynamically.

One of the aspects of element class names that make them unique—and a challenge to deal with—is that each element can be assigned any number of class names. In HTML, the class attribute is used to supply these names as a space-delimited string. For example,

```
<div class="someClass anotherClass yetAnotherClass"></div>
```

Unfortunately, rather than manifesting themselves as an array of names in the DOM element's corresponding className property, the class names appear as that same space-delimited string. How disappointing, and how cumbersome! This means that whenever we want to add class names to or remove class names from an element that already has class names, we need to parse the string to determine the individual names when reading it and be sure to restore it to valid space-delimited format when writing it.

> **NOTE**   The list of class names is considered *unordered*; that is, the order of the names within the space-delimited list has no semantic meaning.

Although it's not a monumental task to write code to handle all that, it's always a good idea to abstract such details behind an API that hides the mechanical details of such operations. Luckily, jQuery has already done that for us.

Adding class names to all the elements of a matched set is an easy operation with the following addClass() method:

Method syntax: addClass

addClass(names)
Adds the specified class name or class names to all elements in the wrapped set.

Parameters
names   (String|Function) Specifies the class name, or a space-delimited string of names, to be added. If a function, the function is invoked for each wrapped element, with that element set as the function context, and passing two parameters: the element index and the current class value. The function's returned value is used as the class name or names.

Returns
The wrapped set.

Removing class names is just as straightforward with the following removeClass() method:

Method syntax: removeClass

`removeClass(names)`

Removes the specified class name or class names from each element in the wrapped set.

Parameters

names   (String|Function) Specifies the class name, or a space-delimited string of names, to be removed. If a function, the function is invoked for each wrapped element, setting that element as the function context, and passing two parameters: the element index, and the class value prior to any removal. The function's returned value is used as the class name or names to be removed.

Returns

The wrapped set.

Often, we may want to switch a set of styles back and forth, perhaps to indicate a change between two states or for any other reasons that make sense with our interface. jQuery makes this easy with the `toggleClass()` method.

Method syntax: toggleClass

`toggleClass(names)`

Adds the specified class name if it doesn't exist on an element, or removes the name from elements that already possess the class name. Note that each element is tested individually, so some elements may have the class name added, and others may have it removed.

Parameters

names   (String|Function) Specifies the class name, or a space-delimited string of names, to be toggled. If a function, the function is invoked for each wrapped element, passing that element as the function context. The function's returned value is used as the class name or names.

Returns

The wrapped set.

One situation where the `toggleClass()` method is most useful is when we want to switch visual renditions between elements quickly and easily. Let's consider a "zebra-striping" example in which we want to give alternating rows of a table different colors. And imagine that we have some valid reason to swap the colored background from the odd rows to the even rows (and perhaps back again) when certain events occur. The `toggleClass()` method would make it almost trivial to add a class name to every other row, while removing it from the remainder.

Let's give it a whirl. In the file chapter3/zebra.stripes.html, you'll find a page that presents a table of vehicle information. Within the script defined for that page, a function is defined as follows:

```
function swapThem() {
  $('tr').toggleClass('striped');
}
```

This function uses the `toggleClass()` method to toggle the class named `striped` for all `<tr>` elements. We also defined the following ready handler:

```
$(function(){/

    $("table tr:nth-child(even)").addClass("striped");
    $("table").mouseover(swapThem).mouseout(swapThem);
});
```

The first statement in the body of this handler applies the class `striped` to every other row of the table using the `nth-child` selector that we learned about in the previous chapter. The second statement establishes event handlers for mouseover and mouseout events that both call the same `swapThem` function. We'll be learning all about event handling in the next chapter, but for now the important point is that whenever the mouse enters or leaves the table, the following line of code ends up being executed:

```
$('tr').toggleClass('striped');
```

The result is that every time the mouse cursor enters or leaves the table, all `<tr>` elements with the class `striped` will have the class removed, and all `<tr>` elements without the class will have it added. This (somewhat annoying) activity is shown in the two parts of figure 3.2.

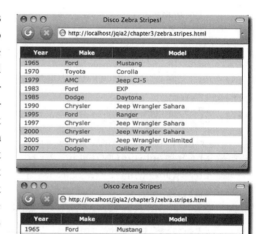

Figure 3.2   **The presence or absence of the striped class is toggled whenever the mouse cursor enters or leaves the table.**

Toggling a class based upon whether the elements already possess the class or not is a very common operation, but so is toggling the class based on some other arbitrary condition. For this more general case, jQuery provides another variant of the `toggleClass()` method that lets us add or remove a class based upon an arbitrary Boolean expression:

Method syntax: toggleClass

`toggleClass(names,switch)`

Adds the specified class name if the `switch` expression evaluates to `true`, and removes the class name if the switch expression evaluates to `false`.

Parameters

`names`   (String|Function) Specifies the class name, or a space-delimited string of names, to be toggled. If a function, the function is invoked for each wrapped element, setting that element as the function context, and passing two parameters: the element index and the current class value. The function's returned value is used as the class name or names.

`switch`   (Boolean) A control expression whose value determines if the class will be added to the elements (if `true`) or removed (if `false`).

Returns

The wrapped set.

It's extremely common to need to determine whether an element has a particular class. We may want to conditionalize our activity based upon whether an element has a certain class or not, or we may just be using it to identify a certain type of element by class.

With jQuery, we can do that by calling the `hasClass()` method:

```
$("p:first").hasClass("surpriseMe")
```

This method will return `true` if any element in the matched set has the specified class. The syntax of this method is as follows:

Method syntax: hasClass

hasClass(name)
Determines if any element of the matched set possesses the passed class name.

Parameters
name   (String) The class name to be checked.

Returns
Returns `true` if any element in the wrapped set possesses the passed class name; `false` otherwise.

Recalling the `is()` method from chapter 2, we could achieve the same thing with

```
$("p:first").is(".surpriseMe")
```

But arguably, the `hasClass()` method makes for more readable code, and internally, `hasClass()` is more efficient.

Another commonly desired ability is to obtain the list of classes defined for a particular element as an array instead of the cumbersome space-separated list. We could try to achieve that by writing

```
$("p:first").attr("className").split(" ");
```

Recall that the `attr()` method will return `undefined` if the attribute in question doesn't exist, so this statement will throw an error if the <p> element doesn't possess any class names.

We could solve this by first checking for the attribute, and if we wanted to wrap the entire thing in a repeatable, useful jQuery extension, we could write

```
$.fn.getClassNames = function() {
  var name = this.attr("className");
  if (name != null) {
    return name.split(" ");
  }
  else {
    return [];
  }
};
```

Don't worry about the specifics of the syntax for extending jQuery; we'll go into that in more detail in chapter 7. What's important is that once we define such an extension, we can use `getClassNames()` anywhere in our script to obtain an array of class names or an empty array if an element has no classes. Nifty!

Manipulating the stylistic rendition of elements via CSS class names is a powerful tool, but sometimes we want to get down to the nitty-gritty styles themselves as declared directly on the elements. Let's see what jQuery offers us for that.

3.2.2 Getting and setting styles

Although modifying the class of an element allows us to choose which predetermined set of defined style sheet rules should be applied, sometimes we want to override the style sheet altogether. Applying styles directly on the elements (via the `style` property available on all DOM elements) will automatically override style sheets, giving us more fine-grained control over individual elements and their styles.

The jQuery `css()` method allows us to manipulate these styles, working in a similar fashion to the `attr()` method. We can set an individual CSS style by specifying its name and value, or a series of styles by passing in an object. First, let's look at specifying a single style name and value.

Method syntax: css

`css(name,value)`
Sets the named CSS style property to the specified value for each matched element.

Parameters
name   (String) The name of the CSS property to be set.
value   (String|Number|Function) A string, number, or function containing the property value. If a function is passed as this parameter, it will be invoked for each element of the wrapped set, setting the element as the function context, and passing two parameters: the element index and the current value. The returned value serves as the new value for the CSS property.

Returns
The wrapped set.

As described, the `value` argument accepts a function in a similar fashion to the `attr()` method. This means that we can, for instance, expand the width of all elements in the wrapped set by 20 pixels as follows:

```
$("div.expandable").css("width",function(index, currentWidth) {
   return currentWidth + 20;
});
```

One interesting side note—and yet another example of how jQuery makes our lives easier—is that the normally problematic `opacity` property will work perfectly across browsers by passing in a value between 0.0 and 1.0; no more messing with IE alpha filters, `-moz-opacity`, and the like!

Next, let's look at using the shortcut form of the `css()` method, which works exactly as the shortcut version of `attr()` worked.

Method syntax: css

`css(properties)`

Sets the CSS properties specified as keys in the passed object to their associated values for all matched elements.

Parameters

properties   (Object) Specifies an object whose properties are copied as CSS properties to all elements in the wrapped set.

Returns

The wrapped set.

We've already seen how useful this variant of this method can be in the code of listing 2.1, which we examined in the previous chapter. To save you some page-flipping, here's the relevant passage again:

```
$('<img>',
  {
    src: 'images/little.bear.png',
    alt: 'Little Bear',
    title:'I woof in your general direction',
    click: function(){
      alert($(this).attr('title'));
    }
  })
  .css({
    cursor: 'pointer',
    border: '1px solid black',
    padding: '12px 12px 20px 12px',
    backgroundColor: 'white'
  })
  ...
```

As in the shortcut version of the `attr()` method, we can use functions as values to any CSS property in the `properties` parameter object, and they will be called on each element in the wrapped set to determine the value that should be applied.

Lastly, we can use `css()` with a name passed in to retrieve the computed style of the property associated with that name. When we say *computed* style, we mean the style after all linked, embedded, and inline CSS has been applied. Impressively, this works perfectly across all browsers, even for `opacity`, which returns a string representing a number between 0.0 and 1.0.

Method syntax: css

`css(name)`

Retrieves the computed value of the CSS property specified by name for the first element in the wrapped set.

Parameters

name   (String) Specifies the name of a CSS property whose computed value is to be returned.

Returns

The computed value as a string.

Keep in mind that this variant of the `css()` method always returns a string, so if you need a number or some other type, you'll need to parse the returned value.

That's not always convenient, so for a small set of CSS values that are commonly accessed, jQuery thoughtfully provides convenience methods that access these values and convert them to the most commonly used types.

GETTING AND SETTING DIMENSIONS

When it comes to CSS styles that we want to set or get on our pages, is there a more common set of properties than the element's width or height? Probably not, so jQuery makes it easy for us to deal with the dimensions of the elements as numeric values rather than strings.

Specifically, we can get (or set) the width and height of an element as a number by using the convenient `width()` and `height()` methods. We can set the width or height as follows:

Method syntax: width and height

`width(value)`
`height(value)`
Sets the width or height of all elements in the matched set.

Parameters
  value   (Number|String|Function) The value to be set. This can be a number of pixels, or a string specifying a value in units (such as `px`, `em`, or `%`). If no unit is specified, `px` is the default.
               If a function, the function is invoked for each wrapped element, passing that element as the function context. The function's returned value is used as the value.

Returns
The wrapped set.

Keep in mind that these are shortcuts for the more verbose `css()` function, so

```
$("div.myElements").width(500)
```

is identical to

```
$("div.myElements").css("width",500)
```

We can retrieve the width or height as follows:

Method syntax: width and height

`width()`
`height()`
Retrieves the width or height of the first element of the wrapped set.

Parameters
  none

Returns
The computed width or height as a number in pixels.

The fact that the width and height values are returned from these functions as numbers isn't the only convenience that these methods bring to the table. If you've ever tried to find the width or height of an element by looking at its style.width or style.height property, you were confronted with the sad fact that these properties are only set by the corresponding style attribute of that element; to find out the dimensions of an element via these properties, you have to set them in the first place. Not exactly a paragon of usefulness!

The width() and height() methods, on the other hand, compute and return the size of the element. Knowing the precise dimensions of an element in simple pages that let their elements lay out wherever they end up isn't usually necessary, but knowing such dimensions in highly interactive scripted pages is crucial to be able to correctly place active elements such as context menus, custom tool tips, extended controls, and other dynamic components.

Let's put them to work. Figure 3.3 shows a sample page that was set up with two primary elements: a <div> serving as a test subject that contains a paragraph of text (also with a border and background color for emphasis) and a second <div> in which to display the dimensions.

The dimensions of the test subject aren't known in advance because no style rules specifying dimensions are applied. The width of the element is determined by the width of the browser window, and its height depends on how much room will be needed to display the contained text. Resizing the browser window will cause both dimensions to change.

In our page, we define a function that will use the width() and height() methods to obtain the dimensions of the test subject <div> (identified as testSubject) and display the resulting values in the second <div> (identified as display).

```
function displayDimensions() {
  $('#display').html(
    $('#testSubject').width()+'x'+$('#testSubject').height()
  );
```

We call this function in the ready handler of the page, resulting in the initial display of the values 589 and 60 for that particular size of browser window, as shown in the upper portion of figure 3.3.
We also add a call to the same function in a resize handler on the window that updates the display whenever the browser window is resized, as shown in the lower portion of figure 3.3.

This ability to determine the computed dimensions of an element at any point is crucial to accurately positioning dynamic elements on our pages.

The full code of this page is shown in listing 3.1 and can be found in the file chapter3/dimensions.html.

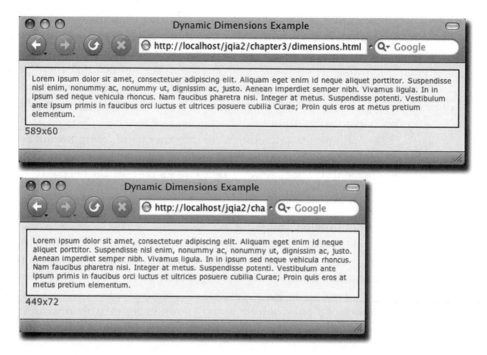

Figure 3.3   The width and height of the test element aren't fixed and depend on the width of the browser window.

Listing 3.1   Dynamically tracking and displaying the dimensions of an element

```
<!DOCTYPE html>
<html>
  <head>
    <title>Dynamic Dimensions Example</title>
    <link rel="stylesheet" type="text/css" href="../styles/core.css"/>
    <style type="text/css">
      body {
        background-color: #eeeeee;
      }
      #testSubject {
        background-color: #ffffcc;
        border: 2px ridge maroon;
        padding: 8px;
        font-size: .85em;
      }
    </style>
    <script type="text/javascript"
            src="../scripts/jquery-1.4.js"></script>
    <script type="text/javascript">
      $(function(){
        $(window).resize(displayDimensions);
        displayDimensions();
      });
```

◁┐ Establishes resize handler that invokes display function

◁┐ Invokes reporting function in document ready handler

```
function displayDimensions() {
  $('#display').html(
    $('#testSubject').width()+'x'+$('#testSubject').height()
  );
}
</script>
</head>

<body>
  <div id="testSubject">
    Lorem ipsum dolor sit amet, consectetuer adipiscing elit.
    Aliquam eget enim id neque aliquet porttitor. Suspendisse
    nisl enim, nonummy ac, nonummy ut, dignissim ac, justo.
    Aenean imperdiet semper nibh. Vivamus ligula. In in ipsum
    sed neque vehicula rhoncus. Nam faucibus pharetra nisi.
    Integer at metus. Suspendisse potenti. Vestibulum ante
    ipsum primis in faucibus orci luctus et ultrices posuere
    cubilia Curae; Proin quis eros at metus pretium elementum.
  </div>
  <div id="display"></div>
</body>
</html>
```

Displays width and height of test subject

Declares test subject with dummy text

Displays dimensions in this area

In addition to the very convenient `width()` and `height()` methods, jQuery also provides similar methods for getting more particular dimension values, as described in table 3.2.

When dealing with the window or document elements, it's recommended to avoid the inner and outer methods and use `width()` and `height()`.

Table 3.2 Additional jQuery dimension-related methods

Method	Description
`innerHeight()`	Returns the "inner height" of the first matched element, which excludes the border but includes the padding.
`innerWidth()`	Returns the "inner width" of the first matched element, which excludes the border but includes the padding.
`outerHeight(margin)`	Returns the "outer height" of the first matched element, which includes the border and the padding. The `margin` parameter causes the margin to be included if it's `true`, or omitted.
`outerWidth(margin)`	Returns the "outer width" of the first matched element, which includes the border and the padding. The `margin` parameter causes the margin to be included if it's `true`, or omitted.

We're not done yet; jQuery also gives us easy support for positions and scrolling values.

POSITIONS AND SCROLLING

jQuery provides two methods for getting the position of an element. Both of these elements return a JavaScript object that contains two properties: `top` and `left`, which, not surprisingly, indicate the top and left values of the element.

The two methods use different origins from which their relative computed values are measured. One of these methods, offset(), returns the position relative to the document:

Method syntax: offset

offset()
Returns the position (in pixels) of the first element in the wrapped set relative to the document origin.

Parameters
none

Returns
A JavaScript object with left and top properties as floats (usually rounded to the nearest integer) depicting the position in pixels relative to the document origin.

The other method, position(), returns values relative to an element's closest offset parent:

Method syntax: position

position()
Returns the position (in pixels) of the first element in the wrapped set relative to the element's closest offset parent.

Parameters
none

Returns
A JavaScript object with left and top properties as integers depicting the position in pixels relative to the closest offset parent.

The *offset parent* of an element is the nearest ancestor that has an explicit positioning rule of either relative or absolute set.

Both offset() and position() can only be used for visible elements, and it's recommended that pixel values be used for all padding, borders, and margins to obtain accurate results.

In addition to element positioning, jQuery gives us the ability to get, and to set, the scroll position of an element. Table 3.3 describes these methods.

All methods in table 3.3 work with both visible and hidden elements.
Now that we've learned how to get and set the styles of elements, let's discuss different ways of modifying their contents.

Table 3.3   The jQuery scroll control methods

Method	Description
scrollLeft()	Returns the horizontal scroll offset of the first matched element.
scrollLeft(value)	Sets the horizontal scroll offset for all matched elements.
scrollTop()	Returns the vertical scroll offset of the first matched element.
scrollTop(value)	Sets the vertical scroll offset for all matched elements.

3.3 *Setting element content*

When it comes to modifying the contents of elements, there's an ongoing debate regarding which technique is better: using DOM API methods or changing the elements' inner HTML.

Although use of the DOM API methods is certainly exact, it's also fairly "wordy" and results in a lot of code, much of which can be difficult to visually inspect. In most cases, modifying an element's HTML is easier and more effective, so jQuery gives us a number of methods to do so.

3.3.1 *Replacing HTML or text content*

First up is the simple `html()` method, which allows us to retrieve the HTML contents of an element when used without parameters or, as we've seen with other jQuery functions, to set its contents when used with a parameter.

Here's how to get the HTML content of an element:

Method syntax: html

`html()`
Obtains the HTML content of the first element in the matched set.

Parameters
   none

Returns
The HTML content of the first matched element. The returned value is identical to accessing the `innerHTML` property of that element.

And here's how to set the HTML content of all matched elements:

Method syntax: html

`html(content)`
Sets the passed HTML fragment as the content of all matched elements.

Parameters
   content   (String|Function) The HTML fragment to be set as the element content. If a function, the function is invoked for each wrapped element, setting that element as the function context, and passing two parameters: the element index and the existing content. The function's returned value is used as the new content.

Returns
The wrapped set.

We can also set or get only the text contents of elements. The `text()` method, when used without parameters, returns a string that's the concatenation of all text. For example, let's say we have the following HTML fragment:

```
<ul id="theList">
  <li>One</li>
  <li>Two</li>
  <li>Three</li>
  <li>Four</li>
</ul>
```

The statement

```
var text = $('#theList').text();
```

results in variable `text` being set to `OneTwoThreeFour`.

Method syntax: text

`text()`
Concatenates all text content of the wrapped elements and returns it as the result of the method.

Parameters
  none

Returns
The concatenated string.

We can also use the `text()` method to set the text content of the wrapped elements. The syntax for this format is as follows:

Method syntax: text

`text(content)`
Sets the text content of all wrapped elements to the passed value. If the passed text contains angle brackets (< and >) or the ampersand (&), these characters are replaced with their equivalent HTML entities.

Parameters
  content   (String|Function) The text content to be set into the wrapped elements. Any angle bracket characters are escaped as HTML entities. If a function, the function is invoked for each wrapped element, setting that element as the function context, and passing two parameters: the element index and the existing text. The function's returned value is used as the new content.

Returns
The wrapped set.

Note that setting the inner HTML or text of elements using these methods will replace contents that were previously in the elements, so use these methods carefully. If you don't want to bludgeon all of an element's previous content, a number of other methods will leave the contents of the elements as they are but modify their contents or surrounding elements. Let's look at them.

3.3.2   *Moving and copying elements*

Manipulating the DOM of a page without the necessity of a page reload opens a world of possibilities for making our pages dynamic and interactive. We've already seen a glimpse of how jQuery lets us create DOM elements on the fly. These new elements can be attached to the DOM in a variety of ways, and we can also move or copy existing elements.

To add content to the end of existing content, the `append()` method is available.

Method syntax: append

`append(content)`

Appends the passed HTML fragment or elements to the content of all matched elements.

Parameters

`content`　(String|Element|jQuery|Function) A string, element, wrapped set, or function specifying the elements of the wrapped set. If a function, the function is invoked for each wrapped element, setting that element as the function context, and passing two parameters: the element index and the previous contents. The function's returned value is used as the content.

Returns

The wrapped set.

This method accepts a string containing an HTML fragment, a reference to an existing or newly created DOM element, or a jQuery wrapped set of elements.

Consider the following simple case:

```
$('p').append('<b>some text<b>');
```

This statement appends the HTML fragment created from the passed string to the end of the existing content of all <p> elements on the page.

A more semantically complex use of this method identifies already-existing elements of the DOM as the items to be appended. Consider the following:

```
$("p.appendToMe").append($("a.appendMe"))
```

This statement moves all links with the class `appendMe` to the end of the child list of all <p> elements with the class `appendToMe`. If there are multiple targets for the operation, the original element is cloned as many times as is necessary and appended to the children of each target. In all cases, the original is removed from its initial location.

This operation is semantically a *move* if one target is identified; the original source element is removed from its initial location and appears at the end of the target's list of children. It can also be a copy-and-move operation if multiple targets are identified, creating enough copies of the original so that each target can have one appended to its children.

In place of a full-blown wrapped set, we can also reference a specific DOM element, as shown:

```
$("p.appendToMe").append(someElement);
```

Although it's a common operation to add elements to the end of an elements content—we might be adding a list item to the end of a list, a row to the end of a table, or simply adding a new element to the end of the document body—we might also have a need to add a new or existing element to the *start* of the target element's contents.

When such a need arises, the `prepend()` method will do the trick.

Method syntax: prepend

`prepend(content)`

Prepends the passed HTML fragment or elements to the content of all matched elements.

Parameters

   `content`   (String|Element|jQuery|Function) A string, element, wrapped set, or function specifying the content to append to the elements of the wrapped set. If a function, the function is invoked for each wrapped element, setting that element as the function context, and passing two parameters: the element index and the previous contents. The function's returned value is used as the content.

Returns

The wrapped set.

Sometimes, we might wish to place elements somewhere other than at the beginning or end of an element's content. jQuery allows us to place new or existing elements anywhere in the DOM by identifying a target element that the source elements are to be placed before, or are to be placed after.

Not surprisingly, the methods are named `before()` and `after()`. Their syntax should seem familiar by now.

Method syntax: before

`before(content)`

Inserts the passed HTML fragment or elements into the DOM as a sibling of the target elements, positioned before the targets. The target wrapped elements must already be part of the DOM.

Parameters

   `content`   (String|Element|jQuery|Function) A string, element, wrapped set, or function specifying the content to insert into the DOM before the elements of the wrapped set. If a function, the function is invoked for each wrapped element, passing that element as the function context. The function's returned value is used as the content.

Returns

The wrapped set.

Method syntax: after

`after(content)`

Inserts the passed HTML fragment or elements into the DOM as a sibling of the target elements positioned after the targets. The target wrapped elements must already be part of the DOM.

Parameters

   `content`   (String|Element|jQuery|Function) A string, element, wrapped set, or function specifying the content to insert into the DOM after the elements of the wrapped set. If a function, the function is invoked for each wrapped element, passing that element as the function context. The function's returned value is used as the content.

Returns

The wrapped set.

These operations are key to manipulating the DOM effectively in our pages, so a Move and Copy Lab Page has been provided so that we can play around with these operations until they're thoroughly understood. This lab is available at chapter3/move.and.copy.lab.html, and its initial display is as shown in figure 3.4.

The left pane of this Lab contains three images that can serve as sources for our move/copy experiments. Select one or more of the images by checking their corresponding checkboxes.

Figure 3.4   The Move and Copy Lab Page will let us inspect the operation of the DOM manipulation methods.

Targets for the move/copy operations are in the right pane and are also selected via checkboxes. Controls at the bottom of the pane allow us to select one of the four operations to apply: append, prepend, before, or after. (Ignore "clone" for now; we'll attend to that later.)

The Execute button causes any source images you have selected to be applied to a wrapped set of the selected set of targets using the specified operation. After execution, the Execute button is replaced with a Restore button that we'll use to put everything back into place so we can run another experiment.

Let's run an "append" experiment.

Select the dog image, and then select Target 2. Leaving the append operation selected, click Execute. The display in figure 3.5 results.

Use the Move and Copy Lab to try various combinations of sources, targets, and the four operations until you have a good feel for how they operate.

Figure 3.5   Cozmo has been added to the end of Target 2 as a result of the append operation.

Sometimes, it might make the code more readable if we could reverse the order of the elements passed to these operations. If we want to move or copy an element from one place to another, another approach would be to wrap the source elements (rather than the target elements), and to specify the targets in the parameters of the method. Well, jQuery lets us do that too by providing analogous operations to the four that we just examined, reversing the order in which sources and targets are specified. They are `appendTo()`, `prependTo()`, `insertBefore()`, and `insertAfter()`, and their syntax is as follows:

Method syntax: appendTo

`appendTo(targets)`

Adds all elements in the wrapped set to the end of the content of the specified target(s).

Parameters

`targets`	(String|Element) A string containing a jQuery selector or a DOM element. Each element of the wrapped set will be appended to the content of each target element.

Returns

The wrapped set.

Method syntax: prependTo

`prependTo(targets)`

Adds all elements in the wrapped set to the beginning of the content of the specified target(s).

Parameters

`targets`	(String|Element) A string containing a jQuery selector or a DOM element. Each element of the wrapped set will be prepended to the content of each target element.

Returns

The wrapped set.

Method syntax: insertBefore

`insertBefore(targets)`

Adds all elements in the wrapped set to the DOM just prior to the specified target(s).

Parameters

`targets`	(String|Element) A string containing a jQuery selector or a DOM element. Each element of the wrapped set will be added before each target element.

Returns

The wrapped set.

Method syntax: insertAfter

`insertAfter (targets)`
Adds all elements in the wrapped set to the DOM just after the specified target(s).

Parameters
`targets`   (String|Element) A string containing a jQuery selector or a DOM element. Each
              element of the wrapped set will be added after each target element.

Returns
The wrapped set.

There's one more thing we need to address before we move on ...

Remember back in the previous chapter when we looked at how to create new HTML fragments with the jQuery $() wrapper function? Well, that becomes a really useful trick when paired with the appendTo(), prependTo(), insertBefore(), and insertAfter() methods. Consider the following:

```
$('<p>Hi there!</p>').insertAfter('p img');
```

This statement creates a friendly paragraph and inserts a copy of it after every image element within a paragraph element. This is an idiom that we've already seen in listing 2.1 and that we'll use again and again on our pages.

Sometimes, rather than inserting elements *into* other elements, we want to do the opposite. Let's see what jQuery offers for that.

3.3.3   *Wrapping and unwrapping elements*

Another type of DOM manipulation that we'll often need to perform is to wrap an element (or series of elements) in some markup. For example, we might want to wrap all links of a certain class inside a <div>. We can accomplish such DOM modifications by using jQuery's wrap() method. Its syntax is as follows:

Method syntax: wrap

`wrap(wrapper)`
Wraps the elements of the matched set with the passed HTML tags or a clone of the passed element.

Parameters
`wrapper`   (String|Element) A string containing the opening and closing tags of the element
              with which to wrap each element of the matched set, or an element to be cloned
              and serve as the wrapper.

Returns
The wrapped set.

To wrap each link with the class surprise in a <div> with the class hello, we could write

```
$("a.surprise").wrap("<div class='hello'></div>")
```

If we wanted to wrap the link in a clone of the first <div> element on the page, we could write

```
$("a.surprise").wrap($("div:first")[0]);
```

When multiple elements are collected in a matched set, the `wrap()` method operates on each one individually. If we'd rather wrap all the elements in the set as a unit, we can use the `wrapAll()` method instead:

Method syntax: wrapAll

wrapAll(wrapper)

Wraps the elements of the matched set, as a unit, with the passed HTML tags or a clone of the passed element.

Parameters

   wrapper   (String|Element) A string containing the opening and closing tags of the element with which to wrap each element of the matched set, or an element to be cloned and serve as the wrapper.

Returns

The wrapped set.

Sometimes we may not want to wrap the elements that are in a matched set, but rather their *contents*. For just such cases, the `wrapInner()` method is available:

Method syntax: wrapInner

wrapInner(wrapper)

Wraps the contents, to include text nodes of the elements in the matched set with the passed HTML tags or a clone of the passed element.

Parameters

   wrapper   (String|Element) A string containing the opening and closing tags of the element with which to wrap each element of the matched set, or an element to be cloned and serve as the wrapper.

Returns

The wrapped set.

The converse operation, removing the parent of a child element, is also possible with the `unwrap()` method: :

Method syntax: unwrap

unwrap()

Removes the parent element of the wrapped elements. The child element, along with any siblings, replaces the parent element in the DOM.

Parameters

   none

Returns

The wrapped set.

Now that we know how to create, wrap, unwrap, copy, and move elements, we may wonder how we make them go away.

3.3.4   *Removing elements*

Just as important as the ability to add, move, or copy elements in the DOM is the ability to remove elements that are no longer needed.

If we want to empty or remove a set of elements, this can be accomplished with the `remove()` method, whose syntax is as follows:

Method syntax: remove

`remove(selector)`
Removes all elements in the wrapped set from the page DOM.

Parameters
`selector`   (String) An optional selector that further filters which elements of the wrapped set are to be removed.

Returns
The wrapped set.

Note that, as with many other jQuery methods, the wrapped set is returned as the result of this method. The elements that were removed from the DOM are still referenced by this set (and hence not yet eligible for garbage collection) and can be further operated upon using other jQuery methods, including the likes of `appendTo()`, `prependTo()`, `insertBefore()`, `insertAfter()`, and any other similar behaviors we'd like.

Note, however, that any jQuery data or events that were bound to the elements are removed when the elements are removed from the DOM using `remove()`. A similar method, `detach()`, also removes the elements from the DOM, but retains any bound events and data.

Method syntax: detach

`detach(selector)`
Removes all elements in the wrapped set from the page DOM, retaining any bound events and jQuery data.

Parameters
`selector`   (Selector) An optional selector string that further filters which elements of the wrapped set are to be detached.

Returns
The wrapped set.

The `detach()` method is the preferred means of removing an element that we'll want to put back into the DOM at a later time with its events and data intact.

To completely empty DOM elements of their contents, we can use the `empty()` method. Its syntax is as follows:

Method syntax: empty

`empty()`

Removes the content of all DOM elements in the matched set.

Parameters

Returns

The wrapped set.

Sometimes, we don't want to move elements, but to copy them ...

3.3.5 *Cloning elements*

One more way that we can manipulate the DOM is to make copies of elements to attach elsewhere in the tree. jQuery provides a handy wrapper method for doing so with its `clone()` method.

Method syntax: clone

`clone(copyHandlers)`

Creates copies of the elements in the wrapped set and returns a new wrapped set that contains them. The elements and any children are copied. Event handlers are optionally copied depending upon the setting of the `copyHandlers` parameter.

Parameters

copyHandlers   (Boolean) If `true`, event handlers are copied. If `false` or omitted, handlers aren't copied.

Returns

The newly created wrapped set.

Making a copy of existing elements with `clone()` isn't useful unless we do something with the carbon copies. Generally, once the wrapped set containing the clones is generated, another jQuery method is applied to stick them somewhere in the DOM. For example,

```
$('img').clone().appendTo('fieldset.photo');
```

This statement makes copies of all image elements and appends them to all <fieldset> elements with the class name `photo`.

A slightly more complex example is as follows:

```
$('ul').clone().insertBefore('#here');
```

This method chain performs a similar operation, but the targets of the cloning operation—all <ul> elements—are copied, *including* their children (it's likely that any <ul> element will have a number of <li> children).

One last example:

```
$('ul').clone().insertBefore('#here').end().hide();
```

This statement performs the same operation as the previous example, but after the insertion of the clones, the end() method is used to select the original wrapped set (the original targets) and hide them. This emphasizes how the cloning operation creates a new set of elements in a new wrapper.

In order to see the clone operation in action, return to the Move and Copy Lab Page. Just above the Execute button is a pair of radio buttons that allow us to specify a cloning operation as part of the main DOM manipulation operation. When the yes radio button is selected, the sources are cloned before the append, prepend, before, or after methods are executed.

Repeat some of the experiments you conducted earlier with cloning enabled, and note how the original sources are unaffected by the operations.

We can insert, we can remove, and we can copy. Using these operations in combination, it'd be easy to concoct higher-level operations such as *replace*. But guess what? We don't need to!

3.3.6   *Replacing elements*

For those times when we want to replace existing elements with new ones, or to move an existing element to replace another, jQuery provides the replaceWith() method.

Method syntax: replaceWith

replaceWith(content)
Replaces each matched element with the specific content.

Parameters
content   (String|Element|Function) A string containing an HTML fragment to become the
           replaced content, or an element reference to be moved to replace the existing
           elements. If a function, the function is invoked for each wrapped element, setting
           that element as the function context and passing no parameters. The function's
           returned value is used as the new content.

Returns
A jQuery wrapped set containing the replaced elements.

Let's say that, under particular circumstances, we want to replace all images on the page that have alt attributes with <span> elements that contain the alt values of the images. Employing each() and replaceWith() we could do it like this:

```
$('img[alt]').each(function(){
  $(this).replaceWith('<span>'+ $(this).attr('alt') +'</span>')
});
```

The each() method lets us iterate over each matching element, and replaceWith() is used to replace the images with generated <span> elements.

The replaceWith() method returns a jQuery wrapped set containing the elements that were removed from the DOM, in case we want to do something other than just discard them. As an exercise, consider how would you augment the example code to reattach these elements elsewhere in the DOM after their removal.

When an existing element is passed to `replaceWith()`, it's detached from its original location in the DOM and reattached to replace the target elements. If there are multiple such targets, the original element is cloned as many times as needed.

At times, it may be convenient to reverse the order of the elements as specified by `replaceWith()` so that the *replacing* element can be specified using the matching selector. We've already seen such complementary methods, such as `append()` and `appendTo()`, that let us specify the elements in the order that makes the most sense for our code.

Similarly, the `replaceAll()` method mirrors `replaceWith()`, allowing us to perform a similar operation, but with the order of specification reversed.

Method syntax: replaceAll

`replaceAll(selector)`

Replaces each element matched by the passed selector with the content of the matched set to which this method is applied.

Parameters

`selector`   (Selector) A selector string expression identifying the elements to be replaced.

Returns

A jQuery wrapped set containing the inserted elements.

As with `replaceWith()`, `replaceAll()` returns a jQuery wrapped set. But this set contains not the replaced elements, but the *replacing* elements. The replaced elements are lost and can't be further operated upon. Keep this in mind when deciding which replace method to employ.

Now that we've discussed handling general DOM elements, let's take a brief look at handling a special type of element: the form elements.

3.4   *Dealing with form element values*

Because form elements have special properties, jQuery's core contains a number of convenience functions for activities such as

- Getting and setting their values
- Serializing them
- Selecting elements based on form-specific properties

These functions will serve us well in most cases, but the Form Plugin—an officially sanctioned plugin developed by members of the jQuery Core Team—provides even more form-related functionality. Learn more about this plugin at http://jquery.malsup.com/form/.

So what's a form element?

When we use the term *form element*, we're referring to the elements that can appear within a form, possess `name` and `value` attributes, and whose values are sent to the server as HTTP request parameters when the form is submitted. Dealing with such elements by hand in script can be tricky because, not only can elements be disabled, but the W3C defines an *unsuccessful* state for controls. This state determines which elements should be ignored during a submission, and it's a tad on the complicated side.

That said, let's take a look at one of the most common operations we'll want to perform on a form element: getting access to its value. jQuery's `val()` method takes care of the most common cases, returning the `value` attribute of a form element for the first element in the wrapped set. Its syntax is as follows:

Method syntax: val

`val()`

Returns the `value` attribute of the first element in the matched set. When the element is a multi-select element, the returned value is an array of all selections.

Parameters
none

Returns
The fetched value or values.

This method, although quite useful, has a number of limitations of which we need to be wary. If the first element in the wrapped set isn't a form element, an empty string is returned, which isn't the most intuitive value that could have been chosen (`undefined` would probably have been clearer). This method also doesn't distinguish between the checked or unchecked states of checkboxes and radio buttons, and will simply return the value of checkboxes or radio buttons as defined by their `value` attribute, regardless of whether they're checked or not.

For radio buttons, the power of jQuery selectors combined with the `val()` method saves the day, as we've already seen in the first example in this book. Consider a form with a radio group (a set of radio buttons with the same name) named `radioGroup` and the following expression:

```
$('[name="radioGroup"]:checked').val()
```

This expression returns the value of the single checked radio button (or `undefined` if none is checked). That's a lot easier than looping through the buttons looking for the checked element, isn't it?

Because `val()` only considers the first element in a wrapped set, it's not as useful for checkbox groups where more than one control might be checked. But jQuery rarely leaves us without recourse. Consider the following:

```
var checkboxValues = $('[name="checkboxGroup"]:checked').map(
  function(){ return $(this).val(); }
).toArray();
```

 Even though we haven't formally covered extending jQuery (that's still four chapters away), you've probably seen enough examples to give it a go. See if you can refactor the preceding code into a jQuery wrapper method that returns an array of any checked checkboxes in the wrapped set.

Although the `val()` method is great for obtaining the value of any single form control element, if we want to obtain the complete set of values that would be submitted through a form submission, we'll be much better off using the serialize() or serializeArray() methods (which we'll see in chapter 8) or the official Form Plugin.

Another common operation we'll perform is to *set* the value of a form element. The val() method is also used bilaterally for this purpose by supplying a value. Its syntax is as follows:

Method syntax: val

val(value)
Sets the passed value as the value of all matched form elements.

Parameters

value   (String|Function) Specifies the value that is to be set as the value property of each form element in the wrapped set. If a function, the function is invoked for each element in the wrapped set, with that element passed as the function context, and two parameters: the element index and the current value of the element. The value returned from the function is taken as the value to be set.

Returns
The wrapped set.

Another way that the val() method can be used is to cause checkbox or radio elements to become checked, or to select options within a <select> element. The syntax of this variant of val() is as follows:

Method syntax: val

val(values)
Causes any checkboxes, radio buttons, or options of <select> elements in the wrapped set to become checked or selected if their value properties match any of the values passed in the values array.

Parameters

values   (Array) An array of values that will be used to determine which elements are to be checked or selected.

Returns
The wrapped set.

Consider the following statement:

```
$('input,select').val(['one','two','three']);
```

This statement will search all the <input> and <select> elements on the page for values that match any of the input strings: *one, two,* or *three*. Any checkboxes or radio buttons that are found to match will become checked, and any options that match will become selected.

This makes val() useful for much more than just the text-based form elements.

3.5   *Summary*

In this chapter, we've gone beyond the art of selecting elements and started manipulating them. With the techniques we've learned so far, we can select elements using powerful criteria, and then move them surgically to any part of the page.

We can choose to copy elements, or to move them, replace them, or even create brand new elements from scratch. We can append, prepend, or wrap any element or set of elements on the page. And we've learned how to manage the values of form elements, all leading to powerful yet succinct logic.

With that behind us, we're ready to start looking into more advanced concepts, starting with the typically messy job of handling events in our pages.

Events are
where it happens!

This chapter covers

- The event models as implemented by the browsers
- The jQuery Event Model
- Binding event handlers to DOM elements
- The `Event` object instance
- Triggering event handlers under script control
- Registering proactive event handlers

Anyone familiar with the Broadway show *Cabaret*, or its subsequent Hollywood film, probably remembers the song "Money Makes the World Go Around." Although this cynical view might be applicable to the physical world, in the virtual realm of the World Wide Web, it's events that make it all happen!

Like many other GUI management systems, the interfaces presented by HTML web pages are *asynchronous* and *event-driven* (even if the HTTP protocol used to deliver them to the browser is wholly synchronous in nature). Whether a GUI is implemented as a desktop program using Java Swing, X11, or the .NET Framework, or as a page in a web application using HTML and JavaScript, the program steps are pretty much the same:

1 Set up the user interface.
2 Wait for something interesting to happen.
3 React accordingly.
4 Go to 2.

The first step sets up the *display* of the user interface; the others define its *behavior*. In web pages, the browser handles the setup of the display in response to the markup (HTML and CSS) that we send to it. The script we include in the page defines the behavior of the interface.

This script takes the form of *event handlers*, also known as *listeners*, that react to the various events that occur while the page is displayed. These events could be generated by the system (timers or the completion of asynchronous requests, for example) but are most often the result of some user activity (such as moving or clicking the mouse, entering text via the keyboard, or even iPhone gestures). Without the ability to react to these events, the World Wide Web's greatest use might be limited to showing pictures of kittens.

Although HTML itself *does* define a small set of built-in semantic actions that require no scripting on our part (such as reloading pages as the result of clicking an anchor tag or submitting a form via a submit button), any other behaviors that we wish our pages to exhibit require us to handle the various events that occur as our users interact with those pages.

In this chapter, we'll examine the various ways that browsers expose these events, how they allow us to establish handlers to control what happens when these events occur, and the challenges that we face due to the multitude of differences between the browser event models. Then we'll see how jQuery cuts through the browser-induced fog to relieve us of these burdens.

Let's start off by examining how browsers expose their event models.

JavaScript you need to know!

One of the great benefits that jQuery brings to web applications is the ability to implement a great deal of scripting-enabled behavior without having to write a whole lot of script ourselves. jQuery handles the nuts-and-bolts details so that we can concentrate on the job of making our applications do what they need to do!

Up to this point, the ride has been pretty painless. You only needed rudimentary JavaScript skills to code and understand the jQuery examples we introduced in the previous chapters. In this chapter and the chapters that follow, you *must* understand a handful of important fundamental JavaScript concepts to make effective use of the jQuery library.

> **continued**
> Depending on your background, you may already be familiar with these concepts, but some page authors may have been able to get pretty far without a firm grasp of these concepts—the very flexibility of JavaScript makes such a situation possible. Before we proceed, it's time to make sure that you've wrapped your head around these core concepts.
>
> If you're already comfortable with the workings of the JavaScript `Object` and `Function` classes, and have a good handle on concepts like *function contexts* and *closures*, you may want to continue reading this and the upcoming chapters. If these concepts are unfamiliar or hazy, we strongly urge you to turn to the appendix to help you get up to speed on these necessary concepts.

4.1　Understanding the browser event models

Long before anyone considered standardizing how browsers would handle events, Netscape Communications Corporation introduced an event-handling model in its Netscape Navigator browser; all modern browsers still support this model, which is probably the best understood and most employed by the majority of page authors.

This model is known by a few names. You may have heard it termed the Netscape Event Model, the Basic Event Model, or even the rather vague Browser Event Model, but most people have come to call it the *DOM Level 0 Event Model.*

> **NOTE**　The term *DOM level* is used to indicate what level of requirements an implementation of the W3C DOM specification meets. There isn't a DOM Level 0, but that term is used to informally describe what was implemented *prior* to DOM Level 1.

The W3C didn't create a standardized model for event handling until DOM Level 2, introduced in November 2000. This model enjoys support from all modern standards-compliant browsers such as Firefox, Camino (as well as other Mozilla browsers), Safari, and Opera. Internet Explorer continues to go its own way and supports a subset of the functionality in the DOM Level 2 Event Model, albeit using a proprietary interface.

Before we see how jQuery makes that irritating fact a non-issue, let's spend some time getting to know how the various event models operate.

4.1.1　The DOM Level 0 Event Model

The DOM Level 0 Event Model is the event model that most web developers employ on their pages. In addition to being somewhat browser-independent, it's fairly easy to use.

Under this event model, event handlers are declared by assigning a reference to a function instance to properties of the DOM elements. These properties are defined to handle a specific event type; for example, a click event is handled by assigning a function to the `onclick` property, and a mouseover event by assigning a function to the `onmouseover` property of elements that support these event types.

The browsers allow us to specify the body of an event handler function as attribute values embedded within the HTML markup of the DOM elements, providing a shorthand for creating event handlers. An example of defining such handlers is shown in listing 4.1. This page can be found in the downloadable code for this book in the file chapter4/dom.0.events.html.

Listing 4.1 Declaring DOM Level 0 event handlers

```
<!DOCTYPE html>
<html>
  <head>
    <title>DOM Level 0 Events Example</title>
    <link rel="stylesheet" type="text/css" href="../styles/core.css"/>
    <script type="text/javascript" src="../scripts/jquery-1.4.min.js"></
     script>
    <script type="text/javascript" src="../scripts/jqia2.support.js"></
     script>
    <script type="text/javascript">
      $(function(){
        $('#example')[0].onmouseover = function(event) {    ❶ Defines the mouseover handler
          say('Crackle!');                                 ❷ Emits text to "console"
        };
      });
    </script>
  </head>

  <body>
    <img id="example" src="example.jpg"                    ❸ Instruments <img> element
         onclick="say('BOOM!');"
         alt="ooooh! ahhhh!"/>
  </body>
</html>
```

In this example, we employ both styles of event handler declaration: declaring under script control and declaring in a markup attribute.

The page first declares a ready handler in which a reference to the image element with the `id` of `example` is obtained (using jQuery), and its `onmouseover` property is set to an inline function ❶. This function becomes the event handler for the element when a mouseover event is triggered on it. Note that this function expects a single parameter to be passed to it. We'll learn more about this parameter shortly.

Within this function, we employ the services of a small utility function, `say()` ❷, that we use to emit text messages to a dynamically created `<div>` element on the page that we'll call the "console." This function is declared within the imported support script file (jqia2.support.js), and will save us the trouble of using annoying and disruptive alerts to indicate when things happen on our page. We'll be using this handy function in many of the examples throughout the remainder of the book.

In the body of the page, we define an `<img>` element upon which we're defining the event handlers. We've already seen how to define a handler under script control in the ready handler ❶, but here we declare a handler for a click event using the `onclick` attribute ❸ of the `<img>` element.

NOTE Obviously we've thrown the concept of Unobtrusive JavaScript out the kitchen window for this example. Long before we reach the end of this chapter, we'll see why we won't need to embed event behavior in the DOM markup anymore!

Loading this page into a browser (found in the file chapter4/dom.0.events.html), waving the mouse pointer over the image a few times, and then clicking the image, results in a display similar to that shown in figure 4.1.

We declared the click event handler in the <img> element markup using the following attribute:

```
onclick="say('BOOM!');"
```

This might lead us to believe that the say() function becomes the click event handler for the element, but that's not really the case. When handlers are declared via HTML markup attributes, an anonymous function is automatically created using the value of the attribute as the function *body*. Assuming that imageElement is a reference to the image element, the construct created as a result of the attribute declaration is equivalent to the following:

```
imageElement.onclick = function(event) {
  say('BOOM!');
};
```

Note how the value of the attribute is used as the body of the generated function, and note that the function is created so that the event parameter is available within the generated function.

Before we move on to examining what that event parameter is all about, we should note that using the attribute mechanism of declaring DOM Level 0 event handlers violates the precepts of Unobtrusive JavaScript that we explored in chapter 1. When using jQuery in our pages, we should adhere to the principles of Unobtrusive

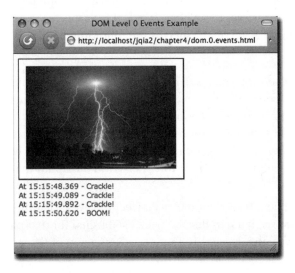

Figure 4.1 Waving the mouse over the image and clicking it results in the event handlers firing and emitting their messages to the console.

JavaScript and avoid mixing behavior defined by JavaScript with display markup. We'll shortly see that jQuery provides a much better way to declare event handlers than either of these means.

But first, let's examine what that `event` parameter is all about.

THE EVENT INSTANCE

When an event handler is fired, an instance of a class named `Event` is passed to the handler as its first parameter in most browsers. Internet Explorer, always the life of the party, does things in its own proprietary way by tacking the `Event` instance onto a global property (in other words, a property on `window`) named `event`.

In order to deal with this discrepancy, we'll often see the following used as the first statement in a non-jQuery event handler:

```
if (!event) event = window.event;
```

This levels the playing field by using feature detection (a concept we'll explore in greater depth in chapter 6) to check if the `event` parameter is `undefined` (or `null`) and assigning the value of the window's `event` property to it if so. After this statement, the `event` parameter can be referenced regardless of how it was made available to the handler.

The properties of the `Event` instance provide a great deal of information regarding the event that has been fired and is currently being handled. This includes details such as which element the event was triggered on, the coordinates of mouse events, and which key was clicked for keyboard events.

But not so fast. Not only does Internet Explorer use a proprietary means to get the `Event` instance to the handler, but it also uses a proprietary definition of the `Event` class in place of the W3C-defined standard—we're not out of the object-detection woods yet.

For example, to get a reference to the target element—the element on which the event was triggered—we access the `target` property in standards-compliant browsers and the `srcElement` property in Internet Explorer. We deal with this inconsistency by employing feature detection with a statement such as the following:

```
var target = (event.target) ? event.target : event.srcElement;
```

This statement tests whether `event.target` is defined and, if so, assigns its value to the local `target` variable; otherwise, it assigns `event.srcElement`. We'll be required to take similar steps for other `Event` properties of interest.

Up until this point, we've acted as if event handlers are only pertinent to the elements that serve as the trigger to an event—the image element of listing 4.1, for example—but events propagate throughout the DOM tree. Let's find out about that.

EVENT BUBBLING

When an event is triggered on an element in the DOM tree, the event-handling mechanism of the browser checks to see if a handler has been established for that particular event on that element and, if so, invokes it. But that's hardly the end of the story.

After the target element has had its chance to handle the event, the event model checks with the parent of that element to see if *it* has established a handler for the event type, and if so, it's also invoked—after which *its* parent is checked, then its parent, then its parent, and on and on, all the way up to the top of the DOM tree. Because the event handling propagates upward like the bubbles in a champagne flute (assuming we view the DOM tree with its root at the top), this process is termed *event bubbling*.

Let's modify the example from listing 4.1 so that we can see this process in action. Consider the code in listing 4.2.

Listing 4.2 Events propagate from the point of origin to the top of the DOM

```
<!DOCTYPE html>
<html id="greatgreatgrandpa">
  <head>
    <title>DOM Level 0 Bubbling Example</title>
    <link rel="stylesheet" type="text/css" href="../styles/core.css"/>
    <script type="text/javascript" src="../scripts/jquery-1.4.js"></script>
    <script type="text/javascript" src="../scripts/jqia2.support.js"></
     script>
    <script type="text/javascript">
      $(function(){
        $('*').each(function(){            ❶ Selects every
          var current = this;                  element on the page
          this.onclick = function(event) {
            if (!event) event = window.event;  ❷ Applies onclick handler to
            var target = (event.target) ?          every selected element
                      event.target : event.srcElement;
            say('For ' + current.tagName + '#'+ current.id +
                ' target is ' +
                target.tagName + '#' + target.id);
          };
        });
      });
    </script>
  </head>

  <body id="greatgrandpa">
    <div id="grandpa">
      <div id="pops">
        <img id="example" src="example.jpg" alt="ooooh! ahhhh!"/>
      </div>
    </div>
  </body>
</html>
```

We do a lot of interesting things in the changes to this example. First, we remove the previous handling of the mouseover event so that we can concentrate on the click event. We also embed the image element that will serve as the target for our event experiment in a couple of nested <div> elements, merely to place the image element artificially deeper within the DOM hierarchy. We also give almost every element in the page a specific and unique id—even the <body> and <html> tags!

Now let's look at even more interesting changes.

In the ready handler for the page, we use jQuery to select all elements on the page and to iterate over each one with the each() method ❶. For each matched element, we record its instance in the local variable current and establish an onclick handler ❷. This handler first employs the browser-dependent tricks that we discussed in the previous section to locate the Event instance and identify the event target, and then emits a console message. This message is the most interesting part of this example.

It displays the tag name and id of the current element, putting *closures* to work (please read the section on closures in the appendix if closures are a subject that gives you heartburn), followed by the id of the target. By doing so, each message that's logged to the console displays the information about the current element of the bubble process, as well as the target element that started the whole shebang.

Loading the page (located in the file chapter4/dom.0.propagation.html) and clicking the image results in the display of figure 4.2.

This clearly illustrates that, when the event is fired, it's delivered first to the target element and then to each of its ancestors in turn, all the way up to the root <html> element.

This is a powerful ability because it allows us to establish handlers on elements at any level to handle events occurring on its descendents. Consider a handler on a <form> element that reacts to any change event on its child elements to effect dynamic changes to the display based upon the elements' new values.

But what if we don't *want* the event to propagate? Can we stop it?

AFFECTING EVENT PROPAGATION AND SEMANTIC ACTIONS

There may be occasions when we want to prevent an event from bubbling any further up the DOM tree. This might be because we're fastidious and we know that we've already accomplished any processing necessary to handle the event, or we may want to forestall unwanted handling that might occur higher up in the chain.

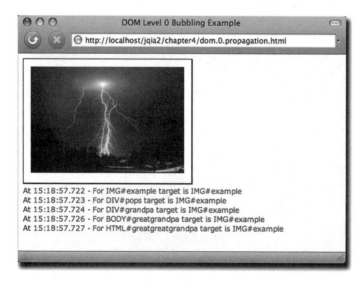

Figure 4.2   The console messages clearly show the propagation of the event as it bubbles up the DOM tree from the target element to the tree root.

Regardless of the reason, we can prevent an event from propagating any higher via mechanisms provided on the Event instance. For standards-compliant browsers, we call the stopPropagation() method of the Event instance to halt the propagation of the event further up the ancestor hierarchy. In Internet Explorer, we set a property named cancelBubble to true in the Event instance. Interestingly, many modern standards-compliant browsers support the cancelBubble mechanism even though it's not part of any W3C standard.

Some events have default semantics associated with them. As examples, a click event on an anchor element will cause the browser to navigate to the element's href, and a submit event on a <form> element will cause the form to be submitted. Should we wish to cancel these semantic actions—sometimes termed the *default actions*—of the event, we simply return the value false from the event handler.

A frequent use for such an action is in the realm of form validation. In the handler for the form's submit event, we can make validation checks on the form's controls and return false if any problems with the data entry are detected.

You may also have seen the following on <form> elements:

```
<form name="myForm" onsubmit="return false;" ...
```

This effectively prevents the form from being submitted in any circumstances except under script control (via form.submit(), which doesn't trigger a submit event)—a common trick used in many Ajax applications where asynchronous requests will be made in lieu of form submissions.

Under the DOM Level 0 Event Model, almost every step we take in an event handler involves using browser-specific detection in order to figure out what action to take. What a headache! But don't put away the aspirin yet—it doesn't get any easier when we consider the more advanced event model.

4.1.2 The DOM Level 2 Event Model

One severe shortcoming of the DOM Level 0 Event Model is that, because a property is used to store a reference to a function that's to serve as an event handler, only one event handler per element can be registered for any specific event type at a time. If we have two things that we want to do when an element is clicked, the following statements aren't going to let that happen:

```
someElement.onclick = doFirstThing;
someElement.onclick = doSecondThing;
```

Because the second assignment replaces the previous value of the onclick property, only doSecondThing is invoked when the event is triggered. Sure, we could wrap both functions in another single function that calls both, but as pages get more complicated, as is quite likely in highly interactive applications, it becomes increasingly difficult to keep track of such things. Moreover, if we use multiple reusable components or libraries in a page, they may have no idea of the event-handling needs of the other components.

We could employ other solutions: implementing the Observable pattern, which establishes a publish/subscribe scheme for the handlers, or even tricks using closures. But all of these add complexity to pages that are likely to already be complex enough.

Besides the establishment of a *standard* event model, the DOM Level 2 Event Model was designed to address these types of problems. Let's see how event handlers, even multiple handlers, are established on DOM elements under this more advanced model.

ESTABLISHING EVENT HANDLERS

Rather than assigning a function reference to an element property, DOM Level 2 event handlers—also termed *listeners*—are established via an element *method*. Each DOM element defines a method named `addEventListener()` that's used to attach event handlers (listeners) to the element. The format of this method is as follows:

```
addEventListener(eventType,listener,useCapture)
```

The `eventType` parameter is a string that identifies the type of event to be handled. These string values are, generally, the same event names we used in the DOM Level 0 Event Model without the *on* prefix: for example: click, mouseover, keydown, and so on.

The `listener` parameter is a reference to the function (or an inline function) that's to be established as the handler for the named event type on the element. As in the basic event model, the `Event` instance is passed to this function as its first parameter.

The final parameter, `useCapture`, is a Boolean whose operation we'll explore in a few moments, when we discuss event propagation in the Level 2 Model. For now, we'll leave it set to `false`.

Let's once again change the example from listing 4.1 to use the more advanced event model. We'll concentrate only on the click event type; this time, we'll establish *three* click event handlers on the image element. The new example code can be found in the file chapter4/dom.2.events.html and is shown in listing 4.3.

Listing 4.3 Establishing event handlers with the DOM Level 2 Event Model

```
<!DOCTYPE html>
<html>
  <head>
    <title>DOM Level 2 Events Example</title>
    <link rel="stylesheet" type="text/css" href="../styles/core.css"/>
    <script type="text/javascript" src="../scripts/jquery-1.4.js"></script>
    <script type="text/javascript" src="../scripts/jqia2.support.js"></
     script>
    <script type="text/javascript">          ❶ Establishes three
      $(function(){                             event handlers!
        var element = $('#example')[0];
        element.addEventListener('click',function(event) {
          say('BOOM once!');
        },false);
        element.addEventListener('click',function(event) {
          say('BOOM twice!');
        },false);
```

```
        element.addEventListener('click',function(event) {
          say('BOOM three times!');
        },false);
      });
    </script>
  </head>

  <body>
    <img id="example" src="example.jpg"/>
  </body>
</html>
```

This code is simple, but it clearly shows how we can establish multiple event handlers on the same element for the same event type—something we were not able to do easily with the Basic Event Model. In the ready handler for the page ❶, we grab a reference to the image element and then establish *three* event handlers for the click event.

Loading this page into a standards-compliant browser (*not* Internet Explorer) and clicking the image results in the display shown in figure 4.3.

Note that even though the handlers fire in the order in which they were established, *this order isn't guaranteed by the standard!* Testers of this code never observed an order other than the order of establishment, but it would be foolish to write code that relies on this order. Always be aware that multiple handlers established on an element may fire in random order.

Now, let's find out what's up with that useCapture parameter.

EVENT PROPAGATION

We saw earlier that, with the Basic Event Model, once an event was triggered on an element the event propagated from the target element upwards in the DOM tree to all the target's ancestors. The advanced Level 2 Event Model also provides this bubbling phase but ups the ante with an additional capture phase.

Under the DOM Level 2 Event Model, when an event is triggered, the event first propagates from the root of the DOM tree down to the target element and then

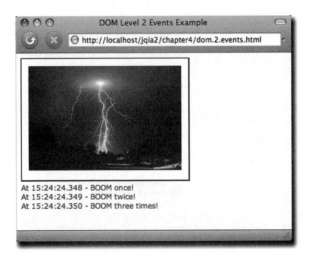

Figure 4.3 Clicking the image once demonstrates that all three handlers established for the click event are triggered.

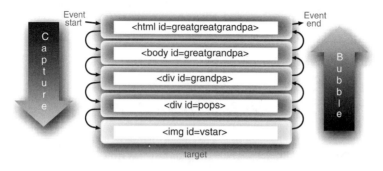

Figure 4.4   Propagation in the DOM Level 2 Event Model traverses the DOM hierarchy twice: once from top to target during capture phase and once from target to top during bubble phase.

propagates again from the target element up to the DOM root. The former phase (root to target) is called *capture phase*, and the latter (target to root) is called *bubble phase*.

When a function is established as an event handler, it can be flagged as a capture handler, in which case it will be triggered during capture phase, or as a bubble handler, to be triggered during bubble phase. As you might have guessed by this time, the useCapture parameter to addEventListener() identifies which type of handler is established. A value of false for this parameter establishes a bubble handler, whereas a value of true registers a capture handler.

Think back a moment to the example of listing 4.2 where we explored the propagation of the Basic Model events through a DOM hierarchy. In that example, we embedded an image element within two layers of <div> elements. Within such a hierarchy, the propagation of a click event with the <img> element as its target would move through the DOM tree as shown in figure 4.4.

Let's put that to the test, shall we? Listing 4.4 shows the code for a page containing the element hierarchy of figure 4.4 (chapter4/dom.2.propagation.html).

Listing 4.4   Tracking event propagation with bubble and capture handlers

```
<!DOCTYPE html>
<html id="greatgreatgrandpa">
  <head>
    <title>DOM Level 2 Propagation Example</title>
    <link rel="stylesheet" type="text/css" href="../styles/core.css"/>
    <script type="text/javascript" src="../scripts/jquery-1.4.js"></script>
    <script type="text/javascript" src="../scripts/jqia2.support.js"></
     script>
    <script type="text/javascript">
      $(function(){
        $('*').each(function(){                      Establishes listeners
          var current = this;                      ❶ on all elements
          this.addEventListener('click',function(event) {
            say('Capture for ' + current.tagName + '#'+ current.id +
              ' target is ' + event.target.id);
          },true);
```

```
            this.addEventListener('click',function(event) {
                say('Bubble for ' + current.tagName + '#'+ current.id +
                    ' target is ' + event.target.id);
            },false);
        });
    });
  </script>
</head>

<body id="greatgrandpa">
  <div id="grandpa">
    <div id="pops">
      <img id="example" src="example.jpg"/>
    </div>
  </div>
  <div id="console"></div>
</body>
</html>
```

This code changes the example of listing 4.2 to use the DOM Level 2 Event Model API to establish the event handlers. In the ready handler ❶, we use jQuery's powerful abilities to run through every element of the DOM tree. On each, we establish two handlers: one capture handler and one bubble handler. Each handler emits a message to the console identifying which type of handler it is, the current element, and the id of the target element.

With the page loaded into a standards-compliant browser, clicking the image results in the display in figure 4.5, showing the progression of the event through the handling phases and the DOM tree. Note that, because we defined both capture and bubble handlers for the target, two handlers were executed for the target and all its ancestor nodes.

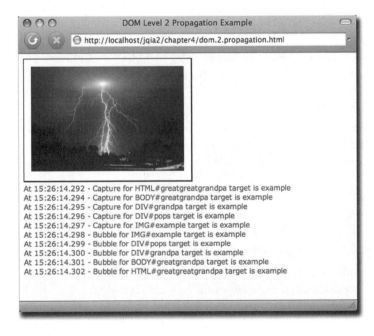

Figure 4.5 Clicking the image results in each handler emitting a console message that identifies the path of the event during both capture and bubble phases.

Well, now that we've gone through all the trouble to understand these two types of handlers, we should know that capture handlers are hardly ever used in web pages. The simple reason for that is that Internet Explorer doesn't support the DOM Level 2 Event Model. Although it *does* have a proprietary model corresponding to the bubble phase of the Level 2 standard, it doesn't support any semblance of a capture phase.

Before we look at how jQuery can help sort all this mess out, let's briefly examine the Internet Explorer Model.

4.1.3   *The Internet Explorer Event Model*

Internet Explorer (IE 6, IE 7, and, most disappointingly, even IE 8) doesn't provide support for the DOM Level 2 Event Model. These versions of Microsoft's browser provide a proprietary interface that closely resembles the bubble phase of the standard model.

Rather than addEventListener(), the Internet Explorer Model defines a method named attachEvent() for each DOM element. This method accepts two parameters similar to those of the standard model:

```
attachEvent(eventName,handler)
```

The first parameter is a string that names the event type to be attached. The standard event names aren't used; the name of the corresponding element property from the DOM Level 0 Model is used—"onclick", "onmouseover", "onkeydown", and so on.

The second parameter is the function to be established as the handler, and as in the Basic Model, the Event instance must be fetched from the window.event property.

What a mess! Even when using the relatively browser-independent DOM Level 0 Model, we're faced with a tangle of browser-dependent choices to make at each stage of event handling. And when using the more capable DOM Level 2 or Internet Explorer Model, we even have to diverge our code when establishing the handlers in the first place.

Well, jQuery is going to make our lives simpler by hiding these browser disparities from us as much as it possibly can. Let's see how!

4.2   *The jQuery Event Model*

Although it's true that the creation of highly interactive applications requires a hefty reliance on event handling, the thought of writing event-handling code on a large scale while dealing with the browser differences is enough to daunt even the most intrepid of page authors.

We could hide the differences behind an API that abstracts the differences away from our page code, but why bother when jQuery has already done it for us?

jQuery's event model implementation, which we'll refer to informally as the jQuery Event Model, exhibits the following features:

- Provides a unified method for establishing event handlers
- Allows multiple handlers for each event type on each element

- Uses standard event-type names: for example, click or mouseover
- Makes the Event instance available as a parameter to the handlers
- Normalizes the Event instance for the most-often-used properties
- Provides unified methods for event canceling and default action blocking

With the notable exception of support for a capture phase, the feature set of the jQuery Event Model closely resembles that of the DOM Level 2 Event Model while supporting both standards-compliant browsers and Internet Explorer with a single API. The omission of the capture phase should not be an issue for the vast majority of page authors who never use it (or even know it exists) due to its lack of support in IE.

Is it really that simple? Let's find out.

4.2.1 Binding event handlers with jQuery

Using the jQuery Event Model, we can establish event handlers on DOM elements with the bind() method. Consider the following simple example:

```
$('img').bind('click',function(event){alert('Hi there!');});
```

This statement binds the supplied inline function as the click event handler for every image on a page. The full syntax of the bind() method is as follows:

Method syntax: bind

bind(eventType,data,handler)
bind(eventMap)
Establishes a function as the event handler for the specified event type on all elements in the matched set.

Parameters

eventType	(String) Specifies the name of the event type or types for which the handler is to be established. Multiple event types can be specified as a space-separated list. These event types can be namespaced with a suffix affixed to the event name with a period character. See the remainder of this section for details.
data	(Object) Caller-supplied data that's attached to the Event instance as a property named data and made available to the handler function. If omitted, the handler function can be specified as the second parameter.
handler	(Function) The function that's to be established as the event handler. When invoked, it will be passed the Event instance, and its function context (this) is set to the current element of the bubble phase.
eventMap	(Object) A JavaScript object that allows handlers for multiple event types to be established in a single call. The property names identify the event type (same as would be used for the eventType parameter), and the property value provides the handler.

Returns
The wrapped set.

Let's put bind() into action. Taking the example of listing 4.3 and converting it from the DOM Level 2 Event Model to the jQuery Event Model, we end up with the code shown in listing 4.5 and found in the file chapter4/jquery.events.html.

Listing 4.5   Establishing advanced event handlers without browser-specific code

```
<!DOCTYPE html>
<html>
  <head>
    <title>jQuery Events Example</title>
    <link rel="stylesheet" type="text/css" href="../styles/core.css"/>
    <script type="text/javascript" src="../scripts/jquery-1.4.js"></script>
    <script type="text/javascript" src="../scripts/jqia2.support.js"></
     script>
    <script type="text/javascript">
      $(function(){
        $('#example')
          .bind('click',function(event) {
            say('BOOM once!');
          })
          .bind('click',function(event) {
            say('BOOM twice!');
          })
          .bind('click',function(event) {
            say('BOOM three times!');
          });
      });
    </script>
  </head>

  <body>
    <img id="example" src="example.jpg"/>
  </body>
</html>
```

❶ Binds three event handlers to the image

The changes to this code, limited to the body of the ready handler, are minor but significant ❶. We create a wrapped set consisting of the target <img> element and apply three bind() methods to it—remember, jQuery chaining lets us apply multiple methods in a single statement—each of which establishes a click event handler on the element.

Loading this page into a standards-compliant browser and clicking the image results in the display of figure 4.6, which, not surprisingly, is the exact same result we saw in figure 4.3 (except for the URL and window caption).

But perhaps more importantly, it also works when loaded into Internet Explorer, as shown in figure 4.7. This was not possible using the code from listing 4.3 without adding browser-specific testing and branching code to use the correct event model for the current browser.

At this point, page authors who have wrestled with mountains of browser-specific event-handling code in their pages are no doubt singing "Happy Days Are Here Again" and spinning in their office chairs. Who could blame them?

Another nifty little event-handling extra that jQuery provides for us is the ability to group event handlers by assigning them to a namespace. Unlike conventional namespacing (which assigns namespaces via a prefix), the event names are namespaced by adding a *suffix* to the event name separated by a period character. In

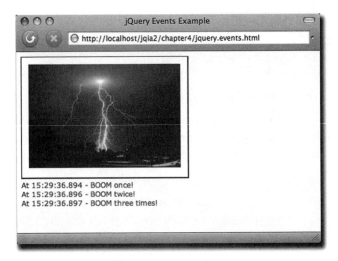

Figure 4.6   Using the jQuery Event Model allows us to specify multiple event handlers just like the DOM Level 2 Event Model.

fact, if you'd like, you can use multiple suffixes to place the event into multiple namespaces.

By grouping event bindings in this way, we can easily act upon them later as a unit.

Take, for example, a page that has two modes: a display mode and an edit mode. When in edit mode, event listeners are placed on many of the page elements, but these listeners aren't appropriate for display mode and need to be removed when the

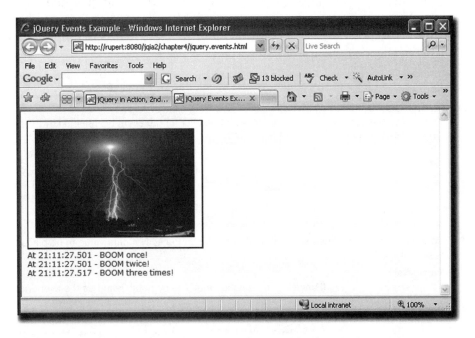

Figure 4.7   The jQuery Event Model allows us to use a unified events API to support events across the standards-compliant browsers as well as Internet Explorer.

page transitions out of edit mode. We could namespace the edit mode events with code such as this:

```
$('#thing1').bind('click.editMode',someListener);
$('#thing2').bind('click.editMode',someOtherListener);
  ...
$('#thingN').bind('click.editMode',stillAnotherListener);
```

By grouping all these bindings into a namespace named `editMode`, we can later operate upon them as a whole. For example, when the page leaves edit mode and it comes time to remove all the bindings, we could do this easily with

```
$('*').unbind('click.editMode');
```

This will remove all `click` bindings (the explanation of the `unbind()` method is coming up in the next section) in the namespace `editMode` for all elements on the page.

Before we leave `bind()`, let's consider one more example:

```
$('.whatever').bind({
  click: function(event) { /* handle clicks */ },
  mouseenter: function(event) { /* handle mouseenters */ },
  mouseleave: function(event) { /* handle mouseleaves */ }
});
```

For occasions when we want to bind multiple event types to an element, we can do it with a single call to `bind()`, as shown.

In addition to the `bind()` method, jQuery provides a handful of shortcut methods to establish specific event handlers. Because the syntax of each of these methods is identical except for the name of the method, we'll save some space and present them all in the following single syntax descriptor:

Method syntax: specific event binding

***eventTypeName*(`listener`)**

Establishes the specified function as the event handler for the event type named by the method's name. The supported methods are as follows:

blur	focusin	mousedown	mouseup
change	focusout	mouseenter	ready
click	keydown	mouseleave	resize
dblclick	keypress	mousemove	scroll
error	keyup	mouseout	select
focus	load	mouseover	submit
			unload

Note that when using these shortcut methods, we can't specify a data value to be placed in the `event.data` property.

Parameters

`listener`   (Function) The function that's to be established as the event handler.

Returns

The wrapped set.

The focusin and focusout events deserve some discussion.

It's not hard to imagine scenarios where we'd want to handle focus and blur events in a central manner. For example, let's say that we wanted to keep track of which fields in a form had been visited. Rather than establishing a handler on each and every element, it'd be handy to establish a single handler on the form. But we can't.

The focus and blur events, by their nature, do not bubble up the DOM tree. Therefore, a focus handler established on the form element would never get invoked.

This is where the focusin and focusout events come in. Handlers established for these events on focusable elements are invoked whenever the element receives or loses focus, as are any such handlers established on the ancestors of the focusable element.

jQuery also provides a specialized version of the bind() method, named one(), that establishes an event handler as a one-shot deal. Once the event handler executes the first time, it's automatically removed as an event handler. Its syntax is similar to the bind() method:

Method syntax: one

`one(eventType,data,listener)`

Establishes a function as the event handler for the specified event type on all elements in the matched set. Once executed, the handler is automatically removed.

Parameters

eventType	(String) Specifies the name of the event type for which the handler is to be established.
data	(Object) Caller-supplied data that's attached to the Event instance for availability to the handler function. If omitted, the handler function can be specified as the second parameter.
listener	(Function) The function that's to be established as the one-time event handler.

Returns

The wrapped set.

These methods give us many choices for binding an event handler to matched elements. And once a handler is bound, we may eventually need to remove it.

4.2.2 Removing event handlers

Typically, once an event handler is established, it remains in effect for the remainder of the life of the page. But particular interactions may dictate that handlers be removed based on certain criteria. Consider, for example, a page where multiple steps are presented, and once a step has been completed, its controls revert to read-only.

For such cases, it would be advantageous to remove event handlers under script control. We've seen that the one() method can automatically remove a handler after it has completed its first (and only) execution, but for the more general case where we'd like to remove event handlers under our own control, jQuery provides the unbind() method.

The syntax of unbind() is as follows:

Method syntax: unbind

`unbind(eventType,listener)`
`unbind(event)`
Removes events handlers from all elements of the wrapped set as specified by the optional passed parameters. If no parameters are provided, all listeners are removed from the elements.

Parameters

`eventType`	(String) If provided, specifies that only listeners established for the specified event type are to be removed.
`listener`	(Function) If provided, identifies the specific listener that's to be removed.
`event`	(Event) Removes the listener that triggered the event described by this `Event` instance.

Returns
The wrapped set.

This method can be used to remove event handlers from the elements of the matched set at various levels of granularity. All listeners can be removed by omitting any parameters, or listeners of a specific type can be removed by providing just that event type.

Specific handlers can be removed by providing a reference to the function originally established as the listener. To do this, a reference to the function must be retained when binding the function as an event listener in the first place. For this reason, when a function that's eventually to be removed as a handler is originally established as a listener, it's either defined as a top-level function (so that it can be referred to by its top-level variable name) or a reference to it is retained by some other means. Supplying the function as an anonymous inline reference would make it impossible to later reference the function in a call to `unbind()`.

That's a situation where using name-spaced events can come in quite handy, as you can unbind all events in a particular namespace without having to retain individual references to the listeners. For example:

```
$('*').unbind('.fred');
```

This statement will remove all event listeners in namespace `fred`.

So far, we've seen that the jQuery Event Model makes it easy to establish (as well as remove) event handlers without worries about browser differences, but what about writing the event handlers themselves?

4.2.3 *Inspecting the Event instance*

When an event handler established with the `bind()` method (or any of its related convenience methods) is invoked, an `Event` instance is passed to it as the first parameter to the function regardless of the browser, eliminating the need to worry about the `window.event` property under Internet Explorer. But that still leaves us dealing with the divergent properties of the `Event` instance, doesn't it?

Thankfully, no, because truth be told, jQuery doesn't really pass the `Event` instance to the handlers.

Screech! (sound of needle being dragged across record).

Yes, we've been glossing over this little detail because, up until now, it hasn't mattered. But now that we've advanced to the point where we're going to examine the instance within handlers, the truth must be told!

In reality, jQuery defines an object of type `jQuery.Event` that it passes to the handlers. But we can be forgiven our simplification, because jQuery copies most of the original `Event` properties to this object. As such, if you only look for the properties that you expected to find on Event, the object is almost indistinguishable from the original `Event` instance.

But that's not the important aspect of this object—what's really valuable, and the reason that this object exists, is that it holds a set of normalized values and methods that we can use independently of the containing browser, ignoring the differences in the `Event` instance.

Table 4.1 lists the `jQuery.Event` properties and methods that are safe to access in a platform-independent manner.

Table 4.1 Browser-independent `jQuery.Event` properties

Name	Description
PROPERTIES	
altKey	Set to `true` if the Alt key was pressed when the event was triggered, `false` if not. The Alt key is labeled Option on most Mac keyboards.
ctrlKey	Set to `true` if the Ctrl key was pressed when the event was triggered, `false` if not.
currentTarget	The current element during the bubble phase. This is the same object that's set as the function context of the event handler.
data	The value, if any, passed as the second parameter to the `bind()` method when the handler was established.
metaKey	Set to `true` if the Meta key was pressed when the event was triggered, `false` if not. The Meta key is the Ctrl key on PCs and the Command key on Macs.
pageX	For mouse events, specifies the horizontal coordinate of the event relative to the page origin.
pageY	For mouse events, specifies the vertical coordinate of the event relative to the page origin.
relatedTarget	For mouse movement events, identifies the element that the cursor left or entered when the event was triggered.
screenX	For mouse events, specifies the horizontal coordinate of the event relative to the screen origin.
screenY	For mouse events, specifies the vertical coordinate of the event relative to the screen origin.

Table 4.1 Browser-independent `jQuery.Event` properties *(continued)*

Name	Description
shiftKey	Set to `true` if the Shift key was pressed when the event was triggered, `false` if not.
result	The most recent non-undefined value returned from a previous event handler.
target	Identifies the element for which the event was triggered.
timestamp	The timestamp, in milliseconds, when the `jQuery.Event` instance was created.
type	For all events, specifies the type of event that was triggered (for example, "click"). This can be useful if you're using one event handler function for multiple events.
which	For keyboard events, specifies the numeric code for the key that caused the event; for mouse events, specifies which button was pressed (1 for left, 2 for middle, 3 for right). This should be used instead of `button`, which can't be relied on to function consistently across browsers.
METHODS	
preventDefault()	Prevents any default semantic action (such as form submission, link redirection, checkbox state change, and so on) from occurring.
stopPropagation()	Stops any further propagation of the event up the DOM tree. Additional events on the current target aren't affected. Works with browser-defined events as well as custom events.
stopImmediatePropagation()	Stops all further event propagation including additional events on the current target.
isDefaultPrevented()	Returns `true` if the `preventDefault()` method has been called on this instance.
isPropagationStopped()	Returns `true` if the `stopPropagation()` method has been called on this instance.
isImmediatePropagationStopped()	Returns `true` if the `stopImmediatePropagation()` method has been called on this instance.

It's important to note that the keycode property isn't reliable across browsers for non-alphabetic characters. For instance, the left arrow key has a code of 37, which works reliably on keyup and keydown events, but Safari returns nonstandard results for these keys on a keypress event.

We can get a reliable, case-sensitive character code in the which property of keypress events. During keyup and keydown events, we can only get a case-insensitive key code (so *a* and *A* both return 65), but we can determine case by checking shiftKey.

Also, if we want to stop the propagation of the event (but not *immediate* propagation), as well as cancel its default behavior, we can simply return false as the return value of the listener function.

All of this gives us the ability to exert fine-grained control over the establishment and removal of event handlers for all the elements that exist within the DOM; but what about elements that don't exist yet, but *will?*

4.2.4 *Proactively managing event handlers*

With the bind() and unbind() methods (and the plethora of convenience methods), we can readily control which event handlers are to be established on the elements of the DOM. The ready handler gives us a convenient place to initially establish handlers on the DOM elements that are created from the HTML markup on the page, or created within the ready handler.

But one of the whole reasons for using jQuery, as we saw in the last chapter, is the ease with which it allows us to dynamically manipulate the DOM. And when we throw Ajax into the mix, a subject that we'll address in chapter 8, it's likely that DOM elements will be coming into and out of existence frequently during the lifetime of the page. The ready handler isn't going to be of much help in managing the event handlers for these dynamic elements that don't exist when the ready handler is executed.

We can certainly manage event handlers on the fly as we use jQuery to manipulate the DOM, but wouldn't it be nice if we could keep all the event management code together in one place?

SETTING UP "LIVE" EVENT HANDLING

jQuery grants our wish with the live() method, which allows us to seemingly proactively establish event handlers for elements that don't even exist yet!

The syntax of live() is as follows:

Method syntax: live

`live(eventType,data,listener)`
Causes the passed listener to be invoked as a handler whenever an event identified by the event type occurs on any element that matches the selector used to create the wrapped set, regardless of whether those elements exist or not when this method is called.

Parameters

eventType	(String) Specifies the name of the event type for which the handler is to be invoked. Unlike bind(), a space-separated list of event types can't be specified.
data	(Object) Caller-supplied data that's attached to the Event instance as a property named data for availability to the handler function. If omitted, the handler function can be specified as the second parameter.
listener	(Function) The function that's to be invoked as the event handler. When invoked, it will be passed the Event instance, and its function context (this) is set to the target element.

Returns
The wrapped set.

If the syntax of this method reminds you of the syntax for the bind() method, you'd be right. This methods looks and acts a lot like bind(), except that when a corresponding event occurs, it will be triggered for all elements that match the selector, even if those elements aren't in existence at the time that live() is called.

For example, we might write

```
$('div.attendToMe').live(
  'click',
    function(event){ alert(this); }
);
```

Throughout the lifetime of the page, a click on any <div> element with class attend-ToMe will result in the handler being invoked as an event handler, complete with a passed event instance. And the preceding code doesn't need to be in a ready handler because, for "live" events, it doesn't matter whether the DOM has been built yet or not.

The live() method makes it amazingly easy to establish all the event handlers needed on the page in one place and at the outset, without having to worry about whether the elements already exist or when the elements will be created.

But some cautions must be exercised when using live(). Because of its similarity to bind(), you might expect "live events" to work in exactly the same manner as native events. But there are differences that may or may not be important on your page.

Firstly, recognize that live events *aren't* native "normal" events. When an event such as a click occurs, it propagates up through the DOM elements as described earlier in this chapter, invoking any event handlers that have been established. Once the event reaches the context used to create the wrapped set upon which live() was called (usually the document), the context checks for elements within itself that match the live selector. The live event handlers are triggered on any elements that match, and this triggered event *doesn't* propagate.

If the logic of your page depends upon propagation and propagation order, live() might not be the best choice—especially if you mix live event handlers with native event handlers established via bind().

Secondly, the live() method can only be used on selectors, and can't be used on derived wrapped sets. For example, both of these expressions are legal:

```
$('img').live( ... )
$('img','#someParent').live( ... )
```

The first will affect all images, the second all images within the context established by #someParent. Note that when a context is specified, it must exist at the time of the call to live().

But the following expression isn't legal

```
$('img').closest('div').live( ... )
```

because it invokes live() on something other than a selector.

Even with these restrictions, live() is tremendously handy on any page with dynamic elements, but we'll see how it becomes *crucial* in pages employing Ajax in chapter 8. Later in this chapter (section 4.3), we'll see live() used extensively in a comprehensive example that employs the handy DOM manipulation methods that we learned about in chapter 3 to create dynamic elements.

REMOVING "LIVE" EVENT HANDLING

Handlers established using `live()` should be unbound with the (rather morbidly named) `die()` method, which bears a strong resemblance to its `unbind()` counterpart:

Method syntax: die

die(eventType, listener)

Removes live event handlers established by `live()`, and prevents the handler from being invoked on any future elements that may match the selector used for the call to `live()`.

Parameters

eventType	(String) If provided, specifies that only listeners established for the specified event type are to be removed.
listener	(Function) If provided, identifies the specific listener that's to be removed.

Returns

The wrapped set.

In addition to allowing us to manage event handling in a browser-independent manner, jQuery provides a set of methods that gives us the ability to trigger event handlers under script control. Let's look at those.

4.2.5 Triggering event handlers

Event handlers are designed to be invoked when browser or user activity triggers the propagation of their associated events through the DOM hierarchy. But there may be times when we want to trigger the execution of a handler under script control. We could define such event handlers as top-level functions so that we can invoke them by name, but as we've seen, defining event handlers as inline anonymous functions is much more common and so darned convenient! Moreover, calling an event handler as a function doesn't cause semantic actions or bubbling to occur.

To provide for this need, jQuery has provided methods that will automatically trigger event handlers on our behalf under script control. The most general of these methods is `trigger()`, whose syntax is as follows:

Method syntax: trigger

trigger(eventType, data)

Invokes any event handlers established for the passed event type for all matched elements.

Parameters

eventType	(String) Specifies the name of the event type for which handlers are to be invoked. This includes namespaced events. You can append the exclamation point (!) to the event type to prevent namespaced events from triggering.
data	(Any) Data to be passed to the handlers as the second parameter (after the event instance).

Returns

The wrapped set.

The `trigger()` method, as well as the convenience methods that we'll introduce in a moment, does its best to simulate the event to be triggered, including propagation through the DOM hierarchy and the execution of semantic actions.

Each handler called is passed a populated instance of `jQuery.Event`. Because there's no real event, properties that report event-specific values, such as the location of a mouse event or the key of a keyboard event, have no value. The `target` property is set to reference the element of the matched set to which the handler was bound.

Just as with actual events, triggered event propagation can be halted via a call to the `jQuery.Event` instance's `stopPropagation()` method, or a `false` value can be returned from any of the invoked handlers.

> **NOTE**   The data parameter passed to the `trigger()` method is *not* the same as the one passed when a handler is established. The latter is placed into the `jQuery.Event` instance as the `data` property; the value passed to `trigger()` (and, as we're about to see, `triggerHandler()`) is passed as a parameter to the listeners. This allows both data values to be used without conflicting with each other.

For cases where we want to trigger a handler, but not cause propagation of the event and execution of semantic actions, jQuery provides the `triggerHandler()` method, which looks and acts just like `trigger()` except that no bubbling or semantic actions will occur. Additionally, no events bound by `live` will be triggered.

Method syntax: triggerHandler

`triggerHandler(eventType,data)`
Invokes any event handlers established for the passed event type for all matched elements without bubbling, semantic actions, or live events.

Parameters

`eventType`	(String) Specifies the name of the event type for which handlers are to be invoked
`data`	(Any) Data to be passed to the handlers as the second parameter (right after the event instance).

Returns
The wrapped set.

In addition to the `trigger()` and `triggerHandler()` methods, jQuery provides convenience methods for triggering most of the event types. The syntax for all these methods is exactly the same except for the method name, and that syntax is as follows:

Method syntax: *eventName*

eventName()

Invokes any event handlers established for the named event type for all matched elements. The supported methods are as follows:

blur	focusin	mousedown	resize
change	focusout	mousenter	scroll
click	keydown	mouseleave	select
dblclick	keypress	mousemove	submit
error	keyup	mouseout	unload
focus	load	mouseover	

Parameters

Returns

The wrapped set.

In addition to binding, unbinding, and triggering event handlers, jQuery offers higher-level functions that further make dealing with events on our pages as easy as possible.

4.2.6 Other event-related methods

Interactive applications often employ interaction styles that are implemented using a combination of behaviors. jQuery provides a few event-related convenience methods that make it easier to use these interaction behaviors on our pages. Let's look at them.

TOGGLING LISTENERS

The first of these is the toggle() method, which establishes a circular progression of click event handlers that are applied on each subsequent click event. On the first click event, the first registered handler is called, on the second click, the second is called, on the third click the third is called, and so on. When the end of the list of established handlers is reached, the first handler becomes the next in line. The toggle() method's syntax is as follows:

Method syntax: toggle

toggle(listener1,listener2, ...)

Establishes the passed functions as a circular list of click event handlers on all elements of the wrapped set. The handlers are called in order on each subsequent click event.

Parameters

listenerN   (Function) One or more functions that serve as the click event handlers for subsequent clicks.

Returns

The wrapped set.

A common use for this convenience method is to toggle the enabled state of an element back and forth on each odd or even click. For this, we'd supply two handlers; one for the odd clicks, and one for the even clicks.

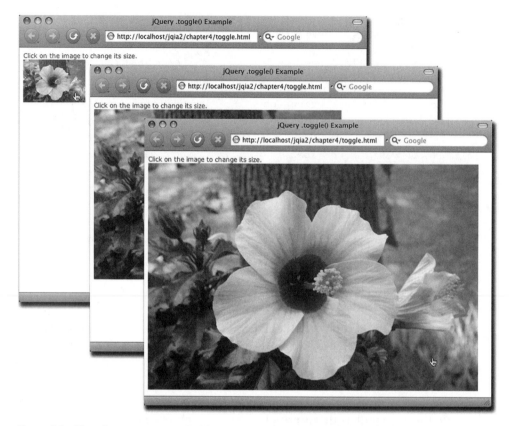

Figure 4.8   jQuery's `toggle()` method lets us predefine a progression of behaviors for click events.

But this method can also be used to create a progression through two or more clicks. Let's consider an example.

Imagine that we have a site in which we want users to be able to view images in one of three sizes: small, medium, or large. The interaction will take place through a simple series of clicks. Clicking on the image bumps it up to its next bigger size, until we reach the largest size, and it reverts back to the smallest.

Examine the progression shown in the time-lapse screenshots in figure 4.8. Each time the image is clicked, it grows to the next bigger size. If one more click were to be made, the image would revert to the smallest size.

The code for this page is shown in listing 4.6 and can be found in file chapter4/toggle.html.

Listing 4.6   Defining a progression of event handlers

```
<!DOCTYPE html>
<html>
  <head>
    <title>jQuery .toggle() Example</title>
    <link rel="stylesheet" type="text/css" href="../styles/core.css"/>
```

```
<script type="text/javascript" src="../scripts/jquery-1.4.js"></script>
<script type="text/javascript">
  $(function(){

    $('img[src*=small]').toggle(          ⟵⌐  Establishes a
      function() {                           └  progression of handlers
        $(this).attr('src',
          $(this).attr('src').replace(/small/,'medium'));
      },
      function() {
        $(this).attr('src',
          $(this).attr('src').replace(/medium/,'large'));
      },
      function() {
        $(this).attr('src',
          $(this).attr('src').replace(/large/,'small'));
      }
    );

  });
</script>
<style type="text/css">
  img {
    cursor: pointer;
  }
</style>
</head>

<body>

  <div>Click on the image to change its size.</div>
  <div>
    <img src="hibiscus.small.jpg" alt="Hibiscus"/>
  </div>

</body>
</html>
```

NOTE If you're like your authors and pay attention to the names of things, you might wonder why this method is named toggle() when that really only makes sense for the case when only two handlers are established. The reason is that in earlier versions of jQuery, this method was limited to only two handlers and was later expanded to accept an arbitrary number of handlers. The name was retained for backwards compatibility.

Another common multi-event scenario that's frequently employed in interactive applications involves mousing into and out of elements.

HOVERING OVER ELEMENTS

Events that inform us when the mouse pointer has entered an area, as well as when it has left that area, are essential to building many of the user interface elements that are commonly presented to users on our pages. Among these element types, cascading menus used as navigation systems are a common example.

A vexing behavior of the mouseover and mouseout event types often hinders the easy creation of such elements: when a mouseout event fires as the mouse is moved

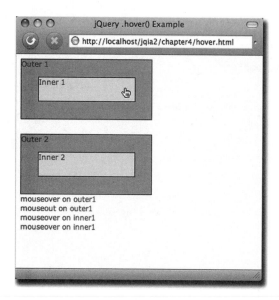

Figure 4.9   This page helps demonstrate when mouse events fire as the mouse pointer is moved over an area and its children.

over an area and its children. Consider the display in figure 4.9 (available in the file chapter4/hover.html).

This page displays two identical (except for naming) sets of areas: an outer area and an inner area. Load this page into your browser as you follow the rest of this section.

For the top set of rectangles on the page, the following script in the ready handler establishes handlers for the mouseover and mouseout events:

```
$('#outer1').bind('mouseover mouseout',report);
$('#inner1').bind('mouseover mouseout',report);
```

This statement establishes a function named `report` as the event handler for both the mouseover and mouseout events.

The `report()` function is defined as follows:

```
function report(event) {
  say(event.type+' on ' + event.target.id);
}
```

This listener merely adds a `<div>` element containing the name of the event that fired to a `<div>` named `console` that's defined at the bottom of the page, allowing us to see when each event fires.

Now, let's move the mouse pointer into the area labeled Outer 1 (being careful not to enter Inner 1). We'll see (from looking at the bottom of the page) that a mouseover event has fired. Move the pointer back out of the area. As expected, we'll see that a mouseout event has fired.

Let's refresh the page to start over, clearing the console.

Now, let's move the mouse pointer into Outer 1 (noting the event), but this time continue inward until the pointer enters Inner 1. As the mouse enters Inner 1, a mouseout event fires for Outer 1. If we wave our pointer to cross back and forth over the boundary between Outer 1 and Inner 1, we'll see a flurry of mouseout and mouseover events. This *is* the defined behavior, even if it's rather unintuitive. Even though the pointer is still within the bounds of Outer 1, when the pointer enters a contained element, the event model considers the transition to be leaving the outer area.

Expected or not, we don't always want that behavior. Often, we want to be informed when the pointer leaves the bounds of the outer area and don't care whether the pointer is over a contained area or not.

Luckily, some of the major browsers support a nonstandard pair of mouse events, mouseenter and mouseleave, first introduced by Microsoft in Internet Explorer. This event pair acts slightly more intuitively, not firing a mouseleave event when moving from an element to a descendant of that element. For browsers not supporting these events, jQuery emulates them so that they work the same across all browsers.

Using jQuery we could establish handlers for this set of events using the following code:

```
$(element).mouseenter(function1).mouseleave(function2);
```

But jQuery also provides a single method that makes it even easier: hover(). The syntax of this method is as follows:

Method syntax: hover

hover(enterHandler, leaveHandler)
hover(handler)
Establishes handlers for the mouseenter and mouseleave events for matched elements. These handlers only fire when the area covered by the elements is entered and exited, ignoring transitions to child elements.

Parameters
enterHandler	(Function) The function to become the mouseenter handler.
leaveHandler	(Function) The function to become the mouseleave handler.
handler	(Function) A single handler to be called for both mouseenter and mouseleave events.

Returns
The wrapped set.

We use the following script to establish mouse event handlers for the second set of areas (Outer 2 and its Inner 2 child) on the hover.html example page:

```
$('#outer2').hover(report);
```

As with the first set of areas, the report() function is established as both the mouseenter and mouseleave handlers for Outer 2. But unlike the first set of areas, when we pass the mouse pointer over the boundaries between Outer 2 and Inner 2, neither of these handlers (for Outer 2) is invoked. This is useful for those situations where we have no need for parent handlers to react when the mouse pointer passes over child elements.

With all these event-handling tools under our belts, let's use what we've learned so far and look at an example page that makes use of them, as well as some of the other jQuery techniques that we've learned from previous chapters!

4.3   *Putting events (and more) to work*

Now that we've covered how jQuery brings order to the chaos of dealing with disparate event models across browsers, let's work on an example page that puts the knowledge we've gained so far to use. This example uses not only events but also some jQuery techniques that we've explored in earlier chapters, including some heavy-weight jQuery method chains. For this comprehensive example, let's pretend that we're videophiles whose collection of DVDs, numbering in the thousands, has become a huge problem. Not only has organization become an issue, making it hard to find a DVD quickly, but all those DVDs in their cases have become a storage problem—they've taken over way too much space and will get us thrown out of the house if the problem isn't solved.

We'll posit that we solved the storage side of the problem by buying DVD binders that hold one hundred DVDs each in much less space than the comparable number of DVDs in their cases. But although that saved us from having to sleep on a park bench, organizing the DVD discs is still an issue. How will we find a DVD that we're looking for without having to manually flip through each binder until we find the one we're seeking?

We can't do something like sort the DVDs in alphabetic order to help quickly locate a specific disc. That would mean that every time we buy a new DVD, we'd need to shift all the discs in perhaps dozens of binders to keep the collection sorted. Imagine the job ahead of us after we buy *Abbott and Costello Go to Mars!*

Well, we've got computers, we've got the know-how to write web applications, and we've got jQuery! So we'll solve the problem by writing a DVD database program to help keep track of what DVDs we have, and where they are.

Let's get to work!

4.3.1   *Filtering large data sets*

Our DVD database program is faced with the same problem facing many other applications, web-delivered or otherwise. How do we allow our users (in this case ourselves) to quickly find the information that they seek?

We could be all low-tech about it and just display a sorted list of all the titles, but that would still be painful to scroll through if there's anything more than a handful of entries. Besides, we want to learn how to do it *right* so that we can apply what we learn to real, customer-facing applications.

So no shortcuts!

Obviously, designing the entire application would be well beyond the scope of this chapter, so what we'll concentrate on is developing a control panel that will allow us to specify filters with which we can tune the list of titles that will be returned when we perform a database search.

We'll want the ability to filter on the DVD title, of course. But we'll also add the ability to filter the search based upon the year that the movie was released, its category, the binder in which we placed the disc, and even whether we've viewed the movie yet or not. (This will help answer the commonly asked question, "What should I watch tonight?")

Your initial reaction may be to wonder what the big deal is. After all, we can just put up a number of fields and be done with it, right?

Well, not so fast. A single field for something like the title is fine if, for example, we wanted to find all movies with the term "creature" in their title. But what if we want to search for either of "creature" or "monster"? Or only movies released in 1957 or 1972?

In order to provide a robust interface for specifying filters, we'll need to allow the user to specify multiple filters for either the same or different properties of the DVD. And rather than try to guess how many filters will be needed, we'll be all swank about it and create them on demand.

For our interface, we're going to steal a page from Apple's user interface playbook and model our interface on the way filters are specified in many Apple applications. (If you're an iTunes user, check out how Smart Playlists are created for an example.)

Each filter, one per "line," is identified by a dropdown (single-selection `<select>` element) that specifies the field that's to be filtered. Based upon the type of that field (string, date, number, and even Boolean) the appropriate controls are displayed on the line to capture information about the filter.

The user is given the ability to add as many of these filters as they like, or to remove previously specified filters.

A picture being worth a thousand words, study the time-progression display of figures 4.10a through 4.10c. They show the filter panel that we'll be building: (a) when initially displayed, (b) after a filter has been specified, and (c) after a number of filters have been specified.

As we can see by inspecting the interactions shown in figures 4.10a through 4.10c, there's going to be a lot of element creation on the fly. Let's take a few moments to discuss how we're going to go about that.

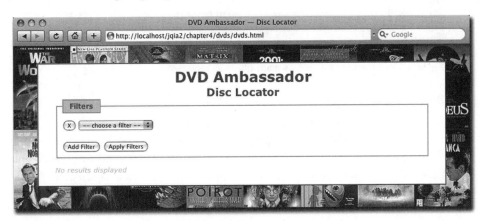

Figure 4.10a The display initially shows a single, unconfigured filter.

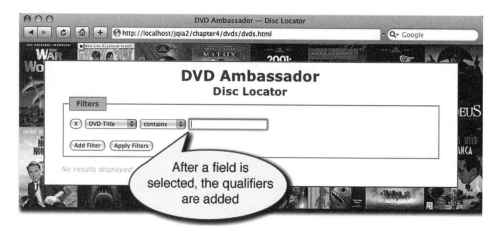

Figure 4.10b   After a filter type is selected, its qualifier controls are added.

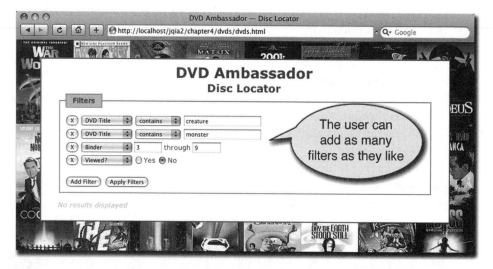

Figure 4.10c   The user can add as many filters as required.

4.3.2   *Element creation by template replication*

We can readily see that to implement this filtering control panel, we're going to need to create a fair number of elements in response to various events. For example, we'll need to create a new filter entry whenever the user clicks the Add Filter button, and new controls that qualify that filter whenever a specific field is selected.

No problem! In the previous chapter we saw how easy jQuery makes it to dynamically create elements using the $() function. And although we'll do some of that in our example, we're also going to explore some higher-level alternatives.

When we're dynamically creating lots of elements, all the code necessary to create those elements and stitch together their relationships can get a bit unwieldy and a bit difficult to maintain, even with jQuery's assistance. (Without jQuery's help, it can be a complete nightmare!) What'd be great would be if we could create a "blueprint" of the complex markup using HTML, and then replicate it whenever we needed an instance of the blueprint.

Yearn, no more! The jQuery `clone()` method gives us just that ability.

The approach that we're going to take is to create sets of "template" markup that represent the HTML fragments we'd like to replicate, and use the `clone()` method whenever we need to create an instance of that template. We don't want these templates to be visible to the end user, so we'll sequester them in a `<div>` element at the end of the page that's hidden from view using CSS.

As an example, let's consider the combination of the "X" button and dropdown that identifies the filterable fields. We'll need to create an instance of this combination every time the user clicks the Add Filter button. The jQuery code to create such a button and `<select>` element, along with its child `<option>` elements, could be considered a tad long, though it would not be too onerous to write or maintain. But it'd be easy to envision that anything more complex would get unwieldy quickly.

Using our template technique, and placing the template markup for that button and dropdown in a parent `<div>` used to hide all the templates, we create markup as follows:

```
<!-- hidden templates -->                ❶ Encloses and hides
<div id="templates">                        all templates        ❷ Defines the
  <div class="template filterChooser">                              filterChooser template
    <button type="button" class="filterRemover" title="Remove this
      filter">X</button>

    <select name="filter" class="filterChooser" title="Select a property to
      filter">
      <option value="" data-filter-type="" selected="selected">
        -- choose a filter --</option>
      <option value="title" data-filter-type="stringMatch">DVD Title</option>
      <option value="category" data-filter-type="stringMatch">Category
      </option>
      <option value="binder" data-filter-type="numberRange">Binder</option>
      <option value="release" data-filter-type="dateRange">Release Date
      </option>
      <option value="viewed" data-filter-type="boolean">Viewed?</option>
    </select>
  </div>

  <!-- more templates go here -->
</div>
```

The outer `<div>` with `id` of `templates` serves as a container for all our templates and will be given a CSS `display` rule of `none` to prevent it from being displayed in the browser ❶.

Within this container, we define another `<div>` which we give the classes `template` and `filterChooser` ❷. We'll use the `template` class to identify templates in general, and the `filterChooser` class to identify this particular template type. We'll see how these classes are used in the code shortly—remember, classes aren't just for CSS anymore!

Also note that each `<option>` in the `<select>` has been given a custom attribute: `data-filter-type`. We'll use this value to determine what type of filter controls need to be used for the selected filter field.

Based upon which filter type is identified, we'll populate the remainder of the filter entry "line" with qualifying controls that are appropriate for the filter type.

For example, if the filter type is `stringMatch`, we'll want to display a text field into which the user can type a text search term, and a dropdown giving them options for how that term is to be applied.

We've set up the template for this set of controls as follows:

```
<div class="template stringMatch">
  <select name="stringMatchType">
    <option value="*">contains</option>
    <option value="^">starts with</option>
    <option value="$">ends with</option>
    <option value="=">is exactly</option>
  </select>
  <input type="text" name="term"/>
</div>
```

Again, we've used the `template` class to identify the element as a template, and we've flagged the element with the class `stringMatch`. We've purposely made it such that this class matches the `data-filter-type` value on the field chooser dropdown.

Replicating these templates whenever, and wherever, we want is easy using the jQuery knowledge under our belts. Let's say that we want to append a template instance to the end of an element that we have a reference to in a variable named `whatever`. We could write

```
$('div.template.filterChooser').children().clone().appendTo(whatever);
```

In this statement, we select the template container to be replicated (using those convenient classes we placed on the template markup), select the child elements of the template container (we don't want to replicate the `<div>`, just its contents), make clones of those children, and then attach them to the end of the contents of the element identified by `whatever`.

See why we keep emphasizing the power of jQuery method chains?

Inspecting the options of the `filterChooser` dropdown, we see that we have a number of other filter types defined: `numberRange`, `dateRange`, and `boolean`. So we define qualifying control templates for those filter types as well with this code:

```
<div class="template numberRange">
  <input type="text" name="numberRange1" class="numeric"/> <span>through
    </span>
  <input type="text" name="numberRange2" class="numeric"/>
</div>

<div class="template dateRange">
  <input type="text" name="dateRange1" class="dateValue"/>
```

```
  <span>through</span>
  <input type="text" name="dateRange2" class="dateValue"/>
</div>

<div class="template boolean">
  <input type="radio" name="booleanFilter" value="true" checked="checked"/>
    <span>Yes</span>
  <input type="radio" name="booleanFilter" value="false"/> <span>No</span>
</div>
```

OK. Now that we've got our replication strategy defined, let's take a look at the primary markup.

4.3.3 *Setting up the mainline markup*

If we refer back to figure 4.10a, we can see that the initial display of our DVD search page is pretty simple: a few headers, a first filter instance, and a couple of buttons. Let's take a look at the HTML markup that achieves that:

```
<div id="pageContent">

  <h1>DVD Ambassador</h1>
  <h2>Disc Locator</h2>

  <form id="filtersForm" action="/fetchFilteredResults" method="post">

    <fieldset id="filtersPane">
      <legend>Filters</legend>
      <div id="filterPane"></div>               ❶ Container for
      <div class="buttonBar">                        filter instances
        <button type="button" id="addFilterButton">Add Filter</button>
        <button type="submit" id="applyFilterButton">Apply Filters</button>
      </div>
    </fieldset>

    <div id="resultsPane">                      ❷ Container for
      <span class="none">No results displayed</span>   search results
    </div>

  </form>

</div>
```

There's nothing too surprising in that markup—or is there? Where, for example, is the markup for the initial filter dropdown? We've set up a container in which the filters will be placed ❶, but it's initially empty. Why?

Well, we're going to need to be able to populate new filters dynamically—which we'll be getting to in just a moment—so why do the work in two places? As we shall see, we'll be able to leverage the dynamic code to initially populate the first filter, so we don't need to explicitly create it in the static markup.

One other thing that should be pointed out is that we've set aside a container to receive the results ❷ (the fetching of which is beyond the scope of this chapter), and we've placed these results *inside* the form so that the results themselves can contain form controls (for sorting, paging, and so on).

OK. We have our very simple, mainline HTML laid out, and we have a handful of hidden templates that we can use to quickly generate new elements via replication. Let's finally get to writing the code that will apply the behavior to our page!

4.3.4   *Adding new filters*

Upon a click of the Add Filter button, we need to add a new filter to the `<div>` element that we've set up to receive it, which we've identified with the `id` of `filterPane`.

Recalling how easy it is to establish event handlers using jQuery, it should be an easy matter to add a click handler to the Add Filter button. But wait! There's something we forgot to consider!

We've already seen how we're going to replicate form controls when users add filters, and we've got a good strategy for easily creating multiple instances of these controls. But eventually, we're going to have to submit these values to the server so it can look up the filtered results in the database. And if we just keep copying the same `name` attributes over and over again for our controls, the server is just going to get a jumbled mess without knowing what qualifiers belong to which filters!

To help out the server-side code (there's a good chance we'll be writing it ourselves in any case) we're going to append a unique suffix to the `name` attribute for each filter entry. We'll keep it simple and use a counter, so that the first filter's controls will all have ".1" appended to their names, the second set ".2", and so on. That way, the server-side code can group them together by suffix when they arrive as part of the request.

> **NOTE** The ".n" suffix format was chosen for this example code because it is simple and conceptually captures what the suffix is trying to represent (groupings of parametric data). Depending upon what you are using for your server-side code, you may wish to choose alternative suffix formats that might work better in conjunction with the data-binding mechanisms that are available to you. For example, the ".n" format would not play particularly well with Java backends using property-based POJO binding mechanisms (a format of "[n]" would be better suited for this environment).

To keep track of how many filters we've added (so we can use the count as the suffix for subsequent filter names), we'll create a global variable, initialized to 0, as follows:

```
var filterCount = 0;
```

"Global variable? I thought those were evil," I hear you say.

Global variables can be a problem *when used incorrectly.* But in this case, this is truly a global value that represents a page-wide concept, and it will never create any conflicts because all aspects of the page will want to access this *single* value in a consistent fashion.

With that set up, we're ready to establish the click handler for the Add Filter button by adding the following code to a ready handler (remember, we don't want to start referencing DOM elements until after we *know* they've been created):

```
$('#addFilterButton').click(function(){
  var filterItem = $('<div>')
    .addClass('filterItem')
    .appendTo('#filterPane')
    .data('suffix','.' + (filterCount++));
  $('div.template.filterChooser')
      .children().clone().appendTo(filterItem)
      .trigger('adjustName');
});
```

① Establishes click handler

② Creates filter entry block

③ Replicates filter dropdown template

④ Triggers custom event

Although this compound statement may look complicated at first glance, it accomplishes a great deal without a whole lot of code. Let's break it down one step at a time.

The first thing that we do in this code is to establish a click handler on the Add Filter button **①** by using the jQuery click() method. It's within the function passed to this method, which will get invoked when the button is clicked, that all the interesting stuff happens.

Because a click of the Add Filter button is going to, well, add a filter, we create a new container for the filter to reside within **②**. We give it the class filterItem not only for CSS styling, but to be able to locate these elements later in code. After the element is created, it's appended to the master filter container that we created with the id value of filterPane.

We also need to record the suffix that we want to add to the control names that will be placed within this container. This value will be used when it comes time to adjust the names of the controls, and this is a good example of a value that's *not* suited for a global variable. Each filter container (class filterItem) will have its own suffix, so trying to record this value globally would require some sort of complex array or map construct so that the various values didn't step all over each other.

Rather, we'll avoid the whole mess by recording the suffix value on the elements themselves using the very handy jQuery data() method. Later, when we need to know what suffix to use for a control, we'll simply look at this data value on its container and won't have to worry about getting it confused with the values recorded on other containers.

The code fragment

```
.data('suffix','.' + (filterCount++))
```

formats the suffix value using the current value of the filterCount variable, and then increments that value. The value is attached to the filterItem container using the name suffix, and we can later retrieve it by that name whenever we need it.

The final statement of the click handler **③** replicates the template that we set up containing the filter dropdown using the replication approach that we discussed in the previous section. You might think that the job is over at this point, but after the cloning and appending, we execute **④** the following fragment:

```
.trigger('adjustName')
```

The trigger() method is used to trigger an event handler for an event named adjustName.

adjustName?

If you thumb through your specifications, you'll find this event listed nowhere! It's not a standard event defined anywhere *but in this page.* What we've done with this code is to trigger a *custom event.*

A custom event is a very useful concept—we can attach code to an element as a handler for a custom event, and cause it to execute by triggering the event. The beauty of this approach, as opposed to directly calling code, is that we can register the custom handlers in advance, and by simply triggering the event, cause any registered handlers to be executed, without having to know where they've been established.

> **Pattern alert!**
>
> The custom event capability in jQuery is a limited example of the Observer pattern, sometimes referred to as the Publish/Subscribe pattern. We *subscribe* an element to a particular event by establishing a handler for that event on that element, and then when the event is *published* (triggered), any subscribed elements in the event hierarchy automatically have their handlers invoked. This can greatly reduce the complexity of code by reducing the *coupling* necessary.
>
> We called this a *limited* example of the Observer pattern because subscribers are limited to elements in the publisher's ancestor hierarchy (as opposed to anywhere in the DOM).

OK, so that will *trigger* the custom event, but we need to define the handler for that event, so within the ready handler, we also establish the code to adjust the control names of the filters:

```
$('.filterItem [name]').live('adjustName',function(){
  var suffix = $(this).closest('.filterItem').data('suffix');
  if (/(\w)+\.(\d)+$/.test($(this).attr('name'))) return;
  $(this).attr('name',$(this).attr('name')+suffix);
});
```

Here we see a use of the `live()` method to proactively establish event handlers. The input elements with `name` attributes will be popping into and out of existence whenever a filter is added or removed, so we employ `live()` to automatically establish and remove the handlers as necessary. That way, we set it up *once*, and jQuery will handle the details whenever an item that matches the `.filterItem[name]` selector is created or destroyed. How easy is that?

We specify our custom event name of `adjustName` and supply a handler to be applied whenever we trigger the custom event. (Because it's a custom event, there's no possibility of it being triggered by user activity the way that, say, a click handler can be.)

Within the handler, we obtain the suffix that we recorded on the `filterItem` container—remember, within a handler, `this` refers to the element upon which the event was triggered, in this case, the element with the `name` attribute. The `closest()` method quickly locates the parent container, upon which we find the suffix value.

We don't want to adjust element names that we've already adjusted once, so we use a regular expression test to see if the name already has the suffix attached, and if so, simply return from the handler.

If the name hasn't been adjusted, we use the `attr()` method to both fetch the original name and set the adjusted name back onto the element.

At this point, it's worth reflecting on how implementing this as a custom event, and using `live()`, creates very loose coupling in our page code. This frees us from having to worry about calling the adjustment code explicitly, or establishing the custom handlers explicitly at the various points in the code when they need to be applied. This not only keeps the code cleaner, it increases the flexibility of the code.

Load this page into your browser and test the action of the Add Filter button. Note how every time you click on the Add Filter button, a new filter is added to the page. If you inspect the DOM with a JavaScript debugger (Firebug in Firefox is great for this), you'll see that the `name` of each `<select>` element has been suffixed with a per-filter suffix, as expected.

But our job isn't over yet. The dropdowns don't yet specify which field is to be filtered. When a selection is made by the user, we need to populate the filter container with the appropriate qualifiers for the filter type for that field.

4.3.5 *Adding the qualifying controls*

Whenever a selection is made from a filter dropdown, we need to populate the filter with the controls that are appropriate for that filter. We've made it easy for ourselves by creating markup templates that we just need to copy when we determine which one is appropriate. But there are also a few other housekeeping tasks that we need to do whenever the value of the dropdown is changed.

Let's take a look at what needs to be done when establishing the change handler for the dropdown:

```
$('select.filterChooser').live('change',function(){          ❶ Establishes change
    var filterType = $(':selected',this).attr('data-filter-type');      handler
    var filterItem = $(this).closest('.filterItem');
    $('.qualifier',filterItem).remove();                      ❷ Removes any old controls
    $('div.template.'+filterType)
        .children().clone().addClass('qualifier')             ❸ Replicates
        .appendTo(filterItem)                                 appropriate template
        .trigger('adjustName');                               ❹ Removes
    $('option[value=""]',this).remove();                      obsolete option
});
```

Once again, we've taken advantage of jQuery's `live()` method to establish a handler up front that will automatically be established at the appropriate points without further action on our part. This time, we've proactively established a change handler for any filter dropdown that comes into being ❶.

TIP The ability to specify change events with `live()` is a new (and welcome) addition to jQuery 1.4.

When the change handler fires, we first collect a few pieces of information: the filter type recorded in the custom `data-filter-type` attribute, and the parent filter container.

Once we've got those values in hand, we need to remove any filter qualifier controls that might already be in the container ❷. After all, the user can change the value of the selected field many times, and we don't want to just keep adding more and more controls as we go along! We'll add the `qualifier` class to all the appropriate elements as they're created (in the next statement), so it's easy to select and remove them.

Once we're sure we have a clean slate, we replicate the template for the correct set of qualifiers ❸ by using the value we obtained from the `data-filter-type` attribute. The `qualifier` class name is added to each created element for easy selection (as we saw in the previous statement). Also note how once again we trigger the `adjustName` custom event to automatically trigger the hander that will adjust the `name` attributes of the newly created controls.

Finally, we want to remove the "choose a filter" `<option>` element from the filter dropdown ❹, because once the user has selected a specific field, it doesn't make any sense to choose that entry again. We *could* just ignore the change event that triggers when the user selects this option, but the best way to prevent a user from doing something that doesn't make sense is to not let them do it in the first place!

Once again, refer to the example page in your browser. Try adding multiple filters, and change their selections. Note how the qualifiers always match the field selection. And if you can view the DOM in a debugger, observe how the `name` attributes are augmented.

Now, for those remove buttons.

4.3.6   *Removing unwanted filters and other tasks*

We've given the user the ability to change the field that any filter will be applied to, but we've also given them a remove button (labeled "X") that they can use to remove a filter completely.

By this time, you should already have realized that this task will be almost trivial with the tools at our disposal. When the button is clicked, all we need to do is find the closest parent filter container, and blow it away!

```
$('button.filterRemover').live('click',function(){
  $(this).closest('div.filterItem').remove();
});
```

And yes, it turns out to be that simple.

On to a few other matters ...

You may recall that when the page is first loaded, an initial filter is displayed, even though we did not include it in the markup. We can easily realize this by simulating a click of the Add Filter button upon page load.

So, in the ready handler we simply add

```
$('#addFilterButton').click();
```

This causes the Add Filter button handler to be invoked, just as if the user had clicked it.

And one final matter. Although it's beyond the scope of this example to deal with submitting this form to the server, we thought we'd give you a tantalizing glimpse of what's coming up in future chapters.

Go ahead and click the Apply Filters button, which you may have noted is a submit button for the form. But rather than the page reloading as you might have expected, the results appear in the <div> element that we assigned the id of resultsPane.

That's because we subverted the submit action of the form with a handler of our own that cancels the form submission and instead makes an Ajax call with the form contents, loading the results into the resultsPane container. We'll see lots more about how easy jQuery makes Ajax in chapter 8, but you might be surprised (especially if you've already done some cross-browser Ajax programming) to see that we can make the Ajax call with just one line of code:

```
$('#filtersForm').submit(function(){
  $('#resultsPane').load('applyFilters',$('#filtersForm').serializeArray());
  return false;
});
```

If you paid attention to those displayed results, you might have noted that the results are the same no matter what filters are specified. Obviously, there's no real database powering this example, so it's really just returning a hard-coded HTML page. But it's easy to imagine that the URL passed to jQuery's load() Ajax method could reference a dynamic PHP, Java servlet, or Rails resource that would return actual results.

That completes the page, at least as far as we wanted to take it for the purposes of this chapter, but as we know ...

4.3.7   *There's always room for improvement*

For our filter form to be considered production-quality, there's still lots of room for improvement.

Below we'll list some additional functionality that this form either requires before being deemed complete, or that would be just plain nice to have. Can you implement these additional features with the knowledge you've gained up to this point?

- Data validation is non-existent in our form. For example, the qualifying fields for the binder range should be numeric values, but we do nothing to prevent the user from entering invalid values. The same problem exists for the date fields.

  We could just punt and let the server-side code handle it—after all, it has to validate the data regardless. But that makes for a less-than-pleasant user experience, and as we've already pointed out, the best way to deal with errors is to prevent them from happening in the first place.

  Because the solution involves inspecting the Event instance—something that wasn't included in the example up to this point—we're going to give you the code to disallow the entry of any characters but decimal digits into the numeric fields. The operation of the code should be evident to you with the knowledge you've gained in this chapter, but if not, now would be a good time to go back and review the key points.

```
$('input.numeric').live('keypress',function(event){
  if (event.which < 48 || event.which > 57) return false;
});
```

- As mentioned, the date fields aren't validated. How would you go about ensuring that only valid dates (in whatever format you choose) are entered? It can't be done on a character-by-character basis as we did with the numeric fields.

  Later in the book, we'll see how the jQuery UI plugin solves this problem for us handily, but for now put your event-handling knowledge to the test!

- When qualifying fields are added to a filter, the user must click in one of the fields to give it focus. Not all that friendly! Add code to the example to give focus to the new controls as they are added.

- The use of a global variable to hold the filter count violates our sensibilities and limits us to one instance of the "widget" per page. Replace it by applying the data() method to an appropriate element, keeping in mind that we may want to use this multiple times on a page.

- Our form allows the user to specify more than one filter, but we haven't defined how these filters are applied on the server. Do they form a disjunction (in which any one filter must match), or a conjunction (in which all filters must match)? Usually, if unspecified, a disjunction is assumed. But how would you change the form to allow the user to specify which?

- What other improvements, either to the robustness of the code or the usability of the interface, would you make? How does jQuery help?

If you come up with ideas that you're proud of, be sure to visit the Manning web page for this book at http://www.manning.com/bibeault2, which contains a link to the discussion forum. You're encouraged to post your solutions for all to see and discuss!

4.4 Summary

Building upon the jQuery knowledge that we've gained so far, this chapter introduced us to the world of event handling.

We learned that there are vexing challenges to implementing event handling in web pages, but such handling is essential for creating pages in interactive web applications. Not insignificant among those challenges is the fact the there are three event models that each operate in different ways across the set of modern popularly used browsers.

The legacy Basic Event Model, also informally termed the DOM Level 0 Event Model, enjoys somewhat browser-independent operation to declare event listeners, but the implementation of the listener functions requires divergent browser-dependent code in order to deal with differences in the Event instance. This event model is probably the most familiar to page authors and assigns event listeners to DOM elements by assigning references to the listener functions to properties of the elements—the `onclick` property, for example.

Although simple, this model limits us to only one listener for any event type on a particular DOM element.

We can avoid this deficiency by using the DOM Level 2 Event Model, a more advanced and standardized model in which an API binds handlers to their event types and DOM elements. Versatile though this model is, it is supported only by standards-compliant browsers such as Firefox, Safari, Camino, and Opera.

For Internet Explorer, even up to IE 8, an API-based proprietary event model that provides a subset of the functionality of the DOM Level 2 Event Model is available.

Coding all event handling in a series of `if` statements—one clause for the standard browsers and one for Internet Explorer—is a good way to drive ourselves to early dementia. Luckily jQuery comes to the rescue and saves us from that fate.

jQuery provides a general `bind()` method to establish event listeners of any type on any element, as well as event-specific convenience methods such as `change()` and `click()`. These methods operate in a browser-independent fashion and normalize the `Event` instance passed to the handlers with the standard properties and methods most commonly used in event listeners.

jQuery also provides the means to remove event handlers or cause them to be triggered under script control, and it even defines some higher-level methods that make implementing common event-handling tasks as easy as possible.

As if all that were not enough, jQuery provides the `live()` method to assign handlers proactively to elements that may not even exist yet, and allows us to specify custom methods to easily register handlers to be invoked when those custom events are published.

We looked at a few examples of using events in our pages, and explored a comprehensive example that demonstrated many of the concepts that we've learned up to this point. In the next chapter, we'll look at how jQuery builds upon these capabilities to put animation and animated effects to work for us.

Energizing pages with animations and effects

This chapter covers

- Showing and hiding elements without animation
- Showing and hiding elements using core animation effects
- Writing custom animations
- Controlling animation and function queuing

Browsers have come a long way since LiveScript—subsequently renamed JavaScript—was introduced to Netscape Navigator in 1995 to allow scripting of web pages.

In those early days, the capabilities afforded to page authors were severely limited, not only by the minimal APIs, but by the sluggishness of scripting engines and low-powered systems. The idea of using these limited abilities for animation and effects was laughable, and for years the only animation was through the use of animated GIF images (which were generally used poorly, making pages more annoying than usable).

My, how times have changed. Today's browser scripting engines are lightning fast, running on hardware that was unimaginable 10 years ago, and they offer a rich variety of capabilities to us as page authors.

But even though the capabilities exist in low-level operations, JavaScript has no easy-to-use animation engine, so we're on our own. Except, of course, that jQuery comes to our rescue, providing a trivially simple interface for creating all sorts of neat effects.

But before we dive into adding whiz-bang effects to our pages, we need to contemplate the question, *should we?* Like a Hollywood blockbuster that's all special effects and no plot, a page that overuses effects can elicit a very different, and negative, reaction than what we intend. Be mindful that effects should be used to *enhance* the usability of a page, not hinder it by just showing off.

With that caution in mind, let's see what jQuery has to offer.

5.1 Showing and hiding elements

Perhaps the most common type of dynamic effect we'll want to perform on an element, or any group of elements, is the simple act of showing or hiding them. We'll get to more fancy animations (like fading an element in or out) in a bit, but sometimes we'll want to keep it simple and pop elements into existence or make them instantly vanish!

The methods for showing and hiding elements are pretty much what we'd expect: show() to show the elements in a wrapped set, and hide() to hide them. We're going to delay presenting their formal syntax for reasons that will become clear in a bit; for now, let's concentrate on using these methods with no parameters.

As simple as these methods may seem, we should keep a few things in mind. First, jQuery hides elements by changing their style.display properties to none. If an element in the wrapped set is already hidden, it will remain hidden but still be returned for chaining. For example, suppose we have the following HTML fragment:

```
<div style="display:none;">This will start hidden</div>
<div>This will start shown</div>
```

If we apply $("div").hide().addClass("fun"), we'll end up with the following:

```
<div style="display:none;" class="fun">This will start hidden</div>
<div style="display:none;" class="fun">This will start shown</div>
```

Note that even though the first element was already hidden, it remains part of the matched set and takes part in the remainder of the method chain.

Second, jQuery shows objects by changing the display property from none to either block or inline. Which of these values is chosen is based upon whether a previously specified explicit value was set for the element or not. If the value was explicit, it's remembered and reverted. Otherwise it's based upon the default state of the display property for the target element type. For example, <div> elements will have their display property set to block, whereas a <span> element's display property will be set to inline.

Let's see about putting these methods to good use.

5.1.1 *Implementing a collapsible "module"*

You're no doubt familiar with sites, some of which aggregate data from other sites, that present you with various pieces of information in configurable "modules" on some sort of "dashboard" page. The iGoogle site is a good example, as shown in figure 5.1.

This site lets us configure much about how the page is presented, including moving the modules around, expanding them to full-page size, specifying configuration information, and even removing them completely. But one thing it doesn't let us do (at least at the time of this writing) is to "roll up" a module into its caption bar so that it takes up less room, without having to remove it from the page.

Let's define our own dashboard modules and one-up Google by allowing users to roll up a module into its caption bar.

First, let's take a look at what we want the module to look like in its normal and rolled-up states, shown in figures 5.2a and 5.2b respectively.

In figure 5.2a, we've created a module with two major sections: a caption bar, and a body. The body contains the data of the module—in this case, random "Lorem ipsum" text. The more interesting caption bar contains a caption for the module and small button that we'll instrument to invoke the roll-up (and roll-down) functionality.

Figure 5.1   iGoogle is an example of a site that presents aggregated information in a series of dashboard modules.

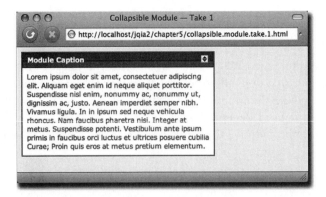

Figure 5.2a We'll create our own dashboard modules, which consist of two parts: a bar with a caption and roll-up button, and a body in which data can be displayed.

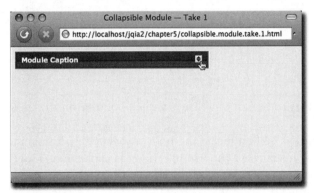

Figure 5.2b When the roll-up button is clicked, the module body disappears as if it had been rolled up into the caption bar.

Once the button is clicked, the body of the module will disappear as if it had been rolled up into the caption bar. A subsequent click will roll down the body, restoring its original appearance.

The HTML markup we've used to create the structure of our module is fairly straightforward. We've applied numerous class names to the elements both for identification as well as for CSS styling.

```
<div class="module">
  <div class="caption">
    <span>Module Caption</span>
    <img src="rollup.gif" alt="rollup" title="rolls up this module"/>
  </div>
  <div class="body">
    Lorem ipsum dolor sit amet, consectetuer adipiscing elit.
    Aliquam eget enim id neque aliquet porttitor. Suspendisse
    nisl enim, nonummy ac, nonummy ut, dignissim ac, justo.
    Aenean imperdiet semper nibh. Vivamus ligula. In in ipsum
    sed neque vehicula rhoncus. Nam faucibus pharetra nisi.
    Integer at metus. Suspendisse potenti. Vestibulum ante
    ipsum primis in faucibus orci luctus et ultrices posuere
    cubilia Curae; Proin quis eros at metus pretium elementum.
  </div>
</div>
```

The entire construct is enclosed in a `<div>` element tagged with the `module` class, and the caption and body constructs are each represented as `<div>` children with the classes `caption` and `body`.

In order to give this module the roll-up behavior, we'll instrument the image in the caption with a click handler that does all the magic. And with the `hide()` and `show()` methods up our sleeves, giving the module this behavior is considerably easier than pulling a quarter out from behind someone's ear.

Let's examine the code placed into the ready handler to take care of the roll-up behavior:

```
$('div.caption img').click(function(){        ❶ Instruments the button
  var body$ = $(this).closest('div.module').find('div.body');   ◁─┐ Finds the
  if (body$.is(':hidden')) {                                      │  related
    body$.show();              ❸ Shows the body                 ❷  body
  }
  else {
    body$.hide();              ❹ Hides the body
  }
});
```

As would be expected, this code first establishes a click handler on the image in the caption ❶.

Within the click handler, we first locate the body associated with the module. We need to find the specific instance of the module body because, remember, we may have many modules on our dashboard page, so we can't just select all elements that have the `body` class. We quickly locate the correct body element by finding the closest `module` container, and using it as the jQuery context, finding the `body` within it using the jQuery expression ❷:

```
$(this).closest('div.module').find('div.body')
```

(If how this expression finds the correct element isn't clear to you, now would be a good time to review the information in chapter 2 regarding finding and selecting elements.)

Once the body is located, it becomes a simple matter of determining whether the body is hidden or shown (the jQuery `is()` method comes in mighty handy here), and either showing or hiding it as appropriate using the `show()` ❸ or `hide()` ❹ method.

> **NOTE** With this code example, we've introduced a convention that many people use when storing references to a wrapped set within a variable: that of using the $ character within the variable name. Some may use the $ as a prefix and some as a suffix (as we have done here—if you think of the $ as representing the word "wrapper," the variable name `body$` can be read as "body wrapper"). In either case, it's a handy way to remember that the variable contains a reference to a wrapped set rather than an element or other type of object.

The full code for this page can be found in file chapter5/collapsible.module.take.1.html and is shown in listing 5.1. (If you surmise that the "take 1" part of this filename indicates that we'll be revisiting this example, you're right!)

Listing 5.1   The first implementation of our collapsible module

```
<!DOCTYPE html>
<html>
  <head>
    <title>Collapsible Module &mdash; Take 1</title>
    <link rel="stylesheet" type="text/css" href="../styles/core.css" />
    <link rel="stylesheet" type="text/css" href="module.css" />
    <script type="text/javascript" src="../scripts/jquery-1.4.js"></script>
    <script type="text/javascript">
      $(function() {

        $('div.caption img').click(function(){
          var body$ = $(this).closest('div.module').find('div.body');
          if (body$.is(':hidden')) {
            body$.show();
          }
          else {
            body$.hide();
          }
        });

      });
    </script>
  </head>

  <body class="plain">

    <div class="module">
      <div class="caption">
        <span>Module Caption</span>
        <img src="rollup.gif" alt="rollup" title="rolls up this module"/>
      </div>
      <div class="body">
        Lorem ipsum dolor sit amet, consectetuer adipiscing elit.
        Aliquam eget enim id neque aliquet porttitor. Suspendisse
        nisl enim, nonummy ac, nonummy ut, dignissim ac, justo.
        Aenean imperdiet semper nibh. Vivamus ligula. In in ipsum
        sed neque vehicula rhoncus. Nam faucibus pharetra nisi.
        Integer at metus. Suspendisse potenti. Vestibulum ante
        ipsum primis in faucibus orci luctus et ultrices posuere
        cubilia Curae; Proin quis eros at metus pretium elementum.
      </div>
    </div>

  </body>

</html>
```

That wasn't difficult at all, was it? But as it turns out, it can be even easier!

5.1.2   *Toggling the display state of elements*

Toggling the display state of elements between revealed and hidden—as we did for the collapsible module example—is such a common occurrence that jQuery defines a method named `toggle()` that makes it even easier.

Let's apply this method to the collapsible module and see how it helps to simplify the code of listing 5.1. Listing 5.2 shows only the ready handler for the refactored page (no other changes are necessary) with the changes highlighted in bold. The complete page code can be found in file chapter5/collapsible.module.take.2.html.

Listing 5.2   The collapsible module code, simplified with `toggle()`

```
$(function() {

  $('div.caption img').click(function(){
    $(this).closest('div.module').find('div.body').toggle();
  });

});
```

Note that we no longer need the conditional statement to determine whether to hide or show the module body; `toggle()` takes care of swapping the displayed state on our behalf. This allows us to simplify the code quite a bit, and the need to store the body reference in a variable simply vanishes.

Instantaneously making elements appear and disappear is handy, but sometimes we want the transition to be less abrupt. Let's see what's available for that.

5.2   *Animating the display state of elements*

Human cognitive ability being what it is, making items pop into and out of existence instantaneously can be jarring to us. If we blink at the wrong moment, we could miss the transition, leaving us to wonder, "What just happened?"

Gradual transitions of a *short* duration help us know what's changing and *how* we got from one state to the other—and that's where the jQuery core effects come in. There are three sets of effect types:

- Show and hide (there's a bit more to these methods than we let on in section 5.1)
- Fade in and fade out
- Slide down and slide up

Let's look more closely at each of these effect sets.

5.2.1   *Showing and hiding elements gradually*

The `show()`, `hide()`, and `toggle()` methods are a tad more complex than we led you to believe in the previous section. When called with no parameters, these methods effect a simple manipulation of the display state of the wrapped elements, causing them to instantaneously be revealed or hidden from the display. But when passed parameters, these effects can be animated so that the changes in display status of the affected elements take place over a period of time.

With that, we're now ready to look at the full syntaxes of these methods.

Method syntax: hide

hide(speed,callback)

Causes the elements in the wrapped set to become hidden. If called with no parameters, the operation takes place instantaneously by setting the display style property value of the elements to none. If a speed parameter is provided, the elements are hidden over a period of time by adjusting their width, height, and opacity downward to zero, at which time their display style property value is set to none to remove them from the display.

An optional callback can be specified, which is invoked when the animation is complete.

Parameters

speed   (Number|String) Optionally specifies the duration of the effect as a number of milliseconds or as one of the predefined strings: "slow", "normal", or "fast". If omitted, no animation takes place, and the elements are immediately removed from the display.

callback   (Function) An optional function invoked when the animation completes. No parameters are passed to this function, but the function context (this) is set to the element that was animated. The callback is fired for each element that undergoes animation.

Returns

The wrapped set.

Method syntax: show

show(speed,callback)

Causes any hidden elements in the wrapped set to be revealed. If called with no parameters, the operation takes place instantaneously by setting the display style property value of the elements to an appropriate setting (one of block or inline).

If a speed parameter is provided, the elements are revealed over a specified duration by adjusting their width, height, and opacity upward to full size and opacity.

An optional callback can be specified that's invoked when the animation is complete.

Parameters

speed   (Number|String) Optionally specifies the duration of the effect as a number of milliseconds or as one of the predefined strings: "slow", "normal", or "fast". If omitted, no animation takes place and the elements are immediately revealed in the display.

callback   (Function) An optional function invoked when the animation is complete. No parameters are passed to this function, but the function context (this) is set to the element that was animated. The callback is fired for each element that undergoes animation.

Returns

The wrapped set.

Method syntax: toggle

`toggle(speed,callback)`

Performs `show()` on any hidden wrapped elements and `hide()` on any non-hidden wrapped elements. See the syntax description of those methods for their semantics.

Parameters

speed   (Number|String) Optionally specifies the duration of the effect as a number of milliseconds or as one of the predefined strings: "slow", "normal", or "fast". If omitted, no animation takes place.

callback   (Function) An optional function invoked when the animation is complete. No parameters are passed to this function, but the function context (`this`) is set to the element that was animated. The callback is fired for each element that undergoes animation.

Returns

The wrapped set.

We can exert a bit more control over the toggling process with another variant of the `toggle()` method:

Method syntax: toggle

`toggle(condition)`

Shows or hides the matched elements based upon the evaluation of the passed condition. If `true`, the elements are shown; otherwise, they're hidden.

Parameters

condition   (Boolean) Determines whether elements are shown (if `true`), or hidden (if `false`).

Returns
The wrapped set.

Let's do a third take on the collapsible module, animating the opening and closing of the sections.

Given the previous information, you'd think that the only change we'd need to make to the code in listing 5.2 would be to change the call to the `toggle()` method to

`toggle('slow')`

And you'd be right.

But not so fast! Because that was just *too* easy, let's take the opportunity to also add some whizz-bang to the module.

Let's say that, to give the user an unmistakable visual clue, we want the module's caption to display a different background when it's in its rolled-up state. We could make the change before firing off the animation, but it'd be much more suave to wait until the animation is finished.

We can't just make the call right after the animation method call because animations *don't block*. The statements following the animated method call would execute immediately, probably even before the animation has had a chance to commence.

Rather, that's where the callback that we can register with the `toggle()` method comes in.

The approach that we'll take is that, after the animation is complete, we'll add a class name to the module to indicate that it's rolled up, and remove the class name when it isn't rolled up. CSS rules will take care of the rest.

Your initial thoughts might have led you to think of using `css()` to add a background style property directly to the caption, but why use a sledgehammer when we have a scalpel?

The "normal" CSS rule for the module caption (found in file chapter5/module.css) is as follows:

```
div.module div.caption {
  background: black url('module.caption.backg.png');
  ...
}
```

We've also added another rule:

```
div.module.rolledup div.caption {
  background: black url('module.caption.backg.rolledup.png');
}
```

This second rule causes the background image of the caption to change whenever its parent module possesses the `rolledup` class. So, in order to effect the change, all we have to do is add or remove the `rolledup` class to the module at the appropriate points.

Listing 5.3 shows the new ready handler code that makes that happen.

Listing 5.3 Animated version of the module, now with a magically changing caption!

```
$(function() {
  $('div.caption img').click(function(){
    $(this).closest('div.module').find('div.body')
      .toggle('slow',function(){
        $(this).closest('div.module')
          .toggleClass('rolledup',$(this).is(':hidden'));
      });
  });
});
```

The page with these changes can be found in file chapter5/collapsible.list.take.3.html.

Knowing how much people like us love to tinker, we've set up a handy tool that we'll use to further examine the operation of these and the remaining effects methods.

INTRODUCING THE JQUERY EFFECTS LAB PAGE

Back in chapter 2, we introduced the concept of lab pages to help us experiment with using jQuery selectors. For this chapter, we've set up a jQuery Effects Lab Page for exploring the operation of the jQuery effects in file chapter5/lab.effects.html.

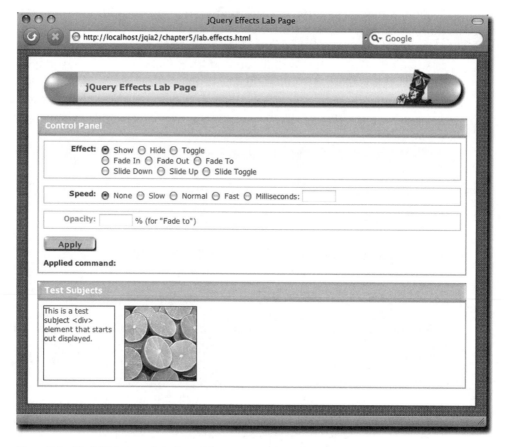

Figure 5.3   The initial state of the jQuery Effects Lab Page, which will help us examine the operation of the jQuery effects methods.

Loading this page into your browser results in the display of figure 5.3.

This Lab consists of two main panels: a control panel in which we'll specify which effect will be applied, and one that contains four test subject elements upon which the effects will act.

"Are they daft?" you might be thinking. "There are only two test subjects."

No, your authors haven't lost it yet. There *are* four elements, but two of them (another <div> with text and another image) are initially hidden.

Let's use this page to demonstrate the operations of the methods we've discussed to this point. Display the page in your browser, and follow along with the ensuing exercises:

- *Exercise 1*—With the controls left as is after the initial page load, click the Apply button. This will execute a show() method with no parameters. The expression that was applied is displayed below the Apply button for your information. Note how the two initially hidden test subject elements appear instantly. If you're wondering why the belt image on the far right appears a bit faded, its opacity has been purposefully set to 50 percent.

- *Exercise 2*—Select the Hide radio button, and click Apply to execute a parameter-less `hide()` method. All of the test subjects immediately vanish. Take special notice that the pane in which they resided has tightened up. This indicates that the elements have been completely removed from the display rather than merely made invisible.

NOTE When we say that an element has been *removed from the display* (here, and in the remainder of our discussion about effects), we mean that the element is no longer being taken into account by the browser's layout manager by setting its CSS `display` style property to `none`. It doesn't mean that the element has been removed from the DOM tree; none of the effects will ever cause an element to be removed from the DOM.

- *Exercise 3*—Select the Toggle radio button, and click Apply. Click Apply again. And again. You'll note that each subsequent execution of `toggle()` flips the presence of the test subjects.
- *Exercise 4*—Reload the page to reset everything to the initial conditions (in Firefox and other Gecko browsers, set focus to the address bar and press the Enter key—simply clicking the reload button won't reset the form elements). Select Toggle, and click Apply. Note how the two initially visible subjects vanish and the two that were hidden appear. This demonstrates that the `toggle()` method applies individually to each wrapped element, revealing the ones that are hidden and hiding those that aren't.
- *Exercise 5*—In this exercise, we'll move into the realm of animation. Refresh the page, leave Show selected, and select Slow for the Speed setting. Click Apply, and carefully watch the test subjects. The two hidden elements, rather than popping into existence, gradually grow from their upper-left corners. If you want to really see what's going on, refresh the page, select Milliseconds for the speed and enter `10000` for the speed value. This will extend the duration of the effect to 10 (excruciating) seconds and give you plenty of time to observe the behavior of the effect.
- *Exercise 6*—Choosing various combinations of Show, Hide, and Toggle, as well as various speeds, experiment with these effects until you feel you have a good handle on how they operate.

Armed with the jQuery Effects Lab Page, and the knowledge of how this first set of effects operates, let's take a look at the next set of effects.

5.2.2 *Fading elements into and out of existence*

If you watched the operation of the `show()` and `hide()` effects carefully, you will have noted that they scaled the size of the elements (either up or down as appropriate) *and* adjusted the opacity of the elements as they grew or shrank. The next set of effects, `fadeIn()` and `fadeOut()`, only affects the opacity of the elements.

Other than the lack of scaling, these methods work in a fashion similar to the animated forms of `show()` and `hide()`. The syntaxes of these methods are as follows:

Method syntax: fadeIn

fadeIn(speed,callback)

Causes any matched elements that are hidden to be shown by gradually changing their opacity to their natural value. This value is either the opacity originally applied to the element, or 100 percent. The duration of the change in opacity is determined by the `speed` parameter. Only hidden elements are affected.

Parameters

speed	(Number|String) Specifies the duration of the effect as a number of milliseconds or as one of the predefined strings: "slow", "normal", or "fast". If omitted, the default is "normal".
callback	(Function) An optional function invoked when the animation completes. No parameters are passed to this function, but the function context (`this`) is set to the element that was animated. This callback is fired individually for each animated element.

Returns

The wrapped set.

Method syntax: fadeOut

fadeOut(speed,callback)

Causes any matched elements that aren't hidden to be removed from the display by gradually changing their opacity to `0` percent and then removing the element from the display. The duration of the change in opacity is determined by the `speed` parameter. Only displayed elements are affected.

Parameters

speed	(Number|String) Specifies the duration of the effect as a number of milliseconds or as one of the predefined strings: "slow", "normal", or "fast". If omitted, the default is "normal".
callback	(Function) An optional function invoked when the animation completes. No parameters are passed to this function, but the function context (`this`) is set to the element that was animated. This callback is fired individually for each animated element.

Returns

The wrapped set.

 Let's have some more fun with the jQuery Effects Lab Page. Display the Lab, and run through a set of exercises similar to those in the previous section but using the Fade In and Fade Out selections (don't worry about Fade To for now; we'll attend to that soon enough).

It's important to note that when the opacity of an element is adjusted, the jQuery `hide()`, `show()`, `fadeIn()`, and `fadeOut()` effects remember the original opacity of an element and honor its value. In the Lab, we purposefully set the initial opacity of the belt image at the far right to 50 percent before hiding it. Throughout all the opacity changes that take place when applying the jQuery effects, this original value is never stomped on.

Run though additional exercises in the Lab until you're convinced that this is so and are comfortable with the operation of the fade effects.

Another effect that jQuery provides is via the `fadeTo()` method. This effect adjusts the opacity of the elements like the previously examined fade effects, but it never removes the elements from the display. Before we start playing with `fadeTo()` in the Lab, here's its syntax.

Method syntax: fadeTo

`fadeTo(speed,opacity,callback)`

Gradually adjusts the opacity of the wrapped elements from their current settings to the new setting specified by `opacity`.

Parameters

speed	(Number|String) Specifies the duration of the effect as a number of milliseconds or as one of the predefined strings: "slow", "normal", or "fast". If omitted, the default is "normal".
opacity	(Number) The target opacity to which the elements will be adjusted, specified as a value from 0.0 to 1.0.
callback	(Function) An optional function invoked when the animation completes. No parameters are passed to this function, but the function context (`this`) is set to the element that was animated. This callback is fired individually for each animated element.

Returns

The wrapped set.

Unlike the other effects that adjust opacity while hiding or revealing elements, `fadeTo()` doesn't remember the original opacity of an element. This makes sense because the whole purpose of this effect is to explicitly change the opacity to a specific value.

Bring up the Lab page, and cause all elements to be revealed (you should know how by now). Then work through the following exercises:

- *Exercise 1*—Select Fade To and a speed value slow enough for you to observe the behavior; 4000 milliseconds is a good choice. Now set the Opacity field (which expects a percentage value between 0 and 100, converted to 0.0 through 1.0 when passed to the method) to `10`, and click Apply. The test subjects will fade to 10 percent opacity over the course of four seconds.

- *Exercise 2*—Set the opacity to `100`, and click Apply. All elements, including the initially semitransparent belt image, are adjusted to full opaqueness.

- *Exercise 3*—Set the opacity to `0`, and click Apply. All elements fade away to invisibility, but note that once they've vanished, the enclosing module doesn't tighten up. Unlike the `fadeOut()` effect, `fadeTo()` never removes the elements from the display, even when they're fully invisible.

Continue experimenting with the Fade To effect until you've mastered its workings. Then we'll be ready to move on to the next set of effects.

5.2.3 *Sliding elements up and down*

Another set of effects that hide or show elements—slideDown() and slideUp()—also works in a similar manner to the hide() and show() effects, except that the elements appear to slide down from their tops when being revealed and to slide up into their tops when being hidden.

As with hide() and show(), the slide effects have a related method that will toggle the elements between hidden and revealed: slideToggle(). The by-now-familiar syntaxes for these methods follow.

Method syntax: slideDown

slideDown(speed,callback)
Causes any matched elements that are hidden to be shown by gradually increasing their vertical size. Only hidden elements are affected.

Parameters

speed   (Number|String) Specifies the duration of the effect as a number of milliseconds or as one of the predefined strings: "slow", "normal", or "fast". If omitted, the default is "normal".

callback   (Function) An optional function invoked when the animation completes. No parameters are passed to this function, but the function context (this) is set to the element that was animated. This callback is fired individually for each animated element.

Returns
The wrapped set.

Method syntax: slideUp

slideUp(speed,callback)
Causes any matched elements that are displayed to be removed from the display by gradually decreasing their vertical size.

Parameters

speed   (Number|String) Specifies the duration of the effect as a number of milliseconds or as one of the predefined strings: "slow", "normal", or "fast". If omitted, the default is "normal".

callback   (Function) An optional function invoked when the animation completes. No parameters are passed to this function, but the function context (this) is set to the element that was animated. This callback is fired individually for each animated element.

Returns
The wrapped set.

Method syntax: slideToggle

`slideToggle(speed,callback)`
Performs `slideDown()` on any hidden wrapped elements and `slideUp()` on any displayed wrapped elements. See the syntax description of those methods for their semantics.

Parameters
`speed`	(Number|String) Optionally specifies the duration of the effect as a number of milliseconds or as one of the predefined strings: "slow", "normal", or "fast". If omitted, the default is "normal".
`callback`	(Function) An optional function invoked when the animation completes. No parameters are passed to this function, but the function context (`this`) is set to the element that was animated. This callback is fired individually for each animated element.

Returns
The wrapped set.

 Except for the manner in which the elements are revealed and hidden, these effects act similarly to the other show and hide effects. Convince yourself of this by displaying the jQuery Effects Lab Page and running through exercises like those we applied using the other effects.

5.2.4 Stopping animations

We may have a reason now and again to stop an animation once it has started. This could be because a user event dictates that something else should occur or because we want to start a completely new animation. The `stop()` command will achieve this for us.

Command syntax: stop

`stop(clearQueue,gotoEnd)`
Halts any animations that are currently in progress for the elements in the matched set.

Parameters
`clearQueue`	(Boolean) If specified and set to `true`, not only stops the current animation, but any other animations waiting in the animation queue. (Animation queue? We'll get to that shortly ...)
`gotoEnd`	(Boolean) If specified and set to `true`, advances the current animation to its logical end (as opposed to merely stopping it).

Returns
The wrapped set.

Note that any changes that have already taken place for any animated elements will remain in effect. If we want to restore the elements to their original states, it's our responsibility to change the CSS values back to their starting values using the `css()` method or similar methods.

By the way, there's also a global flag that we can use to completely disable all animations. Setting the flag `jQuery.fx.off` to `true` will cause all effects to take place immediately without animation. We'll cover this flag more formally in chapter 6 with the other jQuery flags.

Now that we've seen the effects built into core jQuery, let's investigate writing our own!

5.3　*Creating custom animations*

The number of core effects supplied with jQuery is purposefully kept small, in order to keep jQuery's core footprint to a minimum, with the expectation that page authors would use plugins (including jQuery UI which we will begin to explore in chapter 9) to add more animations at their discretion. It's also a surprisingly simple matter to write our own animations.

jQuery publishes the `animate()` wrapper method, which allows us to apply our own custom animated effects to the elements of a wrapped set. Let's take a look at its syntax.

Method syntax: animate

`animate(properties,duration,easing,callback)`
`animate(properties,options)`

Applies an animation, as specified by the `properties` and `easing` parameters, to all members of the wrapped set. An optional callback function can be specified that's invoked when the animation is complete. An alternative format specifies a set of `options` in addition to the `properties`.

Parameters

properties	(Object) An object hash that specifies the values that supported CSS styles should reach at the end of the animation. The animation takes place by adjusting the values of the style properties from the current value for an element to the value specified in this object hash. (Be sure to use camel case when specifying multiword properties.)
duration	(Number|String) Optionally specifies the duration of the effect as a number of milliseconds or as one of the predefined strings: "slow", "normal", or "fast". If omitted or specified as 0, no animation takes place and the elements' specified `properties` are immediately, and synchronously, set to the target values.
easing	(String) The optional name of a function to perform easing of the animation. Easing functions must be registered by name and are often provided by plugins. Core jQuery supplies two easing functions registered as "linear" and "swing". (See chapter 9 for the list of easing functions provided by jQuery UI.)
callback	(Function) An optional function invoked when the animation completes. No parameters are passed to this function, but the function context (`this`) is set to the element that was animated. This callback is fired individually for each animated element.
options	(Object) Specifies the animation parameter values using an object hash. The supported properties are as follows:

- `duration`—See previous description of `duration` parameter.
- `easing`—See previous description of `easing` parameter.
- `complete`—Function invoked when the animation completes.
- `queue`—If `false`, the animation isn't queued and begins running immediately.
- `step`—A callback function called at each step of the animation. This callback is passed the step index and an internal effects object (that doesn't contain much of interest to us as page authors). The function context is set to the element under animation.

Returns

The wrapped set.

We can create custom animations by supplying a set of CSS style properties and target values that those properties will converge towards as the animation progresses. Animations start with an element's original style value and proceed by adjusting that style value in the direction of the target value. The intermediate values that the style achieves during the effect (automatically handled by the animation engine) are determined by the duration of the animation and the easing function.

The specified target values can be absolute values, or we can specify relative values from the starting point. To specify relative values, prefix the value with += or -= to indicate relative target values in the positive or negative direction, respectively.

The term *easing* is used to describe the manner in which the processing and pace of the frames of the animation are handled. By using some fancy math on the duration of the animation and current time position, some interesting variations to the effects are possible. The subject of writing easing functions is a complex, niche topic that's usually only of interest to the most hard-core of plugin authors; we're not going to delve into the subject of custom easing functions in this book. We'll be taking a look at a lot more easing functions in chapter 9 when we examine jQuery UI.

By default, animations are added to a queue for execution (much more on that coming up); applying multiple animations to an object will cause them to run serially. If you'd like to run animations in parallel, set the queue option to false.

The list of CSS style properties that can be animated is limited to those that accept numeric values for which there is a logical progression from a start value to a target value. This numeric restriction is completely understandable—how would we envision the logical progress from a source value to an end value for a non-numeric property such as background-image? For values that represent dimensions, jQuery assumes the default unit of pixels, but we can also specify em units or percentages by including the em or % suffixes.

Frequently animated style properties include top, left, width, height, and opacity. But if it makes sense for the effect we want to achieve, numeric style properties such as font size, margin, padding, and border dimensions can also be animated.

NOTE jQuery UI adds the ability to animate CSS properties that specify a color value. We'll learn all about that when we discuss jQuery UI effects in chapter 9.

In addition to specific values for the target properties, we can also specify one of the strings "hide", "show", or "toggle"; jQuery will compute the end value as appropriate to the specification of the string. Using "hide" for the opacity property, for example, will result in the opacity of an element being reduced to 0. Using any of these special strings has the added effect of automatically revealing or removing the element from the display (like the hide() and show() methods), and it should be noted that "toggle" remembers the initial state so that it can be restored on a subsequent "toggle".

Did you notice that when we introduced the core animations that there was no toggling method for the fade effects? That's easily solved using animate() and "toggle" to create a simple custom animation as follows:

```
$('.animateMe').animate({opacity:'toggle'},'slow');
```

Taking this to the next logical step—creating a wrapper function—could be coded as follows:

```
$.fn.fadeToggle = function(speed){
  return this.animate({opacity:'toggle'},speed);
};
```

Now, let's try our hand at writing a few more custom animations.

5.3.1   A custom scale animation

Consider a simple *scale* animation in which we want to adjust the size of the elements to twice their original dimensions. We'd write such an animation as shown in listing 5.4.

Listing 5.4   A custom scale animation

```
$('.animateMe').each(function(){          ◁┐  Iterates over each
  $(this).animate({                       ❶  matched element
    width: $(this).width() * 2,                       ◁┐  Specifies
    height: $(this).height() * 2                        │  individual
  },                                                   ❷  target values
  2000              ❸  Sets duration
  );
});
```

To implement this animation, we iterate over all the elements in the wrapped set via each() to apply the animation individually to each matched element ❶. This is important because the property values that we need to specify for each element are based upon the individual dimensions for that element ❷. If we always knew that we'd be animating a single element (such as if we were using an id selector) or applying the exact same set of values to each element, we could dispense with each() and animate the wrapped set directly.

Within the iterator function, the animate() method is applied to the element (identified via this) with style property values for width and height set to double the element's original dimensions. The result is that over the course of two seconds (as specified by the duration parameter of 2000 ❸), the wrapped elements (or element) will grow from their original size to twice that size.

Now let's try something a bit more extravagant.

5.3.2   A custom drop animation

Let's say that we want to conspicuously animate the removal of an element from the display, perhaps because it's vitally important to convey to users that the item being removed is *gone* and that they should make no mistake about it. The animation we'll use to accomplish this will make it appear as if the element *drops* off the page, disappearing from the display as it does so.

If we think about it for a moment, we can figure out that by adjusting the top position of the element we can make it move down the page to simulate the drop; adjusting the opacity will make it seem to vanish as it does so. And finally, when all that's done, we can remove the element from the display (similar to the animated `hide()` method).

We can accomplish this drop effect with the code in listing 5.5.

Listing 5.5   A custom drop animation

```
$('.animateMe').each(function(){
  $(this)
    .css('position','relative')          ① Dislodges element
    .animate(                                from static flow
      {
        opacity: 0,
        top: $(window).height() - $(this).height() -    ② Computes drop
            $(this).position().top                          distance
      },
      'slow',
      function(){ $(this).hide(); }       ③ Removes element
    );                                       from display
});
```

There's a bit more going on here than in our previous custom effect. We once again iterate over the element set, this time adjusting the position *and* opacity of the elements. But to adjust the `top` value of an element relative to its original position, we first need to change its CSS `position` style property value to `relative` ①.

Then, for the animation, we specify a target `opacity` of 0 and a computed `top` value. We don't want to move an element so far down the page that it moves below the window's bottom; this could cause scroll bars to be displayed where none may have been before, possibly distracting users. We don't want to draw their attention away from the animation—grabbing their attention is why we're animating in the first place! So we use the height and vertical position of the element, as well as the height of the window, to compute how far down the page the element should drop ②.

When the animation is complete, we want to remove the element from the display, so we specify a callback routine ③ that applies the non-animated `hide()` method to the element (which is available to the function as its function context).

> **NOTE**   We did a little more work than we needed to in this animation, just so we could demonstrate doing something that needs to wait until the animation is complete in the callback function. If we were to specify the value of the opacity property as "hide" rather than 0, the removal of the element(s) at the end of the animation would be automatic, and we could dispense with the callback.

Now let's try one more type of "make it go away" effect for good measure.

5.3.3   A custom puff animation

Rather than dropping elements off the page, let's say we want an effect that makes it appear as if the element dissipates away into thin air like a puff of smoke. To animate such an effect, we can combine a scale effect with an opacity effect, growing the element while fading it away. One issue we need to deal with for this effect is that this dissipation would not fool the eye if we let the element grow in place with its upper-left corner anchored. We want the *center* of the element to stay in the same place as it grows, so in addition to its size we also need to adjust the *position* of the element as part of the animation.

The code for our puff effect is shown in listing 5.6.

Listing 5.6 A custom puff animation

```
$('.animateMe').each(function(){
  var position = $(this).position();
  $(this)
    .css({position: 'absolute',          ❶ Dislodges element
         top: position.top,                 from static flow
         left: position.left})
    .animate(                            ❷ Adjusts element size,
      {                                    position, opacity
        opacity: 'hide',
        width: $(this).width() * 5,
        height: $(this).height() * 5,
        top: position.top - ($(this).height() * 5 / 2),
        left: position.left - ($(this).width() * 5 / 2)
      },
      'normal');
});
```

In this animation, we decrease the opacity to 0 while growing the element to five times its original size and adjusting its position by half that new size, resulting in the center of the element remaining in the same position ❷. We don't want the elements surrounding the animated element to be pushed out while the target element is growing, so we take it out of the layout flow completely by changing its position to absolute and explicitly setting its position coordinates ❶.

Because we specified "hide" for the opacity value, the elements are automatically hidden (removed from the display) once the animation is complete.

Each of these three custom effects can be observed by loading the page at chapter5/custom.effects.html, whose display is shown in figure 5.4.

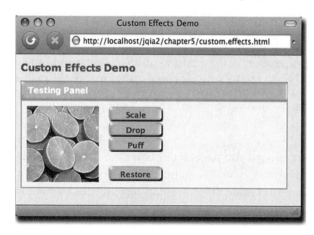

Figure 5.4 The custom effects we developed, Scale, Drop, and Puff, can be observed in action using the buttons provided on this example page.

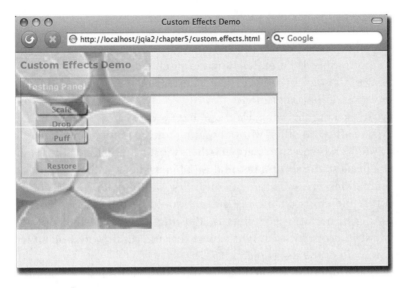

Figure 5.5   The Puff effect expands and moves the image while simultaneously reducing its opacity.

We purposefully kept the browser window to a minimum size for the screenshot, but you'll want to make the window bigger when running this page to properly observe the behavior of the effects. And although we'd love to show you how these effects behave, screenshots have obvious limitations. Nevertheless, figure 5.5 shows the puff effect in progress.

We'll leave it to you to try out the various effects on this page and observe their behavior.

Up until this point, all of the examples we've examined have used a single animation method. Let's discuss how things work when we use more than one.

5.4   *Animations and Queuing*

We've seen how multiple properties of elements can be animated using a single animation method, but we haven't really examined how animations behave when we call simultaneous animation methods.

In this section we'll examine just how animations behave in concert with each other.

5.4.1   *Simultaneous animations*

What would you expect to happen if we were to execute the following code?

```
$('#testSubject').animate({left:'+=256'},'slow');
$('#testSubject').animate({top:'+=256'},'slow');
```

We know that the `animate()` method doesn't block while its animation is running on the page; nor do any of the other animation methods. We can prove that to ourselves by experimenting with this code block:

```
say(1);
$('#testSubject').animate({left:'+=256'},'slow');
say(2);
```

Recall that we introduced the say() function in chapter 4 as a way to spit messages onto an on-page "console" in order to avoid alerts (which would most definitely screw up our observation of the experiment).

If we were to execute this code, we'd see that the messages "1" and "2" are emitted immediately, one after the other, without waiting for the animation to complete.

So, what would we expect to happen when we run the code with two animation method calls? Because the second method isn't blocked by the first, it stands to reason that both animations fire off simultaneously (or within a few milliseconds of each other), and that the effect on the test subject would be the combination of the two effects. In this case, because one effect is adjusting the left style property, and the other the top style property, we might expect that the result would be a meandering diagonal movement of the test subject.

Let's put that to the test. In file chapter5/revolutions.html we've put together an experiment that sets up two images (one of which is to be animated), a button to start the experiment, and a "console" in which the say() function will write its output. Figure 5.6 shows its initial state.

The Start button is instrumented as shown in listing 5.7.

Listing 5.7 Instrumentation for multiple simultaneous animations

```
$('#startButton').click(function(){
  say(1);
  $("img[alt='moon']").animate({left:'+=256'},2500);
  say(2);
  $("img[alt='moon']").animate({top:'+=256'},2500);
```

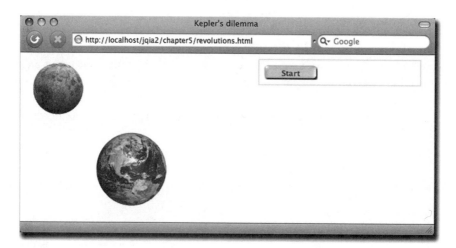

Figure 5.6 Initial state of the page where we'll observe the behavior of multiple, simultaneous animations

```
  say(3);
  $("img[alt='moon']").animate({left:'-=256'},2500);
  say(4);
  $("img[alt='moon']").animate({top:'-=256'},2500);
  say(5);
});
```

In the click handler for the button, we fire off four animations, one after the other, interspersed with calls to say() that show us when the animation calls were fired off.

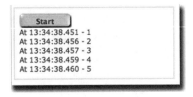

Bring up the page, and click the Start button.

As expected, the console messages "1" through "5" immediately appear on the console as shown in figure 5.7, each firing off a few milliseconds after the previous one.

Figure 5.7   The console messages appear in rapid succession, proving that the animation methods aren't blocking until completion.

But what of the animations? If we examine the code in listing 5.7, we can see that we have two animations changing the top property and two animations changing the left property. In fact, the animations for each property are doing the exact opposite of each other. So what should we expect? Might they just cancel each other out, leaving the Moon (our test subject) to remain completely still?

No. Upon clicking Start, we see that each animation happens serially, one after the other, such that the Moon makes a complete and orderly revolution around the Earth (albeit in a very unnatural square orbit that would have made Kepler's head explode).

What's going on? We've proven via the console messages that the animations aren't blocking, yet they execute serially just as if they were (at least with respect to each other).

What's happening is that, internally, jQuery is queuing up the animations and executing them serially on our behalf.

Refresh the Kepler's Dilemma page to clear the console, and click the Start button three times in succession. (Pause between clicks just long enough to avoid double-clicks.) You'll note how 15 messages get immediately sent to the console, indicating that our click handler has executed three times, and then sit back as the Moon makes three orbits around the Earth.

Each of the 12 animations is queued up by jQuery and executed in order. jQuery maintains a queue on each animated element named fx just for this purpose. (The significance of the queue having a name will become clear in the next section.)

The queuing of animations in this manner means that we can have our cake and eat it too! We can affect multiple properties simultaneously by using a single animate() method that specifies all the animated properties, and we can serially execute any animations we want by simply calling them in order.

What's even better is that jQuery makes it possible for us to create our own execution queues, not just for animations, but for whatever purposes we want. Let's learn about that.

5.4.2   *Queuing functions for execution*

Queuing up animations for serial execution is an obvious use for function queues. But is there a real benefit? After all, the animation methods allow for completion callbacks, so why not just fire off the next animation in the callback of the previous animation?

ADDING FUNCTIONS TO A QUEUE

Let's review the code fragment of listing 5.7 (minus the `say()` invocations for clarity):

```
$("img[alt='moon']").animate({left:'+=256'},2500);
$("img[alt='moon']").animate({top:'+=256'},2500);
$("img[alt='moon']").animate({left:'-=256'},2500);
$("img[alt='moon']").animate({top:'-=256'},2500);
```

Compare that to the equivalent code that would be necessary without function queuing, using the completion callbacks:

```
$('#startButton').click(function(){
  $("img[alt='moon']").animate({left:'+=256'},2500,function(){
    $("img[alt='moon']").animate({top:'+=256'},2500,function(){
      $("img[alt='moon']").animate({left:'-=256'},2500,function(){
        $("img[alt='moon']").animate({top:'-=256'},2500);
      });
    });
  });
});
```

It's not that the callback variant of the code is that much more complicated, but it'd be hard to argue that the original code isn't a lot easier to read (and to write in the first place). And if the bodies of the callback functions were to get substantially more complicated ... Well, it's easy to see how being able to queue up the animations makes the code a lot less complex.

So what if we wanted to do the same thing with our own functions? Well, jQuery isn't greedy about its queues; we can create our own to queue up any functions we'd like to have executed in serial order.

Queues can be created on any element, and distinct queues can be created by using unique names for them (except for `fx` which is reserved for the effects queue). The method to add a function instance to a queue is, unsurprisingly, `queue()`, and it has three variants:

Method syntax: queue

queue(name)
queue(name,function)
queue(name,queue)
The first form returns any queue of the passed name already established on the first element in the matched set as an array of functions.
The second form adds the passed function to the end of the named queue for all elements in the matched set. If such a named queue doesn't exist on an element, it's created.
The last form replaces any existing queue on the matched elements with the passed queue.

Method syntax: queue *(continued)*	

Parameters

name	(String) The name of the queue to be fetched, added to, or replaced. If omitted, the default effects queue of `fx` is assumed.
function	(Function) The function to be added to the end of the queue. When invoked, the function context (`this`) will be set to the DOM element upon which the queue has been established.
queue	(Array) An array of functions that *replaces* the existing functions in the named queue.

Returns

An array of functions for the first form, and the wrapped set for the remaining forms.

The `queue()` method is most often used to add functions to the end of the named queue, but it can also be used to fetch any existing functions in a queue, or to replace the list of functions in a queue. Note that the array form, in which an array of functions is passed to `queue()`, can't be used to add multiple functions to the *end* of a queue because any existing queued functions are removed. (In order to add functions to the queue, we'd fetch the array of functions, merge the new functions, and set the modified array back into the queue.)

EXECUTING THE QUEUED FUNCTIONS

OK, so now we can queue functions up for execution. That's not all that useful unless we can somehow cause the execution of the functions to actually occur. Enter the `dequeue()` method.

Method syntax: dequeue

dequeue(name)

Removes the foremost function in the named queue for each element in the matched set and executes it for each element.

Parameters

name	(String) The name of the queue from which the foremost function is to be removed and executed. If omitted, the default effects queue of `fx` is assumed.

Returns

The wrapped set.

When `dequeue()` is invoked, the foremost function in the named queue for each element in the wrapped set is executed with the function context for the invocation (`this`) being set to the element.

Let's consider the code in listing 5.8.

Listing 5.8 Queuing and dequeuing functions on multiple elements

```html
<html>
  <head>
    <link rel="stylesheet" type="text/css" href="../styles/core.css" />
    <script type="text/javascript" src="../scripts/jquery-1.4.js"></script>
    <script type="text/javascript" src="console.js"></script>
    <script type="text/javascript">
```

```
$(function() {

  $('img').queue('chain',
    function(){ say('First: ' + $(this).attr('alt')); });
  $('img').queue('chain',
    function(){ say('Second: ' + $(this).attr('alt')); });
  $('img').queue('chain',
    function(){ say('Third: ' + $(this).attr('alt')); });
  $('img').queue('chain',
    function(){ say('Fourth: ' + $(this).attr('alt')); });

  $('button').click(function(){
    $('img').dequeue('chain');
  });

});
</script>
</head>

<body>

  <div>
    <img src="earth.png" alt="Earth"/>
    <img src="moon.png" alt="Moon"/>
  </div>

  <button type="button" class="green90x24">Dequeue</button>

  <div id="console"></div>

</body>
</html>
```

❶ Establishes four queued functions

❷ Dequeues one function on each click

In this example (found in file chapter5/queue.html), we have two images upon which we establish queues named chain. In each queue, we place four functions ❶ that identify themselves in order and emit the alt attribute of whatever DOM element is serving as the function context. This way, we can tell which function is being executed, and from which element's queue.

Upon clicking the Dequeue button, the button's click handler ❷ causes a single execution of the dequeue() method.

Go ahead and click the button once, and observe the messages in the console, as shown in figure 5.8.

We can see that the first function we added to the chain queue for the images has been fired twice: once for the Earth image, and once for the Moon image.
Clicking the button more times removes the subsequent functions from the queues one at a time, and executes them until the queues have been emptied; after which, calling dequeue() has no effect.

In this example, the dequeuing of the functions was under manual control—we needed to click the button four times (resulting in four calls to dequeue()) to get all four functions executed. Frequently we may want to trigger the execution of the entire set of queued functions. For such times, a commonly used idiom is to call the dequeue() method *within* the queued function in order to trigger the execution of (in other words, create a chain to) the next queued function.

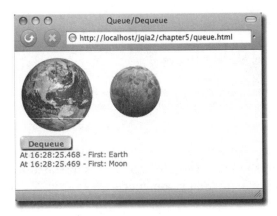

Figure 5.8 Clicking the Dequeue button causes a single queued instance of the function to fire, once for each image that it was established upon.

Consider the following changes to the code in listing 5.8:

```
$('img').queue('chain',
 function(){
   say('First: ' + $(this).attr('alt'));
   $(this).dequeue('chain');
 });
$('img').queue('chain',
   function(){
     say('Second: ' + $(this).attr('alt'));
     $(this).dequeue('chain');
   });
$('img').queue('chain',
   function(){
     say('Third: ' + $(this).attr('alt'));
     $(this).dequeue('chain');
   });
$('img').queue('chain',
   function(){
     say('Fourth: ' + $(this).attr('alt'));
     $(this).dequeue('chain');
   });
```

We've made just such a change to the example in file chapter5/queue.2.html. Bring up that page in your browser, and click the Dequeue button. Note how the single click now triggers the execution of the entire chain of queued functions.

CLEARING OUT UNEXECUTED QUEUED FUNCTIONS

If we want to remove the queued functions from a queue without executing them, we can do that with the `clearQueue()` method:

Method syntax: clearQueue

`clearQueue(name)`

Removes all unexecuted functions from the named queue.

Parameters

name   (String) The name of the queue from which the functions are to be removed without execution. If omitted, the default effects queue of `fx` is assumed.

Returns

The wrapped set.

While similar to the `stop()` animation method, `clearQueue()` is intended for use on general queued functions rather than just animation effects.

DELAYING QUEUED FUNCTIONS

Another queue-oriented activity we might want to perform is to add a delay between the execution of queued functions. The `delay()` method enables that:

Method syntax: delay

`delay(duration,name)`

Adds a delay to all unexecuted functions in the named queue.

Parameters

duration (Number|String) The delay duration in milliseconds, or one of the strings `fast` or `slow`, representing values of 200 and 600 respectively.

name   (String) The name of the queue from which the functions are to be removed without execution. If omitted, the default effects queue of `fx` is assumed.

Returns

The wrapped set.

There's one more thing to discuss regarding queuing functions before moving along ...

5.4.3 *Inserting functions into the effects queue*

We previously mentioned that internally jQuery uses a queue named `fx` to queue up the functions necessary to implement the animations. What if we'd like to add our own functions to this queue in order to intersperse actions within a queued series of effects? Now that we know about the queuing methods, we can!

Think back to our previous example in listing 5.7, where we used four animations to make the Moon revolve around the Earth. Imagine that we wanted to turn the background of the Moon image black after the second animation (the one that moves it downward). If we just added a call to the `css()` method between the second and third animations, as follows,

```
$("img[alt='moon']").animate({left:'+=256'},2500);
$("img[alt='moon']").animate({top:'+=256'},2500);
$("img[alt='moon']").css({'backgroundColor':'black'});
$("img[alt='moon']").animate({left:'-=256'},2500);
$("img[alt='moon']").animate({top:'-=256'},2500);
```

we'd be very disappointed because this would cause the background to change immediately, perhaps even before the first animation had a chance to start.

Rather, consider the following code:

```
$("img[alt='moon']").animate({left:'+=256'},2500);
$("img[alt='moon']").animate({top:'+=256'},2500);
$("img[alt='moon']").queue('fx',
  function(){
    $(this).css({'backgroundColor':'black'});
    $(this).dequeue('fx');
  }
);
$("img[alt='moon']").animate({left:'-=256'},2500);
$("img[alt='moon']").animate({top:'-=256'},2500);
```

Here, we wrap the `css()` method in a function that we place onto the `fx` queue using the `queue()` method. (We could have omitted the queue name, because `fx` is the default, but we made it explicit here for clarity.) This puts our color-changing function into place on the effects queue where it will be called as part of the function chain that executes as the animations progress, between the second and third animations.

But note! After we call the `css()` method, we call the `dequeue()` method on the `fx` queue. This is absolute necessary to keep the animation queue chugging along. Failure to call `dequeue()` at this point will cause the animations to grind to a halt, because nothing is causing the next function in the chain to execute. The unexecuted animations will just sit there on the effects queues until either something causes a dequeue and the functions commence, or the page unloads and everything just gets discarded.

If you'd like to see this process in action, load the page in file chapter5/revolutions.2.html into your browser and click the button.

Queuing functions comes in handy whenever we want to execute functions consecutively, but without the overhead, or complexity, of nesting functions in asynchronous callbacks; something that, as you might imagine, can come in handy when we throw Ajax into the equation.

But that's another chapter.

5.5   Summary

This chapter introduced us to the animated effects that jQuery makes available out of the box, as well as to the `animate()` method that allows us to create our own custom animations.

The `show()` and `hide()` methods, when used without parameters, reveal and conceal elements from the display immediately, without any animation. We can perform animated versions of the hiding and showing of elements with these methods by passing parameters that control the speed of the animation, as well as providing an optional callback that's invoked when the animation completes. The `toggle()` method toggles the displayed state of an element between hidden and shown.

Another set of wrapper methods, `fadeOut()` and `fadeIn()`, also hides and shows elements by adjusting the opacity of elements when removing or revealing them in the display. A third method, fadeTo(), animates a change in opacity for its wrapped elements without removing the elements from the display.

A final set of three built-in effects animates the removal or display of our wrapped elements by adjusting their vertical height: slideUp(), slideDown(), and slideToggle().

For building our own custom animations, jQuery provides the animate() method. Using this method, we can animate any CSS style property that accepts a numeric value, most commonly the opacity, position, and dimensions of the elements. We explored writing some custom animations that remove elements from the page in novel fashions.

We also learned how jQuery queues animations for serial execution, and how we can use the jQuery queuing methods to add our own functions to the effects queue or our own custom queues.

When we explored writing our own custom animations, we wrote the code for these custom effects as inline code within the on-page JavaScript. A much more common, and useful, method is to package custom animations as custom jQuery methods. We'll learn how to do that in chapter 7, and you're encouraged to revisit these effects after you've read that chapter. Repackaging the custom effects we developed in this chapter, and any that you can think up on your own, would be an excellent follow-up exercise.

But before we write our own jQuery extensions, let's take a look at some high-level jQuery functions and flags that will be very useful for general tasks as well as extension writing.

Beyond the DOM
with jQuery utility functions

This chapter covers
- The jQuery browser support information
- Using other libraries with jQuery
- Array manipulation functions
- Extending and merging objects
- Dynamically loading new scripts
- And more ...

Up to this point, we've spent a fair number of chapters examining the jQuery methods that operate upon a set of DOM elements wrapped by the $() function. But you may recall that, way back in chapter 1, we also introduced the concept of *utility functions*—functions namespaced by jQuery/$ that don't operate on a wrapped set. These functions could be thought of as top-level functions except that they're defined on the $ instance rather than window, keeping them *out* of the global namespace.

Generally, these functions either operate upon JavaScript objects *other* than DOM elements (that's the purview of the wrapper methods, after all), or they perform some non-object-related operation (such as an Ajax request).

In addition to functions, jQuery also provides some useful flags that are defined within the jQuery/$ namespace.

You may wonder why we waited until this chapter to introduce these functions and flags. Well, we had two reasons:

- We wanted to guide you into thinking in terms of using jQuery wrapper methods rather than resorting to lower-level operations that might feel more familiar but not be as efficient or as easy to code as using the jQuery wrapper.
- Because the wrapper methods take care of much of what we want to do when manipulating DOM elements on the pages, these lower-level functions are frequently most useful when writing the methods themselves (as well as other extensions) rather than in page-level code. (We'll be tackling how to write our own plugins to jQuery in the next chapter.)

In this chapter, we'll finally get around to formally introducing most of the $-level utility functions, as well as a handful of useful flags. We'll put off talking about the utility functions that deal with Ajax until chapter 8, which deals exclusively with jQuery's Ajax functionality.

We'll start out with those flags we mentioned.

6.1 Using the jQuery flags

Some of the information jQuery makes available to us as page authors, and even plugin authors, is available not via methods or functions but as properties defined on $. Many of these *flags* are focused on helping us divine the capabilities of the current browser, but others help us control the behavior of jQuery at a page-global level.

The jQuery flags intended for public use are as follows:

- `$.fx.off`—Enables or disabled effects
- `$.support`—Details supported features
- `$.browser`—Exposes browser details (officially deprecated)

Let's start by looking at how jQuery lets us disable animations.

6.1.1 Disabling animations

There may be times when we might want to conditionally disable animations in a page that includes various animated effects. We might do so because we've detected that the platform or device is unlikely to deal with them well, or perhaps for accessibility reasons.

In any case, we don't need to resort to writing two pages, one with and one without animations. When we detect we're in an animation-adverse environment, we can simply set the value of $.fx.off to true.

This will *not* suppress any effects we've used on the page; it will simply disable the animation of those effects. For example, the fade effects will show and hide the elements immediately, without the intervening animations.

Similarly, calls to the animate() method will set the CSS properties to the specified final values without animating them.

One possible use-case for this flag might be for certain mobile devices or browsers that don't correctly support animations. In that case, you might want to turn off animations so that the core functionality still works.

The `$.fx.off` flag is a read/write flag. The remaining predefined flags are meant to be read-only. Let's take a look at the flag that gives us information on the environment provided by the user agent (browser).

6.1.2 Detecting user agent support

Thankfully, almost blissfully, the jQuery methods that we've examined so far shield us from having to deal with browser differences, even in traditionally problematic areas like event handling. But when we're the ones writing these methods (or other extensions), we may need to account for the differences in the ways browsers operate so that the users of our extensions don't have to.

Before we dive into seeing how jQuery helps us in this regard, let's talk about the whole concept of browser detection.

WHY BROWSER DETECTION IS HEINOUS

OK, maybe the word *heinous* is too strong, but unless it's absolutely necessary, the browser detection technique should be avoided.

Browser detection might seem, at first, like a logical way to deal with browser differences. After all, it's easy to say, "I know what the set of capabilities of browser X are, so testing for the browser makes perfect sense, right?" But browser detection is full of pitfalls and problems.

One of the major arguments against this technique is that the proliferation of browsers, as well as varying levels of support within versions of the same browser, makes this technique an unscalable approach to the problem.

You could be thinking, "Well, all I need to test for is Internet Explorer and Firefox." But why would you exclude the growing number of Safari users? What about Opera and Google's Chrome? Moreover, there are some niche, but not insignificant, browsers that share capability profiles with the more popular browsers. Camino, for example, uses the same technology as Firefox behind its Mac-friendly UI. And OmniWeb uses the same rendering engine as Safari and Chrome.

There's no need to exclude support for these browsers, but it *is* a royal pain to have to test for them. And that's without even considering differences between versions—IE 6, IE 7, and IE 8, for example.

Yet another reason is that if we test for a specific browser, and a future release fixes that bug, our code may actually stop working. jQuery's alternative approach to this issue (which we'll discuss in the next section) gives browser vendors an incentive to fix the bugs that jQuery has worked around.

A final argument against browser detection (or *sniffing*, as it's sometimes called) is that it's getting harder and harder to know who's who.

Browsers identify themselves by setting a request header known as the *user agent* string. Parsing this string isn't for the faint-hearted. In addition, many browsers now allow their users to spoof this string, so we can't even believe what it tells us after we *do* go though all the trouble of parsing it!

A JavaScript object named `navigator` gives us a partial glimpse into the user agent information, but even *it* has browser differences. We almost need to do browser detection in order to do browser detection!

Stop the madness!

Browser detection is

- Imprecise, accidentally blocking browsers within which our code would actually work
- Unscalable, leading to enormous nested if and if-else statements to sort things out
- Inaccurate, due to users spoofing user agent information

Obviously, we'd like to avoid using it whenever possible.

But what can we do instead?

WHAT'S THE ALTERNATIVE TO BROWSER DETECTION?

If we think about it, we're not *really* interested in which browser anyone is using, are we? The only reason we're even thinking about browser detection is so that we can know which capabilities and features we can use. It's the *capabilities* and *features* of a browser that we're really after; using browser detection is just a ham-handed way of trying to determine what those features and capabilities are.

So why don't we just figure out what those features are rather than trying to infer them from the browser identification? The technique known broadly as *feature detection* allows code to branch based on whether certain objects, properties, or even methods exist.

Let's think back to chapter 4 on event handling as an example. Remember that there are two advanced event-handling models: the W3C standard DOM Level 2 Event Model and the proprietary Internet Explorer Event Model. Both models define methods on the DOM elements that allow listeners to be established, but each uses different method names. The standard model defines the method `addEventListener()`, whereas the IE model defines `attachEvent()`.

Using browser detection, and assuming that we've gone through the pain and aggravation of determining which browser is being used (maybe even correctly), we could write

```
...
complex code to set flags: isIE, isFirefox, and isSafari
...
if (isIE) {
  element.attachEvent('onclick',someHandler);
}
else if (isFirefox || isSafari) {
  element.addEventListener('click',someHandler);
}
else {
  throw new Error('event handling not supported');
}
```

Aside from the fact that this example glosses over whatever necessarily complex code we're using to set the flags `isIE`, `isFirefox`, and `isSafari`, we can't be sure if these flags accurately represent the browser being used. Moreover, this code will throw an error if used in Opera, Chrome, Camino, OmniWeb, or a host of other lesser-known browsers that might perfectly support the standard model.

Consider the following variation of this code:

```
if (element.attachEvent) {
  element.attachEvent('onclick',someHandler);
}
else if (element.addEventListener) {
  element.addEventListener('click',someHandler);
}
else {
  throw new Error('event handling not supported');
}
```

This code doesn't perform a lot of complex, and ultimately unreliable, browser detection, and it automatically supports all browsers that support either of the two competing event models. Much better!

Feature detection is vastly superior to browser detection. It's more reliable, and it doesn't accidentally block browsers that support the capability we're testing for simply because we don't know about the features of that browser, or even of the browser itself. Did you account for Google Chrome in your most recent web application? iCab? Epiphany? Konqueror?

> **NOTE** Even feature detection is best avoided unless absolutely required. If we can come up with a cross-browser solution, it should be preferred over *any* type of branching.

But as superior to browser detection as feature detection may be, it can still be no walk in the park. Branching and detection of any type can still be tedious and painful in our pages, and some feature differences can be decidedly difficult to detect, requiring nontrivial or downright complex checks. jQuery comes to our aid by performing those checks for us and supplying the results in a set of flags that detect the most common user agent features that we might care about.

THE JQUERY BROWSER CAPABILITY FLAGS

The browser capability flags are exposed to us as properties of jQuery's `$.support` object.

Table 6.1 summarizes the flags that are available in this object.

Table 6.1 The `$.support` browser capability flags

Flag property	Description
boxModel	Set to `true` if the user agent renders according to the standards-compliant box model. This flag isn't set until the document is ready. More information regarding the box-model issue is available at http://www.quirksmode.org/css/box.html and at http://www.w3.org/TR/REC-CSS2/box.html.
cssFloat	Set to `true` if the standard `cssFloat` property of the element's `style` property is used.

Table 6.1   The $.support browser capability flags *(continued)*

Flag property	Description
hrefNormalized	Set to true if obtaining the href element attributes returns the value exactly as specified.
htmlSerialize	Set to true if the browser evaluates style sheet references by <link> elements when injected into the DOM via innerHTML.
leadingWhitespace	Set to true if the browser honors leading whitespace when text is inserted via innerHTML.
noCloneEvent	Set to true if the browser does *not* copy event handlers when an element is cloned.
objectAll	Set to true if the JavaScript getElementsByTagName() method returns all descendants of the element when passed "*".
opacity	Set to true if the browser correctly interprets the standard opacity CSS property.
scriptEval	Set to true if the browser evaluates <script> blocks when they're injected via calls to the appendChild() or createTextNode() methods.
style	Set to true if the attribute for obtaining the inline style properties of an element is style.
tbody	Set to true if a browser doesn't automatically insert <tbody> elements into tables lacking them when injected via innerHTML.

Table 6.2 shows the values for each of these flags for the various browser families.

Table 6.2   Browser results for the $.support flags

Flag property	Gecko (Firefox, Camino, etc.)	WebKit (Safari, OmniWeb, Chrome, etc.)	Opera	IE
boxModel	true	true	true	false in quirks mode, true in standards mode
cssFloat	true	true	true	false
hrefNormalized	true	true	true	false
htmlSerialize	true	true	true	false
leadingWhitespace	true	true	true	false
noCloneEvent	true	true	true	false
objectAll	true	true	true	false
opacity	true	true	true	false
scriptEval	true	true	true	false
style	true	true	true	false
tbody	true	true	true	false

As expected, it comes down to the differences between Internet Explorer and the standards-compliant browsers. But lest this lull you into thinking that you can just fall back on browser detection, that approach fails miserably because bugs and differences may be fixed in future versions of IE. And bear in mind that the other browsers aren't immune from inadvertently introducing problems and differences.

Feature detection is always preferred over browser detection when we need to make capability decisions, but it doesn't always come to our rescue. There *are* those rare moments when we'll need to resort to making browser-specific decisions that can only be made using browser detection (we'll see an example in a moment). For those times, jQuery provides a set of flags that allow direct browser detection.

6.1.3 *The browser detection flags*

For those times when only browser detection will do, jQuery provides a set of flags that we can use for branching. They're set up when the library is loaded, making them available even before any ready handlers have executed, and they're defined as properties of an object instance with a reference of $.browser.

Note that even though these flags remain present in jQuery 1.3 and beyond, they're regarded as deprecated, meaning that they could be removed from any future release of jQuery and should be used with that in mind. These flags may have made more sense during the period when browser development had stagnated somewhat, but now that we've entered an era when browser development has picked up the pace, the capability support flags make more sense and are likely to stick around for some time.

In fact, it's recommended that, when you need something more than the core support flags provide, you create new ones of your own. But we'll get to that in just a bit.

The browser support flags are described in table 6.3.

Note that these flags don't attempt to identify the specific browser that's being used. jQuery classifies a user agent based upon which *family* of browsers it belongs to, usually determined by which rendering engine it uses. Browsers within each family will sport the same sets of characteristics, so specific browser identification should not be necessary.

Table 6.3 The $.browser user agent detection flags

Flag property	Description
msie	Set to true if the user agent is identified as any version of Internet Explorer.
mozilla	Set to true if the user agent is identified as any of the Mozilla-based browsers. This includes browsers such as Firefox and Camino.
safari	Set to true if the user agent is identified as any of the WebKit-based browsers, such as Safari, Chrome, and OmniWeb.
opera	Set to true if the user agent is identified as Opera.
version	Set to the version number of the rendering engine for the browser.

The vast majority of commonly used, modern browsers will fall into one of these four browser families, including Google Chrome, which returns `true` for the `safari` flag due to its use of the WebKit engine.

The `version` property deserves special notice because it's not as handy as we might think. The value set in this property isn't the version of the browser (as we might initially believe) but the version of the browser's rendering engine. For example, when executed within Firefox 3.6, the reported version is `1.9.2`—the version of the Gecko rendering engine. This value *is* handy for distinguishing between versions of Internet Explorer, as the rendering engine versions and browser versions match.

We mentioned earlier that there are times when we can't fall back on feature detection and must resort to browser detection. One example of such a situation is when the difference between browsers isn't that they present different object classes or different methods, but that the parameters passed to a method are interpreted differently across the browser implementations. In such a case, there's no object or feature on which to perform detection.

> **NOTE**   Even in these cases, it's possible to set a feature flag by trying the operation in a hidden area of the page (as jQuery does to set some of its feature flags). But that's not a technique we often see used on many pages outside of jQuery.

Let's take the `add()` method of `<select>` elements as an example. It's defined by the W3C as follows (at http://www.w3.org/TR/DOM-Level-2-HTML/html.html#ID-14493106, for those of us who like to look at the specifications):

```
selectElement.add(element,before)
```

For this method, the first parameter identifies an `<option>` or `<optgroup>` element to add to the `<select>` element and the second identifies the existing `<option>` (or `<optgroup>`) before which the new element is to be placed. In standards-compliant browsers, this second parameter is a *reference* to the existing element as specified; in Internet Explorer, however, it's the *ordinal index* of the existing element.

Because there's no way to perform feature detection to determine whether we should pass an object reference or an integer value (short of trying it out, as noted previously), we can resort to browser detection, as shown in the following example:

```
var select = $('#aSelectElement')[0];
select.add(
  new Option('Two and \u00BD','2.5'), $.browser.msie ? 2 : select.options[2]
);
```

In this code, we perform a simple test of the `$.browser.msie` flag to determine whether it's appropriate to pass the ordinal value 2, or the reference to the third option in the `<select>` element.

The jQuery team, however, recommends that we not directly use such browser detection in our code. Rather, it's recommended that we abstract away the browser detection by creating a custom support flag of our own. That way, should the browser support flags vanish, our code is insulated from the change by merely finding another way to set the flag in one location.

For example, somewhere in our own JavaScript library code, we could write

```
$.support.useIntForSelectAdds = $.browser.msie;
```

and use that flag in our code. Should the browser detection flag ever be removed, we'd only have to change our library code; all the code that uses the custom flag would be insulated from the change.

Let's now leave the world of flags and look at the utility functions that jQuery provides.

6.2   *Using other libraries with jQuery*

Back in chapter 1, we introduced a means, thoughtfully provided for us by the jQuery team, to easily use jQuery on the same page as other libraries.

Usually, the definition of the $ global name is the largest point of contention and conflict when using other libraries on the same page as jQuery. As we know, jQuery uses $ as an alias for the `jQuery` name, which is used for every feature that jQuery exposes. But other libraries, most notably Prototype, use the $ name as well.

jQuery provides the `$.noConflict()` utility function to relinquish control of the $ identifier to whatever other library might wish to use it. The syntax of this function is as follows:

Function syntax: $.noConflict

`$.noConflict(jqueryToo)`
Restores control of the $ identifier back to another library, allowing mixed library use on pages using jQuery. Once this function is executed, jQuery features will need to be invoked using the `jQuery` identifier rather than the $ identifier.
Optionally, the `jQuery` identifier can also be given up.
This method should be called after including jQuery but before including the conflicting library.

Parameters
    `jqueryToo`   (Boolean) If provided and set to `true`, the `jQuery` identifier is given up in
                      addition to the $.

Returns
jQuery

Because $ is an alias for `jQuery`, all of jQuery's functionality is still available after the application of `$.noConflict()`, albeit by using the `jQuery` identifier. To compensate for the loss of the brief—yet beloved—$, we can define our own shorter, but nonconflicting, alias for `jQuery`, such as

```
var $j = jQuery;
```

Another idiom we may often see employed is to create an environment where the $ identifier is scoped to refer to the `jQuery` object. This technique is commonly used when extending jQuery, particularly by plugin authors who can't make any assumptions regarding whether page authors have called `$.noConflict()` and who, most certainly, can't subvert the wishes of the page authors by calling it themselves.

This idiom is as follows:

```
(function($) { /* function body here */ })(jQuery);
```

If this notation makes your head spin, don't worry! It's pretty straightforward, even if odd-looking to those encountering it for the first time.

Let's dissect the first part of this idiom:

```
(function($) { /* function body here */ })
```

This part declares a function and encloses it in parentheses to make an expression out of it, resulting in a reference to the anonymous function being returned as the value of the expression. The function expects a single parameter, which it names $; whatever is passed to this function can be referenced by the $ identifier within the body of the function. And because parameter declarations have precedence over any similarly named identifiers in the global scope, any value defined for $ outside of the function is superseded within the function by the passed argument.

The second part of the idiom,

```
(jQuery)
```

performs a function call on the anonymous function passing the `jQuery` object as the argument.

As a result, the $ identifier refers to the `jQuery` object within the body of the function, regardless of whether it's already defined by Prototype or some other library *outside* of the function. Pretty nifty, isn't it?

When employing this technique, the external declaration of $ isn't available within the body of the function.

A variant of this idiom is also frequently used to form a third syntax for declaring a ready handler in addition to the means that we already examined in chapter 1. Consider the following:

```
jQuery(function($) {
  alert("I'm ready!");
});
```

By passing a function as the parameter to the `jQuery` function, we declare it as a ready handler, as we saw in chapter 1. But this time, we declare a single parameter to be passed to the ready handler using the $ identifier. Because jQuery always passes a reference to `jQuery` to a ready handler as its first and only parameter, this guarantees that the $ name refers to `jQuery` inside the ready handler regardless of whatever definition $ might have outside the body of the handler.

Let's prove it to ourselves with a simple test. For the first part of the test, let's examine the HTML document in listing 6.1 (available in chapter6/ready.handler. test.1.html).

Listing 6.1   Ready handler test 1

```
<!DOCTYPE html>
<html>
  <head>
    <title>Hi!</title>
    <script type="text/javascript" src="../scripts/jquery-1.4.js"></script>
    <script type="text/javascript">
      var $ = 'Hi!';
      jQuery(function(){
        alert('$ = '+ $);
      });
    </script>
  </head>
  <body></body>
</html>
```

❷ Declares the ready handler

❶ Overrides $ name with custom value

In this example, we import jQuery, which (as we know) defines the global names jQuery and its alias $. We then redefine the global $ variable to a string value ❶, overriding the jQuery definition. We replace $ with a simple string value for simplicity within this example, but it could be redefined by including another library such as Prototype.

We then define the ready handler ❷ whose only action is to display an alert showing the value of $.

When we load this page, we see the alert displayed, as shown in figure 6.1.

Note that, within the ready handler, the *global* value of $ is in scope and has the expected redefined value resulting from our string assignment. How disappointing if we wanted to use the jQuery definition of $ within the handler.

Now let's make one change to this example document. The following code shows only the portion of the document that has been modified; the minimal change is highlighted in bold. (You can get the full page in chapter6/ready.handler.test.2.html.)

```
<script type="text/javascript">
  var $ = 'Hi!';
  jQuery(function($){
    alert('$ = '+ $);
  });
</script>
```

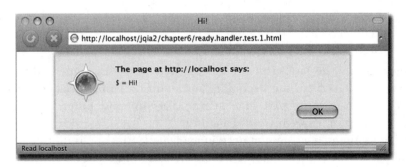

Figure 6.1   The $ says, "Hi!" as its redefinition takes effect within the ready handler.

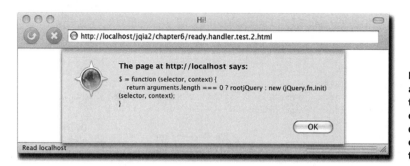

Figure 6.2   The alert now displays the jQuery version of $ because its definition has been enforced within the function.

The only change we made was to add a parameter to the ready handler function named $. When we load this changed version, we see something completely different, as shown in figure 6.2.

Well, that may not have been exactly what we might have predicted in advance, but a quick glance at the jQuery source code shows that, because we declare the first parameter of the ready handler to be $ within that function, the $ identifier refers to the jQuery function that jQuery passes as the sole parameter to all ready handlers (so the alert displays the definition of that function).

When writing reusable components, which might or might not be used in pages where $.noConflict() is used, it's best to take such precautions regarding the definition of $.

A good number of the remaining jQuery utility functions are used to manipulate JavaScript objects. Let's take a good look at them.

6.3   *Manipulating JavaScript objects and collections*

The majority of jQuery features implemented as utility functions are designed to operate on JavaScript objects other than the DOM elements. Generally, anything designed to operate on the DOM is provided as a jQuery wrapper method. Although some of these functions can be used to operate on DOM elements—which *are* JavaScript objects, after all—the focus of the utility functions isn't DOM-centric.

These functions run the gamut from simple string manipulation and type testing to complex collection filtering, serialization of form values, and even implementing a form of object inheritance through property merging.

Let's start with one that's pretty basic.

6.3.1   *Trimming strings*

Almost inexplicably, the JavaScript String type doesn't possess a method to remove whitespace characters from the beginning and end of a string instance. Such basic functionality is customarily part of a String class in most other languages, but JavaScript mysteriously lacks this useful feature.

Yet string trimming is a common need in many JavaScript applications; one prominent example is during form data validation. Because whitespace is invisible on the screen (hence its name), it's easy for users to accidentally enter extra space characters before or after valid entries in text boxes or text areas. During validation, we want to silently trim such whitespace from the data rather than alerting the user to the fact that something they can't see is tripping them up.

To help us out, jQuery defines the `$.trim()` function as follows:

Function syntax: $.trim

`$.trim(value)`

Removes any leading or trailing whitespace characters from the passed string and returns the result.

Whitespace characters are defined by this function as any character matching the JavaScript regular expression `\s`, which matches not only the space character but also the form feed, new line, return, tab, and vertical tab characters, as well as the Unicode character `\u00A0`.

Parameters

value   (String) The string value to be trimmed. This original value isn't modified.

Returns

The trimmed string.

A small example of using this function to trim the value of a text field in-place is

```
$('#someField').val($.trim($('#someField').val()));
```

Be aware that this function doesn't check the parameter we pass to ensure that it's a `String` value, so we'll likely get undefined and unfortunate results (probably a JavaScript error) if we pass any other value type to this function.

Now let's look at some functions that operate on arrays and other objects.

6.3.2 *Iterating through properties and collections*

Oftentimes when we have nonscalar values composed of other components, we'll need to iterate over the contained items. Whether the container element is a JavaScript array (containing any number of other JavaScript values, including other arrays) or instances of JavaScript objects (containing properties), the JavaScript language gives us means to iterate over them. For arrays, we iterate over their elements using the `for` loop; for objects, we iterate over their properties using the `for-in` loop.

We can code examples of each as follows:

```
var anArray = ['one','two','three'];
for (var n = 0; n < anArray.length; n++) {
  //do something here
}
var anObject = {one:1, two:2, three:3};
for (var p in anObject) {
  //do something here
}
```

Pretty easy stuff, but some might think that the syntax is needlessly wordy and complex—a criticism frequently targeted at the `for` loop. We know that, for a wrapped set of DOM elements, jQuery defines the `each()` method, allowing us to easily iterate over the elements in the set without the need for messy `for`-loop syntax. For general arrays and objects, jQuery provides an analogous utility function named `$.each()`.

The really nice thing is that the same syntax is used, whether iterating over the items in an array or the properties of an object.

Function syntax: $.each

`$.each(container,callback)`

Iterates over the items in the passed container, invoking the passed callback function for each.

Parameters

`container` (Array|Object) An array whose items, or an object whose properties, are to be iterated over.

`callback` (Function) A function invoked for each element in the container. If the container is an array, this callback is invoked for each array item; if it's an object, the callback is invoked for each object property.
The first parameter to this callback is the index of the array element or the name of the object property. The second parameter is the array item or property value. The function context (`this`) of the invocation is also set to the value passed as the second parameter.

Returns

The container object.

This unified syntax can be used to iterate over either arrays or objects using the same format. With this function, we can write the previous example as follows:

```
var anArray = ['one','two','three'];
$.each(anArray,function(n,value) {
  //do something here
});

var anObject = {one:1, two:2, three:3};
$.each(anObject,function(name,value) {
  //do something here
});
```

Although using `$.each()` with an inline function may seem like a six-of-one scenario in choosing syntax, this function makes it easy to write reusable iterator functions or to factor out the body of a loop into another function for purposes of code clarity, as in the following:

```
$.each(anArray,someComplexFunction);
```

Note that when iterating over an array or object, we can break out of the loop by returning `false` from the iterator function.

> **NOTE** You may recall that we can also use the `each()` method to iterate over an array, but the `$.each()` function has a slight performance advantage over `each()`. Bear in mind that if you need to be concerned with performance to that level, you'll get the best performance from a good old-fashioned `for` loop.

Sometimes we may iterate over arrays to pick and choose elements to become part of a new array. Although we could use `$.each()` for that purpose, let's see how jQuery makes that even easier.

6.3.3 Filtering arrays

Traversing an array to find elements that match certain criteria is a frequent need of applications that handle lots of data. We might wish to filter the data for items that fall above or below a particular threshold or, perhaps, that match a certain pattern. For any filtering operation of this type, jQuery provides the `$.grep()` utility function.

The name of the `$.grep()` function might lead us to believe that the function employs the use of regular expressions like its namesake, the UNIX `grep` command. But the filtering criterion used by the `$.grep()` utility function isn't a regular expression; it's a callback function provided by the caller that defines the criteria to determine whether a data value should be included or excluded from the resulting set of values. Nothing prevents that callback from *using* regular expressions to accomplish its task, but the use of regular expressions isn't automatic.

The syntax of the function is as follows:

Function syntax: $.grep

`$.grep(array,callback,invert)`
Traverses the passed array, invoking the callback function for each element. The return value of the callback function determines whether the value is collected into a new array returned as the value of the `$.grep()` function. If the `invert` parameter is omitted or `false`, a callback value of `true` causes the data to be collected. If `invert` is `true`, a callback value of `false` causes the value to be collected.
The original array isn't modified.

Parameters
   array   (Array) The traversed array whose data values are examined for collection. This array isn't modified in any way by this operation.

  callback   (Function) A function whose return value determines whether the current data value is to be collected. A return value of `true` causes the current value to be collected, unless the value of the `invert` parameter is `true`, in which case the opposite occurs.
              This function is passed two parameters: the current data value and the index of that value within the original array.

   invert   (Boolean) If specified as `true`, it inverts the normal operation of the function.

Returns
The array of collected values.

Let's say that we want to filter an array for all values that are greater than 100. We'd do that with a statement such as the following:

```
var bigNumbers = $.grep(originalArray,function(value) {
                   return value > 100;
               });
```

The callback function that we pass to `$.grep()` can use whatever processing it likes to determine if the value should be included. The decision could be as easy as this example or, perhaps, even as complex as making synchronous Ajax calls (with the requisite performance hit) to the server to determine if the value should be included or excluded.

Even though the $.grep() function doesn't directly use regular expressions (despite its name), JavaScript regular expressions can be powerful tools in our callback functions to determine whether to include or exclude values from the resultant array. Consider a situation in which we have an array of values and wish to identify any values that don't match the pattern for United States postal codes (also known as Zip Codes).

U.S. postal codes consist of five decimal digits optionally followed by a dash and four more decimal digits. A regular expression for such a pattern would be /^\d{5}(-\d{4})?$/, so we could filter a source array for nonconformant entries with the following:

```
var badZips = $.grep(
                originalArray,
                function(value) {
                  return value.match(/^\d{5}(-\d{4})?$/) != null;
                },
                true);
```

Notable in this example is the use of the String class's match() method to determine whether a value matches the pattern or not and the specification of the invert parameter to $.grep() as true to *exclude* any values that match the pattern.

Collecting subsets of data from arrays isn't the only operation we might perform upon them. Let's look at another array-targeted function that jQuery provides.

6.3.4 *Translating arrays*

Data might not always be in the format that we need it to be. Another common operation that's frequently performed in data-centric web applications is the *translation* of a set of values to another set. Although it's a simple matter to write a for loop to create one array from another, jQuery makes it even easier with the $.map utility function.

Function syntax: $.map

$.map(array,callback)
Iterates through the passed array, invoking the callback function for each array item and collecting the return values of the function invocations in a new array.

Parameters
array   (Array) The array whose values are to be transformed to values in the new array.
callback   (Function) A function whose return values are collected in the new array returned as the result of a call to the $.map() function.
           This function is passed two parameters: the current data value and the index of that value within the original array.

Returns
The array of collected values.

Let's look at a trivial example that shows the $.map() function in action.

```
var oneBased = $.map([0,1,2,3,4],function(value){return value+1;});
```

This statement converts an array of values, a zero-based set of indexes, to a corresponding array of one-based indexes.

An important behavior to note is that if the function returns either null or undefined, the result isn't collected. In such cases, the resulting array will be smaller in length than the original, and one-to-one correspondence between items by order is lost.

Let's look at a slightly more involved example. Imagine that we have an array of strings, perhaps collected from form fields, that are expected to represent numeric values, and that we want to convert this string array to an array of corresponding Number instances. Because there's no guarantee against the presence of an invalid numeric string, we need to take some precautions. Consider the following code:

```
var strings = ['1','2','3','4','S','6'];

var values = $.map(strings,function(value){
  var result = new Number(value);
  return isNaN(result) ? null : result;
});
```

We start with an array of string values, each of which is expected to represent a numeric value. But a typo (or perhaps user entry error) resulted in the letter *S* instead of the expected number *5*. Our code handles this case by checking the Number instance created by the constructor to see if the conversion from string to numeric was successful or not. If the conversion fails, the value returned will be the constant Number.NaN. But the funny thing about Number.NaN is that, by definition, it doesn't equal anything else, *including* itself! Therefore the value of the expression Number.NaN==Number.NaN is false!

Because we can't use a comparison operator to test for NaN (which stands for *Not a Number*, by the way), JavaScript provides the isNaN() method, which we employ to test the result of the string-to-numeric conversion.

In this example, we return null in the case of failure, ensuring that the resulting array contains only the valid numeric values with any error values elided. If we want to collect all the values, we can allow the transformation function to return Number.NaN for bad values.

Another useful behavior of $.map() is that it gracefully handles the case where an *array* is returned from the transformation function, merging the returned value into the resulting array. Consider the following statement:

```
var characters = $.map(
  ['this','that','other thing'],
  function(value){return value.split('');}
);
```

This statement transforms an array of strings into an array of all the characters that make up the strings. After execution, the value of the variable characters is as follows:

```
['t','h','i','s','t','h','a','t','o','t','h','e','r',' ','t','h','i','n','g']
```

This is accomplished by use of the `String.split()` method, which returns an array of the string's characters when passed an empty string as its delimiter. This array is returned as the result of the transformation function and is merged into the resultant array.

jQuery's support for arrays doesn't stop there. There are a handful of minor functions that we might find handy.

6.3.5   *More fun with JavaScript arrays*

Have you ever needed to know if a JavaScript array contained a specific value and, perhaps, even the location of that value in the array?

If so, you'll appreciate the `$.inArray()` function.

Function syntax: $.inArray

`$.inArray(value,array)`
Returns the index position of the first occurrence of the passed value.

Parameters
value   (Object) The value for which the array will be searched.
array   (Array) The array to be searched.

Returns
The index of the first occurrence of the value within the array, or -1 if the value isn't found.

A trivial but illustrative example of using this function is

```
var index = $.inArray(2,[1,2,3,4,5]);
```

This results in the index value of 1 being assigned to the `index` variable.

Another useful array-related function creates JavaScript arrays from other array-like objects. "Other *array-like objects*? What on Earth is an array-like object?" you may ask.

jQuery considers an *array-like object* to be any object that has a length and the concept of indexed entries. This capability is most useful for `NodeList` objects. Consider the following snippet:

```
var images = document.getElementsByTagName("img");
```

This populates the variable `images` with a `NodeList` of all the images on the page.

Dealing with a `NodeList` is a bit of a pain, so converting it to a JavaScript array makes things a lot nicer. The jQuery `$.makeArray` function makes converting the `NodeList` easy.

Function syntax: $.makeArray

`$.makeArray(object)`
Converts the passed array-like object into a JavaScript array.

Parameters
object   (Object) The array-like object (such as a `NodeList`) to be converted.

Returns
The resulting JavaScript array.

This function is intended for use in code that doesn't make much use of jQuery, which internally handles this sort of thing on our behalf. This function also comes in handy when dealing with `NodeList` objects while traversing XML documents without jQuery, or when handling the `arguments` instance within functions (which, you may be surprised to learn, isn't a standard JavaScript array).

Another seldom-used function that might come in handy when dealing with arrays built outside of jQuery is the `$.unique()` function.

Function syntax: $.unique

`$.unique(array)`
Given an array of DOM elements, returns an array of the unique elements in the original array.

Parameters
> `array`   (Array) The array of DOM elements to be examined.

Returns
An array of DOM elements consisting of the unique elements in the passed array.

Again, this is a function that jQuery uses internally to ensure that the lists of elements that we receive contain unique elements. It's intended for use on element arrays created outside the bounds of jQuery.

Want to merge two arrays? No problem; there's the `$.merge` function:

Function syntax: $.merge

`$.merge(array1,array2)`
Merges the values of the second array into the first and returns the result. The first array is modified by this operation and returned as the result.

Parameters
> `array1`   (Array) An array into which the other array's values will be merged.
> `array2`   (Array) An array whose values will be merged into the first array.

Returns
The first array, modified with the results of the merge.

Consider

```
var a1 = [1,2,3,4,5];
var a2 = [5,6,7,8,9];
$.merge(a1,a2);
```

After this sequence executes, a2 is untouched, but a1 contains `[1,2,3,4,5,5,6,7,8,9]`.

Now that we've seen how jQuery helps us to easily work with arrays, let's see how it helps us manipulate plain old JavaScript objects.

6.3.6 *Extending objects*

Although we all know that JavaScript provides some features that make it act in many ways like an object-oriented language, we know that JavaScript isn't what anyone would call purely object-oriented because of the features that it doesn't support. One of these important features is *inheritance*—the manner in which new classes are defined by extending the definitions of existing classes.

A pattern for mimicking inheritance in JavaScript is to extend an object by copying the properties of a base object into the new object, extending the new object with the capabilities of the base.

> **NOTE** If you're an aficionado of "object-oriented JavaScript," you'll no doubt be familiar with extending not only object instances but also their blueprints via the `prototype` property of object constructors. `$.extend()` can be used to effect such constructor-based inheritance by extending `prototype`, as well as object-based inheritance by extending existing object instances (something jQuery does itself internally). Because understanding such advanced topics isn't a requirement in order to use jQuery effectively, this is a subject—albeit an important one—that's beyond the scope of this book.

It's fairly easy to write JavaScript code to perform this extension by copying, but as with so many other procedures, jQuery anticipates this need and provides a ready-made utility function to help us out: `$.extend()`. As we'll see in the next chapter, this function is useful for much more than extending an object. Its syntax is as follows:

Function syntax: $.extend

`$.extend(deep,target,source1,source2, ... sourceN)`
Extends the object passed as `target` with the properties of the remaining passed objects.

Parameters

`deep`	(Boolean) An optional flag that determines whether a deep or shallow copy is made. If omitted or `false`, a shallow copy is executed. If `true`, a deep copy is performed.
`target`	(Object) The object whose properties are augmented with the properties of the source objects. This object is directly modified with the new properties before being returned as the value of the function. Any properties with the same name as properties in any of the source elements are overridden with the values from the source elements.
`source1 ...` `sourceN`	(Object) One or more objects whose properties are added to the `target` object. When more than one source is provided and properties with the same names exist in the sources, sources later in the argument list override those earlier in the list.

Returns
The extended target object.

Let's take a look at this function doing its thing.

We'll set up three objects, a target and two sources, as follows:

```
var target  = { a: 1, b: 2, c: 3 };
var source1 = { c: 4, d: 5, e: 6 };
var source2 = { e: 7, f: 8, g: 9 };
```

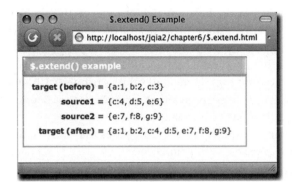

Figure 6.3 The `$.extend()` function merges properties from multiple source objects without duplicates, and gives precedence to instances in reverse order of specification.

Then we'll operate on these objects using `$.extend()` as follows:

```
$.extend(target,source1,source2);
```

This should take the contents of the source objects and merge them into the target. To test this, we've set up this example code in the file chapter6/$.extend.html, which executes the code and displays the results on the page.

Loading this page into a browser results in the display of figure 6.3.

As we can see, all properties of the source objects have been merged into the `target` object. But note the following important nuances:

- Both the `target` and `source1` contain a property named c. The value of c in `source1` replaces the value in the original target.
- Both `source1` and `source2` contain a property named e. Note that the value of e within `source2` overrides the value within `source1` when merged into `target`, demonstrating how objects later in the list of arguments take precedence over those earlier in the list.

Although it's evident that this utility function can be useful in many scenarios where one object must be extended with properties from another object (or set of objects), we'll see a concrete and common use of this feature when learning how to define utility functions of our own in the next chapter.

But before we get to that, we've still got a few other utility functions to examine.

6.3.7 *Serializing parameter values*

It should come as no surprise that in a dynamic, highly interactive application, submitting requests is a common occurrence. Heck, it's one of the things that makes the World Wide Web a web in the first place.

Frequently, these requests will be submitted as a result of a form submission, where the browser formats the request body containing the request parameters on our behalf. Other times, we'll be submitting requests as URLs in the href attribute of <a> elements. In these latter cases, it becomes our responsibility to correctly create and format the query string that contains any request parameters we wish to include with the request.

Server-side templating tools generally have great mechanisms that help us construct valid URLs, but when creating them dynamically on the client, JavaScript doesn't give us much in the way of support. Remember that not only do we need to correctly place all the ampersand (&) and equal signs (=) that format the query string parameters, we need to make sure that each name and value is properly URI-encoded. Although JavaScript provides a handy function for that (`encodeURIComponent()`), the formatting of the query string falls squarely into our laps.

And, as you might have come to expect, jQuery anticipates that burden and gives us a tool to make it easier: the `$.param()` utility function.

Function syntax: $.param

`$.param(params,traditional)`

Serializes the passed information into a string suitable for use as the query string of a submitted request. The passed value can be an array of form elements, a jQuery wrapped set, or a JavaScript object. The query string is properly formatted and each name and value in the string is properly URI-encoded.

Parameters

params	(Array|jQuery|Object) The value to be serialized into a query string. If an array of elements or a jQuery wrapped set is passed, the name/value pairs represented by the included form controls are added to the query string. If a JavaScript object is passed, the object's properties form the parameter names and values.
traditional	(Boolean) An optional flag that forces this function to perform the serialization using the same algorithm used prior to jQuery 1.4. This generally only affects source objects with nested objects. See the sections that follow for more details. If omitted, defaults to `false`.

Returns

The formatted query string.

Consider the following statement:

```
$.param({
  'a thing':'it&s=value',
  'another thing':'another value',
  'weird characters':'!@#$%^&*()_+='
});
```

Here, we pass an object with three properties to the `$.param()` function, in which the names and the values all contain characters that must be encoded within the query string in order for it to be valid. The result of this function call is

```
a+thing=it%26s%3Dvalue&another+thing=another+value
   &weird+characters=!%40%23%24%25%5E%26*()_%2B%3D
```

Note how the query string is formatted correctly and that the non-alphanumeric characters in the names and values have been properly encoded. This might not make the string all that readable to us, but server-side code lives for such strings!

One note of caution: if you pass an array of elements, or a jQuery wrapped set, that contains elements other than those representing form values, you'll end up with a bunch of entries such as

```
&undefined=undefined
```

in the resulting string, because this function doesn't weed out inappropriate elements in its passed argument.

You might be thinking that this isn't a big deal because, after all, if the values are form elements, they're going to end up being submitted by the browser via the form, which is going to handle all of this for us. Well, hold on to your hat. In chapter 8, when we start talking about Ajax, we'll see that form elements aren't always submitted by their forms!

But that's not going to be an issue, because we'll also see later on that jQuery provides a higher-level means (that internally uses this very utility function) to handle this sort of thing in a more sophisticated fashion.

SERIALIZING NESTED PARAMETERS

Trained by years of dealing with the limitations of HTTP and HTML form controls, web developers are conditioned to think of serialized parameters, aka query strings, as a flat list of name/value pairs.

For example, imagine a form in which we collect someone's name and address. The query parameters for such a form might contain names such as `firstName`, `lastName` and `city`. The serialized version of the query string might be:

```
firstName=Yogi&lastName=Bear&streetAddress=123+Anywhere+Lane
  ➡ &city=Austin&state=TX&postalCode=78701
```

The pre-serialized version of this construct would be:

```
{
  firstName: 'Yogi',
  lastName: 'Bear',
  streetAddress: '123 Anywhere Lane',
  city: 'Austin',
  state: 'TX',
  postalCode : '78701'
}
```

As an object, that doesn't really represent the way that we'd think about such data. From a data organization point of view, we might think of this data as two major elements, a name and an address, each with their own properties. Perhaps something along the lines of:

```
{
  name: {
    first: 'Yogi',
    last: 'Bear'
  },
  address: {
    street: '123 Anywhere Lane',
```

```
      city: 'Austin',
      state: 'TX',
      postalCode : '78701'
    }
}
```

But this nested version of the element, though more logically structured than the flat version, doesn't easily lend itself to conversion to a query string.

Or does it?

By using a conventional notation employing square brackets, such a construct could be expressed as the following:

```
name[first]=Yogi&name[last]=Bear&address[street]=123+Anywhere+Lane
    ➥ &address[city]=Austin&address[state]=TX&address[postalCode]=78701
```

In this notation, sub-properties are expressed using square brackets to keep track of the structure. Many server-side frameworks such as RoR (Ruby on Rails) and PHP can handily decode these strings. Java doesn't have any native facility to reconstruct a nested object from such notation, but such a processor would be pretty easy to build.

This is new behavior in jQuery 1.4—older versions of jQuery's $.param() function did not produce anything meaningful when passed a nested construct. If we want to cause $.param() to exhibit the older behavior, the traditional parameter should be passed as true.

We can prove this to ourselves with the $.param() Lab Page provided in file chapter6/lab.$.param.html, and shown in figure 6.4.

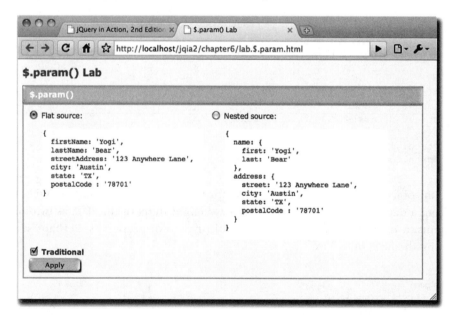

Figure 6.4   The $.param() Lab lets us see how flat and nested objects are serialized using the new and traditional algorithms.

This Lab lets us see how `$.param()` will serialize flat and nested objects, using its new algorithm, as well as the traditional algorithm.

Go ahead and play around with this Lab until you feel comfortable with the action of the function. We even urge you to make a copy of the page and play around with different object structures that you might want to serialize.

6.3.8 Testing objects

You may have noticed that many of the jQuery wrapper methods and utility functions have rather malleable parameter lists; optional parameters can be omitted without the need to include `null` values as placeholders.

Take the `bind()` wrapper method as an example. Its function signature is

```
bind(event,data,handler)
```

But if we have no data to pass to the event, we can simply call `bind()` with the handler function as the second parameter. jQuery handles this by testing the types of the parameters, and if it sees that there are only two parameters, and that a function is passed as the second parameter, it interprets that as the handler rather than as a data argument.

Testing parameters for various types, including whether they are functions or not, will certainly come in handy if we want to create our own functions and methods that are similarly friendly and versatile, so jQuery exposes a number of testing utility functions, as outlined in table 6.4.

Table 6.4 jQuery offers utility functions for testing objects

Function	Description
`$.isArray(o)`	Returns `true` if o is a JavaScript array (but not if o is any other array-like object like a jQuery wrapped set).
`$.isEmptyObject(o)`	Returns `true` if o is a JavaScript object with no properties, including any inherited from `prototype`.
`$.isFunction(o)`	Returns `true` if o is a JavaScript function. Warning: in Internet Explorer, built-in functions such as `alert()` and `confirm()`, as well as element methods are not correctly reported as functions.
`$.isPlainObject(o)`	Returns `true` if o is a JavaScript object created via `{}` or `new Object()`.
`$.isXMLDoc(node)`	Returns `true` if node is an XML document, or a node within an XML document.

Now let's look at a handful of miscellaneous utility functions that don't really fit into any one category.

6.4   *Miscellaneous utility functions*

This section will explore the set of utility functions that each pretty much define their own category. We'll start with one that doesn't seem to do very much at all.

6.4.1   *Doing nothing*

jQuery defines a utility function that does nothing at all. This function could have been named `$.wastingAwayAgainInMargaritaville()`, but that's a tad long so it's named `$.noop()`. It's defined with the following syntax:

Function syntax: $.noop

`$.noop()`
Does nothing.

Parameters
 none
Returns
Nothing.

Hmmm, a function that is passed nothing, does nothing, and returns nothing. What's the point?

Recall how many jQuery methods are passed parameters, or option values, that are optional function callbacks? `$.noop()` serves as a handy default for those callbacks when the user does not supply one.

6.4.2   *Testing for containment*

When we want to test one element for containment within another, jQuery provides the `$.contains()` utility function:

Function syntax: $.contains

`$.contains(container,containee)`
Tests if one element is contained within another with the DOM hierarchy.

Parameters
 container   (Element) The DOM element being tested as containing another element.
 containee   (Element) The DOM element being tested for containment.

Returns
true if the containee is contained within the container; false otherwise.

Hey, wait a minute! Doesn't this sound familiar? Indeed, we discussed the `has()` method back in chapter 2, to which this function bears a striking resemblance.

This function, used frequently internally to jQuery, is most useful when we already have references to the DOM elements to be tested, and there's no need to take on the overhead of creating a wrapped set.

Let's look at another function that closely resembles its wrapper-method equivalent.

6.4.3   *Tacking data onto elements*

Back in chapter 3, we examined the `data()` method, which allows us to assign data to DOM elements. For those cases where we already have a DOM element reference, we can use the low-level utility function `$.data()` to perform the same action:

Function syntax: $.data

`$.data(element,name,value)`

Stores or retrieves data on the passed element using the specified name.

Parameters

element	(Element) The DOM element upon which the data is to be established, or from which the data is to be retrieved.
name	(String) The name with which the data is associated.
value	(Object) The data to be assigned to the element with the given name. If omitted, the named data is retrieved.

Returns

The data value that was stored or retrieved.

As might be expected, we can also remove the data via a utility function:

Function syntax: $.removeData

`$.removeData(element,name)`

Removes data stored on the passed element.

Parameters

element	(Element) The DOM element from which the data is to be removed.
name	(String) The name of the data item to be removed. If omitted, all stored data is removed.

Returns

Nothing.

Now let's turn our attention to one of the more esoteric utility functions—one that lets us have a pronounced effect on how event listeners are called.

6.4.4   *Prebinding function contexts*

As we've seen throughout our examination of jQuery, functions and their contexts play an important role in jQuery-using code. In the coming chapters on Ajax (chapter 8) and jQuery UI (chapters 9 through 11), we'll see an even stronger emphasis on functions, particularly when used as callbacks.

The contexts of functions—what's pointed to by `this`—is determined by how the function is invoked (see the appendix if you want to review this concept). When we want to call a particular function and explicitly control what the function context will be, we can use the `Function.call()` method to invoke the function.

But what if we're not the ones calling the function? What if, for example, the function is a callback? In that case, we're not the ones invoking the function so we can't use `Function.call()` to affect the setting of the function context.

jQuery gives us a utility function by which we can prebind an object to a function such that when the function is invoked, the bound object will become the function context. This utility function is named $.proxy(), and its syntax is as follows:

Function syntax: $.proxy

$.proxy(function,proxy)
$.proxy(proxy,property)
Creates a copy of a function with a prebound proxy object to serve as the function context when the function is invoked as a callback.

Parameters

function	(Function) The function to be prebound with the proxy object.
proxy	(Object) The object to be bound as the proxy function context.
property	(String) The name of the property within the object passed as proxy that contains the function to be bound.

Returns
The new function prebound with the proxy object.

Bring up the example in file chapter6/$.proxy.html. You'll see a display as shown in figure 6.5.

In this example page, a Test button is created within a `<div>` element with an `id` value of `buttonContainer`. When the Normal radio button is clicked, a click handler is established on the button and its container as follows:

```
$('#testButton,#buttonContainer').click(
  function(){ say(this.id); }
);
```

When the button is clicked, we'd expect the established handler to be invoked on the button and, because of event bubbling, on its parent container. In each case, the function context of the invocation should be the element upon which the handler was established.

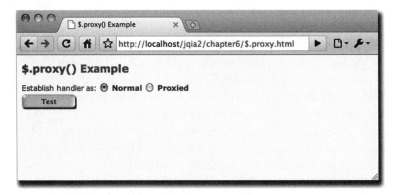

Figure 6.5   The $.proxy example page will help us see the difference between normal and proxied callbacks.

The results of the call to say(this.id) within the handler (which reports the id property of the function context) show that all is as expected—see the top portion of figure 6.6. The handler is invoked twice: first on the button and then on the container, with each element respectively set as the function context.

However, when the Proxy radio button is checked, the handler is established as follows:

```
$('#testButton,#buttonContainer').click(
  $.proxy(function(){ say(this.id); }, $('#controlPanel')[0])
);
```

This establishes the same handler as before, *except* that the handler function has been passed through the $.proxy() utility function, prebinding an object to the handler.

In this case, we bound the element with the id of controlPanel. The bound object does not *have* to be an element—in fact, most often it won't be. We just chose it for this example because it makes the object easy to identify via its id value.

Now when we click the Test button, we see the display at the bottom of figure 6.6, showing that the function context has been forced to be the object that we bound to the handler with $.proxy().

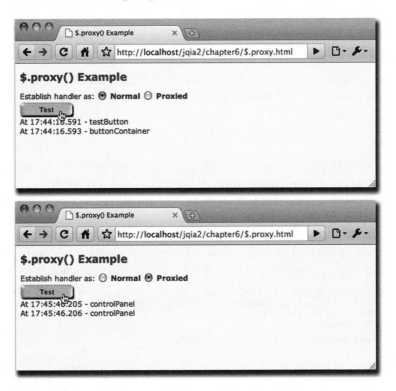

Figure 6.6 This example shows the effects of prebinding an object to the click handler for the Test button.

This ability is really useful for providing data to a callback that it might not normally have access to via closures or other means.

The most common use case for `$.proxy()` is when we want to bind a method of an object as a handler, and have the method's owning object established as the handler's function context exactly as if we had called the method directly. Consider an object such as this:

```
var o = {
  id: 'o',
  hello: function() { alert("Hi there! I'm " + this.id); }
};
```

If we were to call the `hello()` method via `o.hello()`, the function context (`this`) would be o. But if we establish the function as a handler like so,

```
$(whatever).click(o.hello);
```

we find that the function context is the current bubbling element, not o. And if our handler relies upon o, we're rather screwed.

We can unwedge ourselves by using `$.proxy()` to force the function context to be o with one of these two statements:

```
$(whatever).click($.proxy(o.hello,o));
```
or
```
$(whatever).click($.proxy(o,'hello'));
```

Be aware that going this route means that you will not have any way of knowing the current bubble element of the event propagation—the value normally established as the function context.

6.4.5 *Parsing JSON*

JSON has fast become an Internet darling child, threatening to push the more stodgy-seeming XML off the interchange-format pedestal. As most JSON is also valid JavaScript expression syntax, the JavaScript `eval()` function has long been used to convert a JSON string to its JavaScript equivalent.

Modern browsers provide `JSON.parse()` to parse JSON, but not everyone has the luxury of assuming that all of their users will be running the latest and greatest. Understanding this, jQuery provides the `$.parseJSON()` utility function.

Function syntax: $.parseJSON

`$.parseJSON(json)`
Parses the passed JSON string, returning its evaluation.

Parameters
   `json`   (String) The JSON string to be parsed.

Returns
The evaluation of the JSON string.

When the browser supports JSON.parse(), jQuery will use it. Otherwise, it will use a JavaScript trick to perform the evaluation.

Bear in mind that the JSON string must be completely *well-formed*, and that the rules for well-formed JSON are much more strict than JavaScript expression notation. For example, all property names must be delimited by double-quote characters, even if they form valid identifiers. And that's *double*-quote characters—single-quote characters won't cut it. Invalid JSON will result in an error being thrown. See http://www.json.org/ for the nitty-gritty on well-formed JSON.

Speaking of evaluations ...

6.4.6 Evaluating expressions

While the use of eval() is derided by some Internet illuminati, there are times when it's quite useful.

But eval() executes in the current context. When writing plugins and other reusable scripts, we might want to ensure that the evaluation always takes place in the global context. Enter the $.globalEval() utility function.

> ### Function syntax: $.globalEval
>
> **$.globalEval(code)**
> Evaluates the passed JavaScript code in the global context.
>
> **Parameters**
> code (String) The JavaScript code to be evaluated.
>
> **Returns**
> The evaluation of the JavaScript code.

Let's wrap up our investigation of the utility functions with one that we can use to dynamically load new scripts into our pages.

6.4.7 Dynamically loading scripts

Most of the time, we'll load the external scripts that our page needs from script files when the page loads via <script> tags in the <head> of the page. But every now and again, we might want to load a script after the fact under script control.

We might do this because we don't know if the script will be needed until after some specific user activity has taken place, and we don't want to include the script unless it's absolutely needed. Or perhaps we might need to use some information not available at load time to make a conditional choice between various scripts.

Regardless of why we might want to dynamically load new scripts into the page, jQuery provides the $.getScript() utility function to make it easy.

Function syntax: $.getScript

`$.getScript(url,callback)`

Fetches the script specified by the `url` parameter using a `GET` request to the specified server, optionally invoking a callback upon success.

Parameters

`url`   (String) The URL of the script file to fetch. The URL is *not* restricted to the same domain as the containing page.

`callback`   (Function) An optional function invoked after the script resource has been loaded and evaluated, with the following parameters: the text loaded from the resource, and a text status message: "success" if all has gone well.

Returns

The XMLHttpRequest instance used to fetch the script.

Under its covers, this function uses jQuery's built-in Ajax mechanisms to fetch the script file. We'll be covering these Ajax facilities in great detail in chapter 8, but we don't need to know anything about Ajax to use this function.

After fetching, the script in the file is evaluated, any inline script is executed, and any defined variables or functions become available.

> **WARNING** In Safari 2 and older, the script definitions loaded from the fetched file don't become available right away, even in the callback to the function. Any dynamically loaded script elements don't become available until after the script block within which it is loaded relinquishes control back to the browser. If your pages are going to support these older versions of Safari, plan accordingly!

Let's see this in action. Consider the following script file (available in chapter6/new.stuff.js):

```
alert("I'm inline!");
var someVariable = 'Value of someVariable';
function someFunction(value) {
  alert(value);
};
```

This trivial script file contains an inline statement (which issues an alert that leaves no doubt as to when the statement gets executed), a variable declaration, and a declaration for a function that issues an alert containing whatever value is passed to it when executed. Now let's write a page to include this script file dynamically. The page is shown in listing 6.2 and can be found in the file chapter6/$.getScript.html.

Listing 6.2 Dynamically loading a script file and examining the results

```
<!DOCTYPE html>
<html>
  <head>
    <title>$.getScript() Example</title>
    <link rel="stylesheet" type="text/css" href="../styles/core.css" />
    <script type="text/javascript" src="../scripts/jquery-1.4.js"></script>
```

```
<script type="text/javascript"
        src="../scripts/jqia2.support.js"></script>
<script type="text/javascript">
  $(function(){
    $('#loadButton').click(function(){
      $.getScript(
        'new.stuff.js'
        //,function(){$('#inspectButton').click()}
      );
    });
    $('#inspectButton').click(function(){
      someFunction(someVariable);
    });
  });
</script>
</head>

<body>
  <button type="button" id="loadButton">Load</button>
  <button type="button" id="inspectButton">Inspect</button>
</body>
</html>
```

1 Fetches script on clicking **Load** button

2 Displays result on clicking **Inspect** button

3 Contains test buttons

This page defines two buttons **3** that we use to trigger the activity of the example. The first button, labeled Load, causes the new.stuff.js file to be dynamically loaded through use of the `$.getScript()` function **1**. Note that, initially, the second parameter (the callback) is commented out—we'll get to that in a moment.

On clicking the Load button, the new.stuff.js file is loaded, and its content is evaluated. As expected, the inline statement within the file triggers an alert message, as shown in figure 6.7.

Clicking the Inspect button executes its `click` handler **2**, which executes the dynamically loaded `someFunction()` function, passing the value of the dynamically loaded `someVariable` variable. If the alert appears as shown in figure 6.8, we know that both the variable and function are loaded correctly.

If you're still running Safari 2 or older (which is very out-of-date at this point) and would like to observe the behavior of older versions of Safari that we warned you about earlier, make a copy of the HTML file for the page shown in figure 6.8, and

Figure 6.7 The dynamic loading and evaluation of the script file results in the inline alert statement being executed.

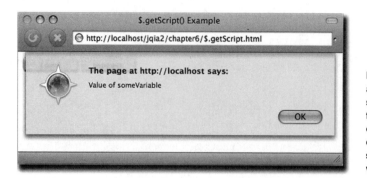

Figure 6.8 The appearance of the alert shows that the dynamic function is loaded correctly, and the correctly displayed value shows that the variable was dynamically loaded.

uncomment the callback parameter to the $.getScript() function. This callback executes the click handler for the Inspect button, calling the dynamically loaded function with the loaded variable as its parameter.

In browsers other than Safari 2, the function and variable loaded dynamically from the script are available within the callback function. But when executed on Safari 2, nothing happens! We need to take heed of this divergence of functionality when using the $.getScript() function in Safari's older versions.

6.5   Summary

In this chapter we surveyed the features that jQuery provides outside of the methods that operate upon a wrapped set of matched DOM elements. These included an assortment of functions, as well as a set of flags, defined directly on the jQuery top-level name (as well as its $ alias).

We saw how jQuery informs us about the capabilities of the containing browser using the various flags in the $.support object. When we need to resort to browser detection to account for differences in browser capabilities and operations beyond what $.support provides, the $.browser set of flags lets us determine within which browser family the page is being displayed. Browser detection should be used only as a last resort when it's impossible to write the code in a browser-independent fashion and the preferred approach of feature detection can't be employed.

Recognizing that page authors may sometimes wish to use other libraries in conjunction with jQuery, jQuery provides $.noConflict(), which allows other libraries to use the $ alias. After calling this function, all jQuery operations must use the jQuery name rather than $.

$.trim() exists to fill the gap left by the native JavaScript String class for trimming whitespace from the beginning and end of string values.

jQuery also provides a set of functions that are useful for dealing with data sets in arrays. $.each() makes it easy to traverse through every item in an array; $.grep() allows us to create new arrays by filtering the data of a source array using whatever filtering criteria we'd like to use; and $.map() allows us to easily apply our own transformations to a source array to produce a corresponding new array with the transformed values.

We can convert `NodeList` instances to JavaScript arrays with `$.makeArray()`, test to see if a value is in an array with `$.inArray()`, and even test if a value is an array itself with `$.isArray()`. We can also test for functions using `$.isFunction()`.

We also saw how jQuery lets us construct properly formatted and encoded query strings with `$.param()`.

To merge objects, perhaps even to mimic a sort of inheritance scheme, jQuery also provides the `$.extend()` function. This function allows us to unite the properties of any number of source objects into a target object.

We also saw a bevy of functions for testing objects to see if they're functions, JavaScript objects, or even empty objects—useful for many situations, but particularly when inspecting variable argument lists.

The `$.proxy()` method can be used to prebind an object to later be used as the function context for an event handler invocation, and the `$.noop()` function can be used to do nothing at all!

And for those times when we want to load a script file dynamically, jQuery defines `$.getScript()`, which can load and evaluate a script file at any point in the lifetime of a page, even from domains other than the page source.

With these additional tools safely tucked away in our toolbox, we're ready to tackle adding our own extensions to jQuery. Let's get to it in the next chapter.

Expand your reach
by extending jQuery

This chapter covers

- Why to extend jQuery with custom code
- Guidelines for effectively extending jQuery
- Writing custom utility functions
- Writing custom wrapper methods

Over the course of the previous chapters, we've seen that jQuery gives us a large toolset of useful methods and functions, and we've also seen that we can easily tie these tools together to give our pages whatever behavior we choose. Sometimes that code follows common patterns we want to use again and again. When such patterns emerge, it makes sense to capture these repeated operations as reusable tools that we can add to our original toolset. In this chapter, we'll explore how to capture these reusable fragments of code as extensions to jQuery.

But before any of that, let's discuss *why* we'd want to pattern our own code as extensions to jQuery in the first place.

7.1   Why extend jQuery?

If you've been paying attention while reading through this book, and you've been reviewing the code examples presented within it, you undoubtedly will have noted that adopting jQuery for use in our pages has a profound effect on how script is written within a page.

jQuery promotes a certain style for a page's code: generally forming a wrapped set of elements and then applying a jQuery method, or chain of methods, to that set. When writing our own code, we can write it however we please, but most experienced developers agree that having all of the code on a site, or at least the great majority of it, adhere to a consistent style is a good practice.

So one good reason to pattern our code as jQuery extensions is to help maintain a consistent code style throughout the site.

Not reason enough? Need more? The whole point of jQuery is to provide a set of reusable tools and APIs. The creators of jQuery carefully planned the design of the library and the philosophy of how the tools are arranged to promote reusability. By following the precedent set by the design of these tools, we automatically reap the benefits of the planning that went into these designs—a compelling second reason to write our code as jQuery extensions.

Still not convinced? The final reason we'll consider (though it's quite possible others could list even more reasons) is that, by extending jQuery, we can leverage the existing code base that jQuery makes available to us. For example, by creating new jQuery methods (wrapper methods), we automatically inherit the use of jQuery's powerful selector mechanism. Why write everything from scratch when we can layer upon the powerful tools jQuery already provides?

Given these reasons, it's easy to see that writing our reusable components as jQuery extensions is a good practice and a smart way of working. In the remainder of this chapter, we'll examine the guidelines and patterns that allow us to create jQuery plugins, and we'll create a few of our own. In the following chapter, which covers a completely different subject (Ajax), we'll see even more evidence that creating our own reusable components as jQuery plugins in real-world scenarios helps to keep the code consistent and makes it a whole lot easier to write those components in the first place.

But first, the guidelines ...

7.2   The jQuery plugin authoring guidelines

> *Sign! Sign! Everywhere a sign!*
> *Blocking out the scenery, breaking my mind.*
> *Do this! Don't do that! Can't you read the sign?*
> —Five Man Electrical Band, 1971

Although the Five Man Electrical Band may have lyrically asserted an anti-establishment stance against rules back in 1971, sometimes rules are a good thing. Without any, chaos would reign.

So it is with the rules—which are more like common-sense guidelines—governing how to successfully extend jQuery with our own plugin code. These guidelines help us ensure that not only does our new code plug into the jQuery architecture properly, but also that it will work and play well with other jQuery plugins, and even other JavaScript libraries.

Extending jQuery takes one of two forms:

- Utility functions defined directly on $ (an alias for `jQuery`)
- Methods to operate on a jQuery wrapped set (what we've been calling jQuery *methods*)

In the remainder of this section, we'll go over some guidelines common to both types of extensions. Then, in the following sections, we'll tackle the guidelines and techniques specific to writing each type of plugin.

7.2.1   *Naming files and functions*

To Tell the Truth was an American game show, first airing in the 1950s, in which multiple contestants claimed to be the same person with the same name, and a panel of celebrities was tasked with determining which of the contestants was in reality the person they all claimed to be. Although fun for a television audience, name collisions aren't fun at all when it comes to programming.

We'll discuss avoiding name collisions *within* our plugins, but first let's address naming the files within which we'll write our plugins so that they don't conflict with other files.

The guideline recommended by the jQuery team is simple but effective, advocating the following format:

- Prefix the filename with *jquery.*
- Follow that with the name of the plugin.
- Optionally, include the major and minor version numbers of the plugin.
- Conclude with *.js.*

For example, if we write a plugin that we want to name "Fred", our JavaScript filename for this plugin could be jquery.fred-1.0.js. The use of the "jquery" prefix eliminates any possible name collisions with files intended for use with other libraries. After all, anyone writing non-jQuery plugins has no business using the "jquery" prefix, but that leaves the plugin name itself still open for contention *within* the jQuery community.

When we're writing plugins for our own use, all we need to do is avoid conflicts with any other plugins that we plan to use. But when writing plugins that we plan to publish for others to use, we need to avoid conflicts with any other plugin that's already published.

The best way to avoid conflicts is to stay in tune with the goings-on within the jQuery community. A good starting point is the page at http://plugins.jquery.com/, but beyond being aware of what's already out there, there are other precautions we can take.

One way to ensure that our plugin filenames are unlikely to conflict with others is to subprefix them with a name that's unique to us or our organization. For example, all of the plugins developed in this book use the filename prefix "jquery.jqia" (*jqia* being short for *jQuery in Action*) to help make sure that they won't conflict with anyone else's plugin filenames, should anyone wish to use them in their own web applications. Likewise, the files for the jQuery Form Plugin begin with the prefix "jquery.form". Not all plugins follow this convention, but as the number of plugins increases, it will become more and more important to follow such conventions.

Similar considerations need to be taken with the *names* we give to our functions, whether they're new utility functions or methods on the jQuery wrappers.

When creating plugins for our own use, we're usually aware of what other plugins we'll use; it's an easy matter to avoid any naming collisions. But what if we're creating our plugins for public consumption? Or what if our plugins, which we initially intended to use privately, turn out to be so useful that we want to share them with the rest of the community?

Once again, familiarity with the plugins that already exist will go a long way in avoiding API collisions, but we also encourage gathering collections of related functions under a common prefix (similar to the proposal for filenames) to avoid cluttering the namespace.

Now, what about conflicts with $?

7.2.2 Beware the $

"Will the real $ please stand up?"

Having written a fair amount of jQuery code, we've seen how handy it is to use the $ alias in place of `jQuery`. But when writing plugins that may end up in other people's pages, we can't be quite so cavalier. As plugin authors, we have no way of knowing whether a web developer intends to use the `$.noConflict()` function to allow the $ alias to be used by another library.

We could employ the sledgehammer approach and use the `jQuery` name in place of the $ alias, but dang it, we *like* using $ and are loath to give up on it so easily.

Chapter 6 introduced an idiom often used to make sure that the $ alias refers to the `jQuery` name in a localized manner without affecting the remainder of the page, and this little trick can also be (and often is) employed when defining jQuery plugins as follows:

```
(function($){
//
// Plugin definition goes here
//
})(jQuery);
```

By passing `jQuery` to a function that defines the parameter as $, $ is guaranteed to reference `jQuery` within the body of the function.

We can now happily use $ to our heart's content in the definition of the plugin.

Before we dive into learning how to add new elements to jQuery, let's look at one more technique plugin authors are encouraged to use.

7.2.3   *Taming complex parameter lists*

Most plugins tend to be simple affairs that require few, if any, parameters. We've seen ample evidence of this in the vast majority of the core jQuery methods and functions, which either take a small handful of parameters or none at all. Intelligent defaults are supplied when optional parameters are omitted, and parameter order can even take on a different meaning when some optional parameters are omitted.

The `bind()` method is a good example; if the optional data parameter is omitted, the listener function, which is normally specified as the third parameter, can be supplied as the second. The dynamic and interpretive nature of JavaScript allows us to write such flexible code, but this sort of thing can start to break down and get complex (both for web developers and ourselves as plugin authors) when the number of parameters grows larger. The possibility of a breakdown increases when many of the parameters are optional.

Consider a somewhat complex function whose signature is as follows:

```
function complex(p1,p2,p3,p4,p5,p6,p7) {
```

This function accepts seven arguments, and let's say that all but the first are optional. There are too many optional arguments to make any intelligent guesses about the intention of the caller when optional parameters are omitted. If a caller of this function is only omitting trailing parameters, this isn't much of a problem, because the optional trailing arguments can be detected as `null`s. But what if the caller wants to specify p7 but let p2 through p6 default? Callers would need to use placeholders for any omitted parameters and write

```
complex(valueA,null,null,null,null,null,valueB);
```

Yuck! Even worse is a call such as

```
complex(valueA,null,valueC,valueD,null,null,valueB);
```

along with other variations of this nature. Web developers using this function are forced to carefully keep track of counting `null`s and the order of the parameters; plus, the code is difficult to read and understand.

But short of not allowing the caller so many options, what can we do?

Again, the flexible nature of JavaScript comes to the rescue; a pattern that allows us to tame this chaos has arisen among the page-authoring communities—the *options hash*. Using this pattern, optional parameters are gathered into a *single* parameter in the guise of a JavaScript `Object` instance, whose property name/value pairs serve as the optional parameters.

Using this technique, our first example could be written as

```
complex(valueA, {p7: valueB});
```

The second would be as follows:

```
complex(valueA, {
  p3: valueC,
  p4: valueD,
  p7: valueB
});
```

Much better!

We don't have to account for omitted parameters with placeholder `null`s, and we also don't need to count parameters; each optional parameter is conveniently labeled so that it's clear exactly what it represents (when we use better parameter names than `p1` through `p7`, that is).

> **NOTE** Some APIs follow this convention of bundling optional parameters into a single `options` parameter (leaving required parameters as standalone parameters), while others bundle the complete set of parameters, required and optional alike, into a single object. Neither approach is deemed more correct than the other, so choose whichever best suits your code.

Although this is obviously a great advantage to the caller of our complex functions, what about the ramifications for *us* as the plugin authors? As it turns out, we've already seen a jQuery-supplied mechanism that makes it easy for us to gather these optional parameters together and merge them with default values. Let's reconsider our complex example function with a required parameter and six options. The new, simplified signature is

```
complex(p1,options)
```

Within our function, we can merge those options with default values with the handy `$.extend()` utility function. Consider the following:

```
function complex(p1,options) {
  var settings = $.extend({
    option1: defaultValue1,
    option2: defaultValue2,
    option3: defaultValue3,
    option4: defaultValue4,
    option5: defaultValue5,
    option6: defaultValue6
  },options||{});
  // remainder of function ...
}
```

By merging the values passed by the web developer in the `options` parameter with an object containing all the available options with their default values, the `settings` variable ends up with the default values superseded by any explicit values specified by the web developer.

> **TIP** Rather than creating a new `settings` variable, we could also just use the `options` reference itself to accumulate the values. That would cut down on one reference on the stack, but let's keep on the side of clarity for the moment.

Note that we guard against an `options` object that's `null` or undefined with `||{}`, which supplies an empty object if `options` evaluates to `false` (as we know `null` and `undefined` do).

Easy, versatile, and caller-friendly!

We'll see examples of this pattern in use later in this chapter and in jQuery functions that will be introduced in chapter 8, but, for now, let's look at how we extend jQuery with our own utility functions.

7.3   *Writing custom utility functions*

In this book, we use the term *utility function* to describe functions defined as properties of jQuery (and therefore $). These functions aren't intended to operate on DOM elements—that's the job of methods defined to operate on a jQuery wrapped set—but to either operate on non-element JavaScript objects or perform some other operation that doesn't specifically operate on any objects. Some examples we've seen of each of these types of function are $.each() and $.noConflict().

In this section, we'll learn how to add our own similar functions.

Adding a function as a property to an Object instance is as easy as declaring the function and assigning it to an object property. (If this seems like black magic to you, and you have not yet read through the appendix, now would be a good time to do so.) Creating a trivial custom utility function should be as easy as

```
$.say = function(what) { alert('I say '+what); };
```

And, in truth, it *is* that easy. But this manner of defining a utility function isn't without its pitfalls; remember our discussion in section 7.2.2 regarding the $? What if some developer includes this function on a page that uses Prototype and has called $.noConflict()? Rather than add a jQuery extension, we'd create a method on Prototype's $() function. (Get thee to the appendix if the concept of a *method* of a function makes your head hurt.)

This isn't a problem for a private function that we know will never be shared, but even then, what if some future changes to the pages reassign the $? It's a good idea to err on the side of caution.

One way to ensure that someone stomping on $ doesn't also stomp on us is to avoid using $ at all. We could write our trivial function as

```
jQuery.say = function(what) { alert('I say '+what); };
```

This seems like an easy way out, but it proves to be less than optimal for more complex functions. What if the function body utilizes lots of jQuery methods and functions internally to get its job done? We'd need to use jQuery rather than $ throughout the function. That's rather wordy and inelegant; besides, once we use the $, we don't want to let it go!

So looking back to the idiom we introduced in section 7.2.2, we can safely write our function as follows:

```
(function($){
  $.say = function(what) { alert('I say '+what); };
})(jQuery);
```

We highly encourage using this pattern (even though it may seem like overkill for such a trivial function) because it protects the use of $ when declaring and defining the function. Should the function ever need to become more complex, we could extend and modify it without wondering whether it's safe to use the $ or not.

With this pattern fresh in our minds, let's implement a nontrivial utility function of our own.

7.3.1 Creating a data manipulation utility function

Often, when emitting fixed-width output, it's necessary to take a numeric value and format it to fit into a fixed-width field (where *width* is defined as the number of characters). Usually such operations will right-justify the value within the fixed-width field and prefix the value with enough *fill characters* to make up any difference between the length of the value and the length of the field.

Let's write such a utility function with the following syntax:

Function syntax: $.toFixedWidth

$.toFixedWidth(value,length,fill)
Formats the passed value as a fixed-width field of the specified length. An optional fill character can be supplied. If the numeric value exceeds the specified length, its higher order digits will be truncated to fit the length.

Parameters
value   (Number) The value to be formatted.
length   (Number) The length of the resulting field.
fill   (String) The fill character used when front-padding the value. If omitted, 0 is used.

Returns
The fixed-width field.

The implementation of this function is shown in listing 7.1.

Listing 7.1 Implementation of the $.toFixedWidth() custom utility function

```
(function($){
  $.toFixedWidth = function(value,length,fill) {
    var result = (value || '').toString();          ❶ Assigns default value
    fill = fill || '0';
    var padding = length - result.length;           ❷ Computes padding
    if (padding < 0) {
      result = result.substr(-padding);             ❸ Truncates if necessary
    }
    else {
      for (var n = 0; n < padding; n++)
        result = fill + result;                      ❹ Pads result
    }
    return result;          ❺ Returns final result
  };
})(jQuery);
```

This function is simple and straightforward. The passed value is converted to its string equivalent, and the fill character is determined either from the passed value or the default of 0 ❶. Then, we compute the amount of padding needed ❷.

If we end up with negative padding (the result is longer than the passed field length), we truncate from the beginning of the result to end up with the specified length ❸; otherwise, we pad the beginning of the result with the appropriate number of fill characters ❹ prior to returning it as the result of the function ❺.

Namespacing utility functions

If you want to make sure that your utility functions aren't going to conflict with anybody else's, you can namespace the functions by creating a namespace object on $ that, in turn, serves as the owner of your functions. For example, if we wanted to namespace all our date formatter functions under a namespace called jQiaDate-Formatter, we'd do the following:

```
$.jQiaDateFormatter = {};
$.jQiaDateFormatter.toFixedWidth = function(value,length,fill) {...};
```

This ensures that functions like toFixedWidth() can never conflict with another similarly named function. (Of course, we still need to worry about conflicting namespaces, but that's easier to deal with.)

Simple stuff, but it serves to show how easily we can add a utility function. And, as always, there's room for improvement. Consider the following exercises:

1 As with most examples in books, the error checking is minimal because we're focusing on the lesson at hand. How would you beef up the function to account for caller errors such as not passing numeric values for value and length? What if they don't pass them at all?

2 We were careful to truncate numeric values that were too long, in order to guarantee that the result was always the specified length. But if the caller passes more than a single-character string for the fill character, all bets are off. How would you handle that?

3 What if you don't want to truncate too-long values?

Now, let's tackle a more complex function in which we can make use of the $.toFixedWidth() function that we just wrote.

7.3.2 *Writing a date formatter*

If you've come to the world of client-side programming from the server, one of the things you may have longed for is a simple date formatter; something that the JavaScript Date type doesn't provide. Because such a function would operate on a Date instance, rather than any DOM element, it's a perfect candidate for a utility function. Let's write one that uses the following syntax:

Function syntax: $.formatDate

`$.formatDate(date,pattern)`

Formats the passed date according to the supplied pattern. The tokens that are substituted in the pattern are as follows:

yyyy: the 4-digit year
yy: the 2-digit year
MMMM: the full name of the month
MMM: the abbreviated name of the month
MM: the month number as a 0-filled, 2-character field
M: the month number
dd: the day of the month as a 0-filled, 2-character field
d: the day of the month
EEEE: the full name of the day of the week
EEE: the abbreviated name of the day of the week
a: the meridian (AM or PM)
HH: the 24-hour clock hour in the day as a 2-character, 0-filled field
H: the 24-hour clock hour in the day
hh: the 12-hour clock hour in the day as a 2-character, 0-filled field
h: the 12-hour clock hour in the day
mm: the minutes in the hour as a 2-character, 0-filled field
m: the minutes in the hour
ss: the seconds in the minute as a 2-character, 0-filled field
s: the seconds in the minute
S: the milliseconds in the second as a 3-character, 0-filled field

Parameters

date   (Date) The date to be formatted.

pattern   (String) The pattern to format the date into. Any characters not matching pattern tokens are copied as-is to the result.

Returns

The formatted date.

The implementation of this function is shown in listing 7.2. We're not going to go into great detail regarding the algorithm used to perform the formatting (after all, this isn't an algorithms book), but we'll use this implementation to point out some interesting tactics that we can use when creating a somewhat complex utility function.

Listing 7.2 Implementation of the `$.formatDate()` custom utility function

```
(function($){
  $.formatDate = function(date,pattern) {             ❶ Implements main
    var result = [];                                     body of the function
    while (pattern.length > 0) {
      $.formatDate.patternParts.lastIndex = 0;
      var matched = $.formatDate.patternParts.exec(pattern);
      if (matched) {
        result.push(
          $.formatDate.patternValue[matched[0]].call(this,date)
        );
        pattern = pattern.slice(matched[0].length);
      } else {
        result.push(pattern.charAt(0));
        pattern = pattern.slice(1);
      }
```

```
    }
    return result.join('');
};
$.formatDate.patternParts =
    /^(yy(yy)?|M(M(M(M)?)?)?|d(d)?|EEE(E)?|a|H(H)?|h(h)?|m(m)?|s(s)?|S)/;

$.formatDate.monthNames = [
    'January','February','March','April','May','June','July',
    'August','September','October','November','December'
];
$.formatDate.dayNames = [
    'Sunday','Monday','Tuesday','Wednesday','Thursday','Friday',
    'Saturday'
];
$.formatDate.patternValue = {
    yy: function(date) {
        return $.toFixedWidth(date.getFullYear(),2);
    },
    yyyy: function(date) {
        return date.getFullYear().toString();
    },
    MMMM: function(date) {
        return $.formatDate.monthNames[date.getMonth()];
    },
    MMM: function(date) {
        return $.formatDate.monthNames[date.getMonth()].substr(0,3);
    },
    MM: function(date) {
        return $.toFixedWidth(date.getMonth() + 1,2);
    },
    M: function(date) {
        return date.getMonth()+1;
    },
    dd: function(date) {
        return $.toFixedWidth(date.getDate(),2);
    },
    d: function(date) {
        return date.getDate();
    },
    EEEE: function(date) {
        return $.formatDate.dayNames[date.getDay()];
    },
    EEE: function(date) {
        return $.formatDate.dayNames[date.getDay()].substr(0,3);
    },
    HH: function(date) {
        return $.toFixedWidth(date.getHours(),2);
    },
    H: function(date) {
        return date.getHours();
    },
    hh: function(date) {
        var hours = date.getHours();
        return $.toFixedWidth(hours > 12 ? hours - 12 : hours,2);
    },
    h: function(date) {
```

② Defines the regular expression

③ Provides name of the months

④ Provides name of the days

⑤ Collects token-to-value translation functions

```
      return date.getHours() % 12;
    },
    mm: function(date) {
      return $.toFixedWidth(date.getMinutes(),2);
    },
    m: function(date) {
      return date.getMinutes();
    },
    ss: function(date) {
      return $.toFixedWidth(date.getSeconds(),2);
    },
    s: function(date) {
      return date.getSeconds();
    },
    S: function(date) {
      return $.toFixedWidth(date.getMilliseconds(),3);
    },
    a: function(date) {
      return date.getHours() < 12 ? 'AM' : 'PM';
    }
  };
})(jQuery);
```

The most interesting aspect of this implementation, aside from a few JavaScript tricks used to keep the amount of code in check, is that the function ❶ needs some ancillary data to do its job. In particular,

- A regular expression used to match tokens in the pattern ❷
- A list of the English names of the months ❸
- A list of the English names of the days ❹
- A set of subfunctions designed to provide the value for each token type, given a source date ❺

We could have included each of these as var definitions within the function body, but that would clutter an already somewhat involved algorithm, and because they're constants, it makes sense to segregate them from variable data.

We don't want to pollute the global namespace, or even the $ namespace, with a bunch of names needed only by this function, so we make these declarations properties of our new function itself. Remember, JavaScript functions are first-class objects, and they can have their own properties like any other JavaScript object.

As for the formatting algorithm itself? In a nutshell, it operates as follows:

1 Creates an array to hold portions of the result.
2 Iterates over the pattern, consuming identified token and non-token characters until it has been completely inspected.
3 Resets the regular expression (stored in $.formatDate.patternParts) on each iteration by setting its lastIndex property to 0.
4 Tests the regular expression for a token match against the current beginning of the pattern.

5   Calls the function in the $.formatDate.patternValue collection of conversion functions to obtain the appropriate value from the Date instance if a match occurs. This value is pushed onto the end of the results array, and the matched token is removed from the beginning of the pattern.

6   Removes the first character from the pattern and adds it to the end of the results array if a token isn't matched at the current beginning of the pattern.

7   Joins the results array into a string and returns it as the value of the function when the entire pattern has been consumed.

Note that the conversion functions in the $.formatDate.patternValue collection make use of the $.toFixedWidth() function that we created in the previous section.

You'll find both of these functions in the file chapter7/jquery.jqia.dateFormat.js and a rudimentary page to test it at chapter7/test.dateFormat.html.

Operating on run-of-the-mill JavaScript objects is all well and good, but the real power of jQuery lies in the wrapper methods that operate on a set of DOM elements collected via the power of jQuery selectors. Next, let's see how we can add our own powerful wrapper methods.

7.4   *Adding new wrapper methods*

The true power of jQuery lies in the ability to easily and quickly select and operate on DOM elements. Luckily, we can extend that power by adding wrapper methods of our own that manipulate selected DOM elements as we deem appropriate. By adding wrapper methods, we automatically gain the use of the powerful jQuery selectors to pick and choose which elements are to be operated on without having to do all the work ourselves.

Given what we know about JavaScript, we probably could have figured out on our own how to add utility functions to the $ namespace, but that's not necessarily true of wrapper functions. There's a tidbit of jQuery-specific information that we need to know: to add wrapper methods to jQuery, we must assign them as properties to an object named fn in the $ namespace.

The general pattern for creating a wrapper function is

```
$.fn.wrapperFunctionName = function(params){function-body};
```

Let's concoct a trivial wrapper method to set the color of the matched DOM elements to blue:

```
(function($){
  $.fn.makeItBlue = function() {
    return this.css('color','blue');
  };
})(jQuery);
```

As with utility functions, we make the declaration within an outer function that guarantees that $ is an alias to jQuery. But unlike utility functions, we create the new wrapper method as a property of $.fn rather than of $.

NOTE If you're familiar with "object-oriented JavaScript" and its prototype-based class declarations, you might be interested to know that `$.fn` is merely an alias for an internal `prototype` property of an object that jQuery uses to create its wrapper objects.

Within the body of the method, the function context (`this`) refers to the wrapped set. We can use all of the predefined jQuery methods on it; in this example, we call the `css()` method on the wrapped set to set the `color` to `blue` for all matched DOM elements.

WARNING The function context (`this`) within the main body of a wrapper method refers to the wrapped set, but when inline functions are declared within this function, they each have their own function contexts. You must take care when using `this` under such circumstances to make sure that it's referring to what you think it is! For example, if you use the `each()` jQuery method with its iterator function, `this` within the iterator function references the DOM element for the current iteration.

We can do almost anything we like to the DOM elements in the wrapped set, but there is one *very* important rule when defining new wrapper methods: unless the function is intended to return a specific value, it should always return the wrapped set as its return value. This allows our new method to take part in any jQuery method chains. In our example, because the `css()` method returns the wrapped set, we simply return the result of the call to `css()`.

In the previous example, we applied the jQuery `css()` method to all the elements in the wrapped set by applying it to `this`. If, for some reason, we need to deal with each wrapped element individually (perhaps because we need to make conditional processing decisions), the following pattern can be used:

```
(function($){
  $.fn.someNewMethod = function() {
    return this.each(function(){
      //
      // Function body goes here -- this refers to individual
      // DOM elements
      //
    });
  };
})(jQuery);
```

In this pattern, the `each()` method is used to iterate over every individual element in the wrapped set. Note that, within the iterator function, `this` refers to the current DOM element rather than the entire wrapped set. The wrapped set returned by `each()` is returned as the new method's value so that this method can participate in chaining.

Let's consider a variation of our previous blue-centric example that deals with each element individually:

```
(function($){
  $.fn.makeItBlueOrRed = function() {
    return this.each(function(){
      $(this).css('color',$(this).is('[id]') ? 'blue' : 'red');
    });
  };
})(jQuery);
```

In this variation, we want to apply the color blue or the color red based upon a condition that's unique to each element (in this case, whether it has an id attribute or not), so we iterate over the wrapped set so that we can examine and manipulate each element individually.

> ### Iteration via methods that accept functions for values
> Note that the "blue or red" example is a tad contrived to show how each() can be used to traverse the individual elements in the wrapped set. Because the css() method accepts a function for its value (which automatically iterates over the elements), the astute among you might have noted that this custom method could also have been written without each() as follows:
>
> ```
> (function($){
>   $.fn.makeItBlueOrRed = function() {
>     return this.css('color', function() {
>       return $(this).is('[id]') ? 'blue' : 'red';
>     });
>   };
> })(jQuery);
> ```
>
> This is a common idiom across the jQuery API; when a function can be passed in place of a value, the function is invoked in an iterative fashion over the elements of the wrapped set.
>
> The variant of the example using each() is illustrative of cases where there's no such automatic iteration of elements.

That's all there is to it, *but* (isn't there always a *but*?) there are some techniques we should be aware of when creating more involved jQuery wrapper methods. Let's define a couple more plugin methods of greater complexity to examine those techniques.

7.4.1 *Applying multiple operations in a wrapper method*

Let's develop another new plugin method that performs more than a single operation on the wrapped set. Imagine that we need to be able to flip the read-only status of text fields within a form and to simultaneously and consistently affect the appearance of the field. We could easily chain a couple of existing jQuery methods together to do this, but we want to be neat and tidy about it and bundle these operations together into a single method.

We'll name our new method setReadOnly(), and its syntax is as follows:

Method syntax: setReadOnly

setReadOnly(state)

Sets the read-only status of wrapped text fields to the state specified by `state`. The opacity of the fields will be adjusted: 100 percent if not read-only, 50 percent if read-only. Any elements in the wrapped set other than text fields are ignored.

Parameters

    state   (Boolean) The read-only state to set. If `true`, the text fields are made read-only; otherwise, the read-only status is cleared.

Returns

The wrapped set.

The implementation of this plugin is shown in listing 7.3 and can be found in the file chapter7/jquery.jqia.setreadonly.js.

Listing 7.3 Implementation of the `setReadOnly()` custom wrapper method

```
(function($){
  $.fn.setReadOnly = function(readonly) {
    return this.filter('input:text')
      .attr('readOnly',readonly)
      .css('opacity', readonly ? 0.5 : 1.0)
      .end();
  };
})(jQuery);
```

This example is only slightly more complicated than our initial example, but it exhibits the following key concepts:

- A parameter is passed that affects how the method operates.
- Four jQuery methods are applied to the wrapped set by use of jQuery chaining.
- The new method can participate in a jQuery chain because it returns the wrapped set as its value.
- The `filter()` method is used to ensure that, no matter what set of wrapped elements the web developer applies this method to, only text fields are affected.
- The `end()` method is invoked so that the original (not the filtered) wrapped set is returned as the value of the call.

How might we put this method to use?

Often, when defining an online order form, we may need to allow the user to enter two sets of address information: one for where the order is to be shipped and one for the billing information. Much more often than not, these two addresses are going to be the same, and making the user enter the same information twice decreases our user-friendliness factor to less than we'd want it to be.

We could write our server-side code to assume that the billing address is the same as the shipping address if the form is left blank, but let's assume that our product manager is a bit paranoid and would like something more overt on the part of the user.

We'll satisfy him by adding a checkbox to the billing address that indicates whether the billing address is the same as the shipping address. When this box is checked, the

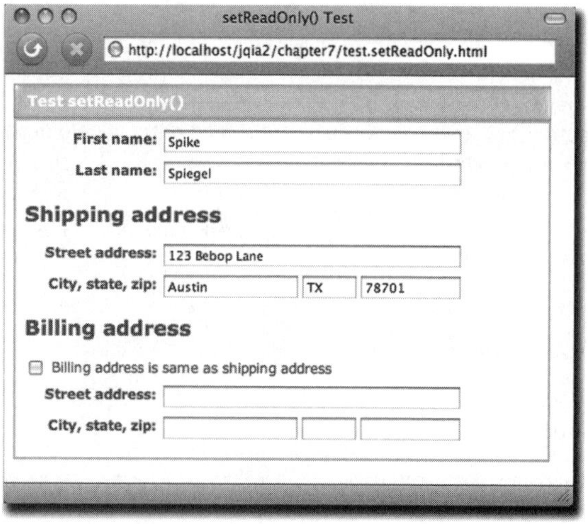

Figure 7.1a Our form for testing the setReadOnly() custom wrapper method before checking the checkbox

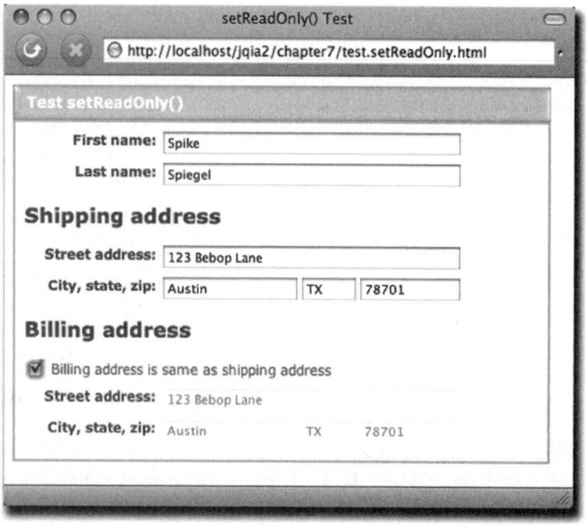

Figure 7.1b Our form for testing the setReadOnly() custom wrapper method after checking the checkbox, showing the results of applying the custom method

billing address fields will be copied from the shipping fields and then made read-only. Unchecking the box will clear the value and read-only status from the fields.

Figure 7.1a shows a test form in its before state, and figure 7.1b shows the after state.

The page for this test form is available in the file chapter7/test.setReadOnly.html and is shown in listing 7.4.

Listing 7.4   Implementation of the test page for the `setReadOnly()` wrapper method

```
<!DOCTYPE html>
<html>
  <head>
    <title>setReadOnly() Test</title>
    <link rel="stylesheet" type="text/css" href="../styles/core.css" />
    <link rel="stylesheet" type="text/css" href="test.setReadOnly.css" />
    <script type="text/javascript" src="../scripts/jquery-1.4.js"></script>
```

```html
  <script type="text/javascript" src="jquery.jqia.setReadOnly.js"></script>
  <script type="text/javascript">
    $(function(){
      $('#sameAddressControl').click(function(){
        var same = this.checked;
        $('#billAddress').val(same ? $('#shipAddress').val():'');
        $('#billCity').val(same ? $('#shipCity').val():'');
        $('#billState').val(same ? $('#shipState').val():'');
        $('#billZip').val(same ? $('#shipZip').val():'');
        $('#billingAddress input').setReadOnly(same);
      });
    });
  </script>
</head>

<body>
  <div class="module">
    <div class="banner">
      <img src="../images/module.left.cap.png" alt="" style="float:left"/>
      <img src="../images/module.right.cap.png" alt=""
           style="float:right"/>
      <h2>Test setReadOnly()</h2>
    </div>
    <div class="body">

      <form name="testForm">
        <div>
          <label>First name:</label>
          <input type="text" name="firstName" id="firstName"/>
        </div>
        <div>
          <label>Last name:</label>
          <input type="text" name="lastName" id="lastName"/>
        </div>
        <div id="shippingAddress">
          <h2>Shipping address</h2>
          <div>
            <label>Street address:</label>
            <input type="text" name="shipAddress" id="shipAddress"/>
          </div>
          <div>
            <label>City, state, zip:</label>
            <input type="text" name="shipCity" id="shipCity"/>
            <input type="text" name="shipState" id="shipState"/>
            <input type="text" name="shipZip" id="shipZip"/>
          </div>
        </div>
        <div id="billingAddress">
          <h2>Billing address</h2>
          <div>
            <input type="checkbox" id="sameAddressControl"/>
            Billing address is same as shipping address
          </div>
          <div>
            <label>Street address:</label>
            <input type="text" name="billAddress"
                   id="billAddress"/>
```

```
        </div>
        <div>
          <label>City, state, zip:</label>
          <input type="text" name="billCity" id="billCity"/>
          <input type="text" name="billState" id="billState"/>
          <input type="text" name="billZip" id="billZip"/>
        </div>
      </div>
    </form>
  </div>
  </div>

  </body>
</html>
```

We won't belabor the operation of this page, as it's relatively straightforward. The only truly interesting aspect of this page is the click handler attached to the checkbox in the ready handler. When the state of the checkbox is changed by a click, we do three things:

1 Copy the checked state into the variable same for easy reference in the remainder of the listener.

2 Set the values of the billing address fields. If they're to be the same, we set the values from the corresponding fields in the shipping address information. If not, we clear the fields.

3 Call the new `setReadOnly()` method on all input fields in the billing address container.

But, oops! We were a little sloppy with that last step. The wrapped set that we create with `$('#billingAddress input')` contains not only the text fields in the billing address block but the checkbox too. The checkbox element doesn't have read-only semantics, but it can have its opacity changed—definitely not our intention!

Luckily, this sloppiness is countered by the fact that we were *not* sloppy when defining our plugin. Recall that we filtered out all but text fields before applying the remainder of the methods in that method. We highly recommend such attention to detail, particularly for plugins that are intended for public consumption.

What are some ways that this method could be improved? Consider making the following changes:

- We forgot about text areas! How would you modify the code to include text areas along with the text fields?
- The opacity levels applied to the fields in either state are hard-coded into the function. This is hardly caller-friendly. Modify the method to allow the levels to be caller-supplied.
- Oh heck, why force the web developer to accept the ability to affect only the opacity? How would you modify the method to allow the developer to determine what the renditions for the fields should be in either state?

Now let's take on an even more complex plugin.

7.4.2 *Retaining state within a wrapper method*

Everybody loves a slideshow!

At least on the web. Unlike hapless after-dinner guests forced to sit through a mind-numbingly endless display of badly focused vacation photos, visitors to a web slideshow can leave whenever they like without hurting anyone's feelings!

For our more complex plugin example, we're going to develop a jQuery method that will easily allow a web developer to whip up a quick slideshow page. We'll create a jQuery plugin, which we'll name *Photomatic*, and then we'll whip up a test page to put it through its paces. When complete, this test page will appear as shown in figure 7.2.

This page sports the following components:

- A set of thumbnail images
- A full-sized photo of one of the images available in the thumbnail list
- A set of buttons for moving through the slideshow manually, and for starting and stopping the automatic slideshow

The behaviors of the page are as follows:

- Clicking any thumbnail displays the corresponding full-sized image.
- Clicking the full-sized image displays the next image.
- Clicking any button performs the following operations:
  - First—Displays the first image

Figure 7.2   The test page that we'll use to put our Photomatic plugin through its paces

- Previous—Displays the previous image
- Next—Displays the next image
- Last—Displays the last image
- Play—Commences moving through the photos automatically until clicked again

■ Any operation that moves past the end of the list of images wraps back to the other end; clicking Next while on the last image displays the first image and vice versa.

We also want to grant web developers as much freedom for layout and styling as possible; we'll define our plugin so that developers can set up the elements in any manner they like and then tell us which page element should be used for each purpose. Furthermore, in order to give web developers as much leeway as possible, we'll define our plugin so that they can provide any wrapped set of images to serve as thumbnails. Usually, thumbnails will be gathered together as in our test page, but developers are free to identify any image on the page as a thumbnail.

To start, let's introduce the syntax for the Photomatic plugin.

Method syntax: photomatic

`photomatic(options)`

Instruments the wrapped set of thumbnails, as well as page elements identified in the `options` hash, to operate as Photomatic controls.

Parameters

`options`   (Object) An object hash that specifies the options for Photomatic. See table 7.1 for details.

Returns

The wrapped set.

Because we have a nontrivial number of parameters for controlling the operation of Photomatic (many of which can be omitted), we utilize an object hash to pass them, as was discussed in section 7.2.3. The possible options that we can specify are shown in table 7.1.

Table 7.1   The options for the Photomatic custom plugin method

Option name	Description
`firstControl`	(Selector|Element) Either a reference to or jQuery selector that identifies the DOM element(s) to serve as a First control. If omitted, no control is instrumented.
`lastControl`	(Selector|Element) Either a reference to or jQuery selector that identifies the DOM element(s) to serve as a Last control. If omitted, no control is instrumented.
`nextControl`	(Selector|Element) Either a reference to or jQuery selector that identifies the DOM element(s) to serve as a Next control. If omitted, no control is instrumented.

Table 7.1   The options for the Photomatic custom plugin method *(continued)*

Option name	Description
`photoElement`	(Selector|Element) Either a reference to or jQuery selector that identifies the `<img>` element that's to serve as the full-sized photo display. If omitted, defaults to the jQuery selector `img.photomaticPhoto`.
`playControl`	(Selector|Element) Either a reference to or jQuery selector that identifies the DOM element(s) to serve as a Play control. If omitted, no control is instrumented.
`previousControl`	(Selector| Element) Either a reference to or jQuery selector that identifies the DOM element(s) to serve as a Previous control. If omitted, no control is instrumented.
`transformer`	(Function) A function used to transform the URL of a thumbnail image into the URL of its corresponding full-sized photo image. If omitted, the default transformation substitutes all instances of `thumbnail` with `photo` in the URL.
`delay`	(Number) The interval between transitions for an automatic slideshow, in milliseconds. Defaults to 3000.

With a nod to the notion of *test-driven development,* let's create the test page for this plugin *before* we dive into creating the Photomatic plugin itself. The code for this page, available in the file chapter7/photomatic/photomatic.html, is shown in listing 7.5.

Listing 7.5   The test page that creates the Photomatic display in figure 7.2

```
<!DOCTYPE html>
<html>
  <head>
    <title>Photomatic Test</title>
    <link rel="stylesheet" type="text/css"
          href="../../styles/core.css">
    <link rel="stylesheet" type="text/css" href="photomatic.css">
    <script type="text/javascript"
            src="../../scripts/jquery-1.4.js"></script>
    <script type="text/javascript"
            src="jquery.jqia.photomatic.js"></script>
    <script type="text/javascript">
      $(function(){
        $('#thumbnailsPane img').photomatic({          ❶ Invokes the
          photoElement: '#photoDisplay',                    Photomatic plugin
          previousControl: '#previousButton',
          nextControl: '#nextButton',
          firstControl: '#firstButton',
          lastControl: '#lastButton',
          playControl: '#playButton',
          delay: 1000
        });
      });
    </script>
  </head>
```

```
<body class="fancy">

  <div id="pageContainer">
    <div id="pageContent">

      <h1>Photomatic Tester</h1>

      <div id="thumbnailsPane">
        <img src="thumbnails/IMG_2212.jpg"/>
        <img src="thumbnails/IMG_2222.jpg"/>
        <img src="thumbnails/IMG_2227.jpg"/>
        <img src="thumbnails/IMG_2235.jpg"/>
        <img src="thumbnails/IMG_2259.jpg"/>
        <img src="thumbnails/IMG_2269.jpg"/>
        <img src="thumbnails/IMG_2273.jpg"/>
        <img src="thumbnails/IMG_2287.jpg"/>
        <img src="thumbnails/IMG_2292.jpg"/>
        <img src="thumbnails/IMG_2296.jpg"/>
        <img src="thumbnails/IMG_2298.jpg"/>
        <img src="thumbnails/IMG_2302.jpg"/>
        <img src="thumbnails/IMG_2310.jpg"/>
        <img src="thumbnails/IMG_2319.jpg"/>
        <img src="thumbnails/IMG_2331.jpg"/>
        <img src="thumbnails/IMG_2335.jpg"/>
      </div>

      <div id="photoPane">
        <img id="photoDisplay" src=""/>
      </div>

      <div id="buttonBar">
        <img src="button.placeholder.png" id="firstButton"
             alt="First" title="First photo"/>
        <img src="button.placeholder.png" id="previousButton"
             alt="Previous" title="Previous photo"/>
        <img src="button.placeholder.png" id="playButton"
             alt="Play/Pause" title="Play or pause slideshow"/>
        <img src="button.placeholder.png" id="nextButton"
             alt="Next" title="Next photo"/>
        <img src="button.placeholder.png" id="lastButton"
             alt="Last" title="Last photo"/>
      </div>

    </div>
  </div>

</body>
</html>
```

❷ Contains thumbnail images

❸ Defines image element for full-sized photos

❹ Contains elements to serve as controls

If that looks simpler than you thought it would, you shouldn't be surprised. By applying the principles of Unobtrusive JavaScript and by keeping all style information in an external style sheet, our markup is tidy and simple. In fact, even the on-page script has a tiny footprint, consisting of a single statement that invokes our plugin ❶.

The HTML markup consists of a container that holds the thumbnail images ❷, an image element (initially sourceless) to hold the full-sized photo ❸, and a collection of images ❹ that will control the slideshow. Everything else is handled by our new plugin.

Let's develop that now.

To start, let's set out a skeleton (we'll fill in the details as we go along). Our starting point should look rather familiar because it follows the same patterns we've been using so far.

```
(function($){
  $.fn.photomatic = function(options) {
  };
})(jQuery);
```

This defines our initially empty wrapper function, which (as expected from our syntax description) accepts a single hash parameter named `options`. First, within the body of the function, we merge these caller settings with the default settings described in table 7.1. This will give us a single `settings` object that we can refer to throughout the remainder of the method.

We perform this merge operation using the following idiom (which we've already seen a few times):

```
var settings = $.extend({
     photoElement: 'img.photomaticPhoto',
     transformer: function(name) {
                    return name.replace(/thumbnail/,'photo');
                  },
     nextControl: null,
     previousControl: null,
     firstControl: null,
     lastControl: null,
     playControl: null,
     delay: 3000
   },options||{});
```

After the execution of this statement, the `settings` variable will contain the defaults supplied by the inline hash object overridden with any values supplied by the caller. Although it's not necessary to include the properties that have no defaults (those with a `null` value), we find it's useful and wise to list all the possible options here if for nothing other than documentation purposes.

We're also going to need to keep track of a few things. In order for our plugin to know what concepts like *next* relative image and *previous* relative image mean, we need not only an ordered list of the thumbnail images, but also an indicator that identifies the *current* image being displayed.

The list of thumbnail images is the wrapped set that this method is operating on—or, at least, it should be. We don't know what the developers collected in the wrapped set, so we want to filter it down to only image elements, which we can easily do with a jQuery selector. But where should we store the list?

We could easily create another variable to hold it, but there's a lot to be said for keeping things corralled. Let's store the list as another property on `settings`, as follows:

```
settings.thumbnails$ = this.filter('img');
```

Filtering the wrapped set (available via `this` in the method) for only image elements results in a new wrapped set (containing only `<img>` elements), which we store in a property of `settings` that we name `thumbnails$` (the trailing dollar sign being a convention that indicates a stored reference to a wrapped set).

Another piece of state that we need to keep track of is the *current* image. We'll do that by maintaining an index into the list of thumbnails by adding another property to `settings` named `current`:

```
settings.current = 0;
```

There is one more setup step that we need to take with regard to the thumbnails. If we're going to keep track of which photo is *current* by keeping track of its index, there will be at least one case (which we'll be examining shortly) where, given a reference to a thumbnail element, we'll need to know its index. The easiest way to handle this is to anticipate this need and use the handy jQuery `data()` method to record a thumbnail's index on each of the thumbnail elements. We do that with the following statement:

```
settings.thumbnails$
  .each(
    function(n) { $(this).data('photomatic-index',n); }
  )
```

This statement iterates through each of the thumbnail images, adding a data element named `photomatic-index` to it that records its order in the list. Now that our initial state is set up, we're ready to move on to the meat of the plugin—instrumenting the controls, thumbnails, and photo display.

Wait a minute! Initial *state*? How can we expect to keep track of state in a *local* variable within a function that's about to finish executing? Won't the variable and all our settings go out of scope when the function returns?

In general, that might be true, but there is one case where such a variable sticks around for longer than its usual scope—when it's part of a *closure*. We've seen closures before, but if you're still shaky on them, please review the appendix. You must understand closures not only for completing the implementation of the Photomatic plugin but also when creating anything but the most trivial of plugins.

When we think about the job remaining, we realize that we need to attach a number of event listeners to the controls and elements that we've taken such great pains to identify to this point. And because the `settings` variable is in scope when we declare the functions that represent those listeners, each listener will be part of a closure that includes the `settings` variable. So we can rest assured that, even though `settings` may appear to be transient, the state that it represents will stick around and be available to all the listeners that we define.

Speaking of those listeners, here's a list of `click` event listeners that we'll need to attach to the various elements:

- Clicking a thumbnail photo will cause its full-sized version to be displayed.
- Clicking the full-sized photo will cause the next photo to be displayed.

- Clicking the element defined as the Previous control will cause the previous image to be displayed.
- Clicking the Next control will cause the next image to be displayed.
- Clicking the First control will cause the first image in the list to be displayed.
- Clicking the Last control will cause the last image in the list to be displayed.
- Clicking the Play control will cause the slideshow to automatically proceed, progressing through the photos using a delay specified in the settings. A subsequent click on the control will stop the slideshow.

Looking over this list, we immediately note that all of these listeners have something in common: they all need to cause the full-sized photo of one of the thumbnail images to be displayed. And being the good and clever coders that we are, we want to factor out that common processing into a function so that we don't need to repeat the same code over and over again.

But how?

If we were writing normal on-page JavaScript, we could define a top-level function. If we were writing object-oriented JavaScript, we might define a method on a JavaScript object. But we're writing a jQuery plugin. Where should we define implementation functions?

We don't want to infringe on either the global namespace, or even the $ namespace, for a function that should only be called internally from our plugin code, so what can we do? Oh, and just to add to our dilemma, let's try to make it so that the function participates in a closure including the settings variable so that we won't have to pass it as a parameter to each invocation.

The power of JavaScript as a *functional* language comes to our aid once again, and allows us to define this new function *within* the plugin function. By doing so, we limit its scope to within the plugin function itself (one of our goals), and because the settings variable is within scope, it forms a closure with the new function (our other goal). What could be simpler?

So we define a function named showPhoto(), which accepts a single parameter indicating the index of the thumbnail that's to be shown full-sized, within the plugin function, as follows:

```
function showPhoto(index) {
  $(settings.photoElement)
    .attr('src',
          settings.transformer(settings.thumbnails$[index].src));
  settings.current = index;
};
```

This new function, when passed the index of the thumbnail whose full-sized photo is to be displayed, uses the values in the settings object (available via the closure created by the function declaration) to do the following:

1 Look up the src attribute of the thumbnail identified by index.
2 Pass that value through the transformer function to convert it from a thumbnail URL to a photo URL.

3 Assign the result of the transformation to the `src` attribute of the full-sized image element.

4 Record the index of the displayed photo as the new current index.

With that handy function available, we're ready to define the listeners that we listed earlier. Let's start by instrumenting the thumbnails themselves, which simply need to cause their corresponding full-size photo to be displayed. We chain a call to the `click()` method to the previous statement that references `settings.thumbnails$`, as follows:

```
.click(function(){
    showPhoto($(this).data('photomatic-index'));
});
```

In this handler, we obtain the value of the thumbnail's index (which we thoughtfully already stored in the `photomatic-index` data element), and call the `showPhoto()` function using it. The simplicity of this handler verifies that all the setup we coded earlier is going to pay off!

Instrumenting the photo display element to show the next photo in the list is just as simple:

```
$(settings.photoElement)
    .attr('title', 'Click for next photo')
    .css('cursor','pointer')
    .click(function(){
        showPhoto((settings.current+1) % settings.thumbnails$.length);
    });
```

We add a thoughtful `title` attribute to the photo so users know that clicking on the photo will progress to the next one, and we set the cursor to indicate that the element is clickable.

We then establish a click handler, in which we call the `showPhoto()` function with the next index value—note how we use the JavaScript modulo operator (%) to wrap around to the front of the list when we fall off the end.

The handlers for the First, Previous, Next, and Last controls all follow a similar pattern: figure out the appropriate index of the thumbnail whose full-sized photo is to be shown, and call `showPhoto()` with that index:

```
$(settings.nextControl).click(function(){
    showPhoto((settings.current+1) % settings.thumbnails$.length);
});
$(settings.previousControl).click(function(){
    showPhoto((settings.thumbnails$.length+settings.current-1) %
            settings.thumbnails$.length);
});
$(settings.firstControl).click(function(){
    showPhoto(0);
});
$(settings.lastControl).click(function(){
    showPhoto(settings.thumbnails$.length-1);
});
```

The instrumentation of the Play control is somewhat more complicated. Rather than showing a particular photo, this control must start a progression through the entire photo set, and then stop that progression on a subsequent click. Let's take a look at the code we use to accomplish that:

```
$(settings.playControl).toggle(
  function(event){
    settings.tick = window.setInterval(
      function(){
        $(settings.nextControl).triggerHandler('click')
      },
      settings.delay);
    $(event.target).addClass('photomatic-playing');
    $(settings.nextControl).click();
  },
  function(event){
    window.clearInterval(settings.tick);
    $(event.target).removeClass('photomatic-playing');
  }
);
```

First, note that we use the jQuery `toggle()` method to easily swap between two different listeners on every other click of the control. That saves us from having to figure out on our own whether we're starting or stopping the slideshow.

In the first handler, we employ the JavaScript-provided `setInterval()` method to cause a function to continually fire off using the `delay` value. We store the handle of that interval timer in the `settings` variable for later reference.

We also add the class `photomatic-playing` to the control so that the web developer can effect any appearance changes using CSS, if desired.

As the last act in the handler, we emulate a click on the Next control to progress to the next photo immediately (rather than having to wait for the first interval to expire).

In the second handler of the `toggle()` invocation, we want to stop the slideshow, so we clear the interval timeout using `clearInterval()` and remove the `photomatic-playing` class from the control.

Bet you didn't think it would be that easy.

We have two final tasks before we can declare success: we need to display the first photo in advance of any user action, and we need to return the original wrapped set so that our plugin can participate in jQuery method chains. We achieve these with

```
showPhoto(0);
return this;
```

Take a moment to do a short Victory Dance; we're finally done!

The completed plugin code, which you'll find in the file chapter7/photomatic/jquery.jqia.photomatic.js, is shown in listing 7.6.

Listing 7.6 The complete implementation of the Photomatic plugin

```
(function($){

  $.fn.photomatic = function(options) {
    var settings = $.extend({
      photoElement: 'img.photomaticPhoto',
      transformer: function(name) {
                    return name.replace(/thumbnail/,'photo');
                },
      nextControl: null,
      previousControl: null,
      firstControl: null,
      lastControl: null,
      playControl: null,
      delay: 3000
    },options||{});
    function showPhoto(index) {
      $(settings.photoElement)
        .attr('src',
              settings.transformer(settings.thumbnails$[index].src));
      settings.current = index;
    }
    settings.current = 0;
    settings.thumbnails$ = this.filter('img');
    settings.thumbnails$
      .each(
        function(n){ $(this).data('photomatic-index',n); }
      )
      .click(function(){
        showPhoto($(this).data('photomatic-index'));
      });
    $(settings.photoElement)
      .attr('title','Click for next photo')
      .css('cursor','pointer')
      .click(function(){
        showPhoto((settings.current+1) % settings.thumbnails$.length);
      });
    $(settings.nextControl).click(function(){
      showPhoto((settings.current+1) % settings.thumbnails$.length);
    });
    $(settings.previousControl).click(function(){
      showPhoto((settings.thumbnails$.length+settings.current-1) %
              settings.thumbnails$.length);
    });
    $(settings.firstControl).click(function(){
      showPhoto(0);
    });
    $(settings.lastControl).click(function(){
      showPhoto(settings.thumbnails$.length-1);
    });
    $(settings.playControl).toggle(
      function(event){
        settings.tick = window.setInterval(
          function(){ $(settings.nextControl).triggerHandler('click'); },
```

```
          settings.delay);
        $(event.target).addClass('photomatic-playing');
        $(settings.nextControl).click();
      },
      function(event){
        window.clearInterval(settings.tick);
        $(event.target).removeClass('photomatic-playing');
      });
    showPhoto(0);
    return this;
  };

})(jQuery);
```

This plugin is typical of jQuery-enabled code; it packs a big wallop in some compact code. But it serves to demonstrate an important set of techniques—using closures to maintain state across the scope of a jQuery plugin and to enable the creation of private implementation functions that plugins can define and use without resorting to any namespace infringements.

Also note that because we took such care to not let state "leak out" of the plugin, we're free to add as many Photomatic widgets to a page as we like, without fear that they will interfere with one another (taking care, of course, to make sure we don't use duplicate id values in the markup).

But is it complete? You be the judge and consider the following exercises:

- Again, error checking and handling has been glossed over. How would you go about making the plugin as bulletproof as possible?
- The transition from photo to photo is instantaneous. Leveraging your knowledge from chapter 5, change the plugin so that photos cross-fade to one another.
- Going one step further, how would you go about allowing the developer to use a custom animation of his or her choice?
- For maximum flexibility, we coded this plugin to instrument HTML elements already created by the user. How would you create an analogous plugin, but with less display freedom, that generated all the required HTML elements on the fly?

You're now primed and ready to write your own jQuery plugins. When you come up with some useful ones, consider sharing them with the rest of the jQuery community. Visit http://plugins.jquery.com/ for more information.

7.5 *Summary*

This chapter introduced us to writing reusable code that extends jQuery.

Writing our own code as extensions to jQuery has a number of advantages. Not only does it keep our code consistent across our web application regardless of whether it's employing jQuery APIs or our own, but it also makes all of the power of jQuery available to our own code.

Following a few naming rules helps avoid naming collisions between filenames, as well as problems that might be encountered when the $ name is reassigned by a page that will use our plugin.

Creating new utility functions is as easy as creating new function properties on $, and new wrapper methods are easily created as properties of $.fn.

If plugin authoring intrigues you, we highly recommend that you download and comb through the code of existing plugins to see how their authors implemented their own features. You'll see how the techniques presented in this chapter are used in a wide range of code, and you'll learn new techniques that are beyond the scope of this book.

Having yet more jQuery knowledge at our disposal, let's move on to learning how jQuery makes incorporating Ajax into our interactive applications practically a no-brainer.

Talk to the server
with Ajax

This chapter covers

- A brief overview of Ajax
- Loading preformatted HTML from the server
- Making general `GET` and `POST` requests
- Exerting fine-grained control over requests
- Setting default Ajax properties
- Handling Ajax events

It can be successfully argued that no single technology shift has transformed the landscape of the web more than Ajax. The ability to make asynchronous requests back to the server without the need to reload entire pages has enabled a whole new set of user-interaction paradigms and made DOM-scripted applications possible.

Ajax is a less recent addition to the web toolbox than many people may realize. In 1998, Microsoft introduced the ability to perform asynchronous requests under script control (discounting the use of `<iframe>` elements for such activity) as an ActiveX control as part of the creation of Outlook Web Access (OWA). Although OWA was a moderate success, few people seemed to take notice of the underlying technology.

A few years passed, and a handful of events launched Ajax into the collective consciousness of the web development community. The non-Microsoft browsers implemented a standardized version of the technology as the XMLHttpRequest (XHR) object; Google began using XHR; and, in 2005, Jesse James Garrett of Adaptive Path coined the term *Ajax* (for Asynchronous JavaScript and XML).

As if they were only waiting for the technologies to be given a catchy name, the web development masses suddenly took note of Ajax in a *big* way, and it has become one of the primary tools by which we can enable DOM-scripted applications.

In this chapter, we'll take a brief tour of Ajax (if you're already an Ajax guru, you might want to skip ahead to section 8.2), and then we'll look at how jQuery makes using Ajax a snap.

Let's start off with a refresher on what Ajax technology is all about.

8.1   Brushing up on Ajax

Although we'll take a quick look at Ajax in this section, please note that this isn't intended as a complete Ajax tutorial or an Ajax primer. If you're completely unfamiliar with Ajax (or worse, think that we're talking about a dishwashing liquid or a mythological Greek hero), we encourage you to familiarize yourself with the technology through resources that are geared toward teaching you *all* about Ajax; the Manning books *Ajax in Action* and *Ajax in Practice* are both excellent examples.

Some people may argue that the term *Ajax* applies to *any* method of making server requests without the need to refresh the user-facing page (such as by submitting a request to a hidden <iframe> element), but most people associate the term with the use of XMLHttpRequest (XHR) or the Microsoft XMLHTTP ActiveX control.

A diagram of the overall process, which we'll examine one step at a time, is shown in figure 8.1.

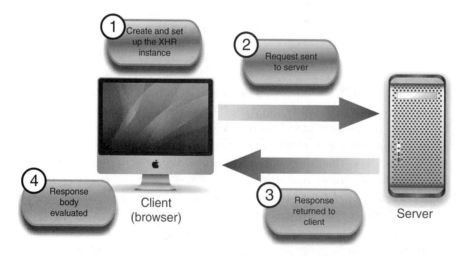

Figure 8.1   The lifecycle of an Ajax request as it makes its way from the client to the server and back again

Let's take a look at how those objects are used to generate requests to the server, beginning with creating an XHR instance.

8.1.1 Creating an XHR instance

In a perfect world, code written for one browser would work in all commonly used browsers. We've already learned that we don't live in that world, and things are no different when it comes to Ajax. There is a standard way to make asynchronous requests via the JavaScript XHR object, and an Internet Explorer proprietary way that uses an ActiveX control. With IE 7, a wrapper that emulates the standard interface is available, but IE 6 requires divergent code.

> **NOTE** jQuery's Ajax implementation—which we'll be addressing throughout the remainder of this chapter—doesn't use the Internet Explorer wrapper, citing issues with improper implementation. Rather, it uses the ActiveX object when available. This is good news for us! By using jQuery for our Ajax needs, we know that the best approaches have been researched and will be utilized.

Once created, the code to set up, initiate, and respond to the request is relatively browser-independent, and creating an instance of XHR is easy for any particular browser. The problem is that different browsers implement XHR in different ways, and we need to create the instance in the manner appropriate for the current browser.

But rather than relying on detecting which browser a user is running to determine which path to take, we'll use the preferred technique of *feature detection* that we introduced in chapter 6. Using this technique, we try to figure out what the browser's features are, not which browser is being used. Feature detection results in more robust code because it can work in any browser that supports the tested feature.

The code in listing 8.1 shows a typical idiom used to instantiate an instance of XHR using this technique.

Listing 8.1 Capability detection resulting in code that can use Ajax in many browsers

```
var xhr;
if (window.ActiveXObject) {                          Tests to see if
  xhr = new ActiveXObject("Microsoft.XMLHTTP");      ActiveX is present
}
else  if (window.XMLHttpRequest) {                   Tests to see if
  xhr = new XMLHttpRequest();                         XHR is defined
}
else {                                               Throws error if there's
  throw new Error("Ajax is not supported by this browser");   no Ajax support
}
```

After it's created, the XHR instance sports a conveniently consistent set of properties and methods across all supporting browser instances. These properties and methods are shown in table 8.1, and the most commonly used of these will be discussed in the sections that follow.

Table 8.1 `XMLHttpRequest` (XHR) methods and properties

Methods	Description
`abort()`	Causes the currently executing request to be cancelled.
`getAllResponseHeaders()`	Returns a single string containing the names and values of all response headers.
`getResponseHeader(name)`	Returns the value of the named response header.
`open(method,url,async, username,password)`	Sets the HTTP method (`GET` or `POST`) and destination URL of the request. Optionally, the request can be declared synchronous, and a username and password can be supplied for requests requiring container-based authentication.
`send(content)`	Initiates the request with the specified (optional) body content.
`setRequestHeader(name,value)`	Sets a request header using the specified name and value.
Properties	**Description**
`onreadystatechange`	The event handler to be invoked when the state of the request changes.
`readyState`	An integer value that indicates the current state of the active request as follows: 0 = UNSENT 1 = OPENED 2 = HEADERS_RECEIVED 3 = LOADING 4 = DONE
`responseText`	The body content returned in the response.
`responseXML`	If the body content is identified as XML, the XML DOM created from the body content.
`status`	The response status code returned from the server. For example: 200 for *success* or 404 for *not found*. See the HTTP specification[a] for the full set of codes.
`statusText`	The status text message returned by the response.

a. HTTP 1.1 status code definitions from RFC 2616:
http://www.w3.org/Protocols/rfc2616/rfc2616-sec10.html#sec10.

NOTE Want to get it from the horse's mouth? The XHR specification can be found at http://www.w3.org/TR/XMLHttpRequest/.

Now that we've got an XHR instance created, let's look at what it takes to set up and fire off the request to the server.

8.1.2　*Initiating the request*

Before we can send a request to the server, we need to perform the following setup steps:

1　Specify the HTTP method, such as (POST or GET)
2　Provide the URL of the server-side resource to be contacted
3　Let the XHR instance know how it can inform us of its progress
4　Provide any body content for POST requests

We set up the first two items by calling the open() method of XHR as follows:

```
xhr.open('GET','/some/resource/url');
```

Note that this method doesn't cause the request to be sent to the server. It merely sets up the URL and HTTP method to be used. The open() method can also be passed a third Boolean parameter that specifies whether the request is to be asynchronous (if true, which is the default) or synchronous (if false). There's seldom a good reason to make the request synchronous (even if doing so means we don't have to deal with callback functions); after all, the asynchronous nature of the request is usually the whole point of making a request in this fashion.

In the third step, we must provide a means for the XHR instance to tap us on the shoulder to let us know what's going on. We accomplish this by assigning a callback function to the onreadystatechange property of the XHR object. This function, known as the *ready state handler*, is invoked by the XHR instance at various stages of its processing. By looking at the settings of the other properties of XHR, we can find out exactly what's going on with the request. We'll take a look at how a typical ready state handler operates in the next section.

The final steps to initiating the request are to provide any body content for POST requests and send it off to the server. Both of these steps are accomplished via the send() method. For GET requests, which typically have no body, no body content parameter is passed, as follows:

```
xhr.send(null);
```

When request parameters are passed to POST requests, the string passed to the send() method must be in the proper format (which we might think of as *query string* format) in which the names and values are properly URI encoded. URI encoding is beyond the scope of this section (and, as it turns out, jQuery is going to handle all of that for us), but if you're curious, do a web search for the term encodeURIComponent, and you'll be suitably rewarded.

An example of such a call is as follows:

```
xhr.send('a=1&b=2&c=3');
```

Now let's see what the ready state handler is all about.

8.1.3   *Keeping track of progress*

An XHR instance informs us of its progress through the ready state handler. This handler is established by assigning a reference to the function to serve as the ready handler to the onreadystatechange property of the XHR instance.

Once the request is initiated via the send() method, this callback will be invoked numerous times as the request makes transitions through its various states. The current state of the request is available as a numeric code in the readyState property (see the description of this property in table 8.1).

That's nice, but more times than not, we're only interested in when the request completes and whether it was successful or not. Frequently we'll see ready handlers implemented using the idiom shown in listing 8.2.

Listing 8.2   Ready state handlers are often written to ignore all but the DONE state

```
xhr.onreadystatechange = function() {           Ignores all but
  if (this.readyState == 4) {               ◁┘   DONE state
    if (this.status >= 200 &&                   Branches on
        this.status < 300) {                    response status
      //success                    ◁┐  Executes
    }                                │  on success
    else {
      //problem                 ◁┐  Executes
    }                             │  on failure
  }
}
```

This code ignores all but the DONE state, and once that has been detected, examines the value of the status property to determine whether the request succeeded or not. The HTTP specification defines all status codes in the 200 to 299 range as success and those with values of 300 or above as various types of failure.

Now let's explore dealing with the response from a completed request.

8.1.4   *Getting the response*

Once the ready handler has determined that the readyState is complete and that the request completed successfully, the body of the response can be retrieved from the XHR instance.

Despite the moniker *Ajax* (where the *X* stands for XML), the format of the response body can be any text format; it's not limited to XML. In fact, most of the time, the response to Ajax requests is a format *other* than XML. It could be plain text or, perhaps, an HTML fragment; it could even be a text representation of a JavaScript object or array in JavaScript Object Notation (JSON) format (which is becoming increasingly popular as an exchange format).

Regardless of its format, the body of the response is available via the responseText property of the XHR instance (assuming that the request completes successfully). If the response indicates that the format of its body is XML by including a content type header specifying a MIME type of text/xml, application/xml, or a MIME type that ends with +xml, the response body will be parsed as XML. The resulting DOM will be available in the responseXML property. JavaScript (and jQuery itself, using its selector API) can then be used to process the XML DOM.

Processing XML on the client isn't rocket science, but—even with jQuery's help—it can still be a pain. Although there are times when nothing but XML will do for returning complex hierarchical data, frequently page authors will use other formats when the full power (and corresponding headache) of XML isn't absolutely necessary.

But some of those other formats aren't without their own pain. When JSON is returned, it must be converted into its runtime equivalent. When HTML is returned, it must be loaded into the appropriate destination element. And what if the HTML markup returned contains <script> blocks that need evaluation? We're not going to deal with these issues in this section because it isn't meant to be a complete Ajax reference and, more importantly, because we're going to find out that jQuery handles most of these issues on our behalf.

At this point, you might want to review the diagram of the whole process shown in figure 8.1.

In this short overview of Ajax, we've identified the following pain points that page authors using Ajax need to deal with:

- Instantiating an XHR object requires browser-specific code.
- Ready handlers need to sift through a lot of uninteresting state changes.
- The response body needs to be dealt with in numerous ways, depending upon its format.

The remainder of this chapter will describe how the jQuery Ajax methods and utility functions make Ajax a lot easier (and cleaner) to use on our pages. There are a lot of choices in the jQuery Ajax API, and we'll start with some of the simplest and most-used tools.

8.2   Loading content into elements

Perhaps one of the most common uses of Ajax is to grab a chunk of content from the server and stuff it into the DOM at some strategic location. The content could be an HTML fragment that's to become the child content of a target container element, or it could be plain text that will become the content of the target element.

Setting up for the examples

Unlike all of the example code that we've examined so far in this book, the code examples for this chapter require the services of a web server to receive the Ajax requests to server-side resources. Because it's well beyond the scope of this book to discuss the operation of server-side mechanisms, we're going to set up some minimal server-side resources that send data back to the client without worrying about doing it for real, treating the server as a "black box"; we don't need or want to know how it's doing its job.

To enable the serving of these smoke-and-mirrors resources, you'll need to set up a web server of some type. For your convenience, the server-side resources have been

continued

set up in two formats: Java Server Pages (JSP) and PHP. The JSP resources can be used if you're running (or wish to run) a servlet/JSP engine; if you want to enable PHP for your web server of choice, you can use the PHP resources.

If you want to use the JSP resources but aren't already running a suitable server, instructions on setting up the free Tomcat web server are included with the sample code for this chapter. You'll find these instructions in the chapter8/tomcat.pdf file. And don't be concerned; even if you've never looked at a single line of Java, it's easier than you might think!

The examples found in the downloaded code are set up to use either of the JSP or PHP resources, depending upon which server you have set up.

Once you have the server of your choice set up, you can hit the URL http://localhost:8080/jqia2/chapter8/test.jsp (to check your Tomcat installation) or http://localhost/jqia2/chapter8/test.php (to check your PHP installation). The latter assumes that you have set up your web server (Apache or any other you have chosen) to use the example code root folder as a document base.

When you can successfully view the appropriate test page, you'll be ready to run the examples in this chapter.

Alternatively, if you don't want to run these examples locally, you can run the example code remotely from http://bibeault.org/jqia2.

Let's imagine that, on page load, we want to grab a chunk of HTML from the server using a resource named someResource, and make it the content of a <div> element with an id of someContainer. For the final time in this chapter, let's look at how we'd do this without jQuery's assistance. Using the patterns we set out earlier in this chapter, the body of the onload handler is as shown in listing 8.3. The full HTML file for this example can be found in the file chapter8/listing.8.3.html.

> **NOTE**   Again, you must run this example using a web server—you can't just open the file in the browser—so the URL should be http://localhost:8080/jqia2/chapter8/listing.8.3.html. Omit the port specification of :8080 if using Apache, and leave it in if using Tomcat.
>
> In future URLs in this chapter we'll use the notation [:8080] to indicate that the port number might or might not be needed, but be sure *not* to include the square brackets as part of the URL.

Listing 8.3   Using native XHR to fetch and include an HTML fragment

```
var xhr;

if(window.ActiveXObject) {
  xhr = new ActiveXObject("Microsoft.XMLHTTP");
  }
else if (window.XMLHttpRequest) {
  xhr = new XMLHttpRequest();
}
```

```
else {
  throw new Error("Ajax is not supported by this browser");
}

xhr.onreadystatechange = function() {
  if (this.readyState == 4) {
    if (this.status >= 200 && this.status < 300) {
      document.getElementById('someContainer')
        .innerHTML = this.responseText;
    }
  }
}

xhr.open('GET','someResource');
xhr.send();
```

Although there's nothing tricky going on here, that's a non-trivial amount of code; 20 lines, without even counting the blank lines that we added for readability.

The equivalent code we'd write as the body of a ready handler using jQuery is as follows:

```
$('#someContainer').load('someResource');
```

We're betting that we know which code you'd rather write and maintain! Let's take a close look at the jQuery method we used in this statement.

8.2.1 *Loading content with jQuery*

The simple jQuery statement at the end of the previous section easily loads content from the server-side resource using one of the most basic, but useful, jQuery Ajax methods: load(). The full syntax description of this method is as follows:

Method syntax: load

load(url,parameters,callback)
Initiates an Ajax request to the specified URL with optional request parameters. A callback function can be specified that's invoked when the request completes and the DOM has been modified. The response text replaces the content of all matched elements.

Parameters

url   (String) The URL of the server-side resource to which the request is sent, optionally modified via selector (explained below).

parameters   (String|Object|Array) Specifies any data that's to be passed as request parameters. This argument can be a string that will be used as the query string, an object whose properties are serialized into properly encoded parameters to be passed to the request, or an array of objects whose name and value properties specify the name/value pairs.
              If specified as an object or array, the request is made using the POST method. If omitted or specified as a string, the GET method is used.

callback   (Function) An optional callback function invoked after the response data has been loaded into the elements of the matched set. The parameters passed to this function are the response text, a status string (usually "success"), and the XHR instance.
              This function will be invoked once for each element in the wrapped set with the target element set as the function context (this).

Returns
The wrapped set.

Though simple to use, this method has some important nuances. For example, when the `parameters` parameter is used to supply the request parameters, the request is made using the POST HTTP method if an object hash or array is used; otherwise, a GET request is initiated. If we want to make a GET request with parameters, we can include them as a query string on the URL. But be aware that when we do so, we're responsible for ensuring that the query string is properly formatted and that the names and values of the request parameters are URI-encoded. The JavaScript `encodeURIComponent()` method is handy for this, or you can employ the services of the jQuery `$.param()` utility function that we covered in chapter 6.

Most of the time, we'll use the `load()` method to inject the complete response into whatever elements are contained within the wrapped set, but sometimes we may want to filter elements coming back as the response. If we want to filter response elements, jQuery allows us to specify a selector on the URL that will be used to limit which response elements are injected into the wrapped elements. We specify the selector by suffixing the URL with a space followed by the selector.

For example, to filter response elements so that only <div> instances are injected, we write

```
$('.injectMe').load('/someResource div');
```

When it comes to supplying the data to be submitted with a request, sometimes we'll be winging it with ad hoc data, but frequently we'll find ourselves wanting to gather data that a user has entered into form controls.

As you might expect, jQuery's got some assistance up its sleeve.

SERIALIZING FORM DATA

If the data that we want to send as request parameters come from form controls, a helpful jQuery method for building a query string is `serialize()`, whose syntax is as follows:

Method syntax: serialize

`serialize()`
Creates a properly formatted and encoded query string from all successful form elements in the wrapped set, or all successful form elements of forms in the wrapped set.

Parameters
  none
Returns
The formatted query string.

The `serialize()` method is smart enough to only collect information from form control elements in the wrapped set, and only from those qualifying elements that are deemed *successful*. A successful control is one that would be included as part of a form submission according to the rules of the HTML specification.[1] Controls such as unchecked checkboxes and radio buttons, dropdowns with no selections, and dis-

---

[1] HTML 4.01 Specification, section 17.13.2, "Successful controls": http://www.w3.org/TR/html401/interact/forms.html#h-17.13.2.

abled controls aren't considered successful and don't participate in form submission, so they're also ignored by serialize().

If we'd rather get the form data in a JavaScript array (as opposed to a query string), jQuery provides the serializeArray() method.

Method syntax: serializeArray

serializeArray()
Collects the values of all successful form controls into an array of objects containing the names and values of the controls.

Parameters
  none
Returns
The array of form data.

The array returned by serializeArray() is composed of anonymous object instances, each of which contains a name property and a value property that contain the name and value of each successful form control. Note that this is (not accidentally) one of the formats suitable for passing to the load() method to specify the request parameter data.

With the load() method at our disposal, let's put it to work solving some common real-world problems that many web developers encounter.

8.2.2 Loading dynamic HTML fragments

Often in business applications, particularly for commerce web sites, we want to grab real-time data from the server in order to present our users with the most up-to-date information. After all, we wouldn't want to mislead customers into thinking that they can buy something that's not available, would we? In this section, we'll begin to develop a page that we'll add to throughout the course of the chapter. This page is part of a web site for a fictitious firm named The Boot Closet, an online retailer of overstock and closeout motorcycle boots. Unlike the fixed product catalogs of other online retailers, this inventory of overstock and closeouts is fluid, depending on what deals the proprietor was able to make that day and what's already been sold from the inventory. It will be important for us to always make sure that we're displaying the latest info!

To begin our page (which will omit site navigation and other boilerplate to concentrate on the lessons at hand), we want to present our customers with a dropdown containing the styles that are currently available and, when a style is selected, display detailed information regarding that style. On initial display, the page will look as shown in figure 8.2.

After the page first loads, a dropdown with the list of styles currently available in the inventory is displayed. When no style is selected, we'll display a helpful message as a placeholder for the selection: "— choose a style —". This invites the user to interact with the dropdown, and when a user selects a boot style from this dropdown, here's what we want to do:

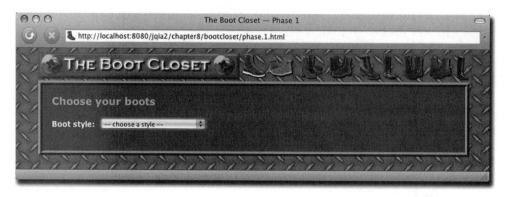

Figure 8.2   The initial display of our commerce page with a simple dropdown inviting customers to click on it

- Display the detailed information about that style in the area below the drop-down.

- Remove the "— choose a style —" entry; once the user picks a style, it's served its purpose and is no longer meaningful.

Let's start by taking a look at the HTML markup for the body that defines this page structure:

```
<body>
  <div id="banner">
    <img src="images/banner.boot.closet.png" alt="The Boot Closet"/>
  </div>
  <div id="pageContent">
    <h1>Choose your boots</h1>             ❶ Contains
    <div>                                     selection
      <div id="selectionsPane">               control
        <label for="bootChooserControl">Boot style:</label> 
        <select id="bootChooserControl" name="bootStyle"></select>
      </div>
      <div id="productDetailPane"></div>    Holds place for
    </div>                                 ❷ product details
  </div>
</body>
```

Not much to it, is there?

As would be expected, we've defined all the visual rendition information in an external style sheet, and (adhering to the precepts of Unobtrusive JavaScript) we've included no behavioral aspects in the HTML markup.

The most interesting parts of this markup are a container ❶ that holds the `<select>` element that will allow customers to choose a boot style, and another container ❷ into which product details will be injected.

Note that the boot style control needs to have its option elements added before the user can interact with the page. So let's set about adding the necessary behavior to this page.

The first thing we'll add is an Ajax request to fetch and populate the boot style dropdown.

NOTE Under most circumstances, initial values such as these would be handled on the server prior to sending the HTML to the browser. But there are circumstances where prefetching data via Ajax may be appropriate, and we're doing that here, if only for instructional purposes.

To add the options to the boot style control, we define a ready handler, and within it we make use of the handy `load()` method:

```
$('#bootChooserControl').load('/jqia2/action/fetchBootStyleOptions');
```

How simple is that? The only complicated part of this statement is the URL, which isn't really all that long or complicated, which specifies a request to a server-side action named `fetchBootStyleOptions`.

One of the nice things about using Ajax (with the ease of jQuery making it even nicer) is that it's completely independent of the server-side technology. Obviously the choice of server-side tech has an influence on the structure of the URLs, but beyond that we don't need to worry ourselves much about what's going to transpire on the server. We simply make HTTP requests, sometimes with appropriate parameter data, and as long as the server returns the expected responses, we could care less if the server is being powered by Java, Ruby, PHP, or even old-fashioned CGI.

In this particular case, we expect that the server-side resource will return the HTML markup representing the boot style options—supposedly from the inventory database. Our faux backend code returns the following as the response:

```
<option value="">&mdash; choose a style &mdash;</option>
<option value="7177382">Caterpillar Tradesman Work Boot</option>
<option value="7269643">Caterpillar Logger Boot</option>
<option value="7332058">Chippewa 9" Briar Waterproof Bison Boot</option>
<option value="7141832">Chippewa 17" Engineer Boot</option>
<option value="7141833">Chippewa 17" Snakeproof Boot</option>
<option value="7173656">Chippewa 11" Engineer Boot</option>
<option value="7141922">Chippewa Harness Boot</option>
<option value="7141730">Danner Foreman Pro Work Boot</option>
<option value="7257914">Danner Grouse GTX Boot</option>
```

This response then gets injected into the `<select>` element, resulting in a fully functional control.

Our next act is to instrument the dropdown so that it can react to changes, carrying out the duties that we listed earlier. The code for that is only slightly more complicated:

```
$('#bootChooserControl').change(function(event){
  $('#productDetailPane').load(
    '/jqia2/action/fetchProductDetails',
    {style: $(event.target).val()},
    function() { $('[value=""]',event.target).remove(); }
  );
});
```

Establishes change handler ❶

❷ Fetches and displays product detail

In this code, we select the boot style dropdown and bind a `change` handler to it ❶. In the callback for the change handler, which will be invoked whenever a customer changes the selection, we obtain the current value of the selection by applying the `val()` method to the event target, which is the `<select>` element that triggered the event. We then once again employ the `load()` method ❷ to the `productDetailPane` element to initiate an Ajax callback to a server-side resource, in this case `fetch-ProductDetails`, passing the style value as a parameter named `style`.

After the customer chooses an available boot style, the page will appear as shown in figure 8.3.

The most notable operation performed in the ready handler is the use of the `load()` method to quickly and easily fetch snippets of HTML from the server and place them within the DOM as the children of existing elements. This method is extremely handy and well suited to web applications that are powered by servers capable of server-side templating with technologies such as JSP and PHP.

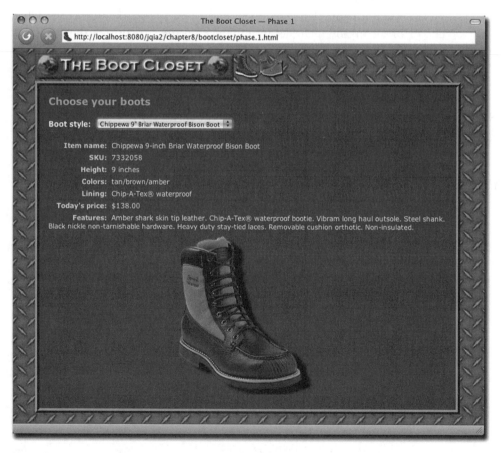

Figure 8.3   The server-side resource returns a preformatted fragment of HTML to display the detailed boot information.

Listing 8.4 shows the complete code for our Boot Closet page, which can be found at http://localhost[:8080]/jqia2/chapter8/bootcloset/phase.1.html. We'll be revisiting this page to add further capabilities to it as we progress through this chapter.

Listing 8.4   The first phase of the Boot Closet commerce page

```html
<!DOCTYPE html>
<html>
  <head>
    <title>The Boot Closet &mdash; Phase 1</title>
    <link rel="stylesheet" type="text/css" href="../../styles/core.css">
    <link rel="stylesheet" type="text/css" href="bootcloset.css">
    <link rel="icon" type="image/gif" href="images/favicon.gif">
    <script type="text/javascript"
            src="../../scripts/jquery-1.4.js"></script>
    <script type="text/javascript"
            src="../../scripts/jqia2.support.js"></script>
    <script type="text/javascript">
      $(function() {

        $('#bootChooserControl')
          .load('/jqia2/action/fetchBootStyleOptions');

        $('#bootChooserControl').change(function(event){
          $('#productDetailPane').load(
            '/jqia2/action/fetchProductDetails',
            {style: $(event.target).val()},
            function() { $('[value=""]',event.target).remove(); }
          );
        });

      });
    </script>
  </head>

  <body>

    <div id="banner">
      <img src="images/banner.boot.closet.png" alt="The Boot Closet"/>
    </div>

    <div id="pageContent">

      <h1>Choose your boots</h1>

      <div>

        <div id="selectionsPane">
          <label for="bootChooserControl">Boot style:</label> 
          <select id="bootChooserControl" name="bootStyle"></select>
        </div>

        <div id="productDetailPane"></div>

      </div>

    </div>

  </body>

</html>
```

The load() method is tremendously useful when we want to grab a fragment of HTML to stuff into the content of an element (or set of elements). But there may be times when we either want more control over how the Ajax request gets made, or we need to do something more esoteric with the returned data in the response body.

Let's continue our investigation of what jQuery has to offer for these more complex situations.

8.3   *Making GET and POST requests*

The load() method makes either a GET or a POST request, depending on how the request parameter data (if any) is provided, but sometimes we want to have a bit more control over which HTTP method gets used. Why should *we* care? Because, just maybe, our *servers* care.

Web authors have traditionally played fast and loose with the GET and POST methods, using one or the other without heeding how the HTTP protocol intends for these methods to be used. The intentions for each method are as follows:

- GET *requests*—Intended to be *idempotent*; the same GET operation, made again and again and again, should return exactly the same results (assuming no other force is at work changing the server state).

- POST *requests*—Can be *non-idempotent*; the data they send to the server can be used to change the model state of the application; for example, adding or updating records in a database or removing information from the server.

A GET request should, therefore, be used whenever the purpose of the request is to merely get data; as its name implies. It may be required to *send* some parameter data to the server for the GET; for example, to identify a style number to retrieve color information. But when data is being sent to the server in order to effect a change, POST should be used.

> **WARNING**   *This is more than theoretical.* Browsers make decisions about caching based upon the HTTP method used, and GET requests are highly subject to caching. Using the proper HTTP method ensures that you don't get crossways with the browser's or server's expectations regarding the intentions of the requests.
>
> This is just a glimpse into the realm of RESTful principles, where other HTTP methods, such as PUT and DELETE, also come into play. But for our purposes, we'll limit our discussion to the GET and POST methods.

With that in mind, if we look back to our phase one implementation of The Boot Closet (in listing 8.4), we discover that *we're doing it wrong*! Because jQuery initiates a POST request when we supply an object hash for parameter data, we're making a POST when we really should be making a GET. If we glance at a Firebug log (as shown in figure 8.4) when we display our page in Firefox, we can see that our second request, submitted when we make a selection from the style dropdown, is indeed a POST.

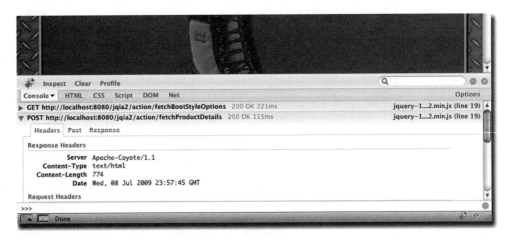

Figure 8.4   An inspection of the Firebug console shows that we're making a POST request when we should be making a GET.

Does it really matter? That's up to you, but if we want to use HTTP in the manner in which it was intended, our request to fetch the boot detail should be a GET rather than a POST.

We could simply make the parameter that specifies the request information a string rather than an object hash (and we'll revisit that a little later), but for now, let's take advantage of another way that jQuery lets us initiate Ajax requests.

Get Firebug

Trying to develop a DOM-scripted application without the aid of a debugging tool is like trying to play concert piano while wearing welding gloves. Why would you do that to yourself?

One important tool to have in your tool chest is *Firebug*, a plugin for the Firefox browser. As shown in figure 8.4, Firebug not only lets us inspect the JavaScript console, it lets us inspect the live DOM, the CSS, the script, and many other aspects of our page as we work through its development.

One feature most relevant for our current purposes is its ability to log Ajax requests along with both the request and response information.

For browsers other than Firefox, there's *Firebug Lite*, which simply loads as a JavaScript library while we're debugging.

You can get Firebug at http://getfirebug.com and Firebug Lite at http://getfire-bug.com/lite.html.

Google's Chrome browser comes built in with Firebug-like debug capabilities, which you can display by opening its Developer Tools (look around the menus for this entry—it keeps moving).

8.3.1 Getting data with GET

jQuery gives us a few means to make GET requests, which unlike load(), aren't implemented as jQuery methods on a wrapped set. Rather, a handful of utility functions are provided to make various types of GET requests. As we pointed out in chapter 1, jQuery utility functions are top-level functions that are namespaced with the jQuery global name (and its $ alias).

When we want to fetch some data from the server and decide what to do with it ourselves (rather than letting the load() method set it as the content of an HTML element), we can use the $.get() utility function. Its syntax is as follows:

Function syntax: $.get

$.get(url,parameters,callback,type)
Initiates a GET request to the server using the specified URL with any passed parameters as the query string.

Parameters

url	(String) The URL of the server-side resource to contact via the GET method.
parameters	(String|Object|Array) Specifies any data that's to be passed as request parameters. This parameter can be a string that will be used as the query string, an object whose properties are serialized into properly encoded parameters to be passed to the request, or an array of objects whose name and value properties specify the name/value pairs.
callback	(Function) An optional function invoked when the request completes successfully. The response body is passed as the first parameter to this callback, interpreted according to the setting of the type parameter, and the text status is passed as the second parameter. A third parameter contains a reference to the XHR instance.
type	(String) Optionally specifies how the response body is to be interpreted; one of html, text, xml, json, script, or jsonp. See the description of $.ajax() later in this chapter for more details.

Returns
The XHR instance.

The $.get() utility function allows us to initiate GET requests with a lot of versatility. We can specify request parameters (if appropriate) in numerous handy formats, provide a callback to be invoked upon a successful response, and even direct how the response is to be interpreted and passed to the callback. If even that's not enough versatility, we'll be seeing a more general function, $.ajax(), later on.

We'll be examining the type parameter in greater detail when we look at the $.ajax() utility function, but for now we'll let it default to html or xml depending upon the content type of the response.

Applying $.get() to our Boot Closet page, we'll replace the use of the load() method with the $.get() function, as shown in listing 8.5.

Listing 8.5 Changing the Boot Closet to use a GET when fetching style details

```
$('#bootChooserControl').change(function(event){
  $.get(
    '/jqia2/action/fetchProductDetails',        Initiates GET
    {style: $(event.target).val()},          ❶ request
    function(response) {
      $('#productDetailPane').html(response);
      $('[value=""]',event.target).remove();      Injects
    }                         ❷ response HTML
  );
});
```

The changes for this second phase of our page are subtle, but significant. We call `$.get()` ❶ in place of `load()`, passing the same URL and the same request parameters. Because `$.get()` does no automatic injection of the response anywhere within the DOM, we need to do that ourselves, which is easily accomplished via a call to the `html()` method ❷.

The code for this version of our page can found at http://localhost[:8080]/jqia2/chapter8/bootcloset/phase.2.html, and when we display it and select a style dropdown, we can see that a GET request has been made, as shown in figure 8.5.

In this example, we returned formatted HTML from the server and inserted it into the DOM, but as we can see from the `type` parameter to `$.get()`, there are many other possibilities than HTML. In fact, the term *Ajax* began its life as the acronym AJAX, where the X stood for XML.

When we pass the `type` as `xml` (remember, we'll be talking about `type` in more detail in a little bit), and return XML from the server, the data passed to the callback is a parsed XML DOM. And although XML is great when we need its flexibility and our data is highly hierarchical in nature, XML can be painful to traverse and to digest its data. Let's see another jQuery utility function that's quite useful when our data needs are more straightforward.

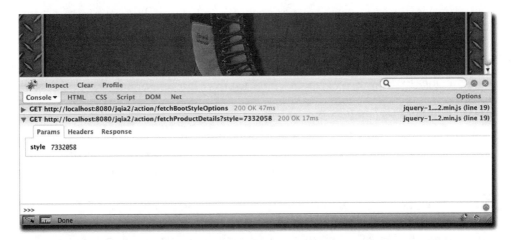

Figure 8.5   Now we can see that the second request is a GET rather than a POST, as befitting the operation.

8.3.2   Getting JSON data

As stated in the previous section, when an XML document is returned from the server, the XML document is automatically parsed, and the resulting DOM is made available to the callback function. When XML is overkill or otherwise unsuitable as a data-transfer mechanism, JSON is often used in its place. One reason for this choice is that JSON is astoundingly easy to digest in client-side scripts. jQuery makes it even easier.

For times when we know that the response will be JSON, the `$.getJSON()` utility function automatically parses the returned JSON string and makes the resulting JavaScript data item available to its callback. The syntax of this utility function is as follows:

Function syntax: $.getJSON

`$.getJSON(url,parameters,callback)`

Initiates a GET request to the server using the specified URL, with any passed parameters as the query string. The response is interpreted as a JSON string, and the resulting data is passed to the callback function.

Parameters

url	(String) The URL of the server-side resource contacted via the GET method.
parameters	(String|Object|Array) Specifies any data that's to be passed as request parameters. This parameter can be a string that will be used as the query string, an object whose properties are serialized into properly encoded parameters to be passed to the request, or an array of objects whose `name` and `value` properties specify the name/value pairs.
callback	(Function) A function invoked when the request completes. The data value resulting from digesting the response body as a JSON representation is passed as the first parameter to this callback, and the status text is passed as the second parameter. A third parameter provides a reference to the XHR instance.

Returns

The XHR instance.

This function, which is simply a convenience function for `$.get()` with a `type` of `json`, is great for those times when we want to get data from the server without the overhead of dealing with XML.

Between `$.get()` and `$.getJSON()`, jQuery gives us some powerful tools when it comes to making GET requests, but man does not live by GETs alone!

8.3.3   Making POST requests

"Sometimes you feel like a nut, sometimes you don't." What's true of choosing between an Almond Joy or a Mounds candy bar is also true of making requests to the server. Sometimes we want to make a GET, but at other times we want (or even need) to make a POST request.

There are any number of reasons why we might choose a POST over a GET. First, the intention of the HTTP protocol is that POST will be used for any non-idempotent requests. Therefore, if our request has the potential to cause a change in the server-side state, resulting in varying responses, it should be a POST. Moreover, accepted practices and conventions aside, a POST operation must sometimes be used when the data to be passed to the server exceeds the small amount that can be passed by URL in a query string—a limit that's a browser-dependent value. And sometimes, the server-side resource we contact may only support POST operations, or it might even perform different functions depending upon whether our request uses the GET or POST method.

For those occasions when a POST is desired or mandated, jQuery offers the $.post() utility function, which operates in a similar fashion to $.get(), except for employing the POST HTTP method. Its syntax is as follows:

Function syntax: $.post

$.post(url,parameters,callback,type)

Initiates a POST request to the server using the specified URL, with any parameters passed within the body of the request.

Parameters

url	(String) The URL of the server-side resource to contact via the POST method.
parameters	(String|Object|Array) Specifies any data that's to be passed as request parameters. This parameter can be a string that will be used as the query string, an object whose properties are serialized into properly encoded parameters to be passed to the request, or an array of objects whose name and value properties specify the name/value pairs.
callback	(Function) A function invoked when the request completes. The response body is passed as the single parameter to this callback, and the status text as the second. A third parameter provides a reference to the XHR instance.
type	(String) Optionally specifies how the response body is to be interpreted; one of html, text, xml, json, script, or jsonp. See the description of $.ajax() for more details.

Returns

The XHR instance.

Except for making a POST request, using $.post() is identical to using $.get(). jQuery takes care of the details of passing the request data in the request body (as opposed to the query string), and sets the HTTP method appropriately.

Now, getting back to our Boot Closet project, we've made a really good start, but there's more to buying a pair of boots than just selecting a style; customers are sure to want to pick which color they want, and certainly they'll need to specify their size. We'll use these additional requirements to show how to solve one of the most-asked questions in online Ajax forums, that of ...

8.3.4 *Implementing cascading dropdowns*

The implementation of cascading dropdowns—where subsequent dropdown options depend upon the selections of previous dropdowns—has become sort of a poster child for Ajax on the web. And although you'll find thousands, perhaps tens of thousands, of solutions, we're going to implement a solution on our Boot Closet page that demonstrates how ridiculously simple jQuery makes it.

We've already seen how easy it was to load a dropdown dynamically with server-powered option data. We'll see that tying multiple dropdowns together in a cascading relationship is only slightly more work.

Let's dig in by listing the changes we need to make in the next phase of our page:

- Add dropdowns for color and size.
- When a style is selected, add options to the color dropdown that show the colors available for that style.
- When a color is selected, add options to the size dropdown that show the sizes available for the selected combination of style and color.
- Make sure things remain consistent. This includes removing the "— please make a selection —" options from newly created dropdowns once they've been used once, and making sure that the three dropdowns never show an invalid combination.

We're also going to revert to using load() again, this time coercing it to initiate a GET rather than a POST. It's not that we have anything against $.get(), but load() just seems more natural when we're using Ajax to load HTML fragments.

To start off, let's examine the new HTML markup that defines the additional dropdowns. A new container for the select elements is defined to contain three labeled elements:

```
<div id="selectionsPane">
  <label for="bootChooserControl">Boot style:</label>
  <select id="bootChooserControl" name="style"></select>
  <label for="colorChooserControl">Color:</label>
  <select id="colorChooserControl" name="color" disabled="disabled"></select>
  <label for="sizeChooserControl">Size:</label>
  <select id="sizeChooserControl" name="size" disabled="disabled"></select>
</div>
```

The previous style selection element remains, but it has been joined by two more: one for color, and one for size, each of which is initially empty and disabled.

That was easy, and it takes care of the additions to the structure. Now let's add the additional behaviors.

The style selection dropdown must now perform double duty. Not only must it continue to fetch and display the boot details when a selection is made, its change handler must now also populate and enable the color selection dropdown with the colors available for whatever style was chosen.

Let's refactor the fetching of the details first. We want to use load(), but we also want to force a GET, as opposed to the POST that we were initiating earlier. In order to have load() induce a GET, we need to pass a string, rather than an object hash, to specify the request parameter data. Luckily, with jQuery's help, we won't have to build that string ourselves. The first part of the change handler for the style dropdown gets refactored like this:

```
$('#bootChooserControl').change(function(event){
  $('#productDetailPane').load(
    '/jqia2/action/fetchProductDetails',
    $(this).serialize()
  );
  // more to follow
});
```
Provides
query string

By using the serialize() method, we create a string representation of the value of the style dropdown, thereby coercing the load() method to initiate a GET, just as we wanted.

The second duty that the change handler needs to perform is to load the color-choice dropdown with appropriate values for the chosen style, and then enable it. Let's take a look at the rest of the code to be added to the handler:

```
$('#colorChooserControl').load(
  '/jqia2/action/fetchColorOptions',
  $(this).serialize(),
  function(){
    $(this).attr('disabled',false);
    $('#sizeChooserControl')
      .attr('disabled',true)
      .html("");
  }
);
```
❶ Fetches and loads
color options

Enables
❷ color control

❸ Disables and
empties size
control

This code should look familiar. It's just another use of load(), this time referencing an action named fetchColorOptions, which is designed to return a set of formatted <option> elements representing the colors available for the chosen style (which we again passed as request data) ❶. This time, we've also specified a callback to be executed when the GET request successfully returns a response.

In this callback, we perform two important tasks. First, we enable the color-chooser control ❷. The call to load() injected the <option> elements, but once populated it would still be disabled if we did not enable it.

Second, the callback disables and empties the size-chooser control ❸. But why? (Pause a moment and think about it.)

Even though the size control will already be disabled and empty the first time the style chooser's value is changed, what about later on? What if, after the customer chooses a style and a color (which we'll soon see results in the population of the size control), he or she changes the selected style? Because the sizes displayed depend upon the combination of style and color, the sizes previously displayed are no longer applicable and don't reflect a consistent view of what's chosen. Therefore, whenever the style changes, we need to blow the size options away and reset the size control to initial conditions.

Before we sit back and enjoy a lovely beverage, we've got more work to do. We still have to instrument the color-chooser dropdown to use the selected style and color values to fetch and load the size-chooser dropdown. The code to do this follows a familiar pattern:

```
$('#colorChooserControl').change(function(event){
  $('#sizeChooserControl').load(
    '/jqia2/action/fetchSizeOptions',
    $('#bootChooserControl,#colorChooserControl').serialize(),
    function(){
      $(this).attr('disabled',false);
    }
  );
});
```

Upon a change event, the size information is obtained via the fetchSizeOptions action, passing both the boot style and color selections, and the size control is enabled.

There's one more thing that we need to do. When each dropdown is initially populated, it's seeded with an <option> element with a blank value and display text along the lines of "— choose a something —". You may recall that in the previous phases of this page, we added code to remove that option from the style dropdown upon selection.

Well, we could add such code to the change handlers for the style and color dropdowns, and add instrumentation for the size dropdown (which currently has none) to add that. But let's be a bit more suave about it.

One capability of the event model that often gets ignored by many a web developer is *event bubbling*. Page authors frequently focus only on the targets of events, and forget that events will bubble up the DOM tree, where handlers can deal with those events in more general ways than at the target level.

If we recognize that removing the option with a blank value from any of the three dropdowns can be handled in the exact same fashion *regardless* of which dropdown is the target of the event, we can avoid repeating the same code in three places by establishing a *single* handler, higher in the DOM, that will recognize and handle the change events.

Recalling the structure of the document, the three dropdowns are contained within a <div> element with an id of selectionsPane. We can handle the removal of the temporary option for all three dropdowns with the following, single listener:

```
$('#selectionsPane').change(function(event){
  $('[value=""]',event.target).remove();
});
```

This listener will be triggered whenever a change event happens on any of the enclosed dropdowns, and will remove the option with the blank value within the context of the target of the event (which will be the changed dropdown). How slick is that?

Using event bubbling to avoid repeating the same code in lower-level handlers can really elevate your script to the big leagues!

With that, we've completed phase three of The Boot Closet, adding cascading dropdowns into the mix as shown in figure 8.6. We can use the same techniques in any pages where dropdown values depend upon previous selections. The page for this phase can be found at URL http://localhost[:8080]/jqia2/chapter8/bootcloset/phase.3.html.

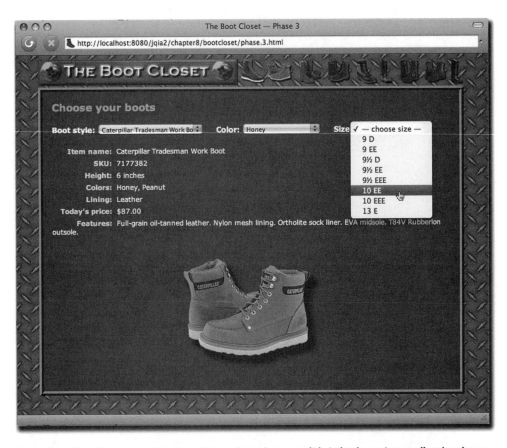

Figure 8.6 The third phase of The Boot Closet shows how easy it is to implement cascading dropdowns.

The full code of the page is now as shown in listing 8.6.

Listing 8.6 The Boot Closet, now with cascading dropdowns!

```
<!DOCTYPE html>
<html>
  <head>
    <title>The Boot Closet &mdash; Phase 3</title>
    <link rel="stylesheet" type="text/css" href="../../styles/core.css">
    <link rel="stylesheet" type="text/css" href="bootcloset.css">
    <link rel="icon" type="image/gif" href="images/favicon.gif">
    <script type="text/javascript"
            src="../../scripts/jquery-1.4.js"></script>

    <script type="text/javascript"
            src="../../scripts/jqia2.support.js"></script>
    <script type="text/javascript">
      $(function() {

        $('#bootChooserControl')
          .load('/jqia2/action/fetchBootStyleOptions');
```

```
    $('#bootChooserControl').change(function(event){
      $('#productDetailPane').load(
        '/jqia2/action/fetchProductDetails',
        $(this).serialize()
      );
      $('#colorChooserControl').load(
        '/jqia2/action/fetchColorOptions',
        $(this).serialize(),
        function(){
          $(this).attr('disabled',false);
          $('#sizeChooserControl')
            .attr('disabled',true)
            .html("");
        }
      );
    });

    $('#colorChooserControl').change(function(event){
      $('#sizeChooserControl').load(
        '/jqia2/action/fetchSizeOptions',
        $('#bootChooserControl,#colorChooserControl').serialize(),
        function(){
          $(this).attr('disabled',false);
        }
      );
    });

    $('#selectionsPane').change(function(event){
      $('[value=""]',event.target).remove();
    });

  });
  </script>
</head>

<body>

  <div id="banner">
    <img src="images/banner.boot.closet.png" alt="The Boot Closet"/>
  </div>

  <div id="pageContent">

    <h1>Choose your boots</h1>

    <div>

      <div id="selectionsPane">
        <label for="bootChooserControl">Boot style:</label>
        <select id="bootChooserControl" name="style"></select>
        <label for="colorChooserControl">Color:</label>
        <select id="colorChooserControl" name="color"
                disabled="disabled"></select>
        <label for="sizeChooserControl">Size:</label>
        <select id="sizeChooserControl" name="size"
                disabled="disabled"></select>
      </div>

      <div id="productDetailPane"></div>
```

```
      </div>

    </div>

  </body>

</html>
```

As we've seen, with the `load()` method and the various GET and POST jQuery Ajax functions at our disposal, we can exert some measure of control over how our request is initiated and how we're notified of its completion. But for those times when we need *full* control over an Ajax request, jQuery has a means for us to get as picky as we want.

8.4   Taking full control of an Ajax request

The functions and methods we've seen so far are convenient for many cases, but there may be times when we want to take the control of all the nitty-gritty details into our own hands.

In this section, we'll explore how jQuery lets us exert such dominion.

8.4.1   Making Ajax requests with all the trimmings

For those times when we want or need to exert fine-grained control over how we make Ajax requests, jQuery provides a general utility function for making Ajax requests, named `$.ajax()`. Under the covers, all other jQuery features that make Ajax requests eventually use this function to initiate the request. Its syntax is as follows:

Function syntax: $.ajax

`$.ajax(options)`
Initiates an Ajax request using the passed options to control how the request is made and callbacks notified.

Parameters
    `options`   (Object) An object whose properties define the parameters for this operation. See table 8.2 for details.

Returns
The XHR instance.

Looks simple, doesn't it? But don't be deceived. The `options` parameter can specify a large range of values that can be used to tune the operation of this function. These options (in general order of their importance and the likelihood of their use) are defined in table 8.2.

Table 8.2   Options for the `$.ajax()` utility function

Name	Description
`url`	(String) The URL for the request.
`type`	(String) The HTTP method to use. Usually either POST or GET. If omitted, the default is GET.

Table 8.2   Options for the `$.ajax()` utility function *(continued)*

Name	Description
data	(String|Object|Array) Defines the values that will serve as the query parameters to be passed to the request. If the request is a GET, this data is passed as the query string. If a POST, the data is passed as the request body. In either case, the encoding of the values is handled by the `$.ajax()` utility function. This parameter can be a string that will be used as the query string or response body, an object whose properties are serialized, or an array of objects whose `name` and `value` properties specify the name/value pairs.
dataType	(String) A keyword that identifies the type of data that's expected to be returned by the response. This value determines what, if any, post-processing occurs upon the data before being passed to callback functions. The valid values are as follows: • `xml`—The response text is parsed as an XML document and the resulting XML DOM is passed to the callbacks. • `html`—The response text is passed unprocessed to the callback functions. Any `<script>` blocks within the returned HTML fragment are evaluated. • `json`—The response text is evaluated as a JSON string, and the resulting object is passed to the callbacks. • `jsonp`—Similar to `json` except that remote scripting is allowed, assuming the remote server supports it. • `script`—The response text is passed to the callbacks. Prior to any callbacks being invoked, the response is processed as a JavaScript statement or statements. • `text`—The response text is assumed to be plain text. The server resource is responsible for setting the appropriate content-type response header. If this property is omitted, the response text is passed to the callbacks without any processing or evaluation.
cache	(Boolean) If `false`, ensures that the response won't be cached by the browser. Defaults to `true` except when `dataType` is specified as either `script` or `jsonp`.
context	(Element) Specifies an element that is to be set as the context of all callbacks related to this request.
timeout	(Number) Sets a timeout for the Ajax request in milliseconds. If the request doesn't complete before the timeout expires, the request is aborted and the error callback (if defined) is called.
global	(Boolean) If `false`, disables the triggering of global Ajax events. These are jQuery-specific custom events that trigger at various points or conditions during the processing of an Ajax request. We'll be discussing them in detail in the upcoming section. If omitted, the default (`true`) is to enable the triggering of global events.
contentType	(String) The content type to be specified on the request. If omitted, the default is `application/x-www-form-urlencoded`, the same type used as the default for form submissions.
success	(Function) A function invoked if the response to the request indicates a success status code. The response body is returned as the first parameter to this function and evaluated according to the specification of the `dataType` property. The second parameter is a string containing a status value—in this case, always `success`. A third parameter provides a reference to the XHR instance.

Table 8.2 Options for the `$.ajax()` utility function *(continued)*

Name	Description
error	(Function) A function invoked if the response to the request returns an error status code. Three arguments are passed to this function: the XHR instance, a status message string (in this case, one of: `error`, `timeout`, `notmodified`, or `parseerror`), and an optional exception object, sometimes returned from the XHR instance, if any.
complete	(Function) A function called upon completion of the request. Two arguments are passed: the XHR instance and a status message string of either `success` or `error`. If either a success or error callback is also specified, this function is invoked after that callback is called.
beforeSend	(Function) A function invoked prior to initiating the request. This function is passed the XHR instance and can be used to set custom headers or to perform other pre-request operations. Returning `false` from this handler will cancel the request.
async	(Boolean) If specified as `false`, the request is submitted as a synchronous request. By default, the request is asynchronous.
processData	(Boolean) If set to `false`, prevents the data passed from being processed into URL-encoded format. By default, the data is URL-encoded into a format suitable for use with requests of type `application/x-www-form-urlencoded`.
dataFilter	(Function) A callback invoked to filter the response data. This function is passed the raw response data and the `dataType` value, and is expected to return the "sanitized" data.
ifModified	(Function) If `true`, allows a request to succeed only if the response content has not changed since the last request, according to the `Last-Modified` header. If omitted, no header check is performed. Defaults to `false`.
jsonp	(String) Specifies a query parameter name to override the default `jsonp` callback parameter name of `callback`.
username	(String) The username to be used in the event of an HTTP authentication request.
password	(String) The password to be used in the case of an HTTP authentication request.
scriptCharset	(String) The character set to be used for `script` and `jsonp` requests when the remote and local content are of different character sets.
xhr	(Function) A callback used to provide a custom implementation of the XHR instance.
traditional	(Boolean) If `true`, the traditional style of parameter serialization is used. See the description of `$.param()` in chapter 6 for details on parameter serialization.

That's a lot of options to keep track of, but it's unlikely that more than a few of them will be used for any one request. Even so, wouldn't it be convenient if we could set default values for these options for pages where we're planning to make a large number of requests?

8.4.2   *Setting request defaults*

Obviously the last question in the previous section was a setup. As you might have suspected, jQuery provides a way for us to define a default set of Ajax properties that will be used when we don't override their values. This can make pages that initiate lots of similar Ajax calls much simpler.

The function to set up the list of Ajax defaults is `$.ajaxSetup()`, and its syntax is as follows:

Method syntax: $.ajaxSetup

`$.ajaxSetup(options)`
Establishes the passed set of option properties as the defaults for subsequent calls to `$.ajax()`.

Parameters

options   (Object) An object instance whose properties define the set of default Ajax options. These are the same properties described for the `$.ajax()` function in table 8.2. This function should not be used to set callback handlers for success, error, and completion. (We'll see how to set these up using an alternative means in an upcoming section.)

Returns
Undefined.

At any point in script processing, usually at page load (but it can be at any point of the page authors' choosing), this function can be used to set up defaults to be used for all subsequent calls to `$.ajax()`.

> **NOTE**   Defaults set with this function aren't applied to the `load()` method. Also, for utility functions such as `$.get()` and `$.post()=`, the HTTP method can't be overridden by these defaults. For example, setting a default `type` of GET won't cause `$.post()` to use the GET HTTP method.

Let's say that we're setting up a page where, for the majority of Ajax requests (made with the utility functions rather than the `load()` method), we want to set up some defaults so that we don't need to specify them on every call. We can, as the first statement in the header `<script>` element, write this:

```
$.ajaxSetup({
  type: 'POST',
  timeout: 5000,
  dataType: 'html'
});
```

This would ensure that every subsequent Ajax call (except as noted previously) would use these defaults, unless explicitly overridden in the properties passed to the Ajax utility function being used.

Now, what about those *global events* we mentioned that were controlled by the `global` option?

8.4.3 Handling Ajax events

Throughout the execution of jQuery Ajax requests, jQuery triggers a series of custom events for which we can establish handlers in order to be informed of the progress of a request, or to take action at various points along the way. jQuery classifies these events as local events and global events.

Local events are handled by the callback functions that we can directly specify using the `beforeSend`, `success`, `error`, and `complete` options of the `$.ajax()` function, or indirectly by providing callbacks to the convenience methods (which, in turn, use the `$.ajax()` function to make the actual requests). We've been handling local events all along, without even knowing it, whenever we've registered a callback function to any jQuery Ajax function.

Global events are those that are triggered like other custom events within jQuery, and for which we can establish event handlers via the `bind()` method (just like any other event). The global events, many of which mirror local events, are: ajaxStart, ajaxSend, ajaxSuccess, ajaxError, ajaxStop, and ajaxComplete.

When triggered, the global events are broadcast to every element in the DOM, so we can establish these handlers on any DOM element, or elements, of our choosing. When executed, the handlers' function context is set to the DOM element upon which the handler was established.

Because we don't need to consider a bubbling hierarchy, we can establish a handler on any element for which it would be convenient to have ready access via `this`. If we don't care about a specific element, we could just establish the handler on the `<body>` for lack of a better location. But if we have something specific to do to an element, such as hide and show animated graphics while an Ajax request is processing, we could establish the handle on that element and have easy access to it via the function context.

In addition to the function context, more information is available via parameters passed to the handlers; most often these are the `jQuery.Event` instance, the XHR instance, and the options passed to `$.ajax()`.

Exceptions to this parameter list will be noted in Table 8.3, which shows the jQuery Ajax events in the order in which they are delivered.

Table 8.3 jQuery Ajax event types

Event name	Type	Description
ajaxStart	Global	Triggered when an Ajax request is started, as long as no other requests are active. For concurrent requests, this event is triggered only for the first of the requests. No parameters are passed.
beforeSend	Local	Invoked prior to initiating the request in order to allow modification of the XHR instance prior to sending the request to the server, or to cancel the request by returning `false`.

Table 8.3   jQuery Ajax event types *(continued)*

Event name	Type	Description
ajaxSend	Global	Triggered prior to initiating the request in order to allow modification of the XHR instance prior to sending the request to the server.
success	Local	Invoked when a request returns a successful response.
ajaxSuccess	Global	Triggered when a request returns a successful response.
error	Local	Invoked when a request returns an error response.
ajaxError	Global	Triggered when a request returns an error response. An optional fourth parameter referencing the thrown error, if any, is passed.
complete	Local	Invoked when a request completes, regardless of status. This callback is invoked even for synchronous requests.
ajaxComplete	Global	Triggered when a request completes, regardless of status. This callback is invoked even for synchronous requests.
ajaxStop	Global	Triggered when an Ajax request completes *and* there are no other concurrent requests active. No parameters are passed.

Once again (to make sure things are clear), local events represent callbacks passed to `$.ajax()` (and its cohorts), whereas global events are custom events that are triggered and can be handled by established handlers, just like other event types.

In addition to using `bind()` to establish event handlers, jQuery also provides a handful of convenience functions to establish the handlers, as follows:

Method syntax: jQuery Ajax event establishers

```
ajaxComplete(callback)
ajaxError(callback)
ajaxSend(callback)
ajaxStart(callback)
ajaxStop(callback)
ajaxSuccess(callback)
```
Establishes the passed callback as an event handler for the jQuery Ajax event specified by the method name.

Parameters

callback   (Function) The function to be established as the Ajax event handler. The function context (`this`) is the DOM element upon which the handler is established. Parameters may be passed as outlined in table 8.3.

Returns

The wrapped set.

Let's put together a simple example of how some of these methods can be used to easily track the progress of Ajax requests. The layout of our test page (it's too simple to be called a Lab) is shown in figure 8.7 and is available at URL http://localhost[:8080]/jqia2/chapter8/ajax.events.html.

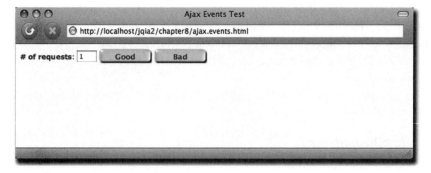

Figure 8.7 The initial display of the page we'll use to examine the jQuery Ajax events by firing multiple events and observing the handlers

This page exhibits three controls: a count field, a Good button, and a Bad button. These buttons are instrumented to issue the number of requests specified by the count field. The Good button will issue requests to a valid resource, whereas the Bad button will issue that number of requests to an invalid resource that will result in failures.

Within the ready handler on the page, we also establish a number of event handlers as follows:

```
$('body').bind(
  'ajaxStart ajaxStop ajaxSend ajaxSuccess ajaxError ajaxComplete',
  function(event){ say(event.type); }
);
```

This statement establishes a handler for each of the various jQuery Ajax event types that emits a message to the on-page "console" (which we placed below the controls), showing the event type that was triggered.

Leaving the request count at 1, click the Good button and observe the results. You'll see that each jQuery Ajax event type is triggered in the order depicted in table 8.3. But to understand the distinctive behavior of the ajaxStart and ajaxStop events, set the count control to 2, and click the Good button. You'll see a display as shown in figure 8.8.

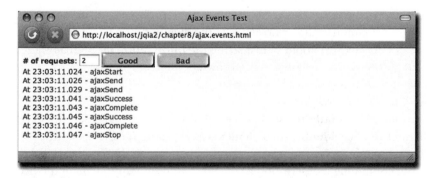

Figure 8.8 When multiple requests are active, the ajaxStart and ajaxStop events are called around the set of requests rather than for each.

Here we can see how, when multiple requests are active, the ajaxStart and ajaxStop events are triggered only once for the entire set of concurrent requests, whereas the other event types are triggered on a per-request basis.

Now try clicking the Bad button to generate an invalid request, and observe the event behavior.

Before we move on to the next chapter, let's put all this grand knowledge to use, shall we?

8.5   *Putting it all together*

It's time for another comprehensive example. Let's put a little of everything we've learned so far to work: selectors, DOM manipulation, advanced JavaScript, events, effects, and Ajax. And to top it all off, we'll implement another custom jQuery method!

For this example, we'll once again return to The Boot Closet page. To review, look back at figure 8.6 to remind yourself where we left off, because we're going to continue to enhance this page.

In the detailed information of the boots listed for sale (evident in figure 8.6), terms are used that our customers may not be familiar with—terms like "Goodyear welt" and "stitch-down construction." We'd like to make it easy for customers to find out what these terms mean, because an informed customer is usually a happy customer. And happy customers buy things! We like that.

We could be all 1998 about it and provide a glossary page that customers navigate to for reference, but that would move the focus away from where we want it—the pages where they can buy our stuff! We could be a *little* more modern about it and open a pop-up window to show the glossary or even the definition of the term in question. But even that's being terribly old-fashioned.

If you're thinking ahead, you might be wondering if we could use the `title` attribute of DOM elements to display a *tooltip* (sometimes called a *flyout*) containing the definition when customers hover over the term with the mouse cursor. Good thinking! That would allow the definition to be shown in-place without requiring customers to move their focus elsewhere.

But the `title` attribute approach presents some problems for us. First, the flyout only appears if the mouse cursor hovers over the element for a few seconds—and we'd like to be a bit more overt about it, displaying the information immediately after clicking a term. But more importantly, some browsers will truncate the text of a `title` flyout to a length far too short for our purposes.

So we'll build our own!

We'll somehow identify terms that have definitions, change their appearance to allow the user to easily identify such elements as clickable (giving them what's termed an "invitation to engage"), and instrument the elements so that a mouse click will display a flyout containing a description of the term. Subsequently clicking the flyout will remove it from the display.

We're also going to write it as a generally reusable plugin, so we need to make sure of two very important things:

- There'll be no hard-coding of anything that's specific to The Boot Closet.
- We'll give the page authors maximum flexibility for styling and layout (within reason).

We'll call our new plugin the *Termifier,* and figures 8.9a through 8.9c display a portion of our page showing the behavior that we'll be adding.

In figure 8.9a, we see the description of the item with the terms "Full-grain" and "oil-tanned" highlighted. Clicking Full-grain causes the Termifier flyout containing the term's definition to be displayed, as shown in figures 8.9b and 8.9c. In the rendition of figure 8.9b, we've supplied some rather simple CSS styling; in figure 8.9c we've gotten a bit more grandiose. We need to make sure that the plugin code allows for such flexibility.

Let's get started.

Figure 8.9a The terms "full-grain" and "oil-tanned" have been instrumented for "termifying" by our handy new plugin.

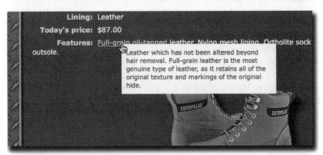

Figure 8.9b The Termifier pane deployed using simple styling specified by CSS external to the plugin.

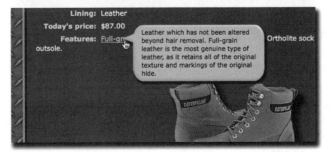

Figure 8.9c The Termifier pane with fancier styling—we need to give a user of our plugin this kind of flexibility.

8.5.1 *Implementing the Termifier*

As you'll recall, adding a jQuery method is accomplished by using the `$.fn` property. Because we've called our new plugin the Termifier, we'll name the method `termifier()`.

The `termifier()` method will be responsible for instrumenting each element in its matched set to achieve the following plan:

- Establish a `click` handler on each matched element that initiates the display of the Termifier flyout.
- Once clicked, the term defined by the current element will be looked up using a server-side resource.
- Once received, the definition of the term will be displayed in a flyout using a fade-in effect.
- The flyout will be instrumented to fade out once clicked within its boundaries.
- The URL of the server-side resource will be the only required parameter; all other options will have reasonable defaults.

The syntax for our plugin is as follows:

Method syntax: termifier

`termifier(url,options)`

Instruments the wrapped elements as Termifier terms. The class name `termified` is added to all wrapped elements.

Parameters

`url`   (String) The URL of the server-side action that will retrieve term definitions.

`options` (Object) Specifies the options as follows:
- `paramName`—The request parameter name to use to send the term to the server-side action. If omitted, a default of `term` is used.
- `addClass`—A class name to be added to the outer container of the generated Termifier pane. This is in addition to the class name `termifier`, which is always added.
- `origin`—An object hash containing the properties `top` and `left` that specify an offset for the Termifier pane from the cursor position. If omitted, the origin is placed exactly at the cursor position.
- `zIndex`—The z-index to assign to the Termifier pane. Defaults to 100.

Returns

The wrapped set.

We'll begin the implementation by creating a skeleton for our new `termifier()` method in a file named `jquery.jqia.termifier.js`:

```
(function($){

  $.fn.termifier = function(actionURL,options) {
    //
    // implementation goes here
    //
    return this;
  };

})(jQuery);
```

This skeleton uses the pattern outlined in the previous chapter to ensure that we can freely use the $ in our implementation, and creates the wrapper method by adding the new function to the fn prototype. Also note how we set up the return value right away to ensure that our new method plays nice with jQuery chaining.

Now, on to processing the options. We want to merge the user-supplied options with our own defaults:

```
var settings = $.extend({
  origin: {top:0,left:0},
  paramName: 'term',
  addClass: null,
  actionURL: actionURL
},options||{});
```

We've seen this pattern before, so we won't belabor its operation, but note how we've added the actionURL parameter value into the settings variable. This collects everything we'll need later into one tidy place for the closures that we'll be creating.

Having gathered all the data, we'll now move on to defining the click handler on the wrapped elements that will create and display the Termifier pane. We start setting that up as follows:

```
this.click(function(event){
  $('div.termifier').remove();
  //
  // create new Termifier here
  //
});
```

When a termified element is clicked, we want to get rid of any previous Termifier panes that are lying around before we create a new one. Otherwise, we could end up with a screen littered with them, so we locate all previous instances and remove them from the DOM.

 NOTE Can you think of another approach that we might have taken to ensure that there is only one Termifier pane ever displayed?

With that, we're now ready to create the structure of our Termifier pane. You might think that all we need to do is create a single <div> into which we can shove the term definition, but although that *would* work, it would also limit the options that we offer the users of our plugin. Consider the example of figure 8.9c, where the text needs to be placed precisely in relation to the background "bubble" image.

So we'll create an outer <div>, and then an inner <div> into which the text will be placed. This won't only be useful for placement; consider the situation of figure 8.10, in which we have a fixed-height construct and text that's longer than will fit. The presence of the inner <div> allows the page author to user the overflow CSS rule to add scrollbars to the flyout text.

Let's examine the code that creates the outer <div>:

Figure 8.10   Having two `<div>` elements to play with gives the page author some leeway to do things like scroll the inner text.

```
$('<div>')                          ❶ Creates outer <div>
  .addClass('termifier' +
    (settings.addClass ? (' ') + settings.addClass : ''))    Adds class
  .css({                                    ❷ name(s)
    position: 'absolute',           Assigns CSS
    top: event.pageY - settings.origin.top,    ❸ positioning
    left: event.pageX - settings.origin.left,
    display: 'none'
  })                                ❹ Removes from
  .click(function(event){              display on click
    $(this).fadeOut('slow');
  })
  .appendTo('body')        ❺ Attaches to DOM
```

In this code, we create a new `<div>` element ❶ and proceed to adjust it. First, we assign the class name `termifier` to the element ❷ so that we can easily find it later, as well as to give the page author a hook onto which to hang CSS rules. If the caller provided an `addClass` option, it's also added.

We then apply some CSS styling ❸. All we do here is the minimum that's necessary to make the whole thing work (we'll let the page author provide any additional styling through CSS rules). The element is initially hidden, and it's absolutely positioned at the location of the mouse event, adjusted by any `origin` provided by the caller. The latter is what allows a page author to adjust the position so that the tip of the bubble's pointer in figure 8.9c appears at the click location.

After that, we establish a click event handler ❹ that removes the element from the display when clicked upon. Finally, the element is attached to the DOM ❺.

OK, so far so good. Now we need to create the inner `<div>`—the one that will carry the text—and append it to the element we just created, so we continue like this:

```
.append(                    ❶ Appends inner to outer <div>
  $('<div>').load(
    settings.actionURL,                           Fetches and
    encodeURIComponent(settings.paramName) + '=' +  ❷ injects definition
      encodeURIComponent($(event.target).text()),
    function(){                                    ❸ Provides term
      $(this).closest('.termifier').fadeIn('slow');
    }                                              Fades Termifier
  )                                                ❹ into view
)
```

Note that this is a continuation of the same statement that created the outer
<div>—have we not been telling you all along how powerful jQuery chaining is?

In this code fragment, we create and append ❶ the inner <div> and initiate an
Ajax request to fetch and inject the definition of the term ❷. Because we're using
load() and want to force a GET request, we need to supply the parameter info as a text
string. We can't rely on serialize() here because we're not dealing with any form
controls, so we make use of JavaScript's encodeURIComponent() method to format the
query string ourselves ❸.

In the completion callback for the request, we find the parent (marked with the
termifier class) and fade it into view ❹.

Before dancing a jig, we need to perform one last act before we can declare our
plugin complete; we must add the class name termified to the wrapped elements to
give the page author a way to style termified elements:

```
this.addClass('termified');
```

There! Now we're done and can enjoy our lovely beverage.

The code for our plugin is shown in its entirety in listing 8.7, and it can be found in
file chapter8/jquery.jqia.termifier.js.

Listing 8.7 The complete implementation of the Termifier plugin

```
(function($){

  $.fn.termifier = function(actionURL,options) {
    var settings = $.extend({
      origin: {top:0,left:0},
      paramName: 'term',
      addClass: null,
      actionURL: actionURL
    },options||{});
    this.click(function(event){
      $('div.termifier').remove();
      $('<div>')
        .addClass('termifier' +
          (settings.addClass ? (' ') + settings.addClass : ''))
        .css({
          position: 'absolute',
          top: event.pageY - settings.origin.top,
          left: event.pageX - settings.origin.left,
          display: 'none'
        })
        .click(function(event){
```

```
        $(this).fadeOut('slow');
      })
      .appendTo('body')
      .append(
        $('<div>').load(
          settings.actionURL,
          encodeURIComponent(settings.paramName) + '=' +
            encodeURIComponent($(event.target).text()),
          function(){
            $(this).closest('.termifier').fadeIn('slow');
          }
        )
      );
    });
    this.addClass('termified');
    return this;
  };

})(jQuery);
```

That was the hard part. The easy part should be putting the Termifier to use on our Boot Closet page—at least, if we did it right. Let's find out if we did.

8.5.2   *Putting the Termifier to the test*

Because we rolled all the complex logic of creating and manipulating the Termifier flyout into the `termifier()` method, using this new jQuery method on the Boot Closet page is relatively simple. But first we have some interesting decisions to make.

For example, we need to decide how to identify the terms on the page that we wish to termify. Remember, we need to construct a wrapped set of elements whose content contains the term elements for the method to operate on. We *could* use a <span> element with a specific class name; perhaps something like this:

```
<span class="term">Goodyear welt</span>
```

In this case, creating a wrapped set of these elements would be as easy as `$('span.term')`.

But some might feel that the <span> markup is a bit wordy. Instead, we'll leverage the little-used <abbr> HTML tag. The <abbr> tag was added to HTML 4 in order to help identify abbreviations in the document. Because the tag is intended purely for identifying document elements, none of the browsers do much with these tags, either in the way of semantics or visual rendition, so it's perfect for our use.

> **NOTE**   HTML 4[2] defines a few more of these semantic tags, such as <cite>, <dfn>, and <acronym>. The HTML 5 draft specification[3] proposal adds even more of these semantic tags, whose purpose is to provide structure rather than provide layout or visual rendition directives. Among such tags are <section>, <article>, and <aside>.

---

[2]   HTML 4.01 specification, http://www.w3.org/TR/html4/.
[3]   HTML 5 draft specification, http://www.w3.org/html/wg/html5/.

Therefore, the first thing we need to do is modify the server-side resource that returns the item details to enclose terms that have glossary definitions in <abbr> tags. Well, as it turns out, the fetchProductDetails action already does that. But because the browsers don't do anything with the <abbr> tag, you might not have even noticed, unless you've already taken a look inside the action file or inspected the action's response. A typical response (for style 7141922) contains this:

```
<div>
  <label>Features:</label> <abbr>Full-grain</abbr> leather uppers. Leather
  lining. <abbr>Vibram</abbr> sole. <abbr>Goodyear welt</abbr>.
</div>
```

Note how the terms "Full-grain", "Vibram", and "Goodyear welt" are identified using the <abbr> tag.

Now, onward to the page itself. Starting with the code of phase three (listing 8.6) as a starting point, let's see what we need to add to the page in order to use the Termifier. We need to bring the new method into the page, so we add the following statement to the <head> section (after jQuery itself has loaded):

```
<script type="text/javascript" src="jquery.jqia.termifier.js"></script>
```

We need to apply the termifier() method to any <abbr> tags added to the page when item information is loaded, so we add a callback to the load() method that fetches the product detail information. That callback uses the Termifier to instrument all <abbr> elements. The augmented load() method (with changes in bold) is as follows:

```
$('#productDetailPane').load(
  '/jqia2/action/fetchProductDetails',
  $('#bootChooserControl').serialize(),
  function(){ $('abbr').termifier('/jqia2/action/fetchTerm'); }
);
```

The added callback creates a wrapped set of all <abbr> elements and applies the termifier() method to them, specifying a server-side action of fetchTerm and letting all options default.

And that's it! (Well, almost.)

CLEANING UP AFTER OURSELVES

Because we wisely encapsulated all the heavy lifting in our reusable jQuery plugin, using it on the page is even easier than pie! And we can as easily use it on any other page or any other site. Now that's what *engineering* is all about!

But there is one little thing we forget. We built into our plugin the removal of any Termifier flyouts when another one is displayed, but what happens if the user chooses a new style? Whoops! We'd be left with a Termifier pane that's no longer relevant. So we need to remove any displayed Termifiers whenever we reload the product detail.

We *could* just add some code to the load() callback, but that seems wrong, tightly coupling the Termifier to the loading of the product details. We'd be happier if we could keep the two decoupled and just listen for an event that tells us when its time to remove any Termifiers.

If the ajaxComplete event came to mind, treat yourself to a Maple Walnut Sundae or whatever other indulgence you use to reward yourself for a great idea. We can listen for ajaxComplete events and remove any Termifiers that exist when the event is tied to the `fetchProductDetails` action:

```
$('body').ajaxComplete(function(event,xhr,options){
  if (options.url.indexOf('fetchProductDetails') != -1) {
    $('div.termifier').remove();
  }
});
```

Now let's take a look at how we applied those various styles to the Termifier flyouts.

TERMIFYING IN STYLE

Styling the elements is quite a simple matter. In our style sheet we can easily apply rules to make the termified terms, and the Termifier pane itself, look like the display of figure 8.9b. Looking in `bootcloset.css`, we find this:

```
abbr.termified {
  text-decoration: underline;
  color: aqua;
  cursor: pointer;
}

div.termifier {
  background-color: cornsilk;
  width: 256px;
  color: brown;
  padding: 8px;
  font-size: 0.8em;
}
```

These rules give the terms a link-ish appearance that invites users to click the terms, and gives the Termifier flyouts the simple appearance shown in figure 8.9b. This version of the page can be found at http://localhost[:8080]/jqia2/chapter8/bootcloset/phase.4a.html.

To take the Termifier panes to the next level, shown in figure 8.9c, we only need to be a little clever and use some of the options we provided in our plugin. For the fancier version, we call the Termifier plugin (within the `load()` callback) with this code:

```
$('#productDetailPane').load(
  '/jqia2/action/fetchProductDetails',
  $('#bootChooserControl').serialize(),
  function(){ $('abbr')
    .termifier(
      '/jqia2/action/fetchTerm',
      {
        addClass: 'fancy',
        origin: {top: 28, left: 2}
      }
    );
  }
);
```

This call differs from the previous example only by specifying that the class name fancy be added to the Termifiers, and that the origin be adjusted so that the tip of the bubble appears at the mouse event location.

To the style sheet we add this (leaving the original rule):

```
div.termifier.fancy {
    background: url('images/termifier.bubble.png') no-repeat transparent;
    width: 256px;
    height: 104px;
}

div.termifier.fancy div {
    height: 86px;
    width: 208px;
    overflow: auto;
    color: black;
    margin-left: 24px;
}
```

This adds all the fancy stuff that can be seen in figure 8.9c.

This new page can be found at http://localhost[:8080]/jqia2/chapter8/boot-closet/phase.4b.html. Our new plugin is useful and powerful, but as always, we can make improvements.

8.5.3 *Improving the Termifier*

Our brand-spankin'-new jQuery plugin is quite useful as is, but it does have some minor issues and the potential for some major improvements. To hone your skills, here's a list of possible changes you could make to this method or to the Boot Closet page:

- Add an option (or options) that allows the page author to control the fade durations or, perhaps, even to use alternate effects.
- The Termifier flyout stays around until the customer clicks it, another one is displayed, or the product details are reloaded. Add a timeout option to the Termifier plugin that automatically makes the flyout go away if it's still displayed after the timeout has expired.
- Clicking the flyout to close it introduces a usability issue, because the text of the flyout can't be selected for cut-and-paste. Modify the plugin so that it closes the flyout if the user clicks anywhere on the page *except* on the flyout.
- We don't do any error handling in our plugin. How would you enhance the code to gracefully deal with invalid caller info, or server-side errors?
- We achieved the appealing drop shadows in our images by using PNG files with partial transparencies. Although most browsers handle this file format well, IE 6 doesn't and displays the PNG files with white backgrounds. To deal with this, we could also supply GIF formats for the images without the drop shadows. Although support for IE 6 is waning (in fact, Google has dropped support for IE 6 as of

March 1, 2010), how would you enhance the page to detect when IE 6 is being used and to replace all the PNG references with their corresponding GIFs?

- While we're talking about the images, we only have one photo per boot style, even when multiple colors are available. Assuming that we have photo images for each possible color, how would you enhance the page to show the appropriate image when the color is changed?

Can you think of other improvements to make to this page or the `termifier()` plugin? Share your ideas and solutions at this book's discussion forum, which you can find at http://www.manning.com/bibeault2.

8.6   Summary

Not surprisingly, this is one of the longest chapters in this book. Ajax is a key part of the new wave of DOM-scripted applications, and jQuery is no slouch in providing a rich set of tools for us to work with.

For loading HTML content into DOM elements, the `load()` method provides an easy way to grab the content from the server and make it the contents of any wrapped set of elements. Whether a GET or POST method is used is determined by how any parameter data to be passed to the server is provided.

When a GET is required, jQuery provides the utility functions `$.get()` and `$.getJSON()`; the latter being useful when JSON data is returned from the server. To force a POST, the `$.post()` utility function can be used.

When maximum flexibility is required, the `$.ajax()` utility function, with its ample assortment of options, lets us control the most minute aspects of an Ajax request. All other Ajax features in jQuery use the services of this function to provide their functionality.

To make managing the bevy of options less of a chore, jQuery provides the `$.ajaxSetup()` utility function that allows us to set default values for any frequently used options to the `$.ajax()` function (and to all of the other Ajax functions that use the services of `$.ajax()`).

To round out the Ajax toolset, jQuery also allows us to monitor the progress of Ajax requests by triggering Ajax events at the various stages, allowing us to establish handlers to listen for those events. We can `bind()` the handlers, or use the convenience methods: `ajaxStart()`, `ajaxSend()`, `ajaxSuccess()`, `ajaxError()`, `ajaxComplete()`, and `ajaxStop()`.

With this impressive collection of Ajax tools under our belts, it's easy to enable rich functionality in our web applications. And remember, if there's something that jQuery doesn't provide, we've seen that it's easy to extend jQuery by leveraging its existing features. Or, perhaps there's already a plugin—official or otherwise—that adds exactly what you need!

Part 2

jQuery UI

In the first part of this book, focusing on the jQuery core library, we made a big deal about how easy it is to extend jQuery. And we were correct to do so, because the ease with which jQuery can be extended is a big deal. And nowhere is it more evident than in the official plugins, the score of available unofficial plugins, and the companion library: jQuery UI.

jQuery UI builds upon the foundation laid by the capabilities of the core library to give us high-level user interface constructs, focused on creating great and intuitive UIs.

We'll start by learning how the library can be obtained and configured—it's not quite as simple as just copying a single file, as we were able to do with the core library. Then we'll take a look at some of the basic capabilities that jQuery UI adds to the features of the core library.

From there we'll see how jQuery UI layers upon the core library, and we'll look at the extended capabilities that it adds, all of which brings us user interface interactions such as the ability to drag and drop, sort, and resize elements. And then, layering further upon that, we'll explore the user interface widgets that jQuery UI adds to our toolbox of input controls.

After finishing this part, and hence the book, you'll be fully prepared to take on just about any user interface project that the web might throw at you. Bring it on!

Introducing jQuery UI: themes and effects

This chapter covers

- An overview of jQuery UI
- Configuring and downloading the jQuery UI library
- Obtaining and creating jQuery UI themes
- Extended effects provided by jQuery UI
- Other extensions to the core library

More than a plugin, but not part of the jQuery core, *jQuery UI* enjoys a status as an official extension of the jQuery core library aimed at providing extended user interface (UI) capabilities to jQuery-enabled web application pages.

The tools available for us to use within the browser environment (JavaScript, DOM manipulation, HTML, and even the core jQuery library) give us low-level abilities to put together pretty much any kind of user interactions we might want to provide for our users. But even so, building complex interactions using basic building blocks can be a large and daunting task. The native JavaScript API for DOM manipulation is tedious in the extreme (luckily we have core jQuery to contend

281

with that), and the set of form controls that HTML provides is rather sparse when compared with desktop environment counterparts.

We can create our own interactions and controls (often called *widgets*) with the help of the jQuery methods we've learned to this point. But the jQuery UI library provides us with a fair number of generally desired extended features or gives us higher-level building blocks to create them ourselves.

Imagine a commonly needed widget such as a progress bar. We could analyze its requirements and figure out how to implement it using core jQuery, but the UI library has already anticipated that need and provides a progress bar widget right out of the box.

Unlike the core jQuery library, jQuery UI is a confederation of loosely coupled elements. We'll see, in the first section of this chapter, how we can download a library that contains all of these pieces, or just the ones we're going to need. These elements fall into three general categories:

- *Effects*—Enhanced effects beyond those provided by the core library
- *Interactions*—Mouse interactions, such as drag and drop, sorting, and the like
- *Widgets*—A set of commonly needed controls, such as progress bars, sliders, dialog boxes, tabs, and so on

It's important to note that the interactions and widgets make heavy use of CSS to "theme" the visible elements. This is an essential tool for making the elements work correctly, as well as to match the design and appearance of our own pages, and it's a topic that we'll be examining later in this chapter.

As you can see, there's a lot there. And because jQuery UI is an important extension to jQuery, we're devoting three chapters to it. We have also provided an extensive set of UI-focused Lab pages—pretty much one for each major area of jQuery UI. These chapters, along with the Labs, should give you a good starting point for using jQuery UI.

Without further blather, let's get going and get our hands on jQuery UI.

9.1 Configuring and downloading the UI library

The jQuery UI library consists of a fairly large number of elements. Depending upon the needs of your application, you might want to use all of these elements, or perhaps just a subset of them. For example, your application might not need to make use of the widgets, but it might need drag-and-drop capability.

The jQuery UI team has provided the ability to construct a library that consists of only the essential required pieces, plus any features that you need for your application. This eliminates the need to load a larger library than your application will use. After all, why load up a bunch of script on every page that's just going to sit there unused?

9.1.1   *Configuring and downloading*

Before we can use the library, we need to download it. The download page for jQuery UI can be found at http://jqueryui.com/download, depicted in figure 9.1. As you can see in the figure, the most recent version as of this writing is jQuery UI 1.8.

On that page, you'll find a list of the available components for the jQuery UI library, each with a checkbox that you can check to select that component. You'll need to check the box for UI Core in order to be able to use any of the interactions and most of the widgets. But don't worry too much about what you select—the page will automatically select dependencies, and it won't let you put together an invalid combination of elements.

Once you've identified the components that you want (for now, we recommend selecting them all for exploratory purposes), pick a theme from the dropdown in the right-most column, and then click the Download button.

Figure 9.1   The jQuery UI download page allows us to configure and download a jQuery UI library configuration customized to the needs of our application.

It doesn't matter which theme you choose at this point; we'll be addressing CSS themes later in this chapter. For now, just pick any theme, though we recommend avoiding the No Theme option at this point. You want to download the CSS rather than building it from scratch. Trust us—you can always replace or tweak it later.

> **NOTE**   The selected theme has no effect on the JavaScript code generated for your component selections. The differences between themes are limited to the style sheet and images associated with the theme.

The jQuery UI library configuration that's provided with the example code for this book contains all components and uses the Cupertino theme.

9.1.2 *Using the UI library*

Once you've clicked the Download button, a set of zipped custom jQuery UI library files is downloaded to your system (exactly where depends upon your browser settings). The zip file contains the following files and folders:

- index.html—An HTML file containing demo samples of the downloaded widgets rendered in the chosen theme. You can use this as a quick check to make sure that the widgets you want are included, and that the theme matches your expectations.
- css—A folder containing a folder that in turn contains the CSS file and images for the theme that you selected. The subfolder will bear the name of the theme that you chose; for example, cupertino or trontastic.
- development-bundle—A folder containing developer resources such as license files, demos, documentation, and other useful files. Explore this at your leisure; there's lots of good stuff there.
- js—A folder containing the generated jQuery UI JavaScript library code, as well as a copy of the core jQuery library.

To use the library, you'll want to copy the theme folder in the css folder, and the jQuery UI library file, jquery-ui-1.8.custom.min.js in the js folder, to the appropriate locations in your web application. You'll also need the jQuery core library file if it's not already present.

> **NOTE**   The name of the JavaScript file will reflect the current version of jQuery UI, so it will change as jQuery UI is updated.

Although the locations in which you place these files can be specific to the needs of your web application, it's important to retain the relationship between the theme's CSS file and its images. Unless you want to change the references to all the images within the CSS file, be sure to leave the theme's images folder in the same folder as the CSS file.

A commonly used application layout, supporting multiple themes, is shown in figure 9.2. Here, we're supporting three of the canned themes available for download.

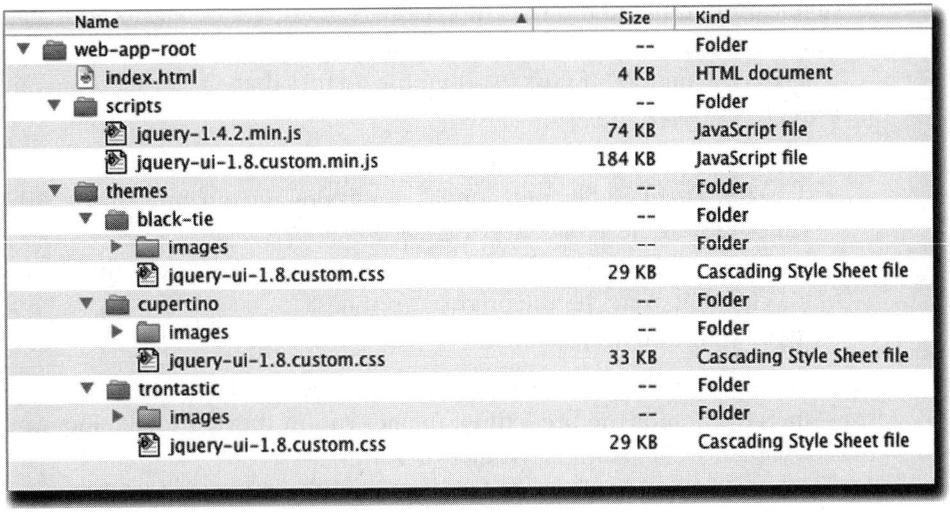

Name	▲	Size	Kind
▼ 📁 web-app-root		--	Folder
📄 index.html		4 KB	HTML document
▼ 📁 scripts		--	Folder
📄 jquery-1.4.2.min.js		74 KB	JavaScript file
📄 jquery-ui-1.8.custom.min.js		184 KB	JavaScript file
▼ 📁 themes		--	Folder
▼ 📁 black-tie		--	Folder
▶ 📁 images		--	Folder
📄 jquery-ui-1.8.custom.css		29 KB	Cascading Style Sheet file
▼ 📁 cupertino		--	Folder
▶ 📁 images		--	Folder
📄 jquery-ui-1.8.custom.css		33 KB	Cascading Style Sheet file
▼ 📁 trontastic		--	Folder
▶ 📁 images		--	Folder
📄 jquery-ui-1.8.custom.css		29 KB	Cascading Style Sheet file

Figure 9.2   A conventional layout for the script and theme files within an application using jQuery UI–your mileage may vary.

Switching between themes is as easy as changing the URLs that reference the CSS files in the application's pages.

Once the files are in place, we can simply import them into our pages with the usual `<link>` and `<script>` tags. For example, we could import the files into the index.html file in the application layout depicted in figure 9.2 with the following markup:

```
<link rel="stylesheet" type="text/css"
      href="themes/black-tie/jquery-ui-1.8.custom.css">
<script type="text/javascript" src="scripts/jquery-1.4.2.min.js"></script>
<script type="text/javascript"
      src="scripts/jquery-ui-1.8.custom.min.js"></script>
```

Switching themes is as easy as changing the theme folder name in the `<link>` tag.

> **NOTE**   If you would like an easy way to allow your users to dynamically switch between themes, check out the Theme Switcher Widget at http://jque-ryui.com/docs/Theming/ThemeSwitcher.

With that, we're ready to start exploring jQuery UI. Within this chapter, we'll begin with a closer look at themes, and then look at the ways jQuery UI extends core methods and capabilities, especially in the area of effects. In the next two chapters, we'll explore the mouse interactions and then the widgets.

9.2   *jQuery themes and styling*

jQuery UI, especially the widget set, relies heavily upon the CSS classes defined within the downloaded CSS file for styling the visible elements that appear on our pages. But, as we'll learn in this and the next two chapters, it also relies heavily upon class names assigned to the elements for much more than just styling.

There are a number of ways to set up the themes that jQuery UI relies upon. Here they are, from easiest to hardest:

- Choose a theme during download and use it verbatim.
- Use the ThemeRoller web application to design your own theme. We'll take a quick look at the ThemeRoller in section 9.2.2.
- Tweak the downloaded theme by modifying the original CSS file, or supplying a CSS file that overrides the original's settings.
- Write your own from scratch.

The last approach isn't recommended. The number of classes to be defined is extensive—the CSS files for the predefined themes run in the 450 to 500 line range—and the consequences of getting it wrong can be dire.

Let's start by taking a look at how the predefined CSS files and class names are organized.

9.2.1 *Overview*

Although the predefined themes are all very nice, it's unlikely that we'd find one that *precisely* matches the look of our own web applications.

We could, of course, pick a canned theme *first*, and use it as the definitive look for our site, but that may not be a luxury we often have. Which one of us has never had a marketing or product manager looking over our shoulder and asking, "What if we make that blue?"

The ThemeRoller, which we'll discuss in the next section, can help us make a theme that has exactly the colors and textures we want for our applications, but even so, we may still need to make page-by-page tweaks. As such, it behooves us to understand how the CSS classes are laid out and used by jQuery UI.

We'll begin by examining how the classes are named.

CLASS NAMING

The class names defined and used by jQuery are extensive, but well organized. They were carefully chosen to convey not only their meaning, but where and how they're used. Even though there are a lot of names, they make logical sense and are easy to manage once you get the hang of how they're constructed.

First, in order to keep from stepping on anyone else's names in the class namespace, all jQuery UI class names begin with the prefix ui-. Names are always in lowercase, and hyphen characters are used to separate words; for example, ui-state-active.

Some classes are used throughout the library. The aforementioned class ui-state-active is a good example. It's used by all components of the UI library to indicate that an element is in an active state. For example, the Tab widget will use it to mark the active table, whereas the Accordion widget will use it to identify the open accordion pane.

When a class is specific to a particular component, be it an interaction or a widget, the name of the component will immediately follow the ui- prefix. For example, classes specific to the Autocomplete widget will all begin with ui-autocomplete, whereas those specific to the Resizable interaction will begin with ui-resizable.

We'll take a closer look at the cross-library class groupings in the remainder of this section. The component-specific classes will be discussed as we examine the various components over the next few chapters. It isn't our intention to cover every one of the hundreds of class names defined by jQuery UI. Rather, we'll look at the most important, and the ones that we're likely to need to know about on our pages.

IDENTIFYING WIDGETS

When widgets are created by the jQuery UI library, some elements that compose the widget may be created by the library, and some may be existing elements that are already resident on the page.

In order to identify the elements that comprise the widgets, jQuery UI uses a set of class names that begin with ui-widget. The class ui-widget is used to identify the *master element* of the widget—usually a container that's the parent of all the elements that form the widget.

Other class names, such as ui-widget-header and ui-widget-content, are used as appropriate for the widget's elements. Just how a widget uses these classes is specific to each widget.

STATE TRACKING

At any point in time, various parts of widget or interaction elements may be in various states. jQuery UI tracks these states, and applies appropriate visual styling to them, via a set of classes that begin with ui-state. These states include ui-state-default, ui-state-active, ui-state-focus, ui-state-highlight, ui-state-error, ui-state-disabled, and ui-state-hover.

We can use these names in our own scripts or CSS to track state or affect the styling of elements in the various states.

ICONS

jQuery UI defines a large number of icons that can be used by various widgets. For example, icon indicators on the tab elements of the Tab widget, or icons directly on Button widgets. Each icon is identified by a class name beginning with ui-icon; for example, ui-icon-person, ui-icon-print, and ui-icon-arrowthick-1-sw.

jQuery UI is very clever regarding how it handles icons. All the individual icon images are defined in a grid on a single image—an *icon sheet*, if you will. That way, once this image has been downloaded and cached by the browser, no further trips to the server are needed to display any of the available icons—and there are a lot of them (173 as this is being written). The icon class definitions merely identify how to move the origin of this sheet image as a background image, causing the desired icon to appear as the background of an element.

We'll be examining icons in greater detail along with the Button widget in chapter 11, but if you want a sneak peek, bring up the file chapter11/buttons/ui-button-icons.html in your browser.

ROUNDED CORNERS

If you've already taken a glimpse at the widgets defined by jQuery UI, you've probably already seen a lot of rounded corners.

jQuery UI applies these corners with a set of class names that define the appropriate browser-specific and CSS3 style rules to cause rounded corners to appear in browsers for which they're supported. Non-supporting browsers will simply not have the rounded corners.

These corner-rounding classes aren't limited to just the JQuery UI widgets! We can use these classes on any element of our page.

Bring up the Rounded Corners Mini-Lab (it's too simple to consider a full Lab page) from the chapter9/lab.rounded-corners.html file in your browser. You'll see the page displayed in figure 9.3.

The checkbox controls allow us to choose which, if any, of the `ui-corner` classes are applied to the test subjects. When a checkbox is checked, the corresponding class name is applied; when unchecked, the class name is removed.

> **NOTE**   Rounded corners of any type aren't supported in Internet Explorer 8 or earlier (they should be as of IE 9), and Firefox (at least as of this writing) doesn't support rounded corners on image elements.

Spend a few moments clicking the various checkboxes to see how the application of the classes affects the corners of the test subjects.

9.2.2 Using the ThemeRoller tool

If you take a quick look through the CSS file generated when we downloaded jQuery UI, you'll probably quickly come to the conclusion that trying to write such a file from scratch would be nothing short of madness. A quick glance at the images accompanying the CSS firmly cements that notion.

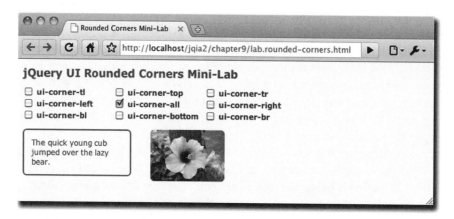

Figure 9.3   The Rounded Corners Mini-Lab lets us see how rounded corners can be applied to elements via simple class assignments.

When one of the canned themes doesn't match what we need for our site, we have some sane choices:

- Pick a canned theme that's close to what we want, and tweak it to our liking.
- Create a theme from scratch using the ThemeRoller tool.

As it turns out, the ThemeRoller tool is the best way to achieve either of these options. With the ThemeRoller tool, we can start from scratch and specify every detail of a theme using an easy and intuitive interface, or we can preload it with one of the predefined themes and adjust it to our liking.

The ThemeRoller can be found at http://jqueryui.com/themeroller/, and it appears as shown in figure 9.4.

We're not going to go into a great deal of detail on using the ThemeRoller—it's pretty easy to figure out. But there are a few things you should know that are worth spending some time on.

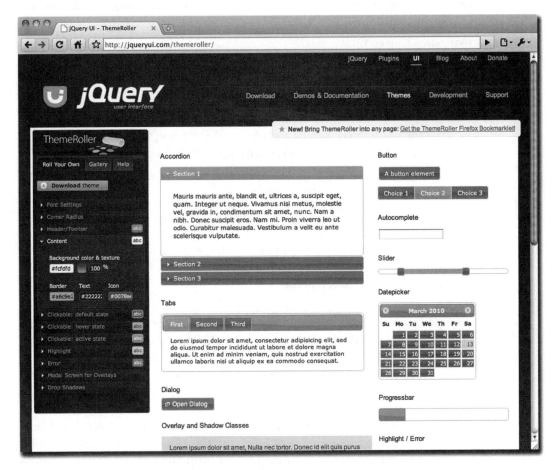

Figure 9.4 The jQuery UI ThemeRoller tool lets us create custom themes interactively with an intuitive and easy-to-use interface.

BASIC THEMEROLLER USAGE

The control panel for the ThemeRoller on left side of the interface has three tabs:

- *Roll Your Own*—This is where we'll do most of the work. The various panels (click on a panel header to open it) let us specify all the details of the theme. Changes are shown in real time in the display area that shows how the settings we make affect the various widgets.
- *Gallery*—Contains a gallery of the canned themes. We'll attend to this one in the next section.
- *Help*—Some help text in case you get stuck.

When we're satisfied with the settings of our theme, the Download Theme button on the Roll Your Own tab sends us to the Build Your Download page so that we can download the custom theme. (The theme settings are passed on the URL as request parameters.)

Clicking the Download button on the Build Your Download page downloads the theme as we discussed in section 9.1.

STARTING WITH A CANNED THEME

Often, one of the canned themes might make a better starting point for a custom theme than starting completely from scratch. If you want to load the settings for one of the predefined themes and make adjustments from there, follow these simple steps:

1 Select the Gallery tab.
2 Peruse the predefined themes and choose the one you want to start with. Click on it and the widgets in the display area will exhibit the theme settings.
3 Return to the Roll Your Own tab. Note that the settings from the predefined theme have been set into the controls.
4 Adjust away to your heart's content.
5 Click Download Theme when the theme is ready.

The downloaded CSS file and images will reflect the settings that you selected for the custom theme, and within the download, the folder containing the theme within the css folder will be named custom-theme.

RELOADING A THEME

Inevitably, just as you're admiring your custom theme in your web application, someone will come along and demand a change. You know the type. But try as you might, you can't find an upload or reload control on the ThemeRoller. Do we really have to start over and recreate a custom theme each time in order to make a change? Of course not.

Within the downloaded CSS file (not right at the top, but somewhere around line 44) you'll find a comment that contains the text, "* To view and modify this theme, visit" followed by a rather long URL. Cut and paste this URL into your browser, and it will bring you to the ThemeRoller page, loaded with the settings for the custom theme (which are encoded onto the URL as request parameters). Any necessary changes can be made to the theme settings and the new files downloaded when ready.

OK, we now have a themed jQuery UI installation ready and waiting to use. Let's dig into the extended effects that jQuery UI provides.

9.3   *jQuery UI Effects*

Back in chapter 5, we saw how easy it is to create custom effects using the jQuery animation engine. jQuery UI takes advantage of the core animation engine to offer us an ample set of effects right out of the box, including some that implement the custom effects that we set up ourselves as exercises.

We'll take a close look at those effects, but we'll also see how jQuery UI infuses these effects into core jQuery by providing extended versions of core methods that normally don't support effects. We'll also see a few new effect-focused methods that jQuery UI provides for us.

But first, let's take a look at the effects.

9.3.1   *The jQuery UI effects*

All of the effects that jQuery UI provides can be used on their own—without other methods—via the `effect()` method. This method launches the effect on the elements of the wrapped set. Here it is:

Method syntax: effect

`effect(type,options,speed,callback)`
Executes the specified effect on the elements of the wrapped set.

Parameters

type	(String) The effect to run. One of `blind`, `bounce`, `clip`, `drop`, `explode`, `fade`, `fold`, `highlight`, `puff`, `pulsate`, `scale`, `shake`, `size`, `slide`, or `transfer`. See table 9.1 for details of these effect types.
options	(Object) Provides the options for the specified effect as defined by the core `animate()` method (see chapter 5). Additionally, each effect has its own set of options that can be specifiedósome common across multiple effectsóas described in table 9.1.
speed	(String|Number) Optionally provides one of `slow`, `normal`, `fast`, or the duration of the effect in milliseconds. If omitted, defaults to `normal`.
callback	(Function) An optional callback function invoked for each element after the effect is completed. No arguments are passed to this function, and the function context is set to the element being animated.

Returns

The wrapped set.

 Although table 9.1 attempts to describe what each effect does, it's a lot clearer to actually see it in action. The jQuery UI Effects Lab has been set up for just this purpose. This Lab page can be found in chapter9/lab.ui-effects.html and appears as shown in figure 9.5.

This Lab lets us see each effect in action. When an effect type is chosen, the options that can be specified with that effect appear in the control panel (using

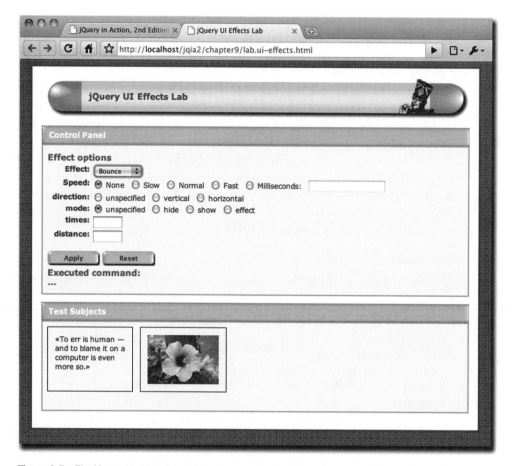

Figure 9.5 The jQuery UI Effects Lab lets us see how the UI effects operate in real time with various options.

jQuery UI effects, of course). As you read through the descriptions of the effects in table 9.1, use this Lab page to see exactly what the effect does, and how the options affect the operation of the effect.

In table 9.1, the various effects are described, along with their options. All effects (except `explode`) accept an `easing` option that specifies the easing function to be used with the effect. We'll examine the concept of easing in the upcoming section 9.3.5.

As you read through the entries in table 9.1, use the jQuery Effects Lab to see each effect in action.

Thinking back to our examination of the `animate()` method in chapter 5, you'll recall how that method allows us to animate CSS properties expressed by numeric values that have a logical progression from a start value to an end value. Color properties, you may recollect, were not among the supported animatable properties.

So how, then, does jQuery UI implement the `highlight` effect, which animates the background color of an element? Let's find out.

Table 9.1   jQuery UI effects

Effect name / Description	Effect-specific options
`blind` Shows or hides the element in the manner of a window blind: by moving the bottom edge down or up, or the right edge to the right or left, depending upon the specified `direction` and `mode`.	`direction`: (String) One of `horizontal` or `vertical`. If omitted, the default is `vertical`. `mode`: (String) One of `show` or `hide` (the default).
`bounce` Causes the element to appear to bounce in the vertical or horizontal direction, optionally showing or hiding the element.	`direction`: (String) One of `up`, `down`, `left`, or `right`. If omitted, the default is `up`. `distance`: (Number) The distance to bounce in pixels. Defaults to 20 pixels. `mode`: (String) One of `effect`, `show`, or `hide`. If omitted, `effect` is used, which simply bounces the element in place without changing the visibility of the element. `times`: (Number) The number of times to bounce. If omitted, the default is 5.
`clip` Shows or hides the element by moving opposite borders of the element together until they meet in the middle, or vice versa.	`direction`: (String) One of `horizontal` or `vertical`. If omitted, the default is `vertical`. `mode`: (String) One of `show` or `hide` (the default).
`drop` Shows or hides the element by making it appear to drop onto, or drop off of, the page.	`direction`: (String) One of `left` (the default), `right`, `up`, or `down`. `distance`: (Number) The distance to move the element. Defaults to half the height or half the width, depending upon the direction that the effect will move the element. `mode`: (String) One of `show` or `hide` (the default).
`explode` Shows or hides the element by splitting it into multiple pieces that move in radial directions as if imploding into, or exploding from, the page.	`mode`: (String) One of `show`, `hide`, or `toggle`. `pieces`: (Number) The number of pieces to be used in the effect. If omitted, a default of 9 is used. Note that the algorithm may optimize your value to a different number.
`fade` Shows or hides the element by adjusting its opacity. This is the same as the core fade effects, but without options.	`mode`: (String) One of `show`, `hide` (the default), or `toggle`.

Table 9.1   jQuery UI effects *(continued)*

Effect name Description	Effect-specific options
`fold` Shows or hides the element by adjusting opposite borders in or out, and then doing the same for the other set of borders.	`horizFirst`: (Boolean) if `true`, the horizontal borders are moved first. If omitted or specified as `false`, the vertical borders are moved first. `mode`: (String) One of `show` or `hide` (the default). `size`: (Number) The size in pixels of the "folded" element. If omitted, the size is set to 15 pixels.
`highlight` Calls attention to the element by momentarily changing its background color while showing or hiding the element.	`color`: (String) The color to use as the highlight. Colors can be expressed as CSS color names such as `orange`, hexadecimal notation such as `#ffffcc` or `#ffc`, or an RGB triplet `rgb(200,200,64)`. `mode`: (String) One of `show` (the default) or `hide`.
`pulsate` Adjusts the opacity of the element on and off before ensuring that the element is shown or hidden as specified.	`mode`: (String) One of `show` (the default) or `hide`. `times`: (Number) The number of times to pulse the element. Defaults to 5.
`puff` Expands or contracts the element in place while adjusting its opacity.	`mode`: (String) One of `show` or `hide` (the default). `percent`: (Number) The target percentage of the `puff` effect. Defaults to 150.
`scale` Expands or contracts the element by a specified percentage.	`direction`: (String) One of `horizontal`, `vertical`, or `both`. If omitted, the default is `both`. `fade`: (Boolean) If specified as `true`, the opacity is adjusted along with the size as appropriate for whether the element is being shown or hidden. `from`: (Object) An object whose `height` and `width` properties specify the starting dimensions. If omitted, the element starts from its current dimensions. `mode`: (String) One of `show`, `hide`, `toggle`, or `effect` (the default). `origin`: (Array) If `mode` is not `effect`, defines the base vanishing point for the effect, specified as a 2-string array. Possible values are: `top`, `middle`, `bottom`, and `left`, `center`, `right`. Defaults to `['middle','center']`. `percent`: (Number) The percentage to scale to. Defaults to `0` for `hide`, and `100` for `show`. `scale`: (String) Which area of the element is to be scaled, specified as one of `box`, which resizes the border and padding; `content`, which resizes the element content; or `both`, which resizes both. Defaults to `both`.

Table 9.1   jQuery UI effects *(continued)*

Effect name Description	Effect-specific options
`shake` Shakes the element back and forth, either vertically or horizontally.	`direction`: (String) One of `up`, `down`, `left`, or `right`. If omitted, the default is `left`. `distance`: (Number) The distance to shake in pixels. Defaults to 20 pixels. `duration`: (Number) The speed of each "shake"; defaults to 140 ms. `mode`: (String) One of `show`, `hide`, `toggle`, or `effect` (the default). `times`: (Number) The number of times to shake. If omitted, the default is 3.
`size` Resizes the element to a specified width and height. Similar to `scale` except for how the target size is specified.	`from`: (Object) An object whose `height` and `width` properties specify the starting dimensions. If omitted, the element starts from its current dimensions. `to`: (Object) An object whose `height` and `width` properties specify the ending dimensions. If omitted, the element starts from its current dimensions. `origin`: (Array) Defines the base vanishing point for the effect, specified as a 2-string array. Possible values are: `top`, `middle`, `bottom`, and `left`, `center`, `right`. Defaults to `['middle', 'center']`. `scale`: (String) Which area of the element is to be scaled, specified as one of `box`, which resizes the border and padding; `content`, which resizes the element content; or `both`, which resizes both. Defaults to `both`. `restore`: (Boolean) Saves and restores certain CSS properties of the elements and their children being animated, and restores them after the effect has been applied. The properties that are saved are undocumented, but include margin and padding settings and are highly dependent upon the other options and environment of the element. Use this option only if some property is not turning out as you intend to see if it rectifies the issue. This option defaults to `false`. (Note that the `scale` effect uses the `size` effect internally, with this option set to `true`).
`slide` Moves the element such that it appears to slide onto or off of the page.	`direction`: (String) One of `up`, `down`, `left`, or `right`. If omitted, the default is `left`. `distance`: (Number) The distance to slide the element. The value should be less than the width or height of the element (depending upon direction), and the default is the current width (for `left` or `right`) or height (for `up` or `down`) of the element. `mode`: (String) One of `show` (the default) or `hide`.
`transfer` Animates a transient outline element that makes the element appear to transfer to another element. The appearance of the outline element must be defined via CSS rules for the `ui-effects-transfer` class, or the class specified as an option.	`className`: (String) An additional class name to be applied to the outline element. Specifying this option doesn't prevent the `ui-effects-transfer` class from being applied. `to`: (String) A jQuery selector for the element to which the element will appear to transfer. There is no default; this option must be specified for the effect to work.

9.3.2   *Extended core animation capabilities*

If we dissect the majority of effects that we've discussed throughout this book, including the list provided by jQuery UI (shown in table 9.1), we can determine that most of them are implemented by changes in the position, dimensions, and opacity of the animated elements. And although that gives us (not to mention jQuery UI) a great deal of latitude for creating effects, the range of effects that can be created is greatly expanded if the ability to animate color is thrown into the mix.

The core jQuery animation engine doesn't possess this ability, so jQuery UI extends the capabilities of the core `animate()` method to allow the animation of CSS properties that specify color values.

The following CSS properties are supported by this augmentation:

- `backgroundColor`
- `borderBottomColor`
- `borderLeftColor`
- `borderRightColor`
- `borderTopColor`
- `color`
- `outlineColor`

And because all effects are eventually executed by this augmented capability, it doesn't matter how the effect is initiated—all means of specifying effects can take advantage of this extended capability. We'll shortly see how this is significant when we examine other extensions to the core library that jQuery UI provides.

9.3.3   *Augmented visibility methods*

As we discussed in chapter 5, the primary visibility methods of core jQuery—`show()`, `hide()`, and `toggle()`—when provided with a duration value, show or hide the target elements with a predefined effect that adjusts the width, height, and opacity of the elements. But what if we want more choices?

jQuery UI gives us that flexibility by extending those methods in core jQuery to accept any of the effects outlined in table 9.1. The extended syntax for these methods is as follows:

Method syntax: extended visibility methods

`show(effect,options,speed,callback)`
`hide(effect,options,speed,callback)`
`toggle(effect,options,speed,callback)`
Shows, hides, or toggles the visibility of the wrapped elements using the specified effect.

Parameters

`effect`	(String) The effect to use when adjusting the element visibility. Any of the effects listed in table 9.1 can be used.
`options`	(Object) Provides the options for the specified effect as described in table 9.1.

Method syntax: extended visibility methods *(continued)*	
speed	(String|Number) Optionally provides one of `slow`, `normal`, `fast`, or the duration of the effect in milliseconds. If omitted, defaults to `normal`.
callback	(Function) An optional callback function invoked for each element after the effect is completed. No arguments are passed to this function, and the function context is set to the element being animated.

Returns
The wrapped set.

Whether you realize it or not, you've already seen an example of using these augmented visibility effects. In the jQuery UI Effects Lab, when the value of the effect dropdown is changed, any option controls not appropriate for the newly selected effect are removed with

```
$(someSelector).hide('puff');
```

And the controls that are appropriate for the selected effect are shown via

```
$(someSelector).show('slide');
```

 As an advanced exercise, make a copy of the jQuery UI Effects Lab, and turn it into the jQuery UI Show, Hide, and Toggle Lab:

- Add a set of radio controls that allow you to select one of the three visibility methods: `show()`, `hide()`, and `toggle()`.
- When the Apply button is clicked, determine which method has been selected, and execute that method in place of the `effect()` method.

The visibility methods aren't the only core methods that jQuery UI extends with added capabilities. Let's see what other core methods are augmented.

9.3.4 *Animating class transitions*

As you might recall, the `animate()` method of core jQuery allows us to specify a set of CSS properties that the animation engine will progressively modify in order to create animated effects. Because CSS classes are collections of CSS properties, it seems a natural extension to allow the animation of class transitions.

And indeed, that's exactly what jQuery UI provides: extensions to the class transition methods `addClass()`, `removeClass()`, and `toggleClass()` to allow animating the changes to the CSS properties. The syntax of the augmented methods is as follows:

Method syntax: extended class methods
`addClass(class,speed,easing,callback)`
`removeClass(class,speed,easing,callback)`
`toggleClass(class,force,speed,easing,callback)`
Adds, removes, or toggles the specified class name on the wrapped elements. If the `speed` parameter is omitted, these methods act exactly like the unextended core methods.

Method syntax: extended class methods (continued)	
Parameters	
class	(String) The CSS class name, or space-delimited list of class names, to be added, removed, or toggled.
speed	(String|Number) Optionally provides one of slow, normal, fast, or the duration of the effect in milliseconds. If omitted, no animated effect takes place.
easing	(String) The name of the easing function to be passed to the animate() method. See the description of animate() in chapter 5 for more information.
callback	(Function) A callback to be invoked when the animation completes. See the description of animate() in chapter 5 for more information.
force	(Boolean) If specified, forces the toggleClass() method to add the class if true, or to remove the class if false.
Returns	
The wrapped set.	

In addition to extending these core class transition methods, jQuery adds a useful new class manipulation method, switchClass(), whose syntax is as follows:

Method syntax: switchClass	
switchClass(removed, added, speed, easing, callback)	
Removes the specified class or classes, while adding the specified class or classes, using a transition effect.	
Parameters	
removed	(String) The CSS class name, or space-delimited list of class names, to be removed.
added	(String) The CSS class name, or space-delimited list of class names, to be added.
speed	(String|Number) Optionally provides one of slow, normal, fast, or the duration of the effect in milliseconds. If omitted, the animate() method determines the default.
easing	(String) The name of the easing function to be passed to the animate() method. See the description of animate() in chapter 5 for more information.
callback	(Function) A callback to be invoked when the animation completes. See the description of animate() in chapter 5 for more information.
Returns	
The wrapped set.	

Between the effect() method and the extensions to the core visibility and class transition methods, jQuery UI gives us a lot of choices regarding how we write code that manipulates elements in an animated manner.

Could we just use the animate() method for all such occasions? Sure we could. But thinking in terms of code clarity, it makes a lot more sense to use a method named hide() to hide an element—even in an animated fashion—than a method named animate(). jQuery UI gives us the ability to use the methods that make the most sense for the context of the code, regardless of whether animation will be used or not.

Another extension that jQuery UI provides in the area of animation is a rather large set of easings beyond that provided by jQuery core.

9.3.5 *Easings*

When we originally discussed animation back in chapter 5, we introduced the concept of easing functions (casually termed *easings*) that control the pace at which animations progress. jQuery core provides two easings: `linear` and `swing`. jQuery UI renames `swing` to `jswing`, adds its own version of `swing`, and adds another 31 easings.

We can specify an easing in any animation method that accepts an options hash. As noted earlier, these options are eventually passed to the `animate()` core method, which all animation methods eventually call to execute the animation or effect. One of those core options is `easing`, which identifies the name of the easing function to be used.

When jQuery UI is loaded, the entire list of available easings is as follows:

- `linear`
- `swing`
- `jswing`
- `easeInQuad`
- `easeOutQuad`
- `easeInOutQuad`
- `easeInCubic`
- `easeOutCubic`
- `easeInOutCubic`
- `easeInQuart`
- `easeOutQuart`

- `easeInOutQuart`
- `easeInQuint`
- `easeOutQuint`
- `easeInOutQuint`
- `easeInSine`
- `easeOutSine`
- `easeInOutSine`
- `easeInExpo`
- `easeOutExpo`
- `easeInOutExpo`
- `easeInCirc`

- `easeOutCirc`
- `easeInOutCirc`
- `easeInElastic`
- `easeOutElastic`
- `easeInOutElastic`
- `easeInBack`
- `easeOutBack`
- `easeInOutBack`
- `easeInBounce`
- `easeOutBounce`
- `easeInOutBounce`

It'd be practically impossible to describe in words how each easing operates—we really need to see them in action to understand how any specific easing affects the progression of an animation. And so the jQuery UI Easings Lab page is available to let us see how the easings operate when applied to the various animations. This Lab is available in file chapter9/lab.ui-easings.html and displays as shown in figure 9.6.

> **NOTE** As an additional resource, the jQuery UI online documentation has SVG-driven examples of the easings, which can be found at http://jqueryui.com/demos/effect/#easing.

This Lab lets us try out the various easings paired with the various effects. For best results in seeing what transpires as each easing function progresses, we recommend trying the following:

1 Choose the easing to be observed.
2 Choose `scale` as the effect. When `scale` is chosen, the `percent` option is hard-coded to `25`.
3 Set the speed to very slow—slower than the `slow` setting. Try 10 seconds (10000 milliseconds) to really see how the scaling of the test subject is affected by the selected easing.

Now let's look at one more utility that jQuery UI provides.

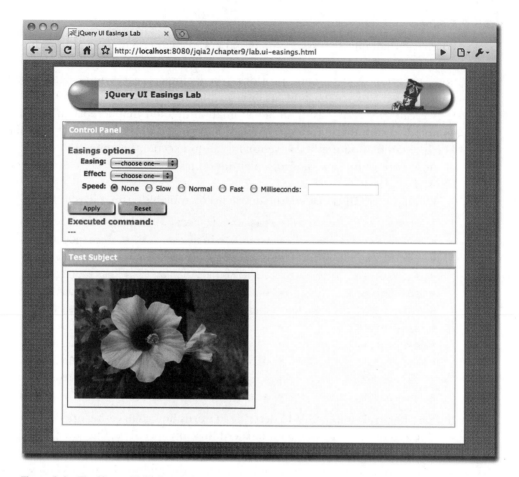

Figure 9.6   The jQuery UI Easings Lab shows us how the various easings operate when applied to an animation effect.

9.4   *Advanced positioning*

CSS positioning gives us the ability to position elements within our pages with relative ease. Throw jQuery into the mix, and it becomes almost trivial—*if* we know *where* we want to position the elements.

For example, if we knew that we wanted an element to be moved to some absolute position, we'd write this:

```
$('#someElement').css({
  position: 'absolute',
  top: 200,
  left: 200
});
```

But what if we wanted to position the element relative to another element? For example, place the element to the right of another element, but with the tops aligned? Or place it below another element with their centers in alignment?

No problem, really. We can grab the dimension and position information of the elements in question using core jQuery methods, do some math, and use the results to absolutely position the target element.

But although it's not a problem, it's rather a fair amount of code, and it could be rather fragile if we're not careful about assumptions made in the formulas that calculate the new position. It probably wouldn't be the most readable code in the world, either; most likely it'd be less than a snap to figure out what that code did by casual inspection, especially for someone who didn't write the formulas in the first place.

jQuery UI gives us a helping hand by providing a method that not only abstracts away the formulas needed to figure out positions relative to other elements (and more, as we'll see), but it does so in a manner that makes the code ultra-readable.

This method is an overloading of the `position()` method we examined in chapter 3 (which obtains the position of an element relative to its offset parent). Here's its syntax:

Method syntax: position

`position(options)`

Absolutely positions the wrapped elements using the information provided by the `options`.

Parameters

options   (Object) Provides the information that specifies how the elements of the wrapped set are to be positioned, as described in table 9.2.

Returns

The wrapped set.

As you may have come to expect, a Lab page has been provided to help observe the operation of the jQuery UI `position()` method: the jQuery UI Positioning Lab, found in chapter9/lab.ui-positioning.html, and shown in figure 9.7.

As you read through the options in table 9.2, use the Positioning Lab to familiarize yourself with the operation of the options. Give yourself bonus points if you can pin the tail in the proper location in one try!

You might be looking at the names of the options and saying to yourself, "What *were* they thinking? at? my? of? What on Earth?"

But there's a method to the madness. If you inspected the generated statement in the Positioning Lab as you were experimenting with it, you've already seen it. If not, consider the following statement:

```
$('#someElement').position({
  my: 'top center',
  at: 'bottom right',
  of: '#someOtherElement'
});
```

It almost reads like an English sentence! Even someone who's never seen a fragment of computer code in his or her life would most likely be able to figure out what this statement does (while wondering why computer gear-heads insist on all that gnarly punctuation).

Most APIs could benefit from a touch of this sort of "madness."

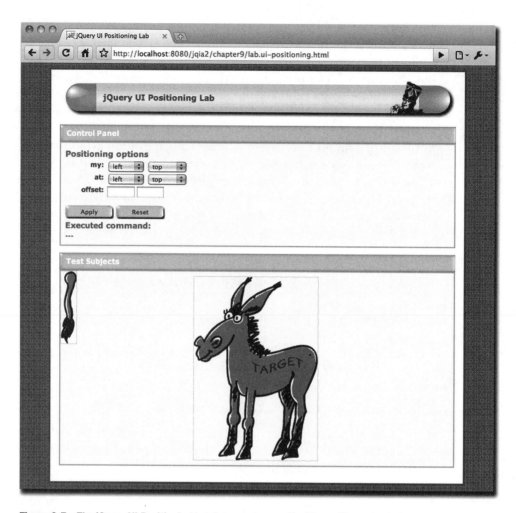

Figure 9.7   The jQuery UI Positioning Lab lets us observe the jQuery UI overload of `position()` in action.

Table 9.2   Options for the jQuery UI `position()` method

Option	Description	In Lab?
my	(String) Specifies the location of the wrapped elements (the ones being re-positioned) to align with the target element or location. Two of: `top`, `left`, `bottom`, `right`, and `center`, separated by a space character, where the first value is the horizontal value, and the second the vertical. If a single value is specified, the other defaults to `center`. Whether the specified single value is considered horizontal or vertical depends upon which value you use (for example, `top` is taken as vertical, while `right` is horizontal). Examples: `top`, or `bottom right`.	✓

Table 9.2 Options for the jQuery UI `position()` method

Option	Description	In Lab?
at	(String) Specifies the location of the target element against which to align the re-positioned elements. Takes the same values as the `my` option. Examples: "`right`", or "`left center`".	✓
of	(Selector|Event) A selector that identifies the target element against which the wrapped elements are to be re-positioned, or an `Event` instance containing mouse coordinates to use as the target location.	✓
offset	(String) Specifies any offset to be added to the calculated position as two pixel values specifying `left` and `top` respectively. Negative offsets are allowed. For example: `10 -20`. If a single value is specified, it applies to both `left` and `top`. Defaults to 0.	✓
collision	(String) Specifies the rules to be applied when the positioned element extends beyond the window in any direction. Accepts two (horizontal followed by vertical) of the following: `flip`: The default, flips the element to the opposing side and runs collision detection again for fit. If neither side fits, `center` is used as a fallback. `fit`: Keeps the element in the desired direction, but adjusts the position such that it will fit. `none`: disables collision detection. If a single value is specified, it applies to both directions.	
using	(Function) A function that replaces the internal function that changes the element position. Called for each wrapped element with a single argument that consists of an object hash with the `left` and `top` properties set to the computed target position, and the element set as the function context.	

9.5 Summary

In this chapter we dove head-first into jQuery UI, and we won't be coming up for air until the end of this book.

We learned that jQuery UI enjoys a special status as an official companion to the core jQuery library, and how to download a customized version of the library (along with one of the predefined themes) from http://jqueryui.com/download. We learned about the contents of the download, and how the library is typically added to a web application's folder structure.

We then discussed the theming capability of the jQuery UI library and how the CSS classes that it defines are laid out, including how they're organized by naming conventions.

We examined the official ThemeRoller online application, located at http://jqueryui.com/themeroller/, which can be used to tweak one of the predefined themes, or to create a new theme entirely from scratch.

The remainder of the chapter examined extensions that JQuery makes to the core library.

We saw how the core animation engine has been extended to provide a good number of named effects that are easily launchable using the new `effect()` method.

We also saw how jQuery UI extends the visibility methods `show()`, `hide()`, and `toggle()` to work in conjunction with these new effects. The same manner of extension has also been applied to the class transition methods: `addClass()`, `removeClass()`, `toggleClass()`, and the newly defined `switchClass()` method.

We then discussed the two and a half dozen easing functions that jQuery adds to be used by the animation engine to control the progression of an animation.

Finally, we looked at an extension to the core `position()` method that allows us, in a remarkably readable fashion, to position elements relative to each other, or to the location of a mouse event.

But we've only just begun. Read on to the next chapter, where we'll learn about another major part of jQuery UI: mouse interactions.

jQuery UI mouse interactions: Follow that mouse!

This chapter covers

- Core mouse interactions
- Implementing drag and drop
- Making things sortable
- Allowing resizing
- Making things selectable

Few usability experts would argue that *direct manipulation* isn't key to good user interfaces. Allowing users to directly interact with elements and immediately see the effects of their activities is a much better user experience than some abstraction that approximates the activities.

Take sorting a list of elements for example. How would we allow users to specify a sort order for the elements? Using just the basic set of controls available in HTML 4, there's not a whole lot of flexibility available to us. Showing the list of elements followed by a text box next to them in which the user must type the ordinal value could hardly be presented as a paragon of usability.

But what if we could allow users to grab and drag the elements within the list to immediately move them around until they're happy with the result? This mechanism, using direct manipulation, is clearly the superior approach, but it's out of reach given only HTML's basic set of controls.

The core interactions—focusing on direct manipulation—are the foundation upon which jQuery UI is built, and they afford us a much greater degree of power and flexibility with regard to the types of user interfaces that we can present to our users.

The core interactions add advanced behavior to our pages that relate to the use of the mouse pointer. We can use these interactions ourselves—as we'll see throughout this chapter—and they're also the bedrock upon which much of the remaining jQuery UI library is built upon.

The core interactions are the following:

- Dragging—Moving things around on a page (section 10.1)
- Dropping—Dropping dragged things onto other things (section 10.2)
- Sorting—Putting things in order (section 10.3)
- Resizing—Changing the size of things (section 10.4)
- Selecting—Making things selectable that aren't normally selectable (section 10.5)

As we'll see while working our way through this chapter, the core interactions build upon one another. To get the most out of this chapter, it's recommended that you work through it sequentially. This may be a long chapter, but there's a level of consistency to the jQuery UI methods, mirrored in the structure of the chapter sections, that makes it easy to work through all the material once you get familiar with how the methods are arranged.

Interacting with the mouse pointer is an integral and core part of any GUI. Although some simple mouse pointer interactions are built into web interfaces (clicking, for example), the web doesn't natively support some advanced interaction styles available to desktop applications. A prime example of this deficiency is the lack of support for drag and drop.

Drag and drop is a ubiquitous interaction technique for desktop user interfaces. For example, in the GUI file manager for any desktop system, we can easily copy files or move them around the filesystem by dragging and dropping them from folder to folder, or even delete them by dragging and dropping them onto a trash or wastebasket icon. But as prevalent as this interaction style is within desktop applications, it's just as sparse in web applications, mainly because modern browsers don't natively support drag and drop. And correctly implementing it is a rather daunting task.

"Daunting?" you might scoff. "A few captured mouse events and some CSS fiddling. What's the big deal?"

Although the high-level concepts aren't that difficult to grasp (especially with the power of jQuery at our disposal), it turns out that implementing the nuances of drag-and-drop support, particularly in a robust and browser-independent manner, can become painful quickly. But in the same way that jQuery and its plugins have eased our pain before, they do so again with direct support for drag and drop.

But before we can drag *and* drop, we first need to learn how to drag, so that's where we'll start.

10.1 *Dragging things around*

Although we'd be hard-pressed to find the term *draggable* in most dictionaries, it's the term that's commonly applied to items that can be dragged about in a drag-and-drop operation. Likewise, it's both the term that jQuery UI uses to describe such elements and the name of the method that applies this ability to elements in a matched set.

But before we introduce the syntax of the draggable() method, let's take some time to talk about a convention used throughout jQuery UI.

In order to keep the incursion into the method namespace as minimal as possible, many of the methods in jQuery serve multiple purposes depending upon the nature of the parameters passed to them. That's not anything particularly new—we've seen quite a bit of that in core jQuery. But jQuery UI takes method overloading to the next level. We'll see that the same method can be used for quite a number of related actions.

The draggable() method is an excellent example. This one method is used to not only make elements draggable, but to control every aspect of the draggability of the elements, including disabling, destroying, and re-enabling the elements' draggability, as well as to set and fetch individual draggability options.

Because the method name will be the same for all these operations, we only have the parameter list to differentiate among the intended operations. Frequently, the differentiator takes the guise of a string, passed as the first parameter, that identifies the operation to be performed.

For example, to disable the draggability of draggable elements, we'd write

```
$('.disableMe').draggable('disable');
```

NOTE If you've been using previous incarnations of jQuery UI, you may remember when distinct methods such as draggableDisable() and draggableDestroy() were defined to provide various operations. Such methods no longer exist, having been replaced by more succinct multipurpose methods such as draggable().

The syntax for the various forms of the draggable() method are as follows:

Command syntax: draggable

draggable(options)
draggable('disable')
draggable('enable')
draggable('destroy')
draggable('option',optionName,value)
Makes the elements in the wrapped set draggable according to the specified options, or performs some other draggability action based upon an operation string passed as the first parameter.

Parameters

options   (Object) An object hash of the options to be applied to the elements in the wrapped set, as described in table 10.1, making them draggable. If omitted (and no other parameters are specified) or empty, the elements become freely draggable anywhere within the window.

Command syntax: draggable *(continued)*

`'disable'`	(String) Temporarily disables the draggability of any draggable elements in the wrapped set. The draggability of the elements isn't removed, and can be restored by calling the `'enable'` variant of this method.
`'enable'`	(String) Re-enables draggability on any draggable elements in the wrapped set whose draggability has been disabled. Note that this method won't *add* draggability to any non-draggable elements.
`'destroy'`	(String) Removes draggability from the elements in the wrapped set.
`'option'`	(String) Allows option values to be set on all elements of the wrapped set, or to be retrieved on the first element of the wrapped set (which should be a draggable element), based upon the remaining parameters. If specified, at least the `optionName` parameter must also be provided.
`optionName`	(String) The name of the option (see table 10.1) whose value is to be set or returned. If a `value` parameter is provided, that value becomes the option's value. If no `value` parameter is provided, the named option's value is returned.
`value`	(Object) The value to be set for the option identified by the `optionName` parameter.

Returns

The wrapped set, except for the case where an option value is returned.

That's a lot of variation to pack into a single method. Let's start digging in by examining how to make things draggable in the first place.

10.1.1 *Making elements draggable*

Looking at the list of variations of the `draggable()` method, we might expect that a call to the `draggable('enable')` method would make the elements in a wrapped set draggable, but we'd be *very mistaken!*

To *make* elements draggable, we need to call the `draggable()` method with a parameter consisting of an object whose properties specify the draggability options (as outlined in table 10.1), or with no parameter at all (to use all default settings). We'll see what the `enable` call does in short order.

When an item is made draggable, the class `ui-draggable` is added to it. This helps not only in allowing us to identify the draggable elements, but as a hook to apply visual clues via CSS should we choose to do so. We can also identify items that are actively being dragged around because the class `ui-draggable-dragging` will be added to a dragged element during a drag operation.

 There are a lot of draggability options, so to help us get familiar with them, a jQuery UI Draggables Lab page has been provided. Bring up the chapter10/draggables/lab.draggables.html page in your browser as you follow along with the rest of this section. You'll see the display shown in figure 10.1.

The options available for the `draggable()` method give us a lot of flexibility and control over exactly how drag operations will take place; they're described in table 10.1. The options represented in the Draggables Lab page are identified in the In Lab column of table 10.1. Be sure to try them out as you go along.

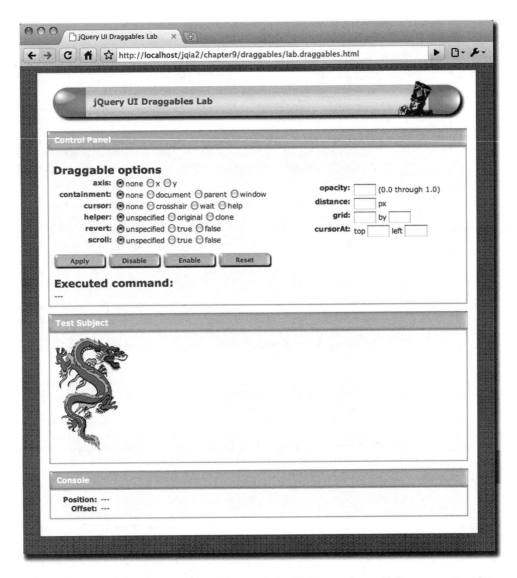

Figure 10.1 The Draggables Lab page will help us to familiarize ourselves with the many options for draggables in the jQuery UI.

Table 10.1 Options for the jQuery UI `draggable()` method

Option	Description	In Lab
addClasses	(Boolean) If specified as `false`, prevents the `ui-draggable` class from being added to draggable elements. We might choose to do this for performance reasons if the class isn't needed and we're adding draggability to many elements on a page. Despite its pluralized name, this option doesn't prevent other classes, such as the `ui-draggable-dragging` class, from being added to elements during a drag operation.	

Table 10.1 Options for the jQuery UI `draggable()` method *(continued)*

Option	Description	In Lab
appendTo	(Element|Selector) When a helper is created (see the `helper` option below), specifies the DOM element to which the helper will be appended. If not specified, any helper is appended to the parent of the draggable element.	
axis	(String) If specified as `x` or `y`, constrains movement during a drag operation to the specified axis. For example, specifying `x` allows movement in the horizontal direction only. If unspecified, or specified as any other values, movement is unconstrained.	✓
cancel	(Selector) Specifies a selector identifying elements that should not allow drag operations to commence. If unspecified, the selector `:input,option` is used. Note that this doesn't prevent these elements from becoming draggable; it merely prevents the elements from being actively dragged around. The elements are still considered draggable and the `ui-draggable` class is added to these elements.	
connectToSortable	(Selector) Identifies a sortable list that this draggable element can be dropped upon in order to become part of that list. If specified, the `helper` option should also be specified as `clone`. This option is in support of sortables, which we'll be taking a look at in section 10.3.	
containment	(Element|Selector|Array|String) Defines an area within which the drag operation will be constrained. If unspecified, or specified as `document`, the movement is unconstrained within the document. The string `window` will constrain movement to the visible viewport, whereas the string `parent` will constrain movement within the element's direct parent. If an element, or selector identifying an element, is specified, movement is constrained within that element. An arbitrary rectangle relative to the document can also be specified as an array of four numbers, identifying the top-left and bottom-right corners of the rectangle as follows: $[x_1,y_1,x_2,y_2]$.	✓
cursor	(String) The CSS name of the mouse pointer cursor to use during a drag operation. If not specified, defaults to `auto`.	✓
cursorAt	(Object) Specifies a relative position for the cursor within the dragged element during a drag operation. Can be specified as an object with one of the `left` or `right` properties, and one of the `top` or `bottom` properties. For example: `cursorAt:{top:5,left:5}` will place the cursor five pixels from the top left of the element while dragging. If unspecified, the cursor remains in the position where it was clicked upon within the element.	✓
delay	(Number) The number of milliseconds to delay after the mousedown event before beginning the drag operation. This can be used to help prevent accidental drags by only reacting if the user maintains the mouse button in the down position for the specified period. By default, the value is 0, meaning that no delay is defined.	

Table 10.1   Options for the jQuery UI `draggable()` method *(continued)*

Option	Description	In Lab
distance	(Number) The number of pixels that must be dragged across before a drag operation is initiated. This can also be used to help prevent accidental drags. If unspecified, the distance defaults to 1 pixel.	✓
drag	(Function) Specifies a function to be established on the draggables as an event handler for drag events. See table 10.2 for more details on this event.	
grid	(Array) An array of two numbers that specifies discrete horizontal and vertical distances that the drag operation will "snap to" during a drag operation. The origin of the grid is the initial position of the dragged element. If unspecified, no grid is defined.	✓
handle	(Element|Selector) Specifies an element, or selector that selects an element, to serve as the trigger for the drag operation. The handle element must be a child of the draggable for this to work correctly. When specified, only a click on the handle element will cause a drag operation to commence. By default, clicking anywhere within the draggable starts the drag.	
helper	(String|Function) If unspecified, or specified as original, the draggable element is moved during a drag operation. If clone is specified, a copy of the draggable item is created and moved around during the drag operation. A function can be specified that gives us the opportunity to create and return a new DOM element to use as the drag helper.	✓
iframeFix	(Boolean|Selector) Prevents <iframe> elements from interfering with a drag operation by preventing them from capturing mousemove events. If specified as true, all iframes are masked during a drag operation. If a selector is provided, any selected iframes are masked.	
opacity	(Number) A value from 0.0 to 1.0 that specifies the opacity of the dragged element or helper. If omitted, the opacity of the element isn't changed during dragging.	✓
refreshPositions	(Boolean) If specified as true, the positions of all droppable elements (which we'll be discussing in section 10.2) are recomputed during every mousemove event of the drag. Use this only if it solves some problems you may be having on highly dynamic pages, because it comes with a heavy performance penalty.	
revert	(Boolean|String) If specified as true, the dragged element will return to its original position at the end of the drag operation. If the string invalid is used, the element reverts only if it has not been dropped onto a droppable; if valid, the element reverts only if dropped onto a droppable. If omitted, or specified as false, the dragged element doesn't return to its original position.	✓
revertDuration	(Number) If revert is true, specifies the number of milliseconds it takes for the dragged element to return to its original position. If omitted, a default value of 500 is used.	
scope	(String) Used to associate draggables with droppables. Draggables with the same scope name as a droppable will automatically be accepted by that droppable. If not specified, a default scope of default is used. (This will make more sense when we discuss droppables.)	

Table 10.1   Options for the jQuery UI `draggable()` method *(continued)*

Option	Description	In Lab
scroll	(Boolean) If set to `false`, prevents the container from auto-scrolling during a drag operation. If omitted, or specified as `true`, auto-scrolling is enabled.	✓
scrollSensitivity	(Number) The distance in pixels from the pointer to the edge of the viewport when auto-scrolling should take place. If omitted, the default is `20` pixels.	
scrollSpeed	(Number) The speed at which auto-scrolling should commence once started. The default value is `20`. Use lower values to slow the scrolling, and higher values to speed it up.	
snap	(Selector|Boolean) Specifies a selector that identifies target elements on the page whose edges the dragged element will "snap to" whenever the dragged element approaches the targets. Specifying `true` is shorthand for the selector `.ui-draggable`, making all other draggables the target elements.	
snapMode	(String) Specifies which side of an edge the dragged object will snap to. The string `outer` specifies that only the outside of the edge will be snapped to, whereas `inner` specifies that only the inside of the edge will be snapped to. The string `both` (the default) will cause either side of the edge to be snapped to.	
snapTolerance	(Number) If snapping is enabled, specifies the distance, in pixels, from an edge at which snapping should occur. The default value is `20` pixels.	
stack	(Object) An object hash that controls z-index stacking of grouped elements during drag operations. Whenever you drag an element, it becomes the highest (by z-index) of all other draggables in that group. A minimum value that the z-index should never fall below can also be specified with the `min` property.	
start	(Function) Specifies a function to be established on the draggables as an event handler for dragstart events. See table 10.2 for more details on this event.	
stop	(Function) Specifies a function to be established on the draggables as an event handler for dragstop events. See table 10.2 for more details on this event.	
zIndex	(Number) Specifies the z-index for the draggables during drag operations. If omitted, the z-index of the draggables is unchanged during drag operations.	

All these options allow us a great deal of flexibility in how drag operations will conduct themselves. But we're not done yet. Draggables also give us the flexibility to control how the rest of our page conducts itself while a drag is under way. Let's see how.

10.1.2 Draggability events

We saw, in table 10.1, that there are three options that let us register event handlers on the draggables themselves: drag, start, and stop. These options are a convenient way to bind event handlers for three custom events that jQuery triggers during various stages of a drag operation: dragstart, drag, and dragstop, all described in table 10.2. This table (and all event-description tables that follow) show the bindable custom

Table 10.2 jQuery UI events triggered for draggables

Event	Option	Description
dragstart	start	Triggered when a drag operation commences
drag	drag	Continuously triggered for mousemove events during a drag operation
dragstop	stop	Triggered when a drag operation terminates

event name, the option name that can be used to specify a handler function, and a description of the event.

Handlers for each of these events can be established on any element in a draggable element's ancestor hierarchy to receive notification whenever any of these events occurs. We might want, for example, to react to dragstart events in some global manner by establishing a handler for that event on the document body:

```
$('body').bind('dragstart',function(event,info){
  say('What a drag!');
});
```

Regardless of where the handler is established, and whether it was established via an option entry or with the bind() method, the handler is passed two parameters: the mouse event instance, and an object whose properties contain information on the current state of the drag event. The properties on this object are as follows:

- helper—A wrapped set containing the element being dragged (either the original element or its clone).
- position—An object whose top and left properties give the position of the dragged element relative to its offset parent. It may be undefined for dragstart events.
- offset—An object whose top and left properties give the position of the dragged element relative to the document page. It may be undefined for dragstart events.

The Draggables Lab page establishes draggable event handlers and uses the information passed to them to show the position of the dragged element in its Console pane.

Once we've made an element draggable using this first form of the draggable() method (in which we pass an options object), we can use the other forms to control the element's draggability.

10.1.3 *Controlling draggability*

As we learned in the previous section, calling the draggable() method with an options hash (or with no parameters at all) establishes the draggability of the wrapped elements. Once an element is draggable, we may have occasion to want to suspend that draggability, but without losing all the options we've taken the effort to set up.

We can temporarily disable an element's draggability by calling the following form of the draggable() method:

```
$('.ui-draggable').draggable('disable');
```

Any draggable elements in the wrapped set will become *temporarily* non-draggable. In the preceding example, we've disabled draggability for all draggables on the page.

To reinstate the draggability of such elements, we'd use this statement:

```
$('.ui-draggable').draggable('enable');
```

This will re-enable the draggability of any draggable elements that have been disabled.

> **WARNING**   As previously discussed, you can't use the `draggable('enable')` method to initially apply draggability to non-draggable elements. The `enable` form of the method will only re-enable the draggability of draggable elements that have been previously disabled.

If we wish to make draggable elements non-draggable permanently, restoring them to predraggable condition, then we'd use this statement:

```
$('.ui-draggable').draggable('destroy');
```

The `destroy` variant of the method removes all vestiges of draggability from the elements.

The final format of the versatile `draggable()` method allows us to set or retrieve individual options at any time during a draggable's lifetime.

For example, to set the `revert` option on a draggable element, use this line:

```
$('.whatever').draggable('option','revert',true);
```

This will set the `revert` option to `true` for the first element in the wrapped set *if* that element is already draggable. Trying to set an option on a non-draggable element won't do anything useful.

If we want to fetch the value of a draggable's option, we could write this:

```
var value = $('.ui-draggable').draggable('option','revert');
```

This will fetch the value of the `revert` option for the first element in the wrapped set if that element is draggable (otherwise, you'll just get `undefined`).

Dragging things around the screen is all well and good, but is it really useful? It's fun for a time, but like playing with a yo-yo (unless we're true aficionados), it loses its charm quickly. In practical applications, we could use it to allow users to move modular elements around the screen (and if we're nice, we'd remember their chosen positions in cookies or other persistence mechanisms), or in games or puzzles. But drag operations truly shine when there's something interesting to drop dragged elements on. So let's see how we can make *droppables* to go with our draggables.

10.2   *Dropping dragged things*

The flip side of the coin from draggables is *droppables*—elements that can accept dragged elements and do something interesting when the draggable is dropped on them. Creating droppable items from page elements is similar to creating draggables; in fact, it's even easier because there are fewer options to worry about.

Like the `draggable()` method, the `droppable()` method has a number of forms: one used to initially create the droppables, and the others to affect the droppable afterwards. This is its syntax:

Command syntax: droppable

`droppable(options)`
`droppable('disable')`
`droppable('enable')`
`droppable('destroy')`
`droppable('option',optionName,value)`

Makes the elements in the wrapped set droppable according to the specified options, or performs some other droppability action based upon an operation string passed as the first parameter.

Parameters

`options`	(Object) An object hash of the options to be applied to the elements in the wrapped set, as described in table 10.3, making them droppable.
`'disable'`	(String) Disables the droppability of any droppable elements in the wrapped set. The droppability of the elements isn't removed and can be restored by calling the `enable` variant of this method.
`'enable'`	(String) Re-enables droppability on any droppable elements in the wrapped set whose droppability has been disabled. Note that this method won't *add* droppability to any non-droppable elements.
`'destroy'`	(String) Removes droppability from the elements in the wrapped set.
`'option'`	(String) Allows option values to be set on all elements of the wrapped set, or to be retrieved from the first element of the wrapped set (which should be a droppable element), based upon the remaining parameters. If specified, at least the `optionName` parameter must also be provided.
`optionName`	(String) The name of the option (see table 10.3) whose value is to be set or returned. If a `value` parameter is provided, that value becomes the option's value. If no `value` parameter is provided, the named option's value is returned.
`value`	(Object) The value to be set for the option identified by the `optionName` parameter.

Returns

The wrapped set, except for the case where an option value is returned.

Let's see what it takes to make elements droppable.

10.2.1 *Making elements droppable*

Elements are made droppable by collecting them into a wrapped set and calling the `droppable()` method with an object hash of options (or no parameters at all to accept the option defaults). When made droppable, the class `ui-droppable` is added to the elements. This is similar to the way we made things draggable, but there are fewer options, as listed in table 10.3.

As with draggables, we've also provided a jQuery UI Droppables Lab page (shown in figure 10.2) that demonstrates most of the droppable options in action.

Figure 10.2   The Droppables Lab page allows us to see the droppable options in action.

Find this page at chapter10/droppables/lab.droppables.html, load it into your browser, and use it to manipulate droppable options as you read through the option descriptions in table 10.3.

Although there are fewer options available for droppables than for draggables, it's also clear that there are more events and states associated with droppables. Let's examine these states and events in detail.

Table 10.3 Options for the jQuery UI `droppable()` method

Option	Description	In Lab
accept	(Selector|Function) Specifies a selector that identifies draggables that are to be accepted for dropping, or a function that filters all draggable elements on the page. The function is invoked for all draggable elements, with a reference to that element as the first parameter. Returning `true` from the function accepts the draggable for dropping. If omitted, all draggable elements are accepted.	✓
activate	(Function) Specifies a function to be established on the droppables as an event handler for dropactivate events, which are triggered when a drag operation starts. See the description of the droppable events in table 10.4 for more details on this event.	✓
activeClass	(String) A class name or names to be added to the droppable whenever a drag operation with an acceptable element is underway. You can specify more than one class name by separating them with space characters. If omitted, no classes are added to the droppable during an acceptable drag operation.	✓
addClasses	(Boolean) If specified as `false`, prevents the `ui-droppable` class from being added to droppable elements. We might choose to do this for performance reasons if the class isn't needed and we're adding droppability to many elements on a page.	
deactivate	(Function) Specifies a function to be established on the droppables as an event handler for dropdeactivate events, which are triggered when a drag operation terminates. See the description of the droppable events in table 10.4 for more details on this event.	✓
drop	(Function) Specifies a function to be established on the droppables as an event handler for drop events. See the description of the droppable events in table 10.4 for more details on this event.	✓
greedy	(Boolean) Droppability events will normally propagate to nested droppables. If this option is set to `true`, this propagation is prevented.	
hoverClass	(String) A class name or names to be added to the droppable whenever an acceptable draggable is hovering over the droppable. Multiple class names can be provided by separating them with space characters. If omitted, no classes are added to the droppable during an acceptable hover.	✓
out	(Function) Specifies a function to be established on the droppables as an event handler for dropout events. See the description of the droppable events in table 10.4 for more details on this event.	✓
over	(Function) Specifies a function to be established on the droppables as an event handler for dropover events. See the description of the droppable events in table 10.4 for more details on this event.	✓
scope	(String) Used to associate draggables with droppables. Draggables with the same scope name as a droppable will automatically be accepted by the droppable. If not specified, a default scope of `default` is used.	

Table 10.3   Options for the jQuery UI `droppable()` method *(continued)*

Option	Description	In Lab
`tolerance`	(String) Controls how a dragged element is considered to be hovering over a droppable. The values are • `fit`—The draggable must be entirely within the droppable. • `pointer`—The mouse pointer must enter the droppable. • `touch`—Any part of the draggable must overlap the droppable. • `intersect`—At least 50 percent of the draggable must overlap the droppable. • If omitted, `intersect` is used as the default.	✓

10.2.2 Droppability events

Keeping track of the states of a drag event is pretty easy; either the element is being dragged or it's not. But when we add dropping into the mix, things become a bit more complex. Not only do we have the draggable to take into account, but also its interaction with the droppables for which it's acceptable.

Because a figure is worth many words, figure 10.3 depicts the states and the events that cause their transitions during a drag-and-drop operation.

Once established as a droppable, a droppable element will be in *inactive* state—it's prepared to accept draggables, but because there's no drag operation underway, all is peaceful and at rest. But once a drag operation starts, things get more interesting:

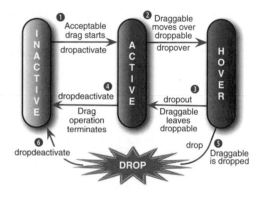

Figure 10.3   **The states and transitions that a droppable can attain depend upon the interaction between the active draggable and the droppable element during a drag-and-drop operation.**

❶ When a drag operation starts for a draggable that's acceptable to the droppable (see the `accept` and `scope` options for what's deemed *acceptable*), a dropactivate event is triggered and the droppable is considered in *active* state.

    Any handlers for dropactivate events (whether established via options or not) will be triggered according to the normal rules of event propagation unless the `greedy` option was specified as `true`, in which case only handlers on droppables will be invoked.

    At this point, any class names provided by the `activeClass` option are applied to the droppable.

❷ If the dragged element is moved such that it satisfies the rules that determine when a draggable is considered hovering over the droppable (as specified by the `tolerance` option), a dropover event is triggered (invoking suitable handlers), and the droppable enters *hover* state.

This is the point at which any class names supplied by a hoverClass option are applied to the droppable.

There are two possible transitions from this point: the drag operation can terminate by the release of the mouse button, or the draggable can continue to be moved.

❸ If the draggable is moved such that it's no longer considered hovering over the droppable (again via the tolerance rules), a dropout event is triggered, and any class names specified by hoverClass are removed.

The droppable returns to active state.

❹ If the drag operation terminates while in active state, a dropdeactivate event is triggered, any classes specified by activeClass are removed, and the droppable reverts to inactive state.

❺ If, however, the drag operation terminates while in hover state, the draggable is considered *dropped* onto the droppable and two events are triggered: drop and dropdeactivate.

❻ The droppable reverts to inactive state, and any classes specified by active-Class are removed.

NOTE The "drop" itself isn't considered a state, but an instantaneous event.

The droppables events are summarized in table 10.4.

Table 10.4 jQuery UI events triggered for droppables

Event	Option	Description
dropactivate	activate	Triggered when a drag operation commences using a draggable that's acceptable to a droppable
dropdeactivate	deactivate	Triggered when a pending drop operation terminates
dropover	over	Triggered when an acceptable draggable moves over a droppable as defined by the droppable's tolerance option
dropout	out	Triggered when a draggable moves off of an accepting droppable
drop	drop	Triggered when a drag operation terminates while over an accepting droppable

All droppable event handlers are passed two parameters: the mouse event instance, and an object whose properties contain information on the current state of the drag-and-drop operation. The properties on this object are as follows:

- helper—A wrapped set containing the helper element being dragged (either the original element or its clone).
- draggable—A wrapped set containing the current draggable element.

- position—An object whose top and left properties give the position of the dragged element relative to its offset parent. May be undefined for dragstart events.

- offset—An object whose top and left properties give the position of the dragged element relative to the document page. May be undefined for drag-start events.

We can use the Droppables Lab to make sure that we understand these events and state transitions. As in the other labs, there's a Control Panel that lets us specify the options to be applied to the droppable after clicking the Apply button. The Disable and Enable buttons serve to disable and enable the droppable (using the appropriate variants of the droppable() method), and the Reset button puts the form back to its initial state and destroys the droppable capability on the Lab's drop target.

In the Test Subjects pane are six draggable elements and an element that will become droppable after clicking the Apply button (which we'll call the *Drop Zone*). Below the Drop Zone are grayed-out text elements that read Activate, Over, Out, Drop, and Deactivate. When a corresponding droppable event is triggered, the appropriate text element, which we'll refer to as an *event indicator*, is momentarily highlighted to indicate that the event has been triggered. (Can you already figure out how that's achieved within the Lab page?)

Let's dig in and get the skinny on droppables using this Lab.

- *Exercise 1*—In this exercise, we're going to begin familiarizing ourselves with the accept option, which is what tells the droppable what constitutes an acceptable draggable. Although this option can be set to any jQuery selector (or even a function that can programmatically make suitability determinations), for the purposes of the lab, we'll concentrate on elements that possess particular class names. In particular, we can specify a selector that includes any of the class names flower, dog, motorcycle, and water by checking the appropriate checkboxes of the accept option controls.

   The six draggable image elements on the left side of the Test Subjects pane are each assigned one or two of these class names based on what appears in the image. For example, the upper-left draggable possesses the class names dog and flower (because both a dog and some flowers appear in the photo), whereas the lower-middle image is defined with the class names motorcycle and water (a Yamaha V-Star and the Colorado River, to be precise).

   Before clicking Apply, try to drag and drop any of these elements on the Drop Zone. Aside from the dragging, not much happens. Carefully observe the event indicators, and note how they don't change. This should be no surprise because, at outset, no droppable even exists on the page.

   Now, leaving all controls in their initial conditions (including all accept checkboxes checked), click the Apply button. The executed command includes an accept option that specifies a selector that matches all four class names.

Once again, try to drag any of the images to the Drop Zone while observing the event indicators. This time, you'll see the Activate indicator briefly highlight, or *throb*, when you begin moving any of the images, indicating that a droppable has noticed that a drag operation has commenced using a draggable that's acceptable for dropping, and has triggered a dropactivate event.

Drag the image over and out of the Drop Zone a number of times. Corresponding dropover and dropout events are triggered (as shown by the corresponding indicators) at the appropriate times. Now, drop the image outside the confines of the Drop Zone, and watch the Deactivate indicator throb.

Finally, repeat the drag operation, but this time drop the image on top of the Drop Zone. The Drop indicator throbs (indicating that the drop event was triggered). Note, also, that the Drop Zone is wired to display the most recent image that was dropped upon it.

- *Exercise 2*—Uncheck all of the accept checkboxes, and click Apply. This results in an accept option consisting of the empty string, which matches nothing. No matter which image you choose, no callback indicators throb, and nothing happens when you drop an image onto the Drop Zone. Without a meaningful accept option, our Drop Zone has become a brick. (Note that this isn't the same as omitting accept, which causes all elements to be acceptable.)

- *Exercise 3*—Check only one accept checkbox, say flower, and note how only images with flowers in them (known to the page because the class name flower was defined for them) are construed to be acceptable items.

 Try again with whatever combinations of acceptable class names you like until you're comfortable with the concept of the accept option.

- *Exercise 4*—Reset the controls, check the activeClass's greenBorder radio button, and click Apply. This supplies an activeClass option to the droppable that specifies a class name that defines (you guessed it) a green border.

 Now, when you begin to drag an image that's acceptable to the droppable (as defined by the accept option), the black border around the Drop Zone is replaced by a green border.

TIP If you have trouble getting this to work for you on your own pages, note that you need to be mindful of CSS precedence rules. When an activeClass class name is applied, it must be able to override the rule that assigns the default visual rendition that you wish to supplant. This is also true of hoverClass. (Sometimes the !important CSS qualifier is needed to override other style rules.)

- *Exercise 5*—Reset the Lab, check the hoverClass radio button labeled bronze, and click Apply. When an acceptable image is dragged over the Drop Zone, the Drop Zone changes to a bronze color.

- *Exercise 6*—For this exercise, choose each of the various tolerance radio buttons, and note how the setting affects when the droppable makes the transition from active to hover (in other words, when a dropover event is triggered). This transition can easily be observed by setting the hoverClass option or when the Over event indicator throbs.

Continue to toy around with the lab page until you fully understand how drag-and-drop operations operate and are affected by the supported options.

Once we have dragging and dropping, we can imagine a whole range of user interactions where drag and drop can be used make things easy and intuitive for the user by letting them directly manipulate page elements. One of those interactions, sorting, is so ubiquitous that jQuery UI provides direct support for it.

10.3 *Sorting stuff*

Arguably, sorting is one of the most useful interactions that utilizes drag and drop. Putting a list of items into a specific order, or even moving them in order between lists, is a rather common interaction technique in desktop applications, but on the web it's either been missing or approximated with a combination of <select> elements and buttons (to move items within, and sometimes between, multiple select lists).

Although such composite controls aren't horrible, it'd be much more intuitive for a user to be able to directly manipulate the elements. Drag and drop gives us that ability, and jQuery UI makes it pretty darn easy.

As with the draggable and droppable capabilities, jQuery UI provides sortability via a single, multi-purpose method, sortable(), whose syntax style should be familiar by now.

Command syntax: sortable

```
sortable(options)
sortable('disable')
sortable('enable')
sortable('destroy')
sortable('option',optionName,value)
sortable('cancel')
sortable('refresh')
sortable('refreshPositions')
sortable('serialize')
sortable('toArray')
```

Makes the elements in the wrapped set sortable according to the specified options, or performs some other sortability action based upon an operation string passed as the first parameter.

Parameters

options	(Object) An object hash of the options to be applied to the elements in the wrapped set, as described in table 10.5, making them sortable.
'disable'	(String) Disables the sortability of any sortable elements in the wrapped set. The sortability of the elements isn't removed and can be restored by calling the enable variant of this method.

Command syntax: sortable *(continued)*	
`'enable'`	(String) Re-enables sortability on any sortable elements in the wrapped set whose sortability has been disabled. Note that this method won't *add* sortability to any non-sortable elements.
`'destroy'`	(String) Removes sortability from the elements in the wrapped set.
`'options'`	(String) Allows option values to be set on all elements of the wrapped set, or to be retrieved on the first element of the wrapped set (which should be a sortable element), based upon the remaining parameters. If specified, at least the `optionName` parameter must also be provided.
`'cancel'`	(String) Cancels the current sort operation. This is most useful within handlers for the sortreceive and sortstop events.
`'refresh'`	(String) Triggers the reloading of items within the sortable element. Calling this method will cause new items added to the sortable to be recognized.
`'refreshPositions'`	(String) This method is used mostly internally to refresh the cached information of the sortable. Unwise use can impair the performance of the operation, so use only within handlers when necessary to solve problems created by outdated cache information.
`'serialize'`	(String) Returns a serialized query string (submitable via Ajax) formed from the sortable. We'll be examining the use of this method in more detail shortly.
`'toArray'`	(String) Returns an array of the `id` values of the sortable elements in sorted order.
`optionName`	(String) The name of the option (see table 10.5) whose value is to be set or returned. If a `value` parameter is provided, that value becomes the option's value. If no `value` parameter is provided, the named option's value is returned.
`value`	(Object) The value to be set for the option identified by the `optionName` parameter.

Returns

The wrapped set, except for the cases where an option value, query string, or array is returned.

That's a few more method variations than in the previous interactions, and we'll examine some of those in detail, but first let's make elements sortable.

10.3.1 *Making things sortable*

We can make pretty much any set of child elements sortable (by applying sortability to their parent), but most often you'll see sortability applied to a list (<ul> or <ol> element) so that its <li> children can be moved around. That makes a lot of semantic sense and also allows the element to degrade gracefully should we decide not to apply sortability.

Nothing prevents us, on the other hand, from applying sortability to the <div> children of a parent <div>, if that makes more sense for our application. We'll see how to do so when we examine the sortability options in table 10.5.

Like the draggable and droppable interactions, sortability is applied by calling the sortable method with no parameters (to accept the defaults), or with an object that provides non-default options.

As jQuery UI Sortables Lab page, chapter10/sortables/lab.sortables.html, is available, which we can use to see the sortability options operate in real time. This Lab page is shown in figure 10.4.

It should come as no surprise that quite a few of the options to sortable simply pass through to the lower-level drag or drop operations. In the interest of saving space, the

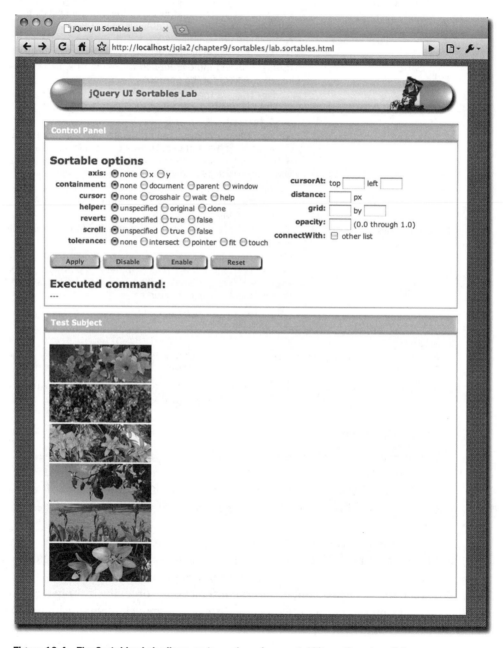

Figure 10.4   The Sortables Lab allows us to apply various sortability options to a list.

description of these options isn't repeated; rather, a reference to the table in which the option is first described is provided.

Most of these options are fairly self-explanatory, but the connectWith option deserves closer attention.

Table 10.5 Options for the jQuery UI `sortable()` method

Option	Description	In Lab
activate	(Function) Specifies a function to be established on the sortables as an event handler for sortactivate events. See table 10.6 for details of this event.	
appendTo	See the draggable operation of the same name in table 10.1. Appending to the body element may solve any issues with overlaying or z-index.	
axis	See the draggable operation of the same name in table 10.1. Frequently, this option is used to constrain movement to the orientation (horizontal or vertical) of the sorted list.	✓
beforeStop	(Function) Specifies a function to be established on the sortables as an event handler for sortbeforeStop events. See table 10.6 for details of this event..	
cancel	See the draggable operation of the same name in table 10.1.	
change	(Function) Specifies a function to be established on the sortables as an event handler for sortchange events. See table 10.6 for details of this event.	
connectWith	(Selector) Identifies another sortable element that can accept items from this sortable. This allows items from one list to be moved to other lists—a frequent and useful user interaction. If omitted, no other element is connected.	✓
containment	See the draggable operation of the same name in table 10.1.	✓
cursor	See the draggable operation of the same name in table 10.1.	✓
cursorAt	See the draggable operation of the same name in table 10.1.	✓
deactivate	(Function) Specifies a function to be established on the sortables as an event handler for sortdeactivate events. See table 10.6 for details of this event.	
delay	See the draggable operation of the same name in table 10.1.	
distance	See the draggable operation of the same name in table 10.1.	✓
dropOnEmpty	(Boolean) If true (the default), dropping items from this sortable on another connected sortable is allowed when that sortable has no elements. Otherwise, dropping is disallowed when empty.	
forceHelperSize	(Boolean) If true, forces the helper to have a size. Defaults to false.	
forcePlaceholderSize	(Boolean) If true, forces the placeholder to have a size. Defaults to false.	

Table 10.5 Options for the jQuery UI `sortable()` method *(continued)*

Option	Description	In Lab
grid	See the draggable operation of the same name in table 10.1.	✓
handle	See the draggable operation of the same name in table 10.1.	
helper	See the draggable operation of the same name in table 10.1.	
items	(Selector) Provides a selector, within the context of the sortable, that identifies what child elements can be sorted. By default, > * is used, which allows all child elements to be selected for sorting.	
opacity	See the draggable operation of the same name in table 10.1.	✓
out	(Function) Specifies a function to be established on the sortables as an event handler for sortout events. See table 10.6 for details of this event.	
over	(Function) Specifies a function to be established on the sortables as an event handler for sortover events. See table 10.6 for details of this event.	
placeholder	(String) A class name that gets applied to the otherwise unstyled placeholder space.	
receive	(Function) Specifies a function to be established on the sortables as an event handler for sortreceive events. See table 10.6 for details of this event.	
remove	(Function) Specifies a function to be established on the sortables as an event handler for sortremove events. See table 10.6 for details of this event.	
revert	See the draggable operation of the same name in table 10.1. The effect, when enabled, is for the drag helper to smoothly slide into place, as opposed to quickly snapping into place.	✓
scroll	See the draggable operation of the same name in table 10.1.	✓
scrollSensitivity	See the draggable operation of the same name in table 10.1.	
scrollSpeed	See the draggable operation of the same name in table 10.1.	
sort	(Function) Specifies a function to be established on the sortables as an event handler for sort events. See table 10.6 for details of this event.	
start	(Function) Specifies a function to be established on the sortables as an event handler for sortstart events. See table 10.6 for details of this event.	
stop	(Function) Specifies a function to be established on the sortables as an event handler for sortstop events. See table 10.6 for details of this event.	
tolerance	See the droppable operation of the same name in table 10.3.	✓
update	(Function) Specifies a function to be established on the sortables as an event handler for sortupdate events. See table 10.6 for details of this event.	4
zIndex	See the draggable operation of the same name in table 10.1.	

10.3.2 *Connecting sortables*

It's readily apparent how useful the sortable capability is for allowing users to order a single list of elements, but it's also a common way to allow them to move items from one list to another. This capability is frequently provided by a combination of two multi-select lists and a button (to move selected items from one list to another), and perhaps even more buttons to control the order of items within each of the lists.

By using jQuery UI sortables, and linking them using the `connectWith` option, we can eliminate all those buttons and present the user with a cleaner direct-manipulation interface. Imagine, perhaps, a page in which we allow users to design reports that they'd like to receive. There may be many possible data columns included in the report, but we can allow users to specify the subset of columns that they'd like included and the order in which they'd like them to appear.

We could include all possible columns in one list, and allow users to drag their desired columns from this list to a second list whose content represents the report's columns in the order in which they're to appear.

Code to set up this complex interaction could be as easy as this:

```
$('#allPossibleColumns').sortable({
  connectWith: '#includedColumns'
});
$('#includedColumns').sortable();
```

In the Sortables Lab page, you can experiment with dragging between two lists by checking the checkbox labeled `connectWith`.

With all those drag and drop operations going on—not to mention elements being moved around within (or between) lists—there are lots of events that we might want to know about so we can hook into what's going on during a sort operation.

10.3.3 *Sortability events*

There's a lot of moving and shaking during a sort operation; drag and drop events are firing, and the DOM is being manipulated—both to move elements around as the sort unfolds, and to handle any placeholder that we may have defined.

If all we care about is allowing the user to sort a list of items and then retrieve the result at a later point (which we'll cover in the next section), we don't need to be very concerned with all the events that are taking place *during* the operation. But, as with draggables and droppables, if we want to hook into the operation during its interesting events, we can define handlers to be notified when these events take place.

As we've seen in the other interactions, we can establish these handlers either locally on the sortable via options passed to `sortable()`, or by establishing the handlers ourselves using `bind()`.

The information passed to these handlers follows the customary interaction format, with the event as the first parameter, and a custom object with interesting information about the operation passed as the second. For sortables, this custom object contains the following properties:

- position—An object whose top and left properties give the position of the dragged element relative to its offset parent
- offset—An object whose top and left properties give the position of the dragged element relative to the document page
- helper—A wrapped set containing the drag helper (often a clone)
- item—A wrapped set containing the sort item
- placeholder—A wrapped set containing the placeholder (if any)
- sender—A wrapped set containing the source sortable when a connected operation takes place between two sortables

Be aware that some of these properties may be undefined or null if they don't make sense for the current state. For example, there is no helper defined for the sortstop event because the drag operation is no longer underway.

The function context for these handlers is the element to which the sortable() method was applied.

The events that are triggered during a sort operation are shown in table 10.6.

Table 10.6   jQuery UI events triggered for sortables

Event	Option	Description
sort	sort	Repeatedly triggered for mousemove events during a sort operation
sortactivate	activate	Triggered on the sortables when a sort operation starts on connected sortables
sortbeforeStop	beforeStop	Triggered when the sort operation is about to end, with the helper and placeholder element reference still valid
sortchange	change	Triggered when the sorted element changes position within the DOM
sortdeactivate	deactivate	Triggered when a connected sort stops, propagated to the connected sortables
sortout	out	Triggered when the sort item is moved away from a connected list
sortover	over	Triggered when a sort item moves into a connected list
sortreceive	receive	Triggered when a connected list has received a sort item from another list
sortremove	remove	Triggered when the sort item is removed from a connected list and is dragged into another
sortstart	start	Triggered when a sort operation starts
sortstop	stop	Triggered when a sort operation has concluded
sortupdate	update	Triggered when a sort operation stops and the position of the item has been changed

Note that a good number of these event types are triggered only during an operation involving connected lists; the number of events fired for a sort within a single list is fairly small.

The sortupdate event may be the most important because it can be used to let us know when a sort that has resulted in something actually changing has taken place. If a sort operation takes place without anything changing, chances are we don't really need to care.

When a sortupdate event fires, we probably want to know what the sorted order of the list is. Let's find out how we can get that information.

10.3.4 *Fetching the sort order*

Any time we want to know what the sorted order of a sortables list is, there are two variants of the `sortable()` method that we can use, depending upon what type of information we need.

The `sortable('toArray')` method returns a JavaScript array of the id values of the sorted items, in their sorted order. We can use this whenever we need to know the order of the items.

If, on the other hand, we want to submit the information as part of a new request, or even an Ajax request, we'd use `sortable('serialize')`, which returns a string suitable for use as a query string or request body, containing the ordered information of the sort elements.

Using this variant requires that you use a specific format for the id values assigned to the sortable's elements (the elements that will be sorted, not the sortable itself). Each id needs to be of the format `prefix_number` where the prefix can be anything you want—as long as it's the same for all the elements—followed by an underscore and a numeric value. When this format is followed, serializing the sortable results in a query string that contains an entry for each sortable where the name is the prefix followed by [], and whose value is the trailing numeric value of the id.

Confused? Don't blame you. Let's turn to the Sortables Lab page for help.

The console at the bottom of the Lab (unseen in figure 10.4 because it's below the bottom of the screen) shows the results of calling the fetch methods after a sort operation (using a sortupdate event handler). The id values assigned to the sort elements are `subject_1` through `subject_6` in top to bottom order, following the formatting rules set out for the `serialize` method.

In the Lab, leaving all options in their default state, click Apply, grab the orange tiger lily image (which has the id value `subject_3`), and drag it such that it becomes the first item in the list. In the console, you'll observe that the array of id values is now as follows:

```
['subject_3', 'subject_1', 'subject_2', 'subject_4', 'subject_5',
    'subject_6']
```

This is exactly what we'd expect, showing the new order of the items with the third item now in the first position.

The result of the serialization is

```
subject[]=3&subject[]=1&subject[]=2&subject[]=4&subject[]=5&subject[]=6
```

This shows how the prefix (`subject`) is used to construct the query parameter names, with the trailing numeric values becoming the parameter values. (The `[]`, by the way, is a common notation meaning "array," which is used to suggest that there are more than one of the same named parameters.)

If this format isn't to your liking, the array of `id`s can always be used as a basis to create your own query strings (in which case `$.param()` would come in quite handy).

As an exercise, hearken back to the "collapsible module" example in chapter 5 (when we animated the rolling up of a body into a caption bar). How would you use sortables to let a user manage the position of a number of these modules (also termed *portlets* by some) in multiple columns?

With sortables, the basic drag and drop interactions have been combined to create a higher-order interaction. Let's see another such interaction that jQuery UI provides.

10.4   *Changing the size of things*

Back in chapter 3, we learned how to change the size of DOM elements using jQuery's methods, and in chapter 5, we even saw how to do so in an animated fashion. jQuery UI also allows us to let our users change the size of elements through direct manipulation.

Thinking again of the collapsible module example, in addition to allowing users to move these modules around on the page, wouldn't it be nice to let them easily assign custom sizes to the modules?

With the interactions we've seen so far, the inclusion of the CSS file generated when you downloaded jQuery UI (which we discussed back in chapter 9) is not necessary. But for the resizable interaction to function, the CSS file must be imported into the page, as in this example:

```
<link rel="stylesheet" type="text/css"
      href="styles/ui-theme/jquery-ui-1.8.custom.css">
```

Other than that detail, the `resizable()` method is as easy to use as the other jQuery UI interactions, and its syntax follows the familiar pattern:

Command syntax: resizable

```
resizable(options)
resizable('disable')
resizable('enable')
resizable('destroy')
resizable('option',optionName,value)
```

Makes the elements in the wrapped set resizable according to the specified options, or performs some other resizable action based upon an operation string passed as the first parameter.

Parameters

options	(Object) An object hash of the options to be applied to the elements in the wrapped set, as described in table 10.7, making them resizable.
'disable'	(String) Disables the resizability of any resizable elements in the wrapped set. The resizability of the elements isn't removed and can be restored by calling the enable variant of this method.
'enable'	(String) Re-enables resizability on any resizable elements in the wrapped set whose resizability has been disabled. Note that this method won't *add* resizability to any non-resizable elements.
'destroy'	(String) Removes resizability from the elements in the wrapped set.
'option'	(String) Allows option values to be set on all elements of the wrapped set, or to be retrieved on the first element of the wrapped set (which should be a resizable element), based upon the remaining parameters. If specified, at least the optionName parameter must also be provided.
optionName	(String) The name of the option (see table 10.7) whose value is to be set or returned. If a value parameter is provided, that value becomes the option's value. If no value parameter is provided, the named option's value is returned.
value	(Object) The value to be set for the option identified by the optionName parameter.

Returns

The wrapped set, except for the cases where an option value, query string, or array is returned.

Nothing much new there—the overloaded interaction method's pattern should be quite familiar by now—so let's take a look at the options available when creating resizable elements.

10.4.1 *Making things resizable*

One size rarely fits all, so as with the other interaction methods, the resizable() method offers a number of options that we can use to customize the interaction to our needs.

 A helpful lab page, the jQuery UI Resizables Lab, is available at chapter10/resizables/lab.resizables.html, and is shown in figure 10.5.

The Control Panel of this lab lets us play around with most of the options available for the resizable() method. Follow along in this Lab as you read through the options list in table 10.7.

As compared with some of the more involved interactions, resizable() has a modest set of options. We'll find the same is true of its events.

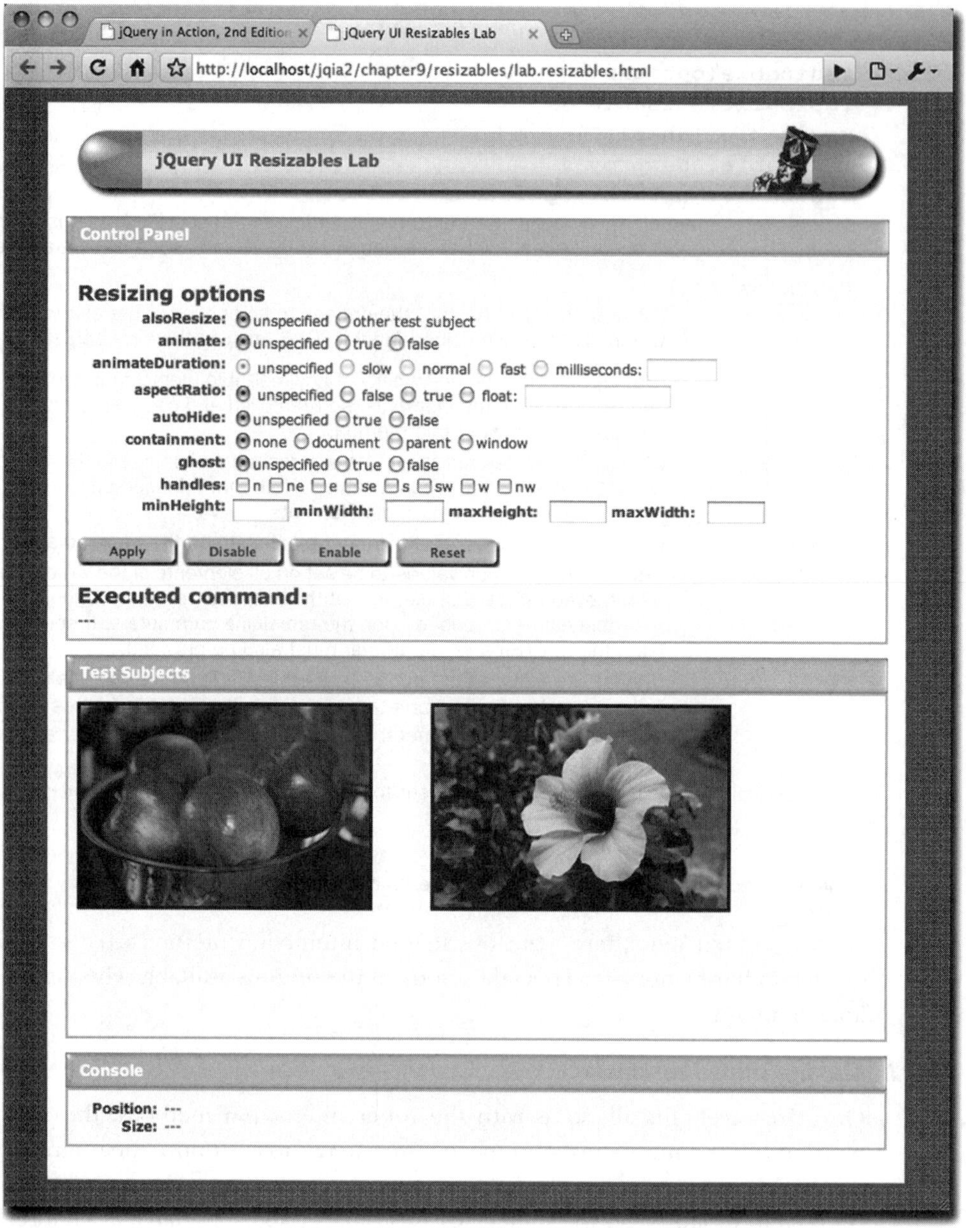

Figure 10.5   The Resizables Lab lets us see the operation of the various resizability options in action.

Table 10.7 Options for the jQuery UI `resizable()` method

Option	Description	In Lab
alsoResize	(Selector|jQuery|Element) Specifies other DOM elements that are to be resized in synchronization with the resizable elements. These other elements don't need to have the `resizable()` method applied to them. If omitted, no other elements are affected.	✓

animate	(Boolean) If `true`, the element itself isn't resized until after the drag operation finishes, at which time the element is resized smoothly via animation. While dragging, a helper with the class `ui-resizable-helper` (unless overridden by the `helper` option, discussed below) is used to show the drag outline. Be sure that this class has a suitable CSS definition or you may not see anything during an animated resize operation.
	For example, the Resizables Lab page uses the following:
	.ui-resizable-helper {
	  border: 1px solid #82bf5a;
	}
	By default, operations aren't animated.
		✓

animateDuration	(Integer|String) When the `animate` option is enabled, defines the duration of the animation. The standard animation strings `slow`, `normal`, or `fast` may be used, or the value can be specified as a number of milliseconds.	✓
animateEasing	(String) Specifies the easing effect to be used when the animate option is enabled. The default is the built-in `swing` easing. See chapter 5 for a more thorough discussion of easing.	
aspectRatio	(Boolean|Float) Specifies whether, and at what ratio, the aspect ratio of the element is to be retained during a resize operation. A value of `true` enforces the original aspect ratio of the element, whereas a floating value can be used to specify the ratio using the formula `width / height`. For example, a 3 to 4 ratio would be specified as 0.75. By default, no aspect ratio is maintained during the operation.	✓
autoHide	(Boolean) If `true`, the handles are hidden except when the mouse hovers over the resizable element. See the `handles` option for more information. By default, the handles are always displayed.	✓
cancel	(Selector) Specifies elements that should be excluded from resizable operations. By default, the selector `:input,option` is used.	
containment	(String|Element|Selector) Specifies an element within which resizing should be constrained. The built-in strings `parent`, or `document` can be specified, a specific element can be supplied, or you can use a selector to identify the containment element. By default, the operation is unconstrained.	✓
delay	See the draggable operation of the same name in table 10.1.	
distance	See the draggable operation of the same name in table 10.1.	
ghost	(Boolean) If `true`, a translucent helper is displayed during a resize operation. The default is `false`.	✓
grid	See the draggable operation of the same name in table 10.1.	

Table 10.7 Options for the jQuery UI `resizable()` method *(continued)*

Option	Description	In Lab
`handles`	(String|Object) Specifies in which directions the elements may be resized. These values can be supplied as a string with a comma-separated list of the possible values: n, ne, e, se, s, sw, w, nw, or all. This format should be used when you want jQuery UI to handle the creation of the handles. If you want to use child elements of the resizable as handles, supply an object with properties that define handles for each of the eight directions: n, ne, e, se, s, sw, w, and nw. The value of the property should be a selector for the element to use as the handle. We'll address the handles a bit more after we talk about events. If omitted, handles are created for the e, se, and s directions.	✓
`helper`	(String) If specified, enables the use of a helper element with the supplied class name during the resize operation. Helpers are enabled by using this option, but can also be implicitly enabled by other options such as `ghost` or `animate`. If implicitly enabled, the default class is `ui-resizable-helper` unless this option is used to override that class name.	
`maxHeight`	(Integer) Specifies a maximum height to which the element can be resized. By default, no maximum is imposed.	✓
`maxWidth`	(Integer) Specifies a maximum width to which the element can be resized. By default, no maximum is imposed.	✓
`minHeight`	(Integer) Specifies a minimum height to which the element can be resized. By default, a value of `10px` is used.	✓
`minWidth`	(Integer) Specifies a minimum width to which the element can be resized. By default, a value of `10px` is used.	✓
`resize`	(Function) Specifies a function to be established on the resizables as an event handler for resize events. See table 10.8 for details of this event.	✓
`start`	(Function) Specifies a function to be established on the resizables as an event handler for resizestart events. See table 10.8 for details of this event.	✓
`stop`	(Function) Specifies a function to be established on the resizables as an event handler for resizestop events. See table 10.8 for details of this event.	✓

10.4.2 *Resizability events*

Only three simple events are triggered during a resize operation to let us know that a resize operation has started, that it's underway, and that it has ended.

The information passed to these event handlers follows the customary interaction format of the event as the first parameter and a custom object with interesting information about the operation passed as the second. For resizables, this custom object contains the following properties:

- `position`—An object whose `top` and `left` properties give the current position of the element relative to its offset parent
- `size`—An object whose `width` and `height` properties give the current size of the element

- `originalPosition`—An object whose `top` and `left` properties give the original position of the element relative to its offset parent
- `originalSize`—An object whose `width` and `height` properties give the original size of the element
- `helper`—A wrapped set containing any helper element

Be aware that some of these properties may be `undefined` or `null` if they don't make sense for the current state. For example, there may be no `helper` defined.

The function context for these handlers is the element to which the `resizable()` method was applied. The specific events that are triggered during a resize operation are summarized in table 10.8.

Table 10.8 jQuery UI events triggered for resizables

Event	Option	Description
resizestart	start	Triggered when a resize operations starts
resize	resize	Repeatedly triggered for mousemove events during the resize operations
resizestop	stop	Triggered when a resize operation terminates

The Resizables Lab uses these events to report the current position and size of the test subject elements in the Console pane of the Lab page.

10.4.3 *Styling the handles*

Although `resizable()` is a fairly simple operation, at least as the jQuery UI interactions go, the handles deserve a bit of discussion of their own.

By default, handles are created for the east, southeast, and south directions, enabling resizing in those directions. Any direction that has no resize handle defined isn't enabled for resizing.

You might initially be confused by the fact that in your pages, as well as in the Resizables Lab, no matter how many directions are enabled, only the southeast corner gets a special "grip" icon when enabled. And yet, all the other specified directions are enabled—they work fine, and the mouse cursor changes shape when the edge of the resizable is hovered over. What's up with the difference?

It's not you, and it's not your code. jQuery UI treats that corner as a special case, adding additional class names to the southeast handle element in addition to what it adds to the other handles.

When any handle is created, it's given the class names `ui-resizable-handle` and `ui-resizable-`*xx*, where *xx* represents the direction that the handle represents (for example, `ui-resizable-n` for the north handle). The southeast corner, deemed special by jQuery UI, also receives the `ui-icon` and `ui-icon-gripsmall-diagonal-se` class names, whose definition (in the default CSS files as generated during the jQuery UI download process) creates the "grip" that appears on that corner. Although you

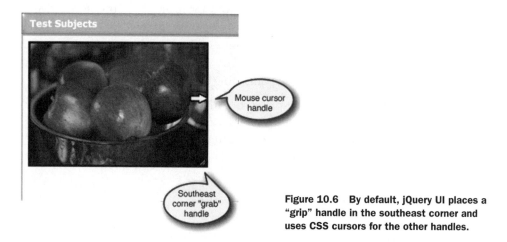

Figure 10.6   By default, jQuery UI places a "grip" handle in the southeast corner and uses CSS cursors for the other handles.

can manipulate the CSS for the handle names to affect how all the handles, including the southeast handle, appear, there is no option to change the class name assignment behavior.

> **NOTE**   The inspiration for the special southeast "grip" handle undoubtedly has its origin in window managers such as that for Mac OS X, which place such a grip on their resizable windows.

Figure 10.6 shows this grip handle, and the CSS handle that the mouse pointer displays when hovered near the resizable east edge.

If you find this too limiting, you can use the more complex version of the `handles` option to define child elements as handles that you can create yourself.

Now let's take a look at the final interaction that jQuery UI provides.

10.5   *Making things selectable*

Most of the interactions that we've examined so far involve direct manipulation of elements in order to change their state in some manner, be it to affect their position, size, or order within the DOM. The `selectable()` interaction gives us the ability to set and clear a "selected" state on any DOM element.

In HTML forms, we're used to using controls such as checkboxes, radio buttons, and yes, `<select>` elements to retain selection state. jQuery UI allows us to retain such state on elements other than these controls.

Think back to the DVD Ambassador example in chapter 4. In that example, we focused on the filtering set of controls, and didn't pay much mind to the results returned from that filtering operation. We're about to change that. As a reminder, a screenshot of that example is shown in figure 10.7.

The results (which, in the example, are the result of a hard-coded HTML fragment that in a real application would be generated from database information) are displayed as a list of elements on the page in a tabular format.

Figure 10.7 Revisiting the DVD Ambassador to instrument its result data set using jQuery UI selectables.

Let's say that we wanted to allow users of DVD Ambassador to select one or more DVD titles and apply some sort of bulk operation upon them: deleting them from the database, for example, or perhaps marking them all as viewed or unviewed.

The traditional approach would be to add a checkbox control to every row, and to use it to indicate that the row is selected. This method is tried and true, but it can present a challenge to the sloppy clickers in the audience because the checkbox creates a small area, usually about 12 by 12 pixels, within which the user must click to toggle the checkbox value.

NOTE In forms, the `<label>` element is often used to associate text with the checkbox, making the combination of the checkbox and label clickable.

User interfaces shouldn't be a game of hand-eye coordination, so we'd like to make it easier on our users. We have the know-how to instrument the *entire row* with a click handler such that when the user clicks *anywhere* on the row, the handler finds the enclosed checkbox and toggles its value. That gives the user a much bigger target to aim for, and the checkbox merely serves as a visual cue, and the means by which the selected state is remembered.

jQuery UI Selectables will allow us to take this a step further, which gives us two distinct advantages:

- The checkbox can be eliminated.
- Users will be able to make multiple selections with a *single* interaction.

The elimination of the checkbox means that we'll need to provide our own visual cues as to whether a row is selectable (without the checkbox, users have lost an important cue that we must make up for), and whether it is selected or not. Changing the background color of the row is a conventional means to indicate changes in status, and it's not a bad idea to also change the cursor shape to one that indicates that something wonderful will happened when the row is clicked upon.

With regards to remembering what's selected and what's not, jQuery UI selectables will maintain selection status using a class name (namely `ui-selected`) placed on selected elements.

Using the checkbox approach, users are limited to selecting and unselecting elements one by one. Although it's common to provide an über-checkbox that toggles the state of all the checkboxes, what if the user want to selects rows 3 through 7? They're stuck with selecting them one at a time.

With selectables, not only can we single-select with a click, but by dragging a rectangular marquee across the elements (or enclosing them, depending on how we set our options) our users will be able to select multiple adjacent elements in one fell swoop—much as we're used to in many desktop applications.

Additionally, selectables allows elements to be *added* to an already selected set by holding down the Control key (the Command key on Macs) while clicking or dragging.

 Now is a good time to bring up the jQuery UI Selectables Lab, found in file chapter10/selectables/lab.selectables.html, and shown in figure 10.8. In this Lab, we use the DVD Ambassador tabular result set as the test subject.

Let's try out a few interactions using the default options.

- *Exercise 1*—Before changing anything or clicking any buttons, wave the mouse cursor over the data table, and try clicking on and dragging over the rows. Note how the cursor pointer retains its normal appearance, and clicking has no effect at all. Dragging just results in the normal browser selection of text.

  Leave the options with their default settings, and click the Apply button. Now note how the mouse cursor changes to the hand pointer when it hovers over any of the data rows. When a DOM element becomes selectable (eligible for selection), jQuery UI places the class `ui-selectee` on the element. In the Lab page, the following CSS rule applies the cursor change:

  ```
  .ui-selectee { cursor: pointer; }
  ```

  Now click on a few rows. Note that as each row is clicked, it changes background color. When an element becomes selected, the class `ui-selected` is applied to it, and the following rule in the Lab page changes its background color:

  ```
  #testSubject .ui-selected { background-color: pink; }
  ```

Figure 10.8   The Selectables Lab uses the HTML results fragment from the DVD Ambassador as its test subject.

Also note that as you click each row, causing it to become selected, any previously selected row becomes unselected.

- *Exercise 2*—Without changing anything or clicking any buttons, select a row and then hold the Control/Command key down while selecting other rows. Note how when the Control/Command key is depressed during a click, any previously selected elements are *not* unselected.

- *Exercise 3*—Without changing anything or clicking any buttons, start a rectangular drag operation that cuts across a number of rows. Be sure that the drag operation starts *within* a row. Note that any row that the drag operation cuts across becomes selected. Pressing the Control/Command key during a drag likewise causes any previous selection to be retained.

That'll do for the moment.

10.5.1 *Creating selectables*

Now that we've seen Selectables in action, let's take a look at the `selectable()` method that makes it all happen:

Command syntax: selectable

`selectable(options)`
`selectable('disable')`
`selectable('enable')`
`selectable('destroy')`
`selectable('option',optionName,value)`
`selectable('refresh')`

Makes the elements in the wrapped set selectable according to the specified options, or performs some other selectable action based upon an operation string passed as the first parameter.

Parameters

`options`	(Object) An object hash of the options to be applied to the elements in the wrapped set, as described in table 10.9, making them selectable.
`'disable'`	(String) Disables the selectability of any selectable elements in the wrapped set. The selectability of the elements isn't removed and can be restored by calling the `enable` variant of this method.
`'enable'`	(String) Re-enables selectability on any selectable elements in the wrapped set whose selectability has been disabled. Note that this method won't *add* selectability to any non-selectable elements.
`'destroy'`	(String) Removes selectability from the elements in the wrapped set.
`'refresh'`	(String) Causes the size and position of the selectable elements to be refreshed. Used mostly when the `autoRefresh` option is disabled.
`'option'`	(String) Allows option values to be set on all elements of the wrapped set, or to be retrieved on the first element of the wrapped set (which should be a selectable element), based upon the remaining parameters. If specified, at least the `optionName` parameter must also be provided.
`optionName`	(String) The name of the option (see table 10.9) whose value is to be set or returned. If a `value` parameter is provided, that value becomes the option's value. If no `value` parameter is provided, the named option's value is returned.
`value`	(Object) The value to be set for the option identified by the `optionName` parameter.

Returns

The wrapped set, except for the cases where an option value, query string, or array is returned.

The options that can be used when creating selectable elements are shown in table 10.9.

Now that we've been introduced to the options, let's try a few more exercises using the Selectables Lab.

Table 10.9   Options for the jQuery UI `selectable()` method

Option	Description	In Lab
autoRefresh	(Boolean) If `true` (the default), the position and size of each selectable item is computed at the beginning of a select operation. Although a selectable operation won't make any changes to the position and size of selectable elements, they might have changed via CSS or scripting on the page. If there are many selectable elements, this option can be disabled for performance, and the `refresh` method can be used to manually recompute the values.	
cancel	See the draggable operation of the same name in table 10.1.	
delay	See the draggable operation of the same name in table 10.1.	
distance	See the draggable operation of the same name in table 10.1.	
filter	(Selector) Specifies a selector that identifies what type of child elements within the elements of the wrapped set become selectable. Each of these elements is marked with the class `ui-selectee`. By default, all children are eligible.	✓
selected	(Function) Specifies a function to be established on the selectables as an event handler for selected events. See table 10.10 for details on this event..	✓
selecting	(Function) Specifies a function to be established on the selectables as an event handler for selecting events. See table 10.10 for details on this event.	✓
start	(Function) Specifies a function to be established on the selectables as an event handler for selectablestart events. This handler is passed the event, but no other information. See table 10.10 for details on this event.	✓
stop	(Function) Specifies a function to be established on the selectables as an event handler for selectablestop events. This handler is passed the event, but no other information. See table 10.10 for details on this event.	✓
tolerance	(String) One of `fit` or `touch` (the default). If `fit`, a drag selection must completely encompass an element for it to be selected. This can be problematic in some layouts because a drag selection must start *within* a selectable. If `touch`, the drag rectangle only needs to intersect any portion of the selectable item.	✓
unselected	(Function) Specifies a function to be established on the selectables as an event handler for unselected events. See table 10.10 for details on this event.	✓
unselecting	(Function) Specifies a function to be established on the selectables as an event handler for unselecting events. See table 10.10 for details on this event.	✓

- *Exercise 4*—Repeat the actions of exercises 1 through 3, except this time observe the Console pane at the bottom of the page. This panel will display the events that take place during the select operations. We'll be discussing what information is passed to these events in the next section.

- *Exercise 5*—In all the exercises so far, we allowed the `filter` option to be specified as `tr`, making the entire data row selectable. Click the Reset button or refresh the page, choose the `td` value for the `filter` option, and click Apply.

  Click within the data table to select various elements. Note that we can now select individual data cells as opposed to entire rows.

- *Exercise 6*—Change the value of the `filter` option to `span`, and click Apply. Now click on the various text values within the data results. Notice that only the text itself is selected rather than the entire cell. (Each text value within the `<td>` elements is enclosed in a `<span>`.)

- *Exercise 7*—Reset the page, choose a `tolerance` value of `touch`, and click Apply. Try various drag selections and note how the behavior hasn't changed; any row that's overlapped by the selection marquee becomes selected.

  Now change the `filter` value to `td` and repeat the exercise, noting how any cell intersected by the marquee becomes selected.

- *Exercise 8*—Leaving the `filter` value set at `td`, choose a `tolerance` value of `fit`, and click Apply. Repeat the drag exercises and note how only cells that are completely enclosed by the marquee become selected.

  Now change the `filter` value to `tr`, click Apply, and try again. Any luck?

  Because a drag selection must begin *within* a selection, the `tolerance` setting requires that a selectable be completely enclosed to become selected, and the rows aren't surrounded by other selectables, this combination makes it almost impossible to select any rows. The lesson? Use a `tolerance` value of `fit` cautiously.

The list of options for `selectable()` is shorter than for the other interactions; in fact, the majority are shortcuts for establishing event handlers for the selectable events. But those events are an important part of the selectables process. Let's examine them.

10.5.2 *Selectable events*

For such a seemingly simple operation, a rich set of events is triggered during a selectable operation. There aren't only events that identify when the operation starts and stops, but when individual elements are selected or unselected, and even when elements are pending a change of selection state.

Unlike the other interaction events, selectable events don't have a fixed construct that's passed to the handlers. Rather, the information, if any at all, is tuned to each event type. Table 10.10 describes the selectable events and what data is passed to them.

If any of these events are unclear, especially the differences between events such as selecting and selected, repeat the exercises in the Selectables Lab, carefully observing the Console Pane to see how the events are triggered as selection operations of various types are carried out.

OK, we have things that are selected. Now what?

Table 10.10   jQuery UI events triggered for selectables

Event	Option	Description
selectablestart	start	Triggered when a selectable operation starts. The event is passed as the first parameter to this handler, and an empty object is passed as the second.
selecting	selecting	Triggered for each selectable element that's about to become selected. The event is passed as the first parameter, and the second parameter is an object with a single property, selecting, that contains a reference to the element that's about to become selected. The class name ui-selecting is added to these elements. If present, the ui-unselecting class is removed. It's not inevitable that an element reported by this event will eventually become selected. If a user drags a marquee that includes an element, that element will be reported by this event. But if the marquee is changed such that the element is no longer included, that element won't become selected.
selected	selected	Triggered for each element that becomes selected. The event is passed as the first parameter, and the second parameter is an object with a single property, selected, that contains a reference to the element that has become selected. The class name ui-selecting is removed and the class ui-selected is added to these elements.
unselecting	unselecting	Triggered for each selected element that's about to become unselected. The event is passed as the first parameter, and the second parameter is an object with a single property, unselecting, that contains a reference to the element that's about to become unselected. The class name ui-unselecting is added to these elements. As with the selecting event, elements reported by this event won't always become unselected.
unselected	unselected	Triggered for each element that becomes unselected. The event is passed as the first parameter, and the second parameter is an object with a single property, unselected, that contains a reference to the element that has become unselected. The class name ui-unselecting is removed from these elements.
selectablestop	stop	Triggered when a selectable operation terminates. The event is passed as the only parameter to this handler.

10.5.3 *Finding the selected and selectable elements*

The selectable event that's bound most often is likely to be selectablestop, which informs us when a selection event has occurred and is concluded. Within handlers for this event, we'll almost invariably want to determine which elements ended up as selected.

Even if we're not interested in the selections when the selection takes place, there almost always comes a time when we need to know what the selections are, such as when it comes time to contact the server.

The traditional state-retaining HTML controls submit their state as part of a form submission without any help on our part. But if we need to communicate the selection state of our selectables as part of a form submission, or even as parameters to an Ajax request, we need to collect the selections.

You may recall that the sortables interaction provided a couple of methods that we could use to determine the final state of the sortables. If we expected the same of selectables, we've been disappointed.

But only momentarily; the selected elements are so easy to obtain using jQuery selectors that a specialized method to fetch them isn't necessary. Because each selected element is marked with the class name `ui-selected`, fetching a wrapped set of all selected elements is as easy as this:

```
$('.ui-selected')
```

If we wanted to only grab selected `<div>` elements, we'd do this:

```
$('div.ui-selected')
```

What we'll probably want to do most often is collect the selected elements so that we can convey the selections to the server, much in the same way that checkboxes or radio buttons are conveyed using request parameters. If we wanted to cause the selections to be submitted to the server as part of a form submission, an easy way to accomplish that is to add hidden `<input>` elements to the form just prior to submission, one for each selected element.

Let's say that in our Selectables Lab, we wanted to submit all selected movie names as a request parameter array named `title[]`. We could accomplish that with the following code placed in the form's submit handler:

```
$('.ui-selected').each(function(){
  $('<input>')
    .attr({
      type: 'hidden',
      name: 'title[]',
      value: $('td:first-child span',this).html()
    })
    .appendTo('#labForm');
});
```

If, instead, we wanted to create a query string to represent the `title[]` request parameter, we could write the following:

```
var queryString = $.param({'title[]':
  $.map($('.ui-selected'),function(element){
    return $('td:first-child span',element).html();
  })
});
```

 As an exercise, write some code that would take the currently selected movie elements and submit them via an Ajax request using $.post(). As another exercise, capture the previous code sample that creates the hidden inputs on the form as a jQuery plugin method.

And that wraps up our examination of the jQuery UI interactions. Let's review what we've learned.

10.6 *Summary*

In this chapter we continued our examination of jQuery UI, focusing on the mouse interaction techniques that it provides.

We began with dragging, which provide a basic interaction used by the remaining interactions: dropping, sorting, resizing, and selecting.

We saw how the dragging interaction lets us free elements from the bounds of their page layout so that we can move them freely about the page. Numerous options are available to customize the dragging behaviors to our needs (as well as to the needs of the remaining interactions).

The dropping interaction gives us something interesting to drop draggables on, in order to provide various user interface semantic actions.

One of those interactions is so common that it's provided as an interaction of its own, sorting, which allows us to drag and drop elements to redefine their position within an ordered list, or even across multiple lists.

Not content with just letting us move things around, the resizing interaction lets us change the size of elements, with plenty of options to customize how and what can be resized.

And finally, we examined selecting, an interaction that lets us apply a persistent selected state to elements that don't intrinsically have selectability.

Together, these interactions give us a lot of power to realize complex, but easy-to-use, user interfaces to present to our users.

But that's not the end of it. These interactions also serve as a basis for even more that jQuery UI has to offer. In the next chapter, we'll continue looking at jQuery UI, this time poking into the user interface widgets that it provides.

jQuery UI widgets: Beyond HTML controls

This chapter covers

- Extending the set of HTML controls with jQuery UI widgets
- Augmenting HTML buttons
- Using slider and datepicker controls for numeric and date input
- Showing progress visually
- Simplifying long lists with autocompleters
- Organizing content with tabs and accordions
- Creating dialog boxes

Since the dawn of the web, developers have been constrained by the limited set of controls afforded by HTML. Although that set of controls runs the gamut from simple text entry through complex file selection, the variety of provided controls pales in comparison to those available to desktop application developers. HTML 5 promises to expand this set of controls, but it may be some time before support appears in all major browsers.

For example, how often have you heard the HTML <select> element referred to as a "combo box," a desktop control to which it bears only a passing resemblance? The real combo box is a very useful control that appears often in desktop applications, yet web developers have been denied its advantages.

But as computers have become more powerful, browsers have increased their capabilities, and DOM manipulation has become a commonplace activity, clever web developers have been taking up the slack. By creating extended controls—either augmenting the existing HTML controls or creating controls from scratch using basic elements—the developer community has shown nothing short of sheer ingenuity in using the tools at hand to make the proverbial lemonade from lemons.

Standing on the shoulders of core jQuery, jQuery UI brings this ingenuity to us, as jQuery users, by providing a set of custom controls to solve common input problems that have traditionally been difficult to solve using the basic control set. Be it making standard elements play well (and look good) in concert with other elements, accepting numeric values within a range, allowing the specification of date values, or giving us new ways to organize our content, jQuery UI offers a valuable set of widgets that we can use on our pages to make data entry a much more pleasurable experience for our users (all while making it easier on us as well).

Following our discussion of the core interactions provided by jQuery UI, we'll continue our exploration by seeing how jQuery UI fills in some gaps that the HTML control set leaves by providing custom controls (widgets) that give us more options for accepting user input. In this chapter, we'll explore the following jQuery UI widgets:

- Buttons (section 11.1)
- Sliders (section 11.2)
- Progress bars (section 11.3)
- Autocompleters (section 11.4)
- Datepickers (section 11.5)
- Tabs (section 11.6)
- Accordions (section 11.7)
- Dialog boxes (section 11.8)

Like the previous chapter, this is a long one! And as with interactions, the jQuery UI methods that create widgets follow a distinct pattern that makes them easy to understand. But unlike interactions, the widgets pretty much stand on their own, so you can choose to skip around the sections in this chapter in any order you like.

We'll start with one of the simpler widgets that lets us modify the style of existing control elements: buttons.

11.1 Buttons and buttonsets

At the same time that we lament the lack of variety in the set of HTML 4 controls, it offers a great number of button controls, many of which overlap in function.

There's the `<button>` element, and no less than six varieties of the `<input>` element that sport button semantics: `button`, `submit`, `reset`, `image`, `checkbox`, and `radio`. Moreover, the `<button>` element has subtypes of `button`, `submit`, and `reset`, whose semantics overlap those of the corresponding input element types.

NOTE   Why are there so many HTML button types? Originally, only the `<input>` button types were available, but as they could only be defined with a simple text string, they were deemed limiting. The `<button>` element was added later; it can contain other elements and thereby offers more rendering possibilities. The simpler `<input>` varieties were never deprecated, so we've ended up with the plethora of overlapping button types.

All these buttons types offer varying semantics, and they're very useful within our pages. But, as we'll see when we explore more of the jQuery UI widget set, their default visual style may not blend well with the styles that the various widgets exhibit.

11.1.1 *Button appearance within UI themes*

Remember back when we downloaded jQuery UI near the beginning of chapter 9? We were given a choice of various themes to download, each of which applies a different look to the jQuery UI elements.

To make our buttons match these styles, we *could* poke around the CSS file for the chosen theme and try to find styles that we could apply to the button elements to bring them more into line with how the other elements look. But as it turns out, we don't have to—jQuery UI provides a means to augment our button controls so their appearance matches the theme without changing the semantics of the elements. Moreover, it will also give them hover styles that will change their appearance slightly when the mouse pointer hovers over them—something the unstyled buttons lack.

The `button()` method will modify individual buttons to augment their appearance, while the `buttonset()` method will act upon a set of buttons (most often a set of radio buttons or checkboxes) not only to theme them, but to make them appear as a cohesive unit.

Consider the display in figure 11.1.

This page fragment shows the unthemed display of some individual button elements, and some groupings of checkboxes, radio buttons, and `<button>` elements. All perfectly functional, but not exactly visually exciting.

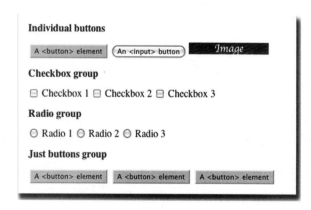

Figure 11.1 Various button elements without any styling—rather boring, wouldn't you say?

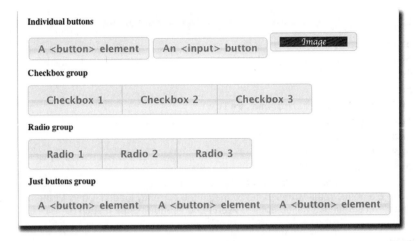

Figure 11.2 After a style makeover, our buttons are dressed in their best and ready to hit the town!

After applying the button() method to the individual buttons, and the buttonset() method to the button groups (in a page using the Cupertino theme), the display changes to that shown in figure 11.2.

After styling, the new buttons make those shown in figure 11.1 look positively Spartan.

Not only has the appearance of the buttons been altered to match the theme, the groups have been styled so that the buttons in the group form a visual unit to match their logical grouping. And even though the radio buttons and checkboxes have been restyled to look like "normal" buttons, they still retain their semantic behaviors. We'll see that in action when we introduce the jQuery UI Buttons Lab.

This theme's styling is one we'll become very familiar with as we progress through the jQuery UI widgets in the remainder of this chapter.

But first we'll take a look at the methods that apply this styling to the button elements.

11.1.2 Creating themed buttons

The methods that jQuery UI provides to create widgets follow the same style we saw in the previous chapter for the interaction methods: calling the button() method and passing an options hash creates the widget in the first place, and calling the same method again but passing a string that identifies a widget-targeted operation modifies the widget.

The syntax for the button() and buttonset() methods is similar to the methods we investigated for the UI interactions:

Command syntax: button and buttonset

```
button(options)
button('disable')
button('enable')
button('destroy')
button('option',optionName,value)
buttonset(options)
buttonset('disable')
buttonset('enable')
buttonset('destroy')
buttonset('option',optionName,value)
```

Themes the elements in the wrapped set to match the currently loaded jQuery UI theme. Button appearance and semantics will be applied even to non-button element such as `<span>` and `<div>`.

Parameters

options	(Object) An object hash of the options to be applied to the elements in the wrapped set, as described in table 11.1, making them themed buttons.
'disable'	(String) Disables click events for the elements in the wrapped set.
'enable'	(String) Re-enables button semantics for the elements in the wrapped set.
'destroy'	(String) Reverts the elements to their original state, before applying the UI theme.
'option'	(String) Allows option values to be set on all elements of the wrapped set, or to be retrieved from the first element of the wrapped set (which should be a jQuery UI button element), based upon the remaining parameters. If specified, at least the `optionName` parameter must also be provided.
optionName	(String) The name of the option (see table 11.1) whose value is to be set or returned. If a `value` parameter is provided, that value becomes the option's value. If no `value` parameter is provided, the named option's value is returned.
value	(Object) The value to be set for the option identified by the `optionName` parameter.

Returns

The wrapped set, except for the case where an option value is returned.

To apply button *theming* to a set of elements, we call the `button()` or `buttonset()` method with a set of options, or with no parameter to accept the default options. Here's an example:

```
$(':button').button({ text: true });
```

NOTE The word "theming" isn't in the dictionary, but it's what jQuery UI uses, so we're running with it.

The options that are available to use when creating buttons are shown in table 11.1.

 The `button()` method comes with plenty of options, and you can try them out in the Buttons Lab page, which you'll find in chapter11/buttons/lab.buttons.html and is shown in figure 11.3.

Follow along in this Lab as you read through the options list in table 11.1.

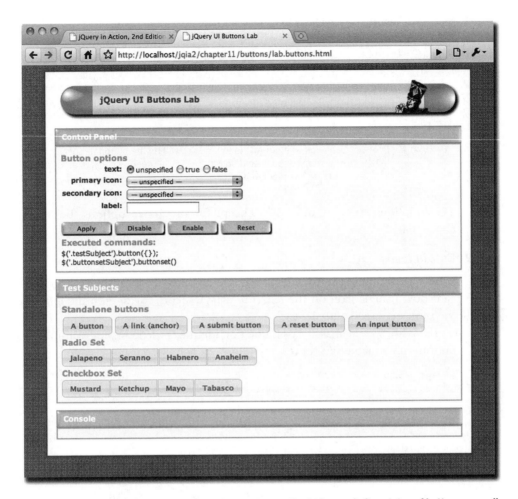

Figure 11.3 The jQuery UI Buttons Lab page lets us see the before and after states of buttons, as well as fiddle with the options.

Table 11.1 Options for the jQuery UI buttons and buttonsets

Option	Description	In Lab?
icons	(Object) Specifies that one or two icons are to be displayed in the button: primary icons to the left, secondary icons to the right. The primary icon is identified by the `primary` property of the object, and the secondary icon is identified by the `secondary` property. The values for these properties must be one of the 174 supported call names that correspond to the jQuery button icon set. We'll discuss these in a moment. If omitted, no icons are displayed.	✓

Table 11.1   Options for the jQuery UI buttons and buttonsets *(continued)*

Option	Description	In Lab?
`label`	(String) Specifies text to display on the button that overrides the natural label. If omitted, the natural label for the element is displayed. In the case of radio buttons and checkboxes, the natural label is the `<label>` element associated with the control.	✓
`text`	(Boolean) Specifies whether text is to be displayed on the button. If specified as `false`, text is suppressed if (and only if) the `icons` option specifies at least one icon. By default, text is displayed.	✓

These options are straightforward except for the `icons` options. Let's chat a little about that.

11.1.3 Button icons

jQuery UI supplies a set of 174 themed icons that can be displayed on buttons. You can show a single icon on the left (the primary icon), or one on the left and one on the right (as a secondary icon).

Icons are specified as a class name that identifies the icon. For example, to create a button with an icon that represents a little wrench, we'd use this code:

```
$('#wrenchButton').button({
  icons: { primary: 'ui-icon-wrench' }
});
```

If we wanted a star on the left, and a heart on the right, we'd do this:

```
$('#weirdButton').button({
  icons: { primary: 'ui-icon-star', secondary: 'ui-icon-heart' }
});
```

Because we all know how many words a picture is worth, rather than just listing the available icon names here, we've provided a page that creates a button for each of the icons, labeled with the name of the icon. You'll find this page at chapter11/buttons/ui-button-icons.html, and it's shown in figure 11.4.

You might want to keep this page handy for whenever you want to find an icon to use on your buttons.

11.1.4 Button events

Unlike the interactions and the remainder of the widgets, there are no custom events associated with jQuery UI buttons.

Because these widgets are merely themed versions of existing HTML 4 controls, the native events can be used as if the buttons had not been augmented. To handle button clicks, we simply continue to handle click events for the buttons.

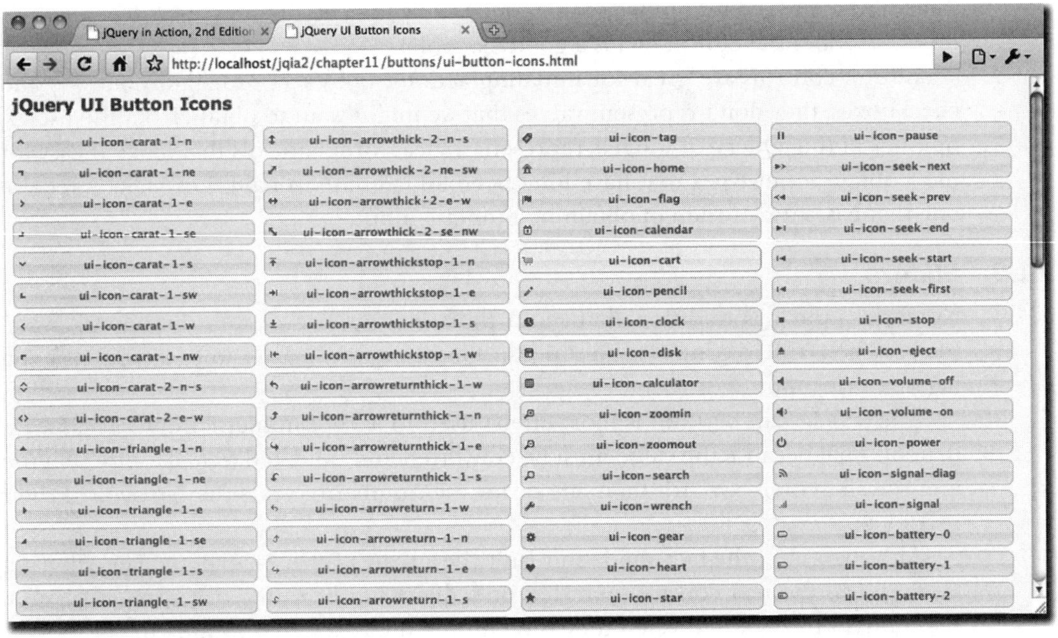

Figure 11.4 The jQuery UI Button Icons page lets us see all the available button icons along with their names.

11.1.5 *Styling buttons*

The whole purpose of using the jQuery UI `button()` and `buttonset()` methods is to make the buttons match the chosen jQuery UI theme. It's as if we took the buttons and sent them to appear on *What Not to Wear* (a popular US and UK TV makeover reality show); they start out drab and homely and emerge looking fabulous! But even so, we may want to fine-tune those styled elements to make them work better on our pages. For example, the text of the buttons on the Buttons Icon page was made smaller to fit the buttons on the page.

jQuery UI augments or creates new elements when creating widgets, and it applies class names to the elements that match the style rules in the theme's CSS style sheet. We can use these class names ourselves to augment or override the theme definitions on our pages.

For example, in the Button Icons page, the button text's font size was adjusted like this:

```
.ui-button-text { font-size: 0.8em; }
```

The class name `ui-button-text` is applied to the `<span>` element that contains the button text.

It would be nearly impossible to cover all the permutations of elements, options, and class names for the widgets created by jQuery UI, so we're not even going to try. Rather, the approach that we'll take is to provide, for each widget type, some tips on some of the most common styling that we're likely to need on our pages. The previous tip on restyling the button text is a good example.

Button controls are great for initiating actions, but except for radio buttons and checkboxes, they don't represent values that we might want to obtain from the user. A number of the jQuery UI widgets represent logical form controls that make it easy for us to obtain input types that have long been an exercise in pain. Let's take a look at one that eases the burden of obtaining numeric input.

11.2   Sliders

Numeric input has traditionally been a thorn in the side of web developers everywhere. The HTML 4 control set just doesn't have a control that's well suited to accepting numeric input.

A text field can be (and is most often) used to accept numeric input. This is less than optimal because the value must be converted and validated to make sure that the user doesn't enter "xyz" for their age or for the number of years they've been at their residence.

Although after-the-fact validation isn't the greatest of user experiences, filtering the input to the text control such that only digits can be entered has its own issues. Users might be confused when they keep hitting the *A* key and nothing happens.

In desktop applications, a control called a *slider* is often used whenever a numeric value within a certain range is to be obtained. The advantage of a slider over text input is that it becomes impossible for the user to enter a bad value. Any value that they can pick with the slider is valid.

jQuery UI brings us a slider control so that we can share that advantage.

11.2.1   Creating slider widgets

A slider generally takes the form of a "trough" that contains a handle. The handle can be moved along the trough to indicate the value selected within the range, or the user can click within the trough to indicate where the handle should move to within the range.

Sliders can be arranged either horizontally or vertically. Figure 11.5 shows an example of a horizontal slider from a desktop application.

Unlike the `button()` method, sliders aren't created by augmenting an existing HTML control. Rather, they're composited from basic elements like `<div>` and `<a>`. The target `<div>` element is styled to form the trough of the slider, and anchor elements are created within it to form the handles.

The slider widget can possess any number of handles and can therefore represent any number of values. Values are specified using an array, with one entry for each handle. However, as the single-handle case is so much more common than the multi-handle case, there are methods and options that *treat* the slider as if it had a single value.

Figure 11.5   Sliders can be used to represent a range of values; in this example, from minimum to full brightness.

This prevents us from having to deal with arrays of a single element for the way that we'll use sliders most often. Thanks jQuery UI team! We appreciate it!

This is the method syntax for the `slider()` method:

Command syntax: slider

```
slider(options)
slider('disable')
slider('enable')
slider('destroy')
slider('option',optionName,value)
slider('value',value)
slider('values',index,values)
```

Transforms the target elements (`<div>` elements recommended) into a slider control.

Parameters

options	(Object) An object hash of the options to be applied to the elements in the wrapped set, as described in table 11.2 making them sliders.
'disable'	(String) Disables slider controls.
'enable'	(String) Re-enables disabled slider controls.
'destroy'	(String) Reverts any elements transformed into slider controls to their previous state.
'option'	(String) Allows option values to be set on all elements of the wrapped set, or to be retrieved from the first element of the wrapped set (which should be a slider element), based upon the remaining parameters. If specified, at least the optionName parameter must also be provided.
optionName	(String) The name of the option (see table 11.2) whose value is to be set or returned. If a value parameter is provided, that value becomes the option's value. If no value parameter is provided, the named option's value is returned.
value	(Object) The value to be set for the option identified by the optionName parameter (when used with 'option'), the value to be set for the slider (if used with 'value'), or the value to be set for the handles (if used with 'values').
'value'	(String) If value is provided, sets that value for the single-handle slider and returns that value ; otherwise the slider's current value is returned.
'values'	(String) For sliders with multiple handles, gets or sets the value for specific handles, where the index parameter must be specified to identify the handles. If the values parameter is provided, sets the value for the handles. The values of the specified handles are returned.
index	(Number|Array) The index, or array of indexes, of the handles to which new values are to be assigned.

Returns

The wrapped set, except for the case where an option or handle value is returned.

When creating a slider, there are a good variety of options for creating slider controls with various behaviors and appearance.

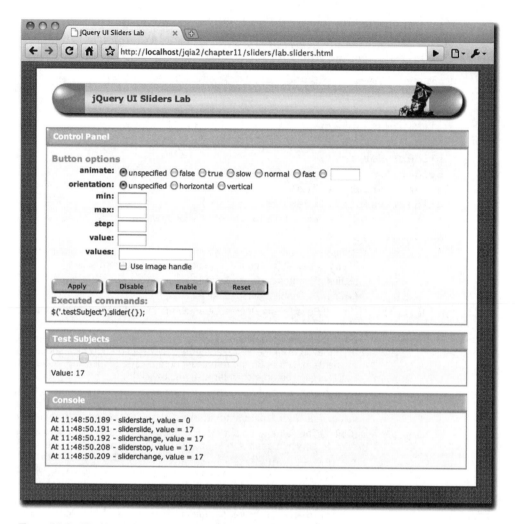

Figure 11.6   The jQuery UI Sliders Lab shows the various ways that jQuery UI sliders can be set up and manipulated.

 While you're reading through the options in table 11.2, bring up the Sliders Lab in file chapter11/sliders/lab.sliders.html (shown in figure 11.6), and follow along, trying out the various options.

Now let's explore the events that slider controls can trigger.

Table 11.2 Options for the jQuery UI sliders

Option	Description	In Lab?
animate	(Boolean|String|Number) If `true`, causes the handle to move smoothly to a position clicked to within the trough. Can also be a duration value or one of the strings `slow`, `normal`, or `fast`. By default, the handle is moved instantaneously.	✓
change	(Function) Specifies a function to be established on the slider as an event handler for slidechange events. See the description of the slider events in table 11.3 for details on the information passed to this handler.	✓
max	(Number) Specifies the upper value of the range that the slider can attain—the value represented when the handle is moved to the far right (for horizontal sliders) or top (for vertical sliders). By default, the maximum value of the range is 100.	✓
min	(Number) Specifies the lower value of the range that the slider can attain—the value represented when the handle is moved to the far left (for horizontal sliders) or bottom (for vertical sliders). By default, the minimum value of the range is 0.	✓
orientation	(String) One of `horizontal` or `vertical`. Defaults to `horizontal`.	✓
range	(Boolean|String) If specified as `true`, and the slider has exactly two handles, an element that can be styled is created between the handles. If the slider has a single handle, specifying `min` or `max` creates a range element from the handle to the beginning or end of the slider respectively. By default, no range element is created.	✓
start	(Function) Specifies a function to be established on the sliders as an event handler for slidestart events. See the description of the slider events in table 11.3 for details on the information passed to this handler.	✓
slide	(Function) Specifies a function to be established on the slider as an event handler for slide events. See the description of the slider events in table 11.3 for details on the information passed to this handler.	✓
step	(Number) Specifies discrete intervals between the minimum and maximum values that the slider is allowed to represent. For example, a step value of 2 would allow only even numbers to be selected. The step value should evenly divide the range. By default, `step` is 1 so that all values can be selected.	✓
stop	(Function) Specifies a function to be established on the slider as an event handler for slidestop events. See the description of the slider events in table 11.3 for details on the information passed to this handler.	✓
value	(Number) Specifies the initial value of a single-handle slider. If there are multiple handles (see the `values` options), specifies the value for the first handle. If omitted, the initial value is the `minimum` value of the slider.	✓

Table 11.2 Options for the jQuery UI sliders *(continued)*

Option	Description	In Lab?
values	(Array) Causes multiple handles to be created and specifies the initial values for those handles. This option should be an array of possible values, one for each handle. For example, [10,20,30] will cause the slider to have three handles with initial values of 10, 20, and 30. If omitted, only a single handle is created.	✓

11.2.2 Slider events

As with the interactions, most of the jQuery UI widgets trigger custom events when interesting things happen to them. We can establish handlers for these events in one of two ways. We can bind handlers in the customary fashion at any point in the ancestor hierarchy, or we can specify the handler as an option, which is what we saw in the previous section.

For example, we might want to handle sliders' slide events in a global fashion on the body element:

```
$('body').bind('slide',function(event,info){ ... });
```

This allows us to handle slide events for all sliders on the page using a single handler. If the handler is specific to an instance of a slider, we might use the slide option instead when we create the slider:

```
$('#slider').slider({ slide: function(event,info){ ... } });
```

This flexibility allows us to establish handlers in the way that best suits our pages.

As with the interaction events, each event handler is passed two parameters: the event instance, and a custom object containing information about the control. Isn't consistency wonderful?

The custom object contains the following properties:

- handle—A reference to the <a> element for the handle that's been moved.
- value—The current value represented by the handle being moved. For single-handle sliders, this is considered the value of the slider.
- values—An array of the current values of all sliders; this is only present for multi-handled sliders.

In the Sliders Lab, the value and values properties are used to keep the value display below the slider up to date.

The events that sliders can trigger are summarized in table 11.3.

The slidechange event is likely to be the one of most interest because it can be used to keep track of the slider's value or values.

Let's say that we have a single-handled slider whose value needs to be submitted to the server upon form submission. Let's also suppose that a hidden input with a name

Table 11.3 Events for the jQuery UI sliders

Event	Option	Description
slide	slide	Triggered for mousemove events whenever the handle is being dragged through the trough. Returning `false` cancels the slide.
slidechange	change	Triggered whenever a handle's value changes, either through user action or programmatically.
slidestart	start	Triggered when a slide starts.
slidestop	stop	Triggered when a slide stops.

of `sliderValue` is to be kept up to date with the slide value so that when the enclosing form is submitted, the slider's value acts like just another form control. We could establish an event on the form as follows:

```
$('form').bind('slidechange',function(event,info){
  $('[name="sliderValue"]').val(info.value);
});
```

Here's a quick exercise for you to tackle:

- *Exercise 1*—The preceding code is fine as long as there is only one slider in the form. Change the preceding code so that it can work for multiple sliders. How would you identify which hidden input element corresponds to the individual slider controls?

Now let's add some style to our sliders.

11.2.3 Styling tips for sliders

When an element is transformed into a slider, the class `ui-slider` is added to it. Within this element, `<a>` elements will be created to represent the handles, each of which will be given the `ui-slider-handle` class. We can use these class names to augment the styles of these elements as we choose.

> **TIP** Can you guess why anchor elements are used to represent the handles? Time's up—it's so that the handles are focusable elements. In the Sliders Lab, create a slider and set focus to a handle by clicking upon it. Now use the left and right arrow keys and see what happens.

Another class that will be added to the slider element is either `ui-slider-horizontal` or `ui-slider-vertical`, depending upon the orientation of the slider. This is a useful hook we can use to adjust the style of the slider based upon orientation. In the Sliders Lab, for example, you'll find the following style rules, which adjust the dimensions of the slider as appropriate to its orientation:

```
.testSubject.ui-slider-horizontal {
  width: 320px;
  height: 8px;
}
```

```
.testSubject.ui-slider-vertical {
   height: 108px;
   width: 8px;
}
```

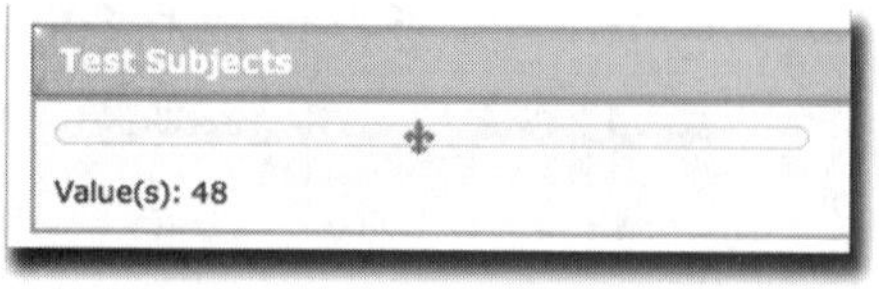

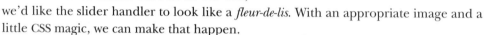

The class name `testSubject` is the class that's used within the Lab to identify the element to be transformed into the slider.

Figure 11.7   With a PNG image and a little CSS magic, we can make the slider handle look like whatever we want.

Here's another neat tip: let's suppose that in order to match the rest of our site, we'd like the slider handler to look like a *fleur-de-lis*. With an appropriate image and a little CSS magic, we can make that happen.

In the Sliders Lab, reset everything, check the checkbox labeled Use Image Handle, and click Apply. The slider looks as shown in figure 11.7.

Here's how it was done. First, a PNG image with a transparent background and containing the *fleur-de-lis* was created, named handle.png. 18 by 18 pixels seems like a good size. Then the following style rule was added to the page:

```
.testSubject a.ui-slider-handle.fancy {
   background: transparent url('handle.png') no-repeat 0 0;
   border-width: 0;
}
```

Finally, after the slider was created, the `fancy` class was added to the handle.

```
$('.testSubject .ui-slider-handle').addClass('fancy');
```

One last tip: if you create a range element via the `range` option, you can style it using the `ui-widget-header` class. We do so in the Lab page with this line:

```
.ui-slider .ui-widget-header { background-color: orange; }
```

Sliders are a great way to let users enter numeric values in a range without a lot of aggravation on our part or the user's. Let's take a look at another widget that can help us keep our users happy.

11.3   *Progress bars*

Little irks a user more than sitting through a long operation without knowing whether anything is really happening behind the scenes. Although users are somewhat more accustomed to waiting for things in web applications than in desktop applications, giving them feedback that their data is actually being processed makes for much happier, less anxious users.

It's also beneficial to our applications. Nothing good can come of a frustrated user clicking away on our interface and yelling, "Where's my data!" at the screen. The flurry of resulting requests will at best help to bog down our servers, and at worst can cause problems for the backend code.

When a fairly accurate and deterministic means of determining the completion percentage of a lengthy operation is available, a progress bar is a great way to give the user feedback that something is happening.

When not to use progress bars

Even worse than making the user guess when an operation will complete is lying to them about it.

Progress bars should only be used when a reasonable level of accuracy is possible. It's never a good idea to have a progress bar that reaches 10 percent and suddenly jumps to the end (leading users to believe that the operation may have aborted in midstream), or even worse, to be pegged at 100 percent long before the operation actually completes.

If you can't determine an accurate completion percentage, a good alternative to a progress bar is just some indication that something might take a long time; perhaps a text display along the lines of "Please wait while your data is processed—this may take a few minutes ...", or perhaps an animation that gives the illusion of activity while the lengthy operation progresses.

For the latter, a handy website at http://www.ajaxload.info/ generates GIF animations that you can tailor to match your theme.

Visually, a progress bar generally takes the form of a rectangle that gradually "fills" from left to right with a visually distinct inner rectangle to indicate the completion percentage of an operation. Figure 11.8 shows an example progress bar depicting an operation that's a bit less than half complete.

Figure 11.8 A progress bar shows the completion percentage of an operation by "filling" the control from left to right.

jQuery UI provides an easy-to-use progress bar widget that we can use to let users know that our application is hard at work performing the requested operation. Let's see just how easy it is to use.

11.3.1 Creating progress bars

Not surprisingly, progress bars are created using the progressbar() method, which follows the same pattern that's become so familiar:

Command syntax: progressbar

```
progressbar(options)
progressbar('disable')
progressbar('enable')
progressbar('destroy')
progressbar('option',optionName,value)
progressbar('value',value)
```
Transforms the wrapped elements (`<div>` elements recommended) into a progress bar widget.

Parameters

options	(Object) An object hash of the options to be applied to the created progress bars, as described in table 11.4.
'disable'	(String) Disables a progress bar.

Command syntax: progressbar *(continued)*	
`'enable'`	(String) Re-enables a disabled progress bar.
`'destroy'`	(String) Reverts the elements made into progress bar widgets to their original state.
`'option'`	(String) Allows option values to be set on all elements of the wrapped set, or to be retrieved from the first element of the wrapped set (which should be a progress bar element), based upon the remaining parameters. If specified, at least the `optionName` parameter must also be provided.
`optionName`	(String) The name of the option (see table 11.4) whose value is to be set or returned. If a `value` parameter is provided, that value becomes the option's value. If no `value` parameter is provided, the named option's value is returned.
`value`	(String|Number) The value to be set for the option identified by the `optionName` parameter (when used with `'option'`), or the value between 0 and 100 to be set for the progress bar (if used with `'value'`).
`'value'`	(String) If `value` is provided, sets that value for the progress bar; otherwise the progress bar's current value is returned.

Returns

The wrapped set, except for the case where a value is returned.

Progress bars are conceptually simple widgets, and this simplicity is reflected in the list of options available for the `progressbar()` method. There are only two, as shown in table 11.4.

Table 11.4   Options for the jQuery UI progress bars

Option	Description
`change`	(Function) Specifies a function to be established on the progress bar as an event handler for progressbarchange events. See the description of the progress bar events in table 11.5 for details on the information passed to this handler.
`value`	(Number) Specifies the initial value of the progress bar; 0, if omitted.

Once a progress bar is created, updating its value is as easy as calling the `value` variant of the method:

```
$('#myProgressbar').progressbar('value',75);
```

Attempting to set a value greater than 100 will result in the value being set to 100. Similarly, attempting to set a value that's a negative number will result in a value of 0.

The options are simple enough, as are the events defined for progress bars.

11.3.2   *Progress bar events*

The single event defined for progress bars is shown in table 11.5.

Catching the `progressbarchange` event could be useful in updating a text value on the page that shows the exact completion percentage of the control, or for any other reason that the page might need to know when the value changes.

Table 11.5 Events for the jQuery UI progress bars

Event	Option	Description
`progressbarchange`	`change`	Called whenever the value of the progress bar changes. Two parameters are passed: the event instance, and an empty object. The latter is passed in order to be consistent with the other jQuery UI events, but no information is contained within the object.

The progress bar is so simple—only two options and one event—that a Lab page for this control has not been provided. Rather, we thought we'd create a plugin that automatically updates a progress bar as a lengthy operation progresses.

11.3.3 An auto-updating progress bar plugin

When we fire off an Ajax request that's likely to take longer to process than a normal person's patience will accept, and we know that we can deterministically obtain the completion percentage, it's a good idea to comfort the user by displaying a progress bar.

Let's think of the steps we'd run through to accomplish this:

1 Fire off the lengthy Ajax operation.
2 Create a progress bar with a default value of 0.
3 At regular intervals, fire off additional requests that take the pulse of the lengthy operation and return the completion status. It's imperative that this operation be quick and accurate.
4 Use the result to update the progress bar and any text display of the completion percentage.

Sounds pretty easy, but there are a few nuances to take into account, such as making sure that the interval timer is destroyed at the right time.

DEFINING THE AUTO-PROGRESSBAR WIDGET

As this widget is something that could be generally useful across many pages, and because there are non-trivial details to take into account, creating a plugin that's going to handle this for us sounds like a great idea.

We call our plugin the auto-progressbar, and its method, `autoProgressbar()`, is defined as follows:

Command syntax: autoProgressbar

`autoProgressbar(options)`
`autoProgressbar('stop')`
`autoProgressbar('destroy')`
`autoProgressbar('value',value)`
Transforms the wrapped elements (`<div>` elements recommended) into a progress bar widget.

Parameters

`options`   (Object) An object hash of the options to be applied to the created progress bars, as described in table 11.6.

Command syntax: autoProgressbar *(continued)*	
'stop'	(String) Stops the auto-progressbar widget from checking the completion status.
'destroy'	(String) Stops the auto-progressbar widget and reverts the elements made into the progress bar widget to their original state.
'value'	(String) If value is provided, sets that value for the progress bar; otherwise the progress bar's current value is returned.
value	(String|Number) A value between 0 and 100 to be set for the progress bar used with the 'value' method.

Returns

The wrapped set, except for the case where a value is returned.

The options that we'll define for our plugin are shown in table 11.6.

Table 11.6   Options for the `autoProgressbar()` plugin method

Option	Description
pulseUrl	(String) Specifies the URL of a server-side resource that will check the pulse of the backend operation that we want to monitor. If this option is omitted, the method performs no operation. The response from this resource must consist of a numeric value in the range of 0 through 100 indicating the completion percentage of the monitored operation.
pulseData	(Object) Any data that should be passed to the resource identified by the `pulseUrl` option. If omitted, no data is sent.
interval	(Number) The duration, in milliseconds, between pulse checks. The default is 1000 (1 second).
change	(Function) A function to be established as the progressbarchange event handler.

Let's get to it.

CREATING THE AUTO-PROGRESSBAR

As usual, we'll start with a skeleton for the method that follows the rules and practices we laid out in chapter 7. (Review chapter 7 if the following doesn't seem familiar.) In a file named jquery.jqia2.autoprogressbar.js we write this outline:

```
(function($){
  $.fn.autoProgressbar = function(settings,value) {

//implementation will go here

    return this;
  };

})(jQuery);
```

The first thing we'll want to do is check to see if the first parameter is a string or not. If it's a string, we'll use the string to determine which method to process. If it's not a string, we'll assume it's an options hash. So we add the following conditional construct:

```
if (typeof settings === "string") {
  // process methods here
```

```
}
else {
 // process options here
}
```

Because processing the options is the meat of our plugin, we'll start by tackling the
`else` part. First, we'll merge the user-supplied options with the set of default options,
as follows:

```
settings = $.extend({
  pulseUrl: null,
  pulseData: null,
  interval: 1000,
  change: null
},settings||{});
if (settings.pulseUrl == null) return this;
```

As in previous plugins that we've developed, we use the `$.extend()` function to merge
the objects. Note also that we continue with the practice of listing *all* options in the
default hash, even if they have a `null` value. This makes for a nice place to see all the
options that the plugin supports.

   After the merge, if the `pulseUrl` option hasn't been specified, we return, performing no operation—if we don't know how to contact the server, there's not much we
can do.

   Now it's time to actually create the progress bar widget:

```
this.progressbar({value:0,change:settings.change});
```

Remember, within a plugin, `this` is a reference to the wrapped set. We call the jQuery
UI progress bar method on this set, specifying an initial value of 0, and passing on any
change handler that the user supplied.

   Now comes the interesting part. For each element in the wrapped set (chances are
there will only be one, but why limit ourselves?) we want to start an interval timer that
will check the status of the lengthy operation using the supplied `pulseUrl`. Here's the
code we use for that:

```
this.each(function(){                          Iterates over
  var bar$ = $(this);                        ❶ wrapped set           ❷ Stores interval
  bar$.data(                                                            handle on widget
    'autoProgressbar-interval',
    window.setInterval(function(){              ❸ Starts interval timer
      $.ajax({                                                         Fires off
        url: settings.pulseUrl,                                     ❹ Ajax request
        data: settings.pulseData,
        global: false,                           ❺ Receives
        dataType: 'json',                            completion
        success: function(value){                    status
          if (value != null) bar$.autoProgressbar('value',value);
          if (value == 100) bar$.autoProgressbar('stop');
        }
      });
    },settings.interval));
});
```

There's a lot going on here, so let's take it one step at a time.

We want each progress bar that will be created to have its own interval timer. Why a user would want to create multiple auto-progressbars may be beyond us, but it's the jQuery way to let them have their rope. We use the each() method ❶ to deal with each wrapped element separately.

For both readability, as well as for use within closures that we'll later create, we capture the wrapped element in the bar$ variable.

We then want to start the interval timer, but we need to keep in mind that later on we're going to want to stop the timer. So we need to store the handle that identifies the timer somewhere that we can easily get at later. jQuery's data() method comes in handy for this ❷, and we use it to store the handle on the bar element with a name of autoProgressbar-interval.

A call to JavaScript's window.setInterval() function starts the timer ❸. To this function we pass an inline function that we want to execute on every tick of the timer, and the interval value that we obtain from the interval option.

Within the timer callback, we fire off an Ajax request ❹ to the URL supplied by the pulseUrl option, with any data supplied via pulseData. We also turn off global events (these requests are happening behind the scenes, and we don't want to confuse the page by triggering global Ajax events that it should know nothing about), and specify that we'll be getting JSON data back as the response.

Finally, in the success callback for the request ❺, we update the progress bar with the completion percentage (which was returned as the response and passed to the callback). If the value has reached 100, indicating that the operation has completed, we stop the timer by calling our own stop method.

After that, implementing the remaining methods will seem easy. In the *if* part of the high-level conditional statement (the one that checked to see if the first parameter was a string or not), we write this:

```
switch (settings) {                                    ❶ Switches on
  case 'stop':                                            string value      ❷ Implements
    this.each(function(){                                                      stop method
      window.clearInterval($(this).data('autoProgressbar-interval'))
    });
    break;
  case 'value':                                                          Implements
    if (value == null) return this.progressbar('value');                 value method
    this.progressbar('value',value);
    break;                                                               Implements
  case 'destroy':                                                        destroy method
    this.autoProgressbar('stop');
    this.progressbar('destroy');                         Does nothing for
    break;                                               unsupported
  default:                                               strings
    break;
}
```

In this code fragment, we switch to different processing algorithms based on the string in the settings parameter ❶, which should contain one of: stop, value, or destroy.

For stop we want to kill off all the interval timers that we created for the elements in the wrapped set ❷. We retrieve the timer handle, which we conveniently stored as data on the element, and pass it to the window.clearInterval() method to stop the timer.

If the method was specified as value, we simply pass the value along to the value method of the progress bar widget.

When destroy is specified, we want to stop the timer, so we just call our own stop method (why copy and paste the same code twice?), and then we destroy the progress bar.

And we're done! Note how whenever we return from any call to our method, we return the wrapped set so that our plugin can participate in jQuery chaining just like any other chainable method.

The full implementation of this plugin can be found in file chapter11/progress-bars/jquery.jqia2.autoprogressbar.js.

Let's now turn our attention to testing our plugin.

TESTING THE AUTO-PROGRESSBAR PLUGIN

The file chapter11/progressbars/autoprogressbar-test.html contains a test page that uses our new plugin to monitor the completion progress of a long-running Ajax operation. In the interest of saving some space, we won't examine every line of code in that file, but we will concentrated on the portions relevant to using our plugin.

First, let's look at the markup that creates the DOM structures of note:

```html
<div>
  <button type="button" id="startButton" class="green90x24">Start</button>
  (starts a lengthy operation)
</div>

<div>
  <div id="progressBar"></div>
  <span id="valueDisplay">&mdash;</span>
</div>

<div>
  <button type="button" id="stopButton" class="green90x24">Stop</button>
  (stops the progress bar pulse checking)
</div>
```

This markup creates four primary elements:

- A Start button that will start a lengthy operation and use our plugin to monitor its progress.
- A <div> to be transformed into the progress bar.
- A <span> to show the completion percentage as text.
- A Stop button that will stop the progress bar from monitoring the lengthy operation.

In action, our test page will look like figure 11.9.

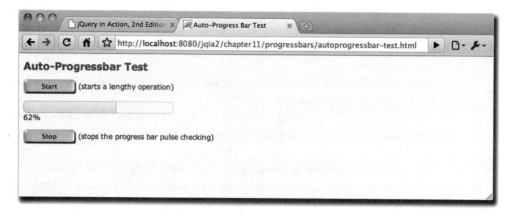

Figure 11.9   The auto-progressbar is monitoring a long-running operation on the server.

NOTE   Because this example uses server-side Ajax operations, it must be run from the Tomcat instance that we set up for the example in chapter 8 (note the 8080 port in the URL). Alternatively, you can run this example remotely by visiting http://www.bibeault.org/jqia2/chapter11/progressbars/autopro-gressbar-test.html.

Instrumenting the Start button is the most important operation on this page, and that's accomplished with the following script:

```
$('#startButton').click(function(){                          ❶ Kicks off the long-
  $.post('/jqia2/lengthyOperation',function(){                   running process
    $('#progressBar')
      .autoProgressbar('stop')                               ❷ Finalizes
      .autoProgressbar('value',100);                            operation
  });
  $('#progressBar').autoProgressbar({                        ❸ Creates the monitoring
    pulseUrl: '/jqia2/checkProgress',                           progress bar
    change: function(event) {
      $('#valueDisplay').text$('#progressBar').autoProgressbar ('value') +
      '%');
    }
  });
});
```

Within the click handler for the Start button, we do two things: kick off the lengthy operation, and create the auto-progressbar.

We post to the URL /jqia2/lengthyOperation, which identifies a process on the server that takes approximately 12 seconds to complete ❶. We'll get to the success callback in a moment, but first let's skip ahead to the creation of the auto-progressbar.

We call our new plugin ❸ with values that identify a server-side resource, /jqia2/checkProgress, which identifies the process that checks the status of our long-running process and returns the completion percentage as its response. How this is done on the server is completely dependent upon how the backend of the web application is written and that's well beyond the scope of this discussion. (For our example, two separate servlets are used, using the servlet session to keep track of progress.) The change handler for the progress bar causes the onscreen display of the completion value to be updated.

Now let's backtrack to the success handler for the long-running operation ❷. When the operation completes, we want to do two things: stop the progress bar, and make sure that the progress bar reflects that the operation is 100 percent done. We easily accomplish this by first calling the `stop` method of our plugin, followed by a call to the `value` method. The change handler for the progress bar will update the text display accordingly.

We've created a really useful plugin using a progress bar. Now let's discuss some styling tips for progress bars.

11.3.4 *Styling progress bars*

When an element is transformed into a progress bar, the class name `ui-progressbar` is added to it, and the `<div>` element created within this element to depict the value is classed with `ui-progressbar-value`. We can use these class names for CSS rules that augment the style of these elements as we see fit.

For example, you might want to fill the background of the inner element with an interesting pattern, rather than the theme's solid color:

```
.ui-progressbar-value {
  background-image: url(interesting-pattern.png);
}
```

Or you could make the progress bar even more dynamic by supplying an animated GIF image as the background image.

Progress bars calm the psyches of our users by letting them know how their operations are progressing. Next, let's delight our users by limiting how much they need to type to find what they're looking for.

11.4 *Autocompleters*

The contemporary acronym *TMI*, standing for "too much information," is usually used in conversation to mean that a speaker has revealed details that are a tad too intimate for the listening audience. In the world of web applications, "too much information" refers not to the nature of the information, but the *amount*.

Although having the vast amount of information that's available on the web at our fingertips is a great thing, it really is possible to have too much information—it's easy to get overwhelmed when fed a deluge of data. Another colloquial expression that describes this phenomenon is "drinking from a fire hose."

When designing user interfaces, particularly those for web applications, which have the ability to access huge amounts of data, it's important to avoid flooding a user with too much data or too many choices. When presenting large data sets, such as report data, good user interfaces give the user tools to gather data in ways that are useful and helpful. For example, filters can be employed to weed out data that isn't relevant to the user, and large sets of data can be paged so that they're presented in digestible chunks. This is exactly the approach taken by our DVD Ambassador example.

As an example, let's consider a data set that we'll be using in this section: a list of DVD titles, which is a data set consisting of 937 titles. It's a large set of data, but still a small slice of larger sets of data (such as the list of all DVDs ever made, for example).

Suppose we wished to present this list to users so that they could pick their favorite flick. We could set up an HTML `<select>` element that they could use to choose a title, but that would hardly be the friendliest thing to do. Most usability guidelines recommend presenting no more than a dozen or so choices to a user at a time, let alone many hundreds! And usability concerns aside, how practical is it to send such a large data set to the page each time it's accessed by potentially hundreds, thousands, or even millions of users on the web?

jQuery UI helps us solve this problem with an *autocomplete* widget—a control that acts a lot like a `<select>` dropdown, but filters the choices to present only those that match what the user is typing into a control.

11.4.1 *Creating autocomplete widgets*

The jQuery autocomplete widget augments an existing `<input>` text element to fetch and present a menu of possible choices that match whatever the user types into the input field. What constitutes a match depends on the options we supply to the widget upon creation. Indeed, the autocomplete widget gives us a great deal of flexibility in how to provide the list of possible choices, and how to filter them given the data supplied by the user.

The syntax for the `autocomplete()` method is as follows:

Command syntax: autocomplete

```
autocomplete(options)
autocomplete('disable')
autocomplete('enable')
autocomplete('destroy')
autocomplete('option',optionName,value)
autocomplete('search',value)
autocomplete('close')
autocomplete('widget')
```

Transforms the `<input>` elements in the wrapped set into an autocomplete control.

Parameters

options	(Object) An object hash of the options to be applied to the elements in the wrapped set, as described in table 11.7, making them autocompleters.
'disable'	(String) Disables autocomplete controls.
'enable'	(String) Re-enables disabled autocomplete controls.
'destroy'	(String) Reverts any elements transformed into autocomplete controls to their previous state.
'option'	(String) Allows option values to be set on all elements of the wrapped set, or to be retrieved from the first element of the wrapped set (which should be an autocomplete element), based upon the remaining parameters. If specified, at least the optionName parameter must also be provided.

Command syntax: autocomplete *(continued)*	
`optionName`	(String) The name of the option (see table 11.7) whose value is to be set or returned. If a `value` parameter is provided, that value becomes the option's value. If no `value` parameter is provided, the named option's value is returned.
`value`	(Object) The value to be set for the option identified by the `optionName` parameter (when used with `'option'`), or the search term (if used with `'search'`).
`'search'`	(String) Triggers a search event using the specified `value`, if present, or the content of the control. Supply an empty string to see a menu of all possibilities.
`'close'`	(String) Closes the autocomplete menu, if open.
`'widget'`	(String) Returns the autocomplete element (the one annotated with the `ui-autocomplete` class name).

Returns

The wrapped set, except for the case where an option, element, search result, or handle value is returned.

For such a seemingly complex control, the list of options available for autocomplete controls is rather sparse, as described in table 11.7.

Table 11.7   Options for the jQuery UI autocompleters

Option	Description	In Lab?
`change`	(Function) Specifies a function to be established on the autocompleters as an event handler for autocompletechange events. See the description of the autocomplete events in table 11.8 for details on the information passed to this handler.	✓
`close`	(Function) Specifies a function to be established on the autocompleters as an event handler for autocompleteclose events. See the description of the autocomplete events in table 11.8 for details on the information passed to this handler.	✓
`delay`	(Number) The number of milliseconds to wait before trying to obtain the matching values (as specified by the `source` option). This can help reduce thrashing when non-local data is being obtained by giving the user time to enter more characters before the search is initiated. If omitted, the default is 300 (0.3 seconds).	✓
`disabled`	(Boolean) If specified and `true`, the widget is initially disabled.	
`focus`	(Function) Specifies a function to be established on the autocompleters as an event handler for autocompletefocus events. See the description of the autocomplete events in table 11.8 for details on the information passed to this handler.	✓
`minLength`	(Number) The number of characters that must be entered before trying to obtain the matching values (as specified by the `source` option). This can prevent too large a value set from being presented when a few characters isn't enough to whittle the set down to a reasonable level. The default value is 1 character.	✓
`open`	(Function) Specifies a function to be established on the autocompleters as an event handler for autocompleteopen events. See the description of the autocomplete events in table 11.8 or details on the information passed to this handler.	✓

Table 11.7   Options for the jQuery UI autocompleters *(continued)*

Option	Description	In Lab?
search	(Function) Specifies a function to be established on the autocompleters as an event handler for autocompletesearch events. See the description of the autocomplete events in table 11.8 for details on the information passed to this handler.	✓
select	(Function) Specifies a function to be established on the autocompleters as an event handler for autocompleteselect events. See the description of the autocomplete events in table 11.8 for details on the information passed to this handler.	✓
source	(String|Array|Function) Specifies the manner in which the data that matches the input data is obtained. A value must be provided or the autocomplete widget won't be created. This value can be a string representing the URL of a server resource that will return matching data, an array of local data from which the value will be matched, or a function that serves as a general callback from providing the matching values. See section 11.4.2 for more information on this option.	✓

As you might have guessed, an Autocompleters Lab (shown in figure 11.10) has been provided. Load it from chapter11/autocompleters/lab.autocompleters.html and follow along as you review the options.

> **NOTE**   In this Lab, the URL variant of the source option requires the use of server-side Ajax operations. It must be run from the Tomcat instance we set up for the example in chapter 8 (note the 8080 port in the URL). Alternatively, you can run this example remotely by visiting http://www.bibeault.org/jqia2/chapter11/autocompleters/lab.autocompleters.html.

Except for source, these options are all fairly self-explanatory. Leaving the source option at its default setting, use the Autocompleters Lab to observe the events that transpire and the behavior of the minLength and delay options until you feel that you have grasped them.

Now let's see what it takes to provide source data for this widget.

11.4.2 *Autocomplete sources*

The autocomplete widget gives us a lot of flexibility for providing the data values that match whatever the user types in.

Source data for the autocompleters takes the form of an array of candidate items, each of which has two properties:

- A value property that represents the actual values. These are the strings that are matched against as the user types into the control, and they're the values that will be injected into the control when a menu item is selected.
- A label property that represents the value, usually as a shorter form. These strings are what is displayed in the autocomplete menu, and they don't participate in the default matching algorithms.

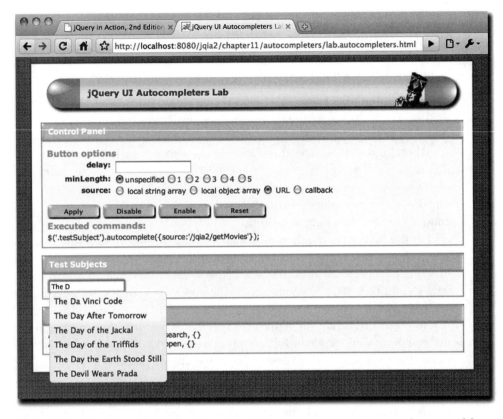

Figure 11.10   The jQuery UI Autocompleters Lab shows us how a large result set can be narrowed down as more data is entered.

This data can come from a variety of sources.

For cases where the data set is fairly small (dozens, not hundreds or more), the data can be provided as a local array. The following example is taken from the Auto-completers Lab and provides candidate data that uses usernames as labels and full names as the values:

```
var sourceObjects = [
  { label: 'bear', value: 'Bear Bibeault'},
  { label: 'yehuda', value: 'Yehuda Katz'},
  { label: 'genius', value: 'Albert Einstein'},
  { label: 'honcho', value: 'Pointy-haired Boss'},
  { label: 'comedian', value: 'Charlie Chaplin'}
];
```

When displayed, the labels (usernames) are what appear in the autocomplete menu, but matching is performed on the *values* (full names), and the value is what is set into the control upon selection.

This is handy when we want to represent longer data with shorter values in the menus, but for many cases, perhaps even most, the label and the value will be the same. For these common cases, jQuery UI lets us specify the data as an array of strings, and takes the string value to be both the label and the value.

> **TIP** When providing objects, if only one of `label` or `value` is specified, the provided data is automatically used for both `label` and `value`.

The entries don't have to be in any particular order (such as sorted) for the widget to work correctly, and matching entries will be displayed in the menu in the order that they appear within the array.

When local data is used, the matching algorithm is such that any candidate value that contains what the user has typed, called the *term*, is deemed to match. If this isn't what you want—let's say you only want to match values that *begin* with the term—fear not! There are two more-general ways to supply the source data that give us complete control over the matching algorithm.

For the first of these schemes, the source can be specified as the URL of a server-side resource that returns a response containing the data values that match the term, which is passed to the resource as a request parameter named `term`. The returned data should be a JSON response that evaluates to one of the formats supported for local data, usually an array of strings.

Note that this variant of `source` is expected to perform the search and return *only* the matching elements—no further processing of the data will take place. Whatever values are returned are displayed in the autocomplete menu.

When we need maximum flexibility, another scheme can be used: a callback function can be supplied as the `source` option, and it's called whenever data is needed by the widget. This callback is invoked with two parameters:

- An object with a single property, `term`, that contains the term to be matched.
- A callback function to be called, which is passed the matching results to be displayed. This set of results can be either of the formats accepted as local data, usually an array of strings.

This callback mechanism offers the most flexibility, because we can use whatever mechanisms and algorithms we want to turn the term into a set of matching elements. A skeleton for how to use this variant of `source` is as follows:

```
$('#control').autocomplete({
  source: function(request,response) {
    var term = request.term;
    var results;

    // algorithm here to fill results array

    response(results);
  }
});
```

As with the URL variant of `source`, the result should contain only those values that are to be displayed in the autocomplete menu.

Play around with the source options in the Autocompleters Lab. A few things to note about the different source options in the Lab:

- The local string option provides a list of 79 values, all of which begin with the letter F.
- The local object option provides a short list of usernames for labels, and full names as values. Note how the matching occurs on the *values*, not the labels. (Hint: enter the letter *b*.)
- For the URL variant, the backend resource only matches values that *begin* with the term. It uses a different algorithm than when local values are supplied (in which the term can appear anywhere within the string). This difference is intentional and is intended to emphasize that the backend resource is free to employ whatever matching criteria it likes.
- The callback variant simply returns the entire value set of 79 F-titles provided by the local option. Make a copy of the Lab page, and modify the callback to play around with whatever algorithm you'd like to filter the returned values.

Various events are triggered while an autocomplete widget is doing its thing. Let's see what those are.

11.4.3 *Autocomplete events*

During an autocomplete operation, a number of custom events are triggered, not only to inform us of what's going on, but to give us a chance to cancel certain aspects of the operation.

As with other jQuery UI custom events, two parameters are passed to the event handlers: the event and a custom object. This custom object is empty except for auto-completefocus, autocompletechange, and autocompleteselect events. For the focus, change, and select events, this object contains a single property named item, which in turn contains the properties label and value, representing the label and value of the focused or selected value. For all the event handlers, the function context (this) is set to the <input> element.

Table 11.8 Events for the jQuery UI autocompleters

Event	Option	Description
autocompletechange	change	Triggered when the value of the <input> element is changed based upon a selection. When triggered, this event will always come after the autocompleteclose event is triggered.
autocompleteclose	close	Triggered whenever the autocomplete menu closes.
autocompletefocus	focus	Triggered whenever one of the menu choices receives focus. Unless canceled (for example, by returning false), the focused value is set into the <input> element.

Table 11.8   Events for the jQuery UI autocompleters *(continued)*

Event	Option	Description
`autocompleteopen`	`open`	Triggered after the data has been readied and the menu is about to open.
`autocompletesearch`	`search`	Triggered after any `delay` and `minLength` criteria have been met, just before the mechanism specified by `source` is activated. If canceled, the search operation is aborted.
`autocompleteselect`	`select`	Triggered when a value is selected from the autocomplete menu. Canceling this event prevents the value from being set into the `<input>` element (but doesn't prevent the menu from closing).

The Autocompleters Lab uses all of these events to update the console display as the events are triggered.

Now let's take a look at dressing up our autocompleters.

11.4.4 *Autocompleting in style*

As with the other widgets, autocompleters inherit style elements from the jQuery UI CSS theme via the assignment of class names to the elements that compose the autocompleter.

When an `<input>` element is transformed into an autocompleter, the class `ui-autocomplete-input` is added to it.

When the autocomplete menu is created, it's created as an unordered list element (`<ul>`) with class names `ui-autocomplete` and `ui-menu`. The values within the menu are created as `<li>` elements with class name `ui-menu-item`. And within those list items, anchor elements are created that get the `ui-state-hover` class when hovered over.

We can use these classes to hook our own styles onto the autocomplete elements.

For example, let's say that we want to give the autocomplete menu a slight level of transparency. We could do that with this style rule:

```
.ui-autocomplete.ui-menu { opacity: 0.9; }
```

Be careful with that. Make it *too* transparent and it becomes unreadable.

The autocomplete menu can end up pretty big if there are lots of matches. If we'd like to fit more entries in less space, we can shrink the font size of the entries with a rule like this:

```
.ui-autocomplete.ui-menu .ui-menu-item { font-size: 0.75em; }
```

Note that `ui-menu-item` isn't a class name specific to the autocompleter (if it were, it would have the text `autocomplete` within it), so we qualify it with `ui-autocomplete` and `ui-menu` to make sure we don't inadvertently apply the style to other elements on the page.

What if we really wanted to make hovered items stand out? We could change their border to red:

```
.ui-autocomplete.ui-menu a.ui-state-hover { border-color: red; }
```

Autocompleters let us let our users hone down large datasets quickly, preventing information overload. Now let's see how we can simplify yet another long-standing pain point in data entry: dates.

11.5 Date pickers

Entering date information has been another traditional source of anxiety for web developers and frustration for end users. A number of approaches have been tried using the basic HTML 4 controls, all of which have their drawbacks.

Many sites will present the user with a simple text input into which the date must be entered. But even if we include instructions such as, "Please enter the date in dd/mm/yyyy format", people still tend to get it wrong. And so, apparently, do some web developers. How many times have you wanted to throw your computer across the room upon discovering, after 15 failed attempts, that you had to include leading zeroes when entering a single digit date or month value?

Another approach uses three dropdowns, one each for month, day, and year. Although this vastly reduces the possibility of user error, it's clumsy and requires a lot of clicks to choose a date. And developers still need to guard against entries such as February 31.

When people think of dates, they think of calendars, so the most natural way to have them enter a date is to let them pick it from a calendar display.

Frequently called *calendar controls* or *date pickers*, scripts to create these controls have been around for some time, but they've generally been cantankerous to configure, and awkward to use on pages, including trying to match styling. Leave it to jQuery and jQuery UI to make it easy with jQuery UI datepickers.

11.5.1 Creating jQuery datepickers

Creating a jQuery datepicker is easy, especially if you take the default values. It may only seem complex because there are lots of options for configuring the datepicker in the manner that best suits our applications.

As with other jQuery UI elements, the `datepicker()` exposes the basic set of UI methods and also offers some specific methods to control the element after creation:

Command syntax: datepicker

```
datepicker(options)
datepicker('disable')
datepicker('enable')
datepicker('destroy')
datepicker('option',optionName,value)
datepicker('dialog',dialogDate,onselect,options,position)
datepicker('isDisabled')
datepicker('hide',speed)
datepicker('show')
datepicker('getDate')
datepicker('setDate',date)
datepicker('widget')
```

Transforms the `<input>`, `<div>`, and `<span>` elements in the wrapped set into a datepicker control. For `<input>` elements, the datepicker is displayed on focus; for other elements, creates an inline datepicker.

Parameters

`options`	(Object) An object hash of the options to be applied to the elements in the wrapped set, as described in table 11.9, making them datepickers.
`'disable'`	(String) Disables datepicker controls.
`'enable'`	(String) Re-enables disabled datepicker controls.
`'destroy'`	(String) Reverts any elements transformed into datepicker controls to their previous state.
`'option'`	(String) Allows option values to be set on all elements of the wrapped set, or to be retrieved from the first element of the wrapped set (which should be a datepicker element), based upon the remaining parameters. If specified, at least the `optionName` parameter must also be provided.
`optionName`	(String) The name of the option (see table 11.9) whose value is to be set or returned. If a `value` parameter is provided, that value becomes the option's value. If no `value` parameter is provided, the named option's value is returned.
`value`	(Object) The value to be set for the option identified by the `optionName` parameter.
`'dialog'`	(String) Displays a jQuery UI dialog box containing a datepicker.
`dialogDate`	(String|Date) Specifies the initial date for the datepicker in the dialog box as a string in the current date format (see the description of the `dateFormat` option in table 11.9) or a `Date` instance.
`onselect`	(Function) If specified, defines a callback to be invoked with the date text and datepicker instance when a date is selected.
`position`	(Array|Event) An array specifying the position of the dialog box as `[left,top]`, or a mouseevent `Event` instance from which the position will be determined. If omitted, the dialog box is centered in the window.
`'isDisabled'`	(String) Returns `true` or `false` reporting whether the datepicker is currently disabled or not.
`'hide'`	(String) Closes the datepicker.

Command syntax: datepicker *(continued)*

speed	(String|Number) One of `slow`, `normal`, or `fast`, or a value in milliseconds that controls the animation closing the datepicker.
`'show'`	(String) Opens the datepicker.
`'getDate'`	(String) Returns the currently selected date for the datepicker. This value can be `null` if no value has yet been selected.
`'setDate'`	(String|Date) Sets the specified date as the current date of the datepicker.
date	(String|Date) Sets the date for the datepicker. This value can be a `Date` instance, or a string that identifies an absolute or relative date. Absolute dates are specified using the date format for the control (specified by the `dateFormat` option, see table 11.9), or a string of values specifying a date relative to today. The values are numbers followed by `m` for month, `d` for day, `w` for week, and `y` for year. For example, tomorrow is `+1d`, and a week and a half could be `+1w +4d`. Both positive and negative values can be used.
`'widget'`	(String) The datapicker widget element; the one annotated with the `ui-datapicker` class name.

Returns

The wrapped set, except for the cases where values are returned, as described above.

Seemingly to make up for the Spartan set of options available for autocompleters, datepickers offer a dizzying array of options that make it the most configurable widget in the jQuery UI set. Don't get too overwhelmed; frequently the defaults are just what we want. But the options are there in case we need to change the way the datepicker works to better fit into our sites.

 But all those options do make for a rather complicated Datepickers Lab page—as shown in figure 11.11. You'll find it in file chapter11/datepickers/lab.datepickers.html.

As you work your way through the generous set of options described in table 11.9, try them out in the Datepickers Lab.

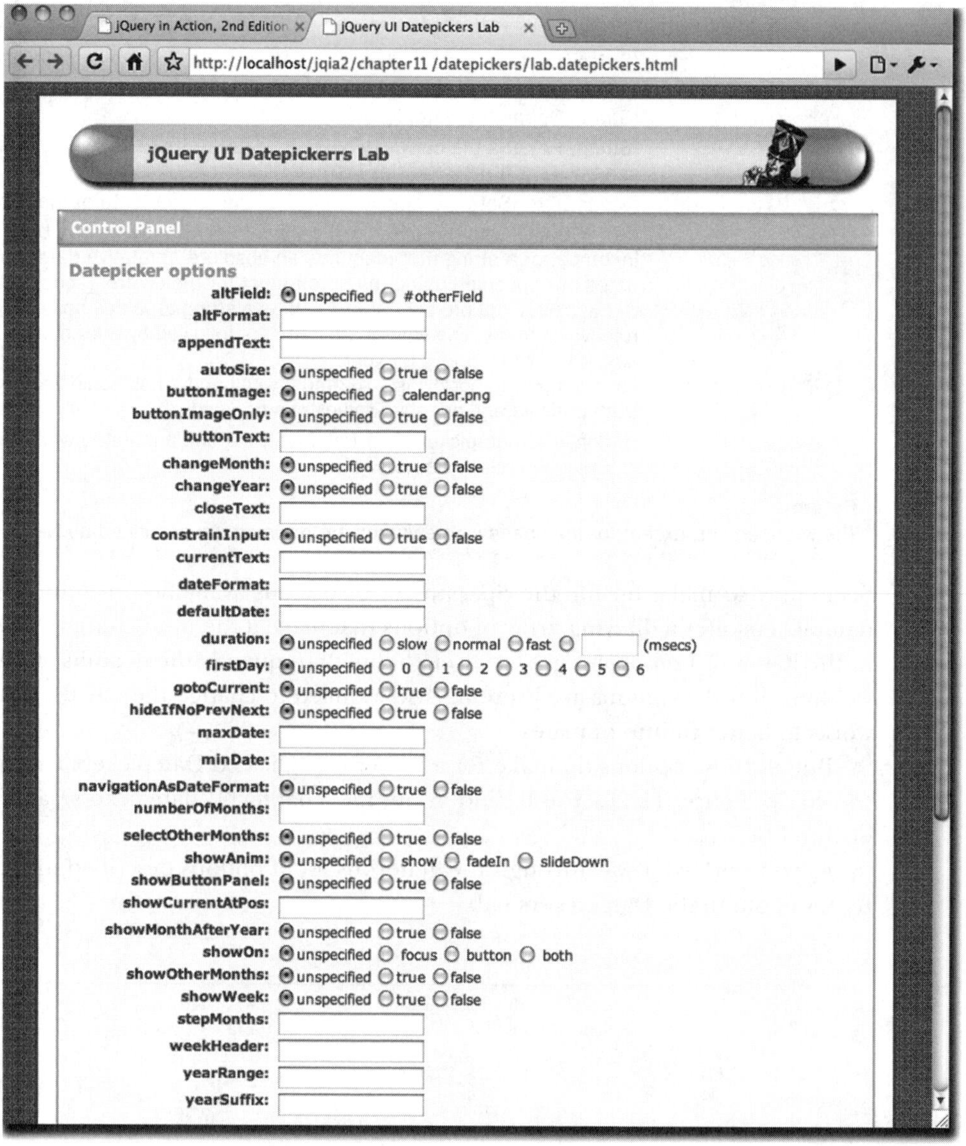

Figure 11.11   The jQuery UI Datepickers Lab helps us grasp the copious variety of options available for datepicker controls (too many to fit into one screenshot).

Table 11.9 Options for the jQuery UI datepickers

Option	Description	In Lab?
altField	(Selector) Specifies a jQuery selector for a field that's to also be updated with any date selections. The altFormat option can be used to set the format for this value. This is quite useful for setting date values into a hidden input element to be submitted to the server, while displaying a more user-friendly format to the user.	✓
altFormat	(String) When an altField is specified, provides the format for the value to be written to the alternate element. The format of this value is the same as for the $.datepicker.formatDate() utility function—see its description in section 11.5.2 for details.	✓
appendText	(String) A value to be placed after the <input> element, intended to show instructions to the user. This value is displayed within a <span> element created with the class name ui-datepicker-append, and can contain HTML markup.	✓
autoSize	(Boolean) If true, the size of the <input> element is adjusted to accommodate the datepicker's date format as set with the dateFormat option. If omitted, no resize takes place.	✓
beforeShow	(Function) A callback that's invoked just before a datepicker is displayed, with the <input> element and datepicker instance passed as parameters. This function can return an options hash used to modify the datepicker.	✓
beforeShowDay	·(Function) A callback that's invoked for each day in the datepicker just before it's displayed, with the date passed as the only parameter. This can be used to override some of the default behavior of the day elements. This function must return a three-element array, as follows: · [0]—true to make the date selectable, false otherwise · [1]—A space-delimited string of CSS class names to be applied, or an empty string to apply none · [2]—An optional string to apply a tooltip to the day element	
buttonImage	(String) Specifies the path to an image to be displayed on the button enabled by setting the showOn option to one of button or both. If buttonText is also provided, the button text becomes the alt attribute of the button.	✓
buttonImageOnly	(Boolean) If true, specifies that the image specified by buttonImage is to appear standalone (not on a button). The showOn option must still be set to one of button or both for the image to appear.	✓
buttonText	(String) Specifies the caption for the button enabled by setting the showOn option to one of button or both. If buttonImage is also specified, this text becomes the alt attribute of the image.	✓
calculateWeek	(Function) A custom function to calculate and return the week number for a date passed as the lone parameter. The default implementation is that provided by the $.datepicker.iso8601Week() utility function.	

Table 11.9   Options for the jQuery UI datepickers *(continued)*

Option	Description	In Lab?
changeMonth	(Boolean) If `true`, a month dropdown is displayed, allowing the user to directly change the month without using the arrow buttons to step through them. If omitted, no dropdown is displayed.	✓
changeYear	(Boolean) If `true`, a year dropdown is displayed, allowing the user to directly change the year without using the arrow buttons to step through them. If omitted, no dropdown is displayed.	✓
closeText	(String) If the button panel is displayed via the `showButtonPanel` option, specifies the text to replace the default caption of Done for the close button.	✓
constrainInput	(Boolean) If `true` (the default), text entry into the `<input>` element is constrained to characters allowed for the date format of the control (see `dateFormat`).	✓
currentText	(String) If the button panel is displayed via the `showButtonPanel` option, specifies the text to replace the default caption of Today for the current button.	✓
dateFormat	(String) Specifies the date format to be used. See section 11.5.2 for details.	✓
dayNames	(Array) A 7-element array providing the full day names with the 0th element representing Sunday. Can be used to localize the control. The default set is the full day names in English.	
dayNamesMin	(Array) A 7-element array providing the minimal day names with the 0th element representing Sunday, used as column headers. Can be used to localize the control. The default set is the first two letters of the English day names.	
dayNamesShort	(Array) A 7-element array providing the short day names with the 0th element representing Sunday. Can be used to localize the control. The default set is the first three letters of the English day names.	
defaultDate	(Date|Number|String) Sets the initial date for the control, overriding the default value of today, if the `<input>` element has no value. This can be a `Date` instance, the number of days from today, or a string specifying an absolute or relative date. See the description of the `date` parameter in the method syntax for the `datapicker()` method for more details.	✓
disabled	(Boolean) If specified and `true`, the widget is initially disabled.	
duration	(String|Number) Specifies the speed of the animation that makes the datepicker appear. Can be one of `slow`, `normal`, (the default) or `fast`, or the number of milliseconds for the animation to span.	✓
firstDay	(Number) Specifies which day is considered the first day of the week, and will be displayed as the left-most column. Sunday (the default) is 0, Saturday is 6.	✓
gotoCurrent	(Boolean) If `true`, the current day link is set to the selected date, overriding the default of today.	✓

Table 11.9 Options for the jQuery UI datepickers *(continued)*

Option	Description	In Lab?
hideIfNoPrevNext	(Boolean) If `true`, hides the next and previous links (as opposed to merely disabling them) when they aren't applicable, as determined by the settings of the `minDate` and `maxDate` options. Defaults to `false`.	✓
isRTL	(Boolean) If `true`, the localizations specify a right-to-left language. Used by localized version of this control. Defaults to `false`.	
maxDate	(Date|Number|String) Sets the maximum selectable date for the control. This can be a `Date` instance, the number of days from today, or a string specifying an absolute or relative date. See the description of the `date` parameter in the datepicker `setDate` method syntax for more details.	✓
minDate	(Date|Number|String) Sets the minimum selectable date for the control. This can be a `Date` instance, the number of days from today, or a string specifying an absolute or relative date. See the description of the `date` parameter in the method syntax for the `datapicker()` method for more details.	✓
monthNames	(Array) A 12-element array providing the full month names with the 0th element representing January. Can be used to localize the control. The default set is the full month names in English.	
monthNamesShort	(Array) A 12-element array providing the short month names with the 0th element representing January. Can be used to localize the control. The default set is the first three letters of the English month names.	✓
navigationAsDateFormat	(Boolean) If `true`, the navigation links for `nextText`, `prevText`, and `currentText` are passed through the `$.datepicker.formatDate()` function prior to display. This allows date formats to be supplied for those options that get replaced with the relevant values. Defaults to `false`.	✓
nextText	(String) Specifies the text to replace the default caption of Next for the next month navigation link. Note that the ThemeRoller replaces this text with an icon.	✓
numberOfMonths	(Number|Array) The number of months to show in the datepicker, or a 2-element array specifying the number of rows and columns for a grid of months. For example, `[3,2]` will display 6 months in a 3-row by 2-column grid. By default, a single month is shown.	✓
onChangeMonthYear	(Function) A callback that's invoked when the datepicker moves to a new month or year, with the selected year, month (1-based), and datepicker instance passed as parameters, and the function context is set to the input field element.	
onClose	(Function) A callback invoked whenever a datepicker is closed, passed the selected date as text (the empty string if there is no selection), and the datepicker instance, and the function context is set to the input field element.	

Table 11.9   Options for the jQuery UI datepickers *(continued)*

Option	Description	In Lab?
onSelect	(Function) A callback invoked whenever a date is selected, passed the selected date as text (the empty string if there is no selection), and the datepicker instance, and the function context is set to the input field element.	
prevText	(String) Specifies the text to replace the default caption of Prev for the previous month navigation link. (Note that the ThemeRoller replaces this text with an icon.)	✓
selectOtherMonths	(Boolean) If true, days shown before or after the displayed month(s) are selectable. Such days aren't displayed unless the showOtherMonths option is true. By default, the days aren't selectable.	✓
shortYearCutoff	(Number|String) If a number, specifies a value between 0 and 99 years before which any 2-digit year values will be considered to belong to the previous century. For example, if specified as 50, the year 39 would be considered to be 2039, and the year 52 would be interpreted as 1952. If a string, the value undergoes a numeric conversion and is added to the current year. The default is +10 which represents 10 years from the current year.	
showAnim	(String) Sets the name of the animation to be used to show and hide the datepicker. If specified, must be one of show (the default), fadeIn, slideDown, or any of the jQuery UI show/hide animations.	✓
showButtonPanel	(Boolean) If true, a button panel at the bottom of the datepicker is displayed, containing current and close buttons. The caption of these buttons can be provided via the currentText and closeText options. Defaults to false.	✓
showCurrentAtPos	(Number) Specifies the 0-based index, starting at the upper left, of where the month containing the current date should be placed within a multi-month display. Defaults to 0.	?✓
showMonthAfterYear	(Boolean) If true, the positions of the month and year are reversed in the header of the datepicker. Defaults to false.	✓
showOn	(String) Specifies what triggers the display of the datepicker as one of focus, button, or both. focus (default) causes the datepicker to display when the <input> element gains focus, whereas button causes a button to be created after the <input> element (but before any appended text) that triggers the datepicker when clicked. The button's appearance can be varied with the buttonText, buttonImage, and buttonImageOnly options. both causes the trigger button to be created, and for focus events to also trigger the datepicker.	✓
showOptions	(Object) When a jQuery UI animation is specified for the showAnim option, provides an option hash to be passed to that animation.	

Table 11.9   Options for the jQuery UI datepickers *(continued)*

Option	Description	In Lab?
showOtherMonths	(Boolean) If true, dates before or after the first and last days of the current month are displayed. These dates aren't selectable unless the selectOtherMonths option is also set to true. Defaults to false.	✓
showWeek	(Boolean) If true, the week number is displayed in a column to the left of the month display. The calculateWeek option can be used to alter the manner in which this value is determined. Defaults to false.	✓
stepMonths	(Number) Specifies how many months to move when one of the month navigation controls is clicked. By default, a single month is stepped.	✓
weekHeader	(String) The text to display for the week number column, overriding the default value of Wk, when showWeek is true.	✓
yearRange	(String) When changeYear is true, specifies limits on which years are displayed in the dropdown in the form from:to. The values can be absolute or relative (for example: 2005:+2, for 2005 through 2 years from now). The prefix c can be used to make relative values offset from the selected year rather than the current year (example: c-2:c+3).	✓
yearSuffix	(String) Text that's displayed after the year in the datepicker header.	✓

Still with us?

Although that may seem rather overwhelming when taken as a whole, the vast majority of options for the datepickers are used only when needed to override default values, which are usually exactly what we want. It's not uncommon to create datepickers while specifying no options at all.

11.5.2   Datepicker date formats

A number of the datepicker options listed in table 11.9 employ a string that represents a *date format*. These are strings that specify a pattern for formatting and parsing dates. Character patterns within the string represent parts of dates (for example, y for year, and MM for full month name) or simply template (literal) text.

Table 11.10 shows the character patterns used within date format patterns and what they represent.

Table 11.10   Date format character patterns

Patterns	Description
d	Date within month without leading zeroes
dd	2-digit date within month with leading zeroes for values less than 10
o	Day of the year without leading zeroes

Table 11.10   Date format character patterns (continued)

Patterns	Description
oo	3-digit day within the year with leading zeroes for values less than 100
D	Short day name
DD	Full day name
m	Month of the year with no leading zeroes, where January is 1
mm	2-digit month within the year with leading zeroes for values less than 10
M	Short month name
MM	Full month name
y	2-digit year with leading zeroes for values less than 10
yy	4-digit year
@	Number of milliseconds since January 1, 1970
!	Number of 100 ns ticks since January 1, year 1
' '	Single quote character
'...'	Literal text (quoted with single quotes)
Anything else	Literal text

The datepicker defines some well-known date format patterns as constant values, as shown in table 11.11.

We'll be addressing these patterns again when we discuss the datepicker utility functions in section 11.5.4.

Now let's turn our attention to the events that datepickers trigger.

Constant	Pattern
$.datepicker.ATOM	yy-mm-dd
$.datepicker.COOKIE	D, dd M yy
$.datepicker.ISO_8601	yy-mm-dd
$.datepicker.RFC_822	D, d M y
$.datepicker.RFC_850	DD, dd-M-y
$.datepicker.RFC_1036	D, d M y
$.datepicker.RFC_1123	D, d M yy
$.datepicker.RFC_2822	D, d M yy
$.datepicker.RSS	D, d M y
$.datepicker.TICKS	!
$.datepicker.TIMESTAMP	@
$.datepicker.W3C	yy-mm-dd

Table 11.11 Date format pattern constants

11.5.3 *Datepicker events*

Surprise! There aren't any!

The datepicker code in jQuery UI 1.8 is some of the oldest in the code base, and it hasn't been updated to adhere to the modern event-triggering conventions that the other widgets follow. Expect this to change in a future version of jQuery UI, to the point that the jQuery UI roadmap (which you can find at http://wiki.jqueryui.com/ Roadmap) states that the widget will be completely rewritten for version 2.0.

For now, the options that allow us to specify callbacks when interesting things happen to a datepicker are `beforeShow`, `beforeShowDay`, `onChangeMonthYear`, `onClose`, and `onSelect`. All the callbacks invoked via these options have the `<input>` elements set as their function contexts.

Although datepickers may lack the event triggering that other widgets sport, they do give us some extras: a handful of useful utility functions. Let's see what those can do for us.

11.5.4 *Datepicker utility functions*

Dates can be cantankerous data types. Just think of the nuances of dealing with years and leap years, months of differing lengths, weeks that don't divide into months evenly, and all the other oddities that plague date information. Luckily for us, the JavaScript `Date` implementation handles most of those details for us. But there are a few areas where it falls short—the formatting and parsing of date values being two of them.

The jQuery UI datepicker steps up to the plate and fills in those gaps. In the guise of utility functions, jQuery UI provides the means to not only format and parse date values, but also to make the large number of datepicker options a bit easier to handle for pages with more than one datepicker.

Let's start there.

SETTING DATEPICKER DEFAULTS

When our datepickers need to use multiple options to get the look and behavior we want, it seems just plain wrong to cut and paste the same set of options for every datepicker on the page. We could store the `options` object in a global variable and reference it from every datepicker creation, but jQuery UI lets us go one better by providing a means to simply register a set of default options that supersedes the defined defaults. This utility function's syntax is as follows:

Command syntax: $.datepicker.setDefaults

`$.datepicker.setDefaults(options)`
Sets the options passed as the defaults for all subsequently created datepickers.

Parameters
  `options`   (Object) An object hash of the options to be used as the defaults for all
                 datepickers.

Returns
Nothing.

As you'll recall from the list of datepicker options, some of the options specify formats for how date values are to be displayed. That's a useful thing to be able to do in general, and jQuery UI makes it available directly to us.

FORMATTING DATE VALUES

We can format any date value using the `$.datepicker.formatDate()` utility function, defined as follows:

Command syntax: $.datepicker.formatDate

`$.datepicker.formatDate(format,date,options)`
Formats the passed date value as specified by the passed format pattern and options.

Parameters

format	(String) The date format pattern string as described in tables 11.10 and 11.11.
date	(Date) The date value to be formatted.
options	(Object) An object hash of options that supply alternative localization values for day and month names. The possible options are `dayNames`, `dayNamesShort`, `monthNames`, and `monthNamesShort`. See table 11.9 for details of these options. If omitted, the default English names are used.

Returns
The formatted date string.

That sort of obsoletes the date formatter we set up in chapter 7! But that's OK, we learned a lot from that exercise, and we can always use it in projects that don't use jQuery UI.

What other tricks does the datepicker have up its sleeve for us?

PARSING DATE STRINGS

As useful as formatting date values into text strings is, it's just as useful—if not even more so—to convert text strings into date values. jQuery UI gives us that ability with the `$.datepicker.parseDate()` function, whose syntax is as follows:

Command syntax: $.datepicker.parseDate

`$.datepicker.parseDate(format,value,options)`
Converts the passed text value into a date value using the passed format pattern and options.

Parameters

format	(String) The date format pattern string as described in tables 11.10 and 11.11.
value	(String) The text value to be parsed.
options	(Object) An object hash of options that supply alternative localization values for day and month names, as well as specifying how to handle 2-digit year values. The possible options are `shortYearCutoff`, `dayNames`, `dayNamesShort`, `monthNames`, and `monthNamesShort`. See table 11.9 for details of these options. If omitted, the default English names are used, and the rollover year is +10.

Returns
The parsed date value.

There's one more utility function that the datepicker makes available.

GETTING THE WEEK IN THE YEAR

As a default algorithm for the `calculateWeek` option, jQuery UI uses an algorithm defined by the ISO 8601 standard. In the event that we might have some use for this algorithm outside of a datepicker control, it's exposed to use as the `$.datepicker.iso8601Week()` function:

Command syntax: $.datepicker.iso8601Week

`$.datepicker.iso8601Week(date)`
Given a date value, calculates the week number as defined by ISO 8601.

Parameters
> `date`   (Date) The date whose week number is to be calculated.

Returns
The computed week number.

The ISO 8601 definition of week numbering is such that weeks start on Mondays, and the first week of the year is the one that contains January 4th (or in other words, the week containing the first Thursday).

We've seen jQuery UI widgets that allow us to gather data from the user in an intuitive manner, so we're now going to turn our attention to widgets that help us organize our content. If your eyes are getting bleary at this point, now might be a good time to sit back for a moment and enjoy a snack; preferably one containing caffeine.

When you're ready, let's forge on ahead to examine one of the most common organization metaphors on the web—tabs.

11.6   *Tabs*

Tabs probably need no introduction. As a navigation method, they've become ubiquitous on the web, surpassed only by links themselves. Mimicking physical card index tabs, GUI tabs allow us to quickly flip between sets of content logically grouped at the same level.

In the bad old days, switching between tabbed panels required full-page refreshes, but today we can just use CSS to show and hide elements as appropriate, and even employ Ajax to fetch hidden content on an as-needed basis.

As it turns out "just using CSS" turns out to be a fair amount of work to get right, so jQuery UI gives us a ready-made tabs implementation that, of course, matches the downloaded UI theme.

11.6.1   *Creating tabbed content*

Most of the widgets we've examined so far take a simple element, such as a `<button>`, `<div>`, or `<input>`, and transforms it into the target widget. Tabs, by nature, start with a more complex HTML construct.

A canonical construct for a tabset with three tabs should follow this pattern:

```
<div id="tabset">
  <ul>
    <li><a href="#panel1">Tab One</a></li>
    <li><a href="#panel2">Tab Two</a></li>
    <li><a href="#panel3">Tab Three</a></li>
  </ul>
  <div id="panel1">
    ... content ...
  </div>
  <div id="panel2">
    ... content ...
  </div>
  <div id="panel3">
    ... content ...
  </div>
</div>
```

❶ Contains tabs and tab panels

❷ Defines tabs

❸ Provides panels

This construct consists of a <div> element that contains the entire tabset ❶, which consists of two subsections: an unordered list (<ul>) containing list items (<li>) that will become the tabs ❷, and a set of <div> elements, one for each corresponding panel ❸.

Each list item that represents a tab contains an anchor element (<a>) that not only defines the association between the tab and its corresponding panel, but also serves as a focusable element. The href attribute of these anchors specifies an HTML anchor hash, useable as a jQuery id selector, for the panel that it's to be associated with.

Each tab's content can alternatively be fetched from the server via an Ajax request upon first selection. In this case, the href of the anchor element specifies the URL of the active content, and it isn't necessary to include a panel in the tabset.

If we were to create the markup for a three-tab tabset where all the content is fetched from the server, the markup could be as follows:

```
<div id="tabset">
  <ul>
    <li><a href="/url/for/panel1">Tab One</a></li>
    <li><a href="/url/for/panel2">Tab Two</a></li>
    <li><a href="/url/for/panel3">Tab Three</a></li>
  </ul>
</div>
```

In this scenario, three <div> elements serving as panels to hold the dynamic content will be automatically created. You can control the id values assigned to these panel elements by placing a title attribute on the anchor. The value of the title, with spaces replaced by underscores, will be the id of the corresponding panel.

You can precreate the panel using this id, and the tab will be correctly hooked up to it, but if you don't, it will be automatically generated. For example, if we were to rewrite the third tab as,

```
<li><a href="/url/for/panel3" title="a third panel">Tab Three</a></li>
```

the id value of the corresponding panel would be a_third_panel. If such a panel already exists, it will be used; otherwise, it will be created.

Ajax and non-Ajax tabs can be freely mixed in a single tabset.

Once we have the base markup all squared away, we'll create the tabset with the tabs() method, applied to the outer tabset <div> element, whose syntax follows.

Command syntax: tabs

```
tabs(options)
tabs('disable',index)
tabs('enable',index)
tabs('destroy')
tabs('option',optionName,value)
tabs('add',association,label,index)
tabs('remove',index)
tabs('select',index)
tabs('load',index)
tabs('url',index,url)
tabs('length')
tabs('abort')
tabs('rotate',duration,cyclical)
tabs('widget')
```

Transforms tabset markup (as specified earlier in this section) into a set of UI tabs.

Parameters

options	(Object) An object hash of the options to be applied to the tabset, as described in table 11.12.
'disable'	(String) Disables one or all tabs. If a zero-based index is provided, only the identified tab is disabled. Otherwise, the entire tabset is disabled. A backdoor method to disable any set of tabs is to use the data() method to set a data value of disabled.tabs onto the widget element consisting of an array of zero-based indexes of the tabs to be disabled. For example, $('#tabWidget').data('disabled.tabs',[0,3,4]).
'enable'	(String) Re-enables a disabled tab or tabset. If a zero-based index is provided, the identified tab is enabled. Otherwise, the entire tabset is enabled. All tabs can be enabled by using the backdoor trick outlined above, specifying an empty array.
'destroy'	(String) Reverts any elements transformed into tab controls to their previous state.
'option'	(String) Allows option values to be set on all elements of the wrapped set, or to be retrieved from the first element of the wrapped set (which should be a tab element), based upon the remaining parameters. If specified, at least the optionName parameter must also be provided.
optionName	(String) The name of the option (see table 11.12) whose value is to be set or returned. If a value parameter is provided, that value becomes the option's value. If no value parameter is provided, the named option's value is returned.
index	(Number) The zero-based index identifying a tab to be operated upon. Used with disable, enable, remove, select, add, load, and url.

Command syntax: tabs *(continued)*	
'add'	(String) Adds a new tab to the tabset. The index parameter specifies the existing tab before which the new tab will be inserted. If no index is provided, the tab is placed at the end of the tab list.
association	(String) Specifies the association with the panel that will correspond to this tab. This can be an id selector for an existing element to become the panel, or the URL of a server-side resource to create an Ajax tab.
label	(String) The label to assign to the new tab.
'remove'	(String) Removes the indexed tab from the tabset.
'select'	(String) Causes the indexed tab to become the selected tab.
'load'	(String) Forces a reload of the indexed tab, ignoring the cache.
'url'	(String) Changes the association URL for the indexed tab. If the tab isn't an Ajax tab, it becomes one.
url	(String) The URL to a server-side resource that returns a tab's panel content.
'length'	(String) Returns the number of tabs in the first matched tabset in the wrapped set.
'abort'	(String) Aborts any in-progress Ajax tab-loading operations and any running animations.
'rotate'	(String) Sets the tabs to automatically cycle using the specified duration.
duration	(Number) The duration, in milliseconds, between rotations of the tabset. Pass 0 or null to stop an active rotation.
cycle	(Boolean) If true, rotation continues even after a user has selected a tab. Defaults to false.
'widget'	(String) Returns the element serving as the tabs widget, annotated with the ui-tabs class name.

Returns

The wrapped set, except for the cases where values are returned as described above.

As might be expected for such a complex widget, there are a fair number of options (see table 11.12).

 As usual, we've provided a Tabs Lab to help you sort through the tabs() method options. The Lab can be found in file chapter11/tabs/lab.tabs.html, and it's shown in figure 11.12.

NOTE   Because this Lab uses server-side Ajax operations, it must be run from the Tomcat instance we set up for the examples in chapter 8 (note the 8080 port in the URL). Alternatively, you can run this Lab remotely by visiting http://www.bibeault.org/jqia2/chapter11/tabs/lab.tabs.html.

The options available for the tabs() method are shown in table 11.12.

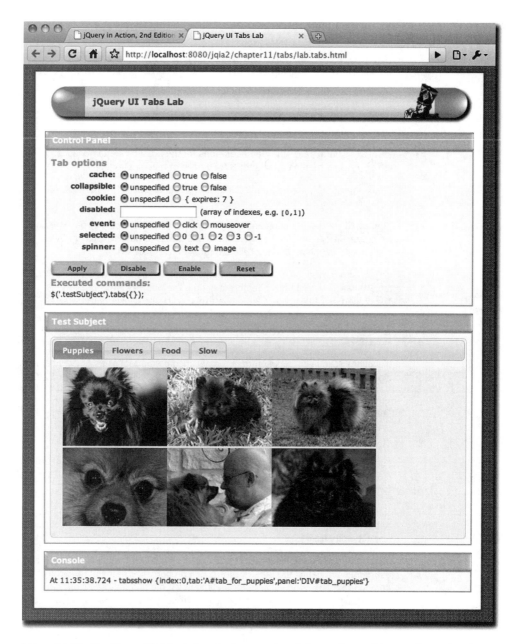

Figure 11.12 The jQuery UI Tabs Lab page shows us how tabs can be used to organize content into panels for serial display.

Table 11.12 Options for the jQuery UI tabs

Option	Description	In Lab?
`add`	(Function) Specifies a function to be established on the tabset as an event handler for tabsadd events. See the description of the tab events in table 11.13 for details on the information passed to this handler.	✓
`ajaxOptions`	(Object) An options hash specifying any additional options to be passed to `$.ajax()` during any Ajax load operations for the tabset. See the description of the `$.ajax()` method in chapter 8 for details of these options.	
`cache`	(Boolean) If `true`, any content loaded via Ajax will be cached. Otherwise, Ajax content is reloaded. Defaults to `false`.	✓
`collapsible`	(Boolean) If `true`, selecting an already selected tab will cause it to become unselected, resulting in no tab being selected and the pane area collapsing. By default, clicking on an already selected tab has no effect.	✓
`cookie`	(Object) If provided, specifies that a cookie should be used to remember which tab was last selected and to restore it upon page load. The properties of this object are those expected by the cookie plugin: `name`, `expires` (in days), `path`, `domain`, and `secure`. Requires that the cookie plugin (http://plugins.jquery.com/project/cookie) be loaded.	✓
`disable`	(Function) Specifies a function to be established on the tabset as an event handler for tabsdisable events. See the description of the tab events in table 11.13 for details on the information passed to this handler.	✓
`disabled`	(Array) An array containing the zero-based indexes of tabs that will be initially disabled. If the `selected` option is not specified (defaults to 0), having 0 as index in this array won't disable the first tab, as it will be selected by default.	✓
`enable`	(Function) Specifies a function to be established on the tabset as an event handler for tabsenable events. See the description of the tab events in table 11.13 for details on the information passed to this handler.	✓
`event`	(String) Specifies the event used to select a tab. Most often this is one of `click` (the default) or `mouseover`, but events such as `mouseout` can also be specified (even if a bit strange).	✓
`fx`	(Object) Specifies an object hash to be suitable for use with `animate()` to be used when animating the tabs. A `duration` property can be used to specify the duration with any value suitable for the animation method: milliseconds, `normal` (the default), `slow`, or `fast`. An `opacity` property can also be specified as a number from 0 to 1.0.	
`idPrefix`	(String) When no `title` attribute is present on a tab anchor, specifies the prefix to use when generating a unique `id` value to assign to the tab panels for dynamic content. If omitted, the prefix `ui-tabs-` is used.	
`load`	(Function) Specifies a function to be established on the tabset as an event handler for tabsload events. See the description of the tab events in table 11.13 for details on the information passed to this handler.	✓

Table 11.12 Options for the jQuery UI tabs *(continued)*

Option	Description	In Lab?
panelTemplate	(String) The HTML template to use when creating tab panels on the fly. This could be the result of an add method or automatic creation for an Ajax tab. By default, the template "`<div></div>`" is used.	
remove	(Function) Specifies a function to be established on the tabset as an event handler for tabsremove events. See the description of the tab events in table 11.13 for details on the information passed to this handler.	✓
select	(Function) Specifies a function to be established on the tabset as an event handler for tabsselect events. See the description of the tab events in table 11.13 for details on the information passed to this handler.	✓
selected	(Number) The zero-based index of the tab to be initially selected. If omitted, the first tab is selected. The value −1 can be used to cause no tabs to be initially selected.	✓
show	(Function) Specifies a function to be established on the tabset as an event handler for tabsshow events. See the description of the tab events in table 11.13 for details on the information passed to this handler.	✓
spinner	(String) A string of HTML to be displayed in an Ajax tab that's fetching remote content. The default is the string "`<em>Loading&#8230;</em>`". (The embedded HTML entity is the Unicode character for an ellipsis.) In order for the spinner to appear, the content of the tabs anchor element must be a `<span>` element. For example, `<li><a href="/jqia2/lengthyTab"><span>Slow</span></a></li>`	✓
tabTemplate	(String) The HTML template to use when creating new tabs via the add method. If omitted, the default of "`<li><a href="#{href}"><span>#{label}</span></a></li>`" is used. Within the template, the tokens `#{href}` and `#{label}` are replaced with the values passed to the add method.	

We trust that you've become experienced enough with the various Lab pages presented throughout this book to not need any help working through the basic options in the Tabs Lab. But there are some important nuances we want to make sure you understand around Ajax tabs, so here are a few Lab exercises that you should do after playing around with the basic options:

- *Exercise 1*—Bring up the Lab and, leaving all controls in their default state, click Apply. The Food and Slow tabs are Ajax tabs whose panels aren't loaded until the tabs are selected.

  Click the Food tab. This tab is simply loaded from an HTML source and appears instantaneously. But note a *tabsload* event in the console. This indicates that the content was loaded from the server.

  Click the Flowers tab and then click the Food tab again. Note how another tabsload event was triggered as the content was loaded again from the server.

- *Exercise 2*—Reset the Lab. Choose the `true` option for `cache`, and click Apply.

  Repeat the actions of exercise 1 and note how, this time, the Food tab is only loaded on its first selection.

- *Exercise 3*—Reset the Lab and, leaving all controls in their default state, click Apply.

  Repeat exercise 1 except click on the Slow tab instead of the Flowers tab. The Slow tab is loaded from a server-side resource that takes about 10 seconds to load. Note how the default spinner value of "Loading ..." is displayed during the lengthy load operation, and how the tabsload event isn't delivered until the content has been received.

- *Exercise 4*—Reset the Lab and, choosing the Image value for the spinner option, click Apply.

  Repeat the actions of exercise 3. This supplies the HTML for an `<img>` element that's displayed in the tab while loading. You can't miss the effect.

11.6.2 *Tab events*

There are many reasons that we may want to be notified when users are clicking on our tabs. For example, we may want to wait to perform some initialization events on tabbed content until the user actually selects the tab. After all, why do a bunch of work on content that the user may not even look at? The same goes with loaded content. There may be tasks we want to perform after the content has been loaded.

To help us get our hooks into the tabs and tabbed content at the appropriate times, the events shown in table 11.13 are triggered at interesting times during the life of the tabset. Each event handler is passed the event instance as the first parameter, and a custom object as the second, whose properties consist of three elements:

- `index`—The zero-based index of the tab associated with the event
- `tab`—A reference to the anchor element for the tab associated with the event
- `panel`—A reference to the panel element for the tab associated with the event

Table 11.13   Events for jQuery UI tabs

Event	Option	Description
tabsadd	add	Triggered when a new tab is added to the tabset.
tabsdisable	disable	Triggered whenever a tab is disabled.
tabsenable	enable	Triggered whenever a tab is enabled.
tabsload	load	Triggered after the content of an Ajax tab is loaded (even if an error occurs).
tabsremove	remove	Triggered when a tab is removed.
tabsselect	select	Triggered when a tab is clicked upon, becoming selected, unless this callback returns `false`, in which case the selections is canceled.
tabsshow	show	Triggered when a tabbed panel is shown

As an example, let's say we wanted to add a class name to all image elements in a tabbed panel that loaded via Ajax. We could do that with a single tabsload handler established on the tabset:

```
$('#theTabset').bind('tabsload',function(event,info){
  $('img',info.panel).addClass('imageInATab');
});
```

The important points to take away from this small example are

- The `info.panel` property references the panel affected.
- The panel's content has been loaded by the time the tabsload event is triggered.

Now let's turn our attention to what CSS class names are added to the elements so we can use them as styling hooks.

11.6.3 *Styling tabs*

When a tabset is created, the following CSS class names are applied to various participating elements:

- `ui-tabs`—Added to the tabset element
- `ui-tabs-nav`—Added to the unordered list element housing the tabs
- `ui-tabs-selected`—Added to the list item representing the selected tab
- `ui-tabs-panel`—Added to the tabbed panels

Do you think that the tabs are too big in their default rendition? Shrink them down to size with a style rules such as this:

```
ul.ui-tabs-nav { font-size: 0.5em; }
```

Do you want your selected tabs to really stand out? Try this:

```
li.ui-tabs-selected a { background-color: crimson; }
```

Tabs are a great and ubiquitous widget for organizing panels of related content so that users only see a single panel at a time. But what if they're a bit *too* ubiquitous and you want to achieve the same goal but with a less common look and feel?

An accordion might be just the widget for you.

11.7 *Accordions*

Although the term *accordion* might conjure images of mustached men playing badly delivered tableside serenades, it's actually an apt name for the widget that presents content panels one at a time (just like tabs) in a layout reminiscent of the bellows of the actual instrument.

Rather than having a set of tabs across the top of an area that displays the panels, accordions present choices as a stacked series of horizontal bars, each of whose content is shown between the associated bar and the next. If you've been using the index page for the code examples (index.html in the root folder), you've already seen an accordion in action, as shown in figure 11.13.

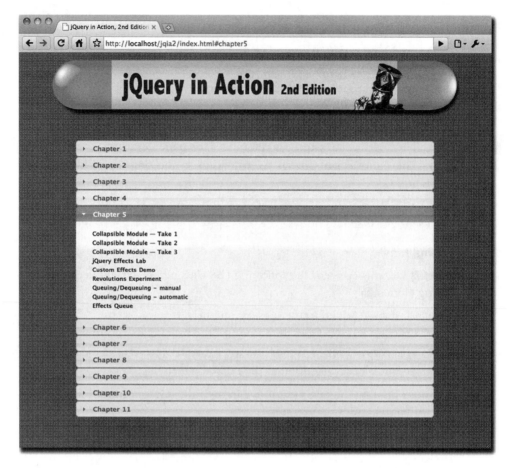

Figure 11.13   We used an accordion widget to organize the links to the many code examples for this book.

Like a tabset, only one panel can be open at a time, and, by default, accordions also adjust the size of the panels so that the widget takes up the same amount of room no matter which panel is open. This makes the accordion a very well-behaved on-page citizen.

Let's take a look at what it takes to create one.

11.7.1 *Creating accordion widgets*

As with the tabset, the accordion expects a particular HTML construct that it will instrument. Because of the different layout of the accordion, and to make sure things degrade gracefully in the absence of JavaScript, the structure of the source for an accordion is rather different from that for a tabset.

The accordion expects an outer container (to which the `accordion()` method is applied) that contains pairs consisting of a header and associated content. Rather than using `href` values to associate content panels to their headers, accordions (by default) expect each header to be followed by its content panel as the next sibling.

A typical construct for an accordion could look like the following:

```
<div id="accordion">

  <h2><a href="#">Header 1</a></h2>
  <div id="contentPanel_1">  ... content ... </div>

  <h2><a href="#">Header 2</a></h2>
  <div id="contentPanel_2">  ... content ... </div>

  <h2><a href="#">Header 3</a></h2>
  <div id="contentPanel_3">  ... content ... </div>

</div>
```

Note that the header text continues to be embedded within an anchor—in order to give the user a focusable element—but the `href` is generally set to # and isn't used to associate the header to its content panel. (There is one option where the anchor's `href` value is significant, but generally they're just set to #.)

The syntax of the `accordion()` method is as follows:

Command syntax: accordion

```
accordion(options)
accordion('disable')
accordion('enable')
accordion('destroy')
accordion('option',optionName,value)
accordion('activate',index)
accordion('widget')
accordion('resize')
```

Transforms the accordion source construct (as specified earlier in this section) into an accordion widget.

Parameters

`options`	(Object) An object hash of the options to be applied to the accordion, as described in table 11.14.
`'disable'`	(String) Disables the accordion.
`'enable'`	(String) Re-enables a disabled accordion.
`'destroy'`	(String) Reverts any elements transformed into an accordion widget to their previous state.
`'option'`	(String) Allows option values to be set on all elements of the wrapped set, or to be retrieved from the first element of the wrapped set (which should be an accordion element), based upon the remaining parameters. If specified, at least the `optionName` parameter must also be provided.
`optionName`	(String) The name of the option (see table 11.14) whose value is to be set or returned. If a `value` parameter is provided, that value becomes the option's value. If no `value` parameter is provided, the named option's value is returned.
`'activate'`	(String) Activates (opens) the content panel identified by the `index` parameter.

Command syntax: accordion *(continued)*	
`index`	(Number|Selector|Boolean) A zero-based index identifying the accordion panel to be activated, a selector identifying the panel, or `false`, which causes all panels to be deactivated if the collapsible option is specified as `true`.
`'widget'`	(String) Returns the accordion widget element; the one annotated with the `ui-accordion` class name.
`'resize'`	(String) Causes the size of the widget to be recomputed. This should be called whenever something occurs that may cause the widget size to change; for example, resizing its container.

Returns

The wrapped set, except for the cases where values are returned as described above.

The short, but capable, list of options available for the `accordion()` method is shown in table 11.14.

Follow along in this Lab as you read through the options list in table 11.14.

Table 11.14 Options for the jQuery UI `accordions`

Option	Description	In Lab?
`active`	(Number|Boolean|Selector|Element|jQuery) Specifies which panel is to be initially open. This can be the zero-based index of the panel, or a means to identify the header element for the panel: an element reference, a selector, or a jQuery wrapped set. If specified as `false`, no panel is initially opened unless the `collapsible` options is set to `false`.	✓
`animated`	(String|Boolean) The name of the animation to be used when opening and closing accordion panels. One of: `slide` (the default), `bounceslide`, or any of the installed easings (if included on the page). If specified as `false`, no animation is used.	✓
`autoHeight`	(Boolean) Unless specified as `false`, all panels are forced to the biggest height needed to accommodate the highest panel, making all panels the same size. Otherwise, panels retain their natural size. Defaults to `true`.	✓
`clearStyle`	(Boolean) If `true`, height and overflow styles are cleared after an animation. The `autoHeight` option must be set to `false` for this to apply.	
`change`	(Function) Specifies a function to be established on the accordion as an event handler for accordionchange events. See the description of the accordion events in table 11.15 for details on the information passed to this handler.	✓
`changestart`	(Function) Specifies a function to be established on the accordion as an event handler for accordionchangestart events. See the description of the accordion events in table 11.15 for details on the information passed to this handler.	✓
`collapsible`	(Boolean) If `true`, clicking on the header for the open accordion panel will cause the panel to close, leaving no panels open. By default, clicks on the open panel's header have no effect.	✓
`disabled`	(Boolean) If specified and `true`, the accordion widget is initially disabled.	

Table 11.14 Options for the jQuery UI accordions *(continued)*

Option	Description	In Lab?
event	(String) Specifies the event used to select an accordion header. Most often this is one of `click` (the default) or `mouseover`, but events such as `mouseout` can also be specified (even if a bit strange).	✓
fillSpace	(Boolean) If `true`, the accordion is sized to completely fill the height of its parent element, overriding any `autoHeight` option value.	
header	(Selector|jQuery) Specifies a selector or element to override the default pattern for identifying the header elements. The default is `"> li > :first-child,> :not(li):even"`. Use this only if you need to use a source construct for the accordion that doesn't conform to the default pattern.	
icons	(Object) An object that defines the icons to use to the left of the header text for opened and closed panels. The icon to use for closed panels is specified as a property named `header`, whereas the icon to use for open panels is specified as a property named `headerSelected`. The values of these properties are strings identifying the icons by class name, as defined earlier for button widgets in section 11.1.3. The defaults are `ui-icon-triangle-1-e` for `header`, and `ui-icon-triangle-1-s` for `headerSelected`.	✓
navigation	(Boolean) If `true`, the current location (`location.href`) is used to attempt to match up to the `href` values of the anchor tags in the accordion headers. This can be used to cause specific accordion panels to be opened when the page is displayed. For example, setting the `href` values to anchor hashes such as `#chapter1` (and so on), will cause the corresponding panel to be opened when the page is displayed if the URL (or bookmark) is suffixed with the same hash value. The index.html page for the code examples uses this technique. Try it out! Visit the page by specifying index.html#chapter3 as part of the URL.	
navigationFilter	(Function) Overrides the default navigation filter used when navigation is `true`. You can use this function to change the behavior described in the `navigation` option description to any of your own choosing. This callback will be invoked with no parameters, and the anchor tag for a header is set as the function context. Return `true` to indicate that a navigation match has occurred.	

 We've provided the Accordions Lab, in file chapter11/accordions/lab/accordions.html, to demonstrate many of the options. It's shown in figure 11.14.

After you've run through the basic options and tried out things in the Accordions Lab, here are a couple of exercises we want to make sure you don't miss:

- *Exercise 1*—Load the Lab and, leaving all settings at their default, click Apply. Select various headers in any order and note how, as the panels open and close, the accordion itself never changes size.
- *Exercise 2*—Reset the Lab, choose `true` for `autoHeight`, and click Apply. Run through the actions of exercise 1, noticing that, this time, when the Flowers panel is opened, the height of the accordion shrinks to fit the smaller content of the Flowers panel.

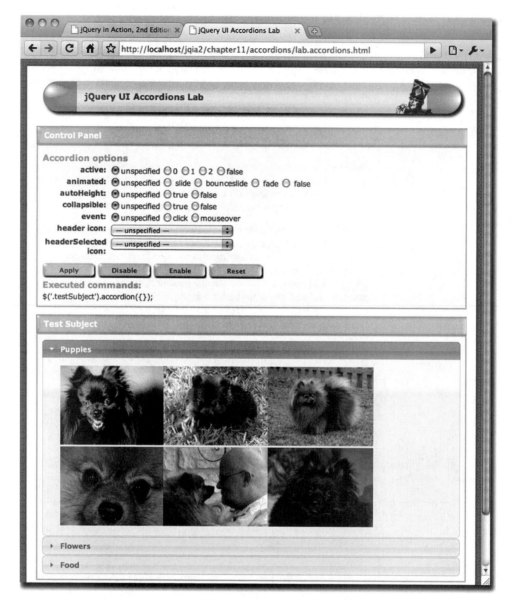

Figure 11.14   The jQuery UI Accordions Lab shows us how we can expose serial content panels to our users in a novel fashion.

Now we're ready to tackle the events that are triggered while an accordion is being manipulated.

11.7.2 Accordion events

Accordions trigger only two event types when the user is opening and closing panels, as described in table 11.15.

Each of the handlers is passed the usual event instance and custom object. The properties of the custom object are the same for both events and consist of the following:

- options—The options passed to the accordion() method when the widget was created.
- oldHeader—A jQuery wrapped set containing the header element of the previously open panel. This may be empty if no panel was opened.
- newHeader—A jQuery wrapped set containing the header element of the panel being opened. This may be empty for collapsible accordions when all panels are being closed.
- oldContent—A jQuery wrapped set containing a reference to the previously open panel.
- newContent—A jQuery wrapped set containing a reference to the panel being opened.

Table 11.15. lists the events generated for accordion widgets.

Table 11.15   Events for jQuery UI accordions

Event	Option	Description
accordionchangestart	changestart	Triggered when the accordion is about to change.
accordionchange	change	Triggered when the accordion has been changed, after the duration of any animation used to change the display.

That's a pretty sparse list of events, and it does offer some challenges. For example, it's disappointing that we get no notification when the initial panel (if any) is opened. We'll see how that makes things a tad harder for us when we try to use these events to instrument the accordion. But before we tackle an example of using these events to add some functionality to our widget, let's examine the CSS class names that jQuery UI adds to the elements that compose the accordion.

11.7.3 *Styling classes for accordions*

As with tabs, jQuery UI adds a number of CSS class names to the elements that go into making an accordion. We can use not only use them as styling hooks, but to find the elements using jQuery selectors. We saw an example of that in the previous section when we learned how to locate the panels involved in the accordion events.

These are the class names that are applied to the accordion elements:

- ui-accordion—Added to the outer container for the accordion (the element upon which accordion() was called).
- ui-accordion-header—Added to all header elements that become the clickable elements.
- ui-accordion-content—Added to all panel elements.

- `ui-accordion-content-active`—Assigned to the currently open panel element, if any.

- `ui-state-active`—Assigned to the header for the currently open panel, if any. Note that this is one of the generic jQuery UI class names shared across multiple widgets.

Using these class names, we can restyle accordion elements as we like, much like we did for tabs. Try your hand at changing the style of the elements: the header text, for example, or maybe the border surrounding the panels.

Let's also see how knowing these class names helps us to add functionality to an accordion widget.

11.7.4 Loading accordion panels using Ajax

One feature that the accordion widget lacks, present in its tabs widget kinfolk, is the innate ability to load content via Ajax. Not wanting our accordions to suffer from an inferiority complex, let's see how we can easily add that ability using the knowledge that we have at hand.

Tabs specify the location of remote content via the `href` of the anchor tags within them. Accordions, on the other hand, ignore the `href` of anchor tags in their header unless the `navigation` option is being used. Knowing this, we'll safely use it to specify the location of any remote content to be loaded for the panel.

This is a good decision because it's consistent with the way that tabs work (consistency is a good thing), and it means we don't have to needlessly introduce custom options or attributes to record the location. We'll leave the anchor `href` of "normal" panels at #.

We want to load the panel content whenever the panel is about to open, so we bind an accordionchangestart event to the accordion(s) on our page with this code:

```
$('.ui-accordion').bind('accordionchangestart',function(event,info){
  if (info.newContent.length == 0) return;
  var href = $('a',info.newHeader).attr('href');
  if (href.charAt(0) != '#') {
    info.newContent.load(href);
    $('a',info.newHeader).attr('href','#');
  }
});
```

In this handler we first locate the opening panel by using the reference provided in `info.newContent`. If there's none (which can happen for collapsible accordions), we simply return.

Then we locate the anchor within the activating header by finding the `<a>` element within the context of the reference provided by `info.newHeader`, and grab its `href` attribute. If it doesn't start with #, we assume it's a remote URL for the panel content.

To load the remote content, we employ the handy `load()` method, and then change the `href` of the anchor to #. This last action prevents us from fetching the content again next time the panel is opened. (To force a load every time, simply remove the `href` assignment.)

When using this handler, we might want to turn autoHeight off if not knowing the size of the largest panel in advance creates a problem. A working example of this approach can be found at chapter11/accordions/ajax/ajax-accordion.html.

As usual, there are always different vectors of approach. Try the following exercise.

- *Exercise 1*—If we wanted to avoid using the href value so that we could use the navigation option, how would you rewrite the example to use custom attributes (or any other tactic of your choosing)?

Accordions give us an alternative to tabbed panels when we want to serially present related content to the user. Now let's wrap up our examination of the widgets, by looking at another widget that lets us present content dynamically.

11.8 Dialog boxes

As a concept, dialog boxes need no introduction. A staple of desktop application design since the inception of the GUI, dialog boxes, whether modeless or modal, are a common means of eliciting information from the user, or delivering information to the user.

In web interfaces, however, they haven't existed as an innate concept except for the built-in JavaScript alert prompt and confirm tools. Deemed inadequate for a variety of reasons—not the least of which is their inability to be styled to conform to the theme of a site—these tools are often ignored except as debugging aids.

Internet Explorer introduced the concept of a web-based dialog box, but it failed to impress the standards community and remains a proprietary solution.

For years, web developers used the window.open() method to create new windows that stood in for dialog boxes. Although fraught with issues, this approach was adequate as a solution for modeless dialog boxes, but truly modal dialog boxes were out of reach.

As JavaScript, browsers, DOM manipulations, and developers themselves have become more capable, it's become possible to use these basic tools to create in-page elements that "float" over the rest of the display—even locking out input in a modal fashion—which better approximates the semantics of modeless and modal dialog boxes.

So although dialog boxes as a concept still don't actually exist in web interfaces, we can do a darned good job of making it seem like they do.

Let's see what jQuery UI provides for us in this area.

11.8.1 Creating dialog boxes

Although the idea of in-page dialog boxes seems simple—just remove some content from the page flow, float it with a high z-index, and put some "chrome" around it—there are lots of details to take into account. Luckily, jQuery UI is going to handle that, allowing us to create modeless and modal dialog boxes, with advanced features such as the ability to be resized and repositioned, with ease.

NOTE The term "chrome" when applied to dialog boxes denotes the frame and widgets that contain the dialog box and allow it to be manipulated. This can include features such as resize borders, title bar, and the omnipresent little "x" icon that closes the dialog box.

Unlike the rather stringent requirements for the tabs and accordion widgets, just about any element can become the body of a dialog box, though a <div> element containing the content that's to become the dialog box's body is most often used.

To create a dialog box, the content to become the body is selected into a wrapped set, and the dialog() method is applied. The dialog() method has the following syntax:

Command syntax: dialog

```
dialog(options)
dialog('disable')
dialog('enable')
dialog('destroy')
dialog('option',optionName,value)
dialog('open')
dialog('close')
dialog('isOpen')
dialog('moveToTop')
dialog('widget')
```

Transforms the elements in the wrapped set into a dialog box by removing them from the document flow and wrapping them in "chrome." Note that creating a dialog box also causes it to automatically be opened unless this is disabled by setting the autoOpen option to false.

Parameters

options	(Object) An object hash of the options to be applied to the dialog box, as described in table 11.16.
'disable'	(String) Disables the dialog box.
'enable'	(String) Re-enables a disabled dialog box.
'destroy'	(String) Destroys the dialog box. Once destroyed, the dialog box can't be reopened. Note that destroying a dialog box doesn't cause the contained elements to be restored to the normal document flow.
'option'	(String) Allows option values to be set on all elements of the wrapped set, or to be retrieved from the first element of the wrapped set (which should be a dialog box element), based upon the remaining parameters. If specified, at least the optionName parameter must also be provided.
optionName	(String) The name of the option (see table 11.16) whose value is to be set or returned. If a value parameter is provided, that value becomes the option's value. If no value parameter is provided, the named option's value is returned.
'open'	(String) Opens a closed dialog box.
'close'	(String) Closes an open dialog box. The dialog box can be reopened at any time with the open method.
'isOpen'	(String) Returns true if the dialog box is open; false otherwise.
'moveToTop'	(String) If multiple dialog boxes exist, moves the dialog box to the top of the stack of dialog boxes.

Command syntax: dialog *(continued)*

`'widget'` (String) Returns the dialog box's widget element; the element annotated with the `ui-dialog` class name.

Returns

The wrapped set, except for the cases where values are returned as described above.

It's important to understand the difference between creating a dialog box and opening one. Once a dialog box is created, it doesn't need to be created again to be reopened after closing. Unless disabled, a dialog box is automatically opened upon creation, but to reopen a dialog box that has been closed, we call `dialog('open')` rather than calling the `dialog()` method with options again.

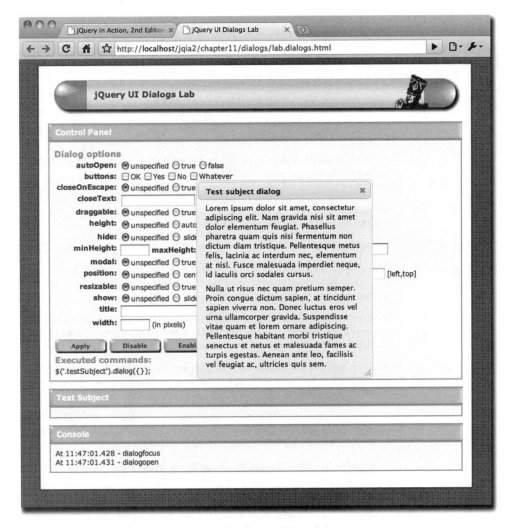

Figure 11.15 The jQuery UI Dialogs Lab lets us try out all the options that are available for jQuery UI dialog boxes.

As usual, a Dialogs Lab has been made available in file chapter11/dialogs/lab.dialogs.html, shown in figure 11.15, so you can try out the `dialog()` method options. Follow along in this Lab as you read through the options list in table 11.16.

Table 11.16   Options for the jQuery UI dialogs

Option	Description	In Lab?
autoOpen	(Boolean) Unless set to `false`, the dialog box is opened upon creation. When `false`, the dialog box will be opened upon a call to `dialog('open')`.	✓
beforeClose	(Function) Specifies a function to be established on the dialog box as an event handler for dialogbeforeClose events. See the description of the dialog events in table 11.17 for details on the information passed to this handler.	✓
buttons	(Object) Specifies any buttons to place at the bottom of the dialog box. Each property in the object serves as the caption for the button, and the value must be a callback function to be invoked when the button is clicked. This handler is invoked with a function context of the dialog box element, and is passed the event instance with the button set as the `target` property. If omitted, no buttons are created for the dialog box. The function context is suitable for use with the `dialog()` method. For example, within a Cancel button, the following could be used to close the dialog box: `$(this).dialog('close');`	✓
close	(Function) Specifies a function to be established on the dialog box as an event handler for dialogclose events. See the description of the dialog events in table 11.17 for details on the information passed to this handler.	✓
closeOnEscape	(Boolean) Unless set to `false`, the dialog box will be closed when the user presses the Escape key while the dialog box has focus.	✓
closeText	(String) Text to replace the default of Close for the close button.	✓
dialogClass	(String) Specifies a space-delimited string of CSS class names to be applied to the dialog box element in addition to the class names that jQuery UI will add. If omitted, no extra class names are added.	
drag	(Function) Specifies a function to be established on the dialog box as an event handler for drag events. See the description of the dialog events in table 11.17 for details on the information passed to this handler.	✓
dragstart	(Function) Specifies a function to be established on the dialog box as an event handler for `dragStart` events. See the description of the dialog events in table 11.17 for details on the information passed to this handler.	
dragstop	(Function) Specifies a function to be established on the dialog box as an event handler for `dragStop` events. See the description of the dialog events in table 11.17 for details on the information passed to this handler.	
draggable	(Boolean) Unless set to `false`, the dialog box is draggable by clicking and dragging its title bar.	✓
focus	(Function) Specifies a function to be established on the dialog box as an event handler for `dialogfocus` events. See the description of the dialog events in table 11.17 for details on the information passed to this handler.	

Table 11.16 Options for the jQuery UI dialogs (continued)

Option	Description	In Lab?
height	(Number|String) The height of the dialog box in pixels, or the string `"auto"` (the default), which allows the dialog box to determine its height based upon its contents.	✓
hide	(String) The effect to be used when the dialog box is closed (as we discussed in chapter 9). By default, none.	✓
maxHeight	(Number) The maximum height, in pixels, to which the dialog box can be resized.	✓
maxWidth	(Number) The maximum width, in pixels, to which the dialog box can be resized.	✓
minHeight	(Number) The minimum height, in pixels, to which the dialog box can be resized. Defaults to 150.	✓
minWidth	(Number) The minimum width, in pixels, to which the dialog box can be resized. Defaults to 150.	✓
modal	(Boolean) If `true`, a semi-transparent "curtain" is created behind the dialog box covering the remainder of the window content, preventing any user interaction. If omitted, the dialog box is modeless.	✓
open	(Function) Specifies a function to be established on the dialog box as an event handler for `dialogopen` events. See the description of the dialog events in table 11.17 for details on the information passed to this handler.	
position	(String|Array) Specifies the initial position of the dialog box. Can be one of the predefined positions: `center` (the default), `left`, `right`, `top`, or `bottom`. Can also be a 2-element array with the left and top values (in pixels) as `[left,top]`, or text positions such as `['right','top']`.	✓
resize	(Function) Specifies a function to be established on the dialog box as an event handler for resize events. See the description of the dialog events in table 11.17 for details on the information passed to this handler.	
resizable	(Boolean) Unless specified as `false`, the dialog box is resizable in all directions.	✓
resizeStart	(Function) Specifies a function to be established on the dialog box as an event handler for `resizeStart` events. See the description of the dialog events in table 11.17 for details on the information passed to this handler.	
resizeStop	(Function) Specifies a function to be established on the dialog box as an event handler for `resizeStop` events. See the description of the dialog events in table 11.17 for details on the information passed to this handler.	
show	(String) The effect to be used when the dialog box is being opened. By default, no effect is used.	✓
stack	(Boolean) Unless specified as `false`, the dialog box will move to the top of any other dialog boxes when it gains focus.	
title	(String) Specifies the text to appear in the title bar of the dialog box chrome. By default, the `title` attribute of the dialog box element will be used as the title.	✓

Table 11.16 Options for the jQuery UI dialogs *(continued)*

Option	Description	In Lab?
`width`	(Number) The width of the dialog box in pixels. If omitted, a default of 300 pixels is used.	✓
`zIndex`	(Number) The initial z-index for the dialog box, overriding the default value of `1000`.	

Most of these options are easy to see in action using the Dialogs Lab, but make sure you run through the differences between modal and modeless dialog boxes.

In the console of the Lab, the various events that are triggered (as the dialog box is interacted with) are displayed in the order that they're received. Let's examine the possible events.

11.8.2 Dialog events

As the user manipulates the dialog boxes we create, various custom events are triggered that let us get our hooks into the page. This gives us the opportunity to perform actions at pertinent times during the life of the dialog box, or even to affect the operation of the dialog box.

The events triggered during dialog box interactions are shown in table 11.17. Each of these handlers is passed the event instance and a custom object. The function context, as well as the event target, is set to the dialog box element.

The custom object passed to the handler depends upon the event type:

- For the drag, dragStart, and dragStop events, the custom object contains properties `offset` and `position`, which in turn contain `left` and `top` properties that identify the position of the dialog box relative to the page or its offset parent respectively.
- For the resize, resizeStart, and resizeStop events, the custom object contains the properties `originalPosition`, `originalSize`, `position`, and `size`. The position properties are objects that contain the expected `left` and `top` properties, while the size properties contain `height` and `width` properties.
- For all other event types, the custom object has no properties.

Table 11.17 Events for jQuery UI dialogs

Event	Option	Description
`dialogbeforeClose`	`beforeClose`	Triggered when the dialog box is about to close. Returning `false` prevents the dialog box from closing—handy for dialog boxes with forms that fail validation.
`dialogclose`	`close`	Triggered after a dialog box has closed.

Table 11.17   Events for jQuery UI dialogs *(continued)*

Event	Option	Description
drag	drag	Triggered repeatedly as a dialog box is moved about during a drag.
dragStart	dragStart	Triggered when a repositioning of the dialog box commences by dragging its title bar.
dragStop	dragStop	Triggered when a drag operation terminates.
dialogfocus	focus	Triggered when the dialog box gains focus.
dialogopen	open	Triggered when the dialog box is opened.
resize	resize	Triggered repeatedly as a dialog box is resized.
resizeStart	resizeStart	Triggered when a resize of the dialog box commences.
resizeStop	resizeStop	Triggered when a resize of the dialog box terminates.

Before we can see a few clever uses of these events, let's examine the class names that jQuery places on the elements that participate in the creation of our dialog boxes.

11.8.3 *Dialog box class names*

As with the other widgets, jQuery UI marks up the elements that go into the structure of the dialog box widget with class names that help us to find the elements, as well as to style them via CSS.

In the case of dialog boxes, the added class names are as follows:

- ui-dialog—Added to the <div> element created to contain the entire widget, including the content and the chrome.
- ui-dialog-titlebar—Added to the <div> element created to house the title and close icon.
- ui-dialog-title—Added to the <span> element contained within the title bar to wrap the title text.
- ui-dialog-titlebar-close—Added to the <a> tag used to encompass the 'x' icon within the title bar.
- ui-dialog-content—Added to the dialog box content element (the element wrapped during the call to dialog()).

It's important to remember that the element passed to the event handlers is the dialog box content element (the one marked with ui-dialog-content), not the generated outer container created to house the widget.

Now let's look at a few ways to specify content that's not already on the page.

11.8.4 *Some dialog box tricks*

Generally, dialog boxes are created from <div> elements that are included in the page markup. jQuery UI takes that content, removes it from the DOM, creates elements that serve as the dialog box chrome, and sets the original elements as the content of the chrome.

But what if we wanted to load the content dynamically upon dialogopen via Ajax? That's actually surprisingly easy with code such as this:

```
$('<div>').dialog({
  open: function(){ $(this).load('/url/to/resource'); },
  title: 'A dynamically loaded dialog'
});
```

In this code, we create a new <div> element on the fly, and turn it into a dialog box just as if it were an existing element. The options specify its title, and a callback for dialogopen events that loads the content element (set as the function context) using the load() method.

In the scenarios we've seen so far, regardless of whether the content already existed on the page or was loaded via Ajax, the content exists within the DOM of the current page. What if we want the dialog box body to be its own page?

Although it's convenient to have the dialog box content be part of the same DOM as its parent, if the dialog box content and the page content need to interact in any way, we might want the dialog box content to be a separate page unto itself. The most common reason may be because the content needs its own styles and scripts that we don't want to include in every parent page in which we plan to use the dialog box.

How could we accomplish this? Is there support in HTML for using a separate page as a part of another page? Of course ... the <iframe> element!

Consider this:

```
$('<iframe src="content.html" id="testDialog">').dialog({
  title: 'iframe dialog',
  buttons: {
    Dismiss: function(){ $(this).dialog('close'); }
  }
});
```

Here we dynamically create an <iframe> element, specifying its source and an id, and make it into a dialog box. The options we pass to the dialog() method give the dialog box its title and a Dismiss button that closes the dialog box. Is this awesome or what?

But our self-admiration is short-lived when we display the dialog box and see a problem. The scrollbar for the <iframe> is clipped by the dialog chrome, as shown in the left half of figure 11.16. What we want, of course, is for the dialog box to appear as shown in the right half of the figure.

Because the <iframe> appears a bit too wide, we could attempt to narrow it with a CSS rule, but to our chagrin, we find that doesn't work. A little digging reveals that a CSS style of width: auto is placed right on the <iframe> element by the dialog() method, defeating any attempt to style the <iframe> indirectly.

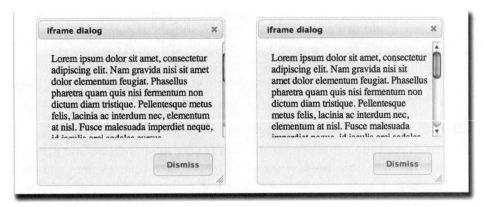

Figure 11.16 Our victory dance was cut short by the clipping of the scroll bar shown at left—how can we fix it as shown at right?

But that's OK. We'll just use a bigger sledgehammer. Let's add the following option to the `dialog()` call:

```
open: function(){
  $(this).css('width','95%');
}
```

This overrides the style placed on the `<iframe>` when the dialog box is opened.

Bear in mind that this approach isn't without its pitfalls. For example, any buttons are created in the parent page, and interaction between the buttons and the page loaded into the `<iframe>` will need to communicate across the two windows.

The source for this example can be found in file chapter11/dialogs/iframe.dialog.html.

11.9 *Summary*

Wow. This was a long chapter, but we learned a great deal from it.

We saw how jQuery UI builds upon the interactions and effects that it provides, and which we explored in the previous chapters, to allow us to create various widgets that help us present intuitive and easy-to-use interfaces to our users.

We learned about the button widget that augments the look and feel of conventional HTML buttons so that they play well in the jQuery UI sandbox.

Widgets that allow our users to enter data types that have traditionally been fraught with problems, namely numeric and date data, are provided in the guise of sliders and datepickers. Autocomplete widgets round out the data entry widgets, letting users quickly filter through large sets of data.

Progress bars give us the ability to communicate completion percentage status to our users in a graphical, easy-to-understand display.

And finally, we saw three widgets that let us organize our content in varying fashions: tabs, the accordion, and the dialog box.

Added to our toolbox, these widgets give us a wider range of possibilities for our interfaces. But that's just the official set of widgets provided by jQuery UI. As we've seen firsthand, jQuery is designed to extend easily, and the jQuery community hasn't been sitting on its hands. Hundreds, if not many thousands, of other plugin controls exist, just waiting for us to discover them. A good place to start is http://plugins.jquery.com/.

11.10 *The end?*

Hardly! Even though we've presented the entire API for jQuery and jQuery UI within the confines of this book, it would have been impossible to show you all the many ways that these broad APIs can be used on our pages. The examples we presented were chosen specifically to lead you down the path of discovering how you can use jQuery to solve the problems that you encounter on a day-to-day basis on your web application pages.

jQuery is a living project. Astoundingly so! Heck, it was quite a chore for your authors to keep up with the rapid developments in the libraries over the course of writing this book. The core library is constantly evolving into a more useful resource, and more and more plugins are appearing on practically a daily basis. And the pace of development for jQuery UI is practically exhausting.

We urge you to keep track of the developments in the jQuery community and sincerely hope that this book has been a great help in starting you on the path to writing better web applications in less time and with less code than you might have ever believed possible.

We wish you health and happiness, and may all your bugs be easily solvable!

appendix:
JavaScript that
you need to know
but might not!

This appendix covers

- Which JavaScript concepts are important for effectively using jQuery
- JavaScript `Object` basics
- How functions are *first-class objects*
- Determining (and controlling) what `this` means
- What's a closure?

One of the great benefits that jQuery brings to our web applications is the ability to implement a great deal of scripting-enabled behavior without having to write a whole lot of script ourselves. jQuery handles the nuts-and-bolts details so that we can concentrate on the job of making our applications do what they need to do!

For the first few chapters in this book, we only needed rudimentary JavaScript skills to code and understand the examples. In the chapters on advanced topics such as event handling, animations, and Ajax, we must understand a handful of fundamental JavaScript concepts to make effective use of the jQuery library. You may find that a lot of things that you, perhaps, took for granted in JavaScript (or took on blind faith) will start to make more sense.

We're not going to go into an exhaustive study of all JavaScript concepts here—that's not the purpose of this book. The purpose of this book is to get us up and running with effective jQuery in the shortest time possible. To that end, this appendix will concentrate on the fundamental concepts that we need to make the most effective use of jQuery in our web applications.

The most important of these concepts is that functions are *first-class objects* in JavaScript, which is a result of the way JavaScript defines and deals with functions. What do we mean by that? In order to understand what it means for a function to be an object, let alone a *first-class* one, we must first make sure that we understand what a JavaScript object is all about. So let's dive right in.

A.1   *JavaScript Object fundamentals*

The majority of object-oriented (OO) languages define a fundamental `Object` type of some kind from which all other objects are derived. In JavaScript, the fundamental `Object` serves as the basis for all other objects, but that's where the comparison stops. At its basic level, the JavaScript `Object` has little in common with the fundamental object defined by most other OO languages.

At first glance, a JavaScript `Object` may seem like a boring and mundane item. Once created, it holds no data and exposes little in the way of semantics. But those limited semantics *do* give it a great deal of potential.

Let's see how.

A.1.1   *How objects come to be*

A new object comes into existence via the `new` operator paired with the `Object` constructor. Creating an object is as easy as this:

```
var shinyAndNew = new Object();
```

It could be even easier (as we'll see shortly), but this will do for now.

But what can we *do* with this new object? It seemingly contains nothing: no information, no complex semantics, nothing. Our brand-new, shiny object doesn't get interesting until we start adding things to it—things known as *properties*.

A.1.2   *Properties of objects*

Like their server-side counterparts, JavaScript objects can contain data and possess methods (well ... sort of, but that's getting ahead of ourselves). Unlike those server-side brethren, these elements aren't predeclared for an object; we create them dynamically as needed.

Take a look at the following code fragment:

```
var ride = new Object();
ride.make = 'Yamaha';
ride.model = 'V-Star Silverado 1100';
ride.year = 2005;
ride.purchased = new Date(2005,3,12);
```

Here we create a new `Object` instance and assign it to a variable named `ride`. We then populate this variable with a number of *properties* of different types: two strings, a number, and an instance of the `Date` type.

We don't need to declare these properties prior to assigning them; they come into being merely by the act of our assigning a value to them. That's mighty powerful juju that gives us a great deal of flexibility. But before we get too giddy, let's remember that flexibility always comes with a price!

For example, let's say that in subsequent code on our scripted HTML page, we want to change the value of the purchase date:

```
ride.purchased = new Date(2005,2,1);
```

No problem ... unless we make an inadvertent typo such as

```
ride.purcahsed = new Date(2005,2,1);
```

There's no compiler to warn us that we've made a mistake; a new property named `purcahsed` is cheerfully created on our behalf, leaving us to wonder later why the new date didn't *take* when we reference the correctly spelled property.

With great power comes great responsibility (where have we heard that before?), so type carefully!

> **NOTE** JavaScript debuggers, like Firebug for Firefox, can be lifesavers when dealing with these issues. Because typos such as these frequently result in no JavaScript errors, relying on JavaScript consoles or error dialog boxes is usually less than effective.

From this example, we've learned that an instance of the JavaScript `Object`, which we'll simply refer to as an *object* from here forward, is a collection of *properties*, each of which consists of a *name* and a *value*. The name of a property is a string, and the value can be any JavaScript object, be it a `Number`, `String`, `Date`, `Array`, basic `Object`, or any other JavaScript object type (including, as we shall see, functions).

This means the primary purpose of an `Object` instance is to serve as a container for a named collection of other objects. This may remind you of concepts in other languages: a Java map for example, or dictionaries or hashes in other languages.

Properties aren't limited to types such as `String` or `Number`. An object property can be another `Object` instance, which in turn has its own set of properties, which can in turn be objects with their own properties, and so on, to any depth that makes sense for the data that we are trying to model.

Let's say that we add a new property to our `ride` instance that identifies the owner of the vehicle. This property is another JavaScript object that contains properties such as the name and occupation of the owner:

```
var owner = new Object();
owner.name = 'Spike Spiegel';
owner.occupation = 'bounty hunter';
ride.owner = owner;
```

To access the nested property, we write this:

```
var ownerName = ride.owner.name;
```

There are no limits to the nesting levels we can employ (except the limits of good sense). When finished—up to this point—our object hierarchy is as shown in figure A.1.

Note how each value in the figure is a distinct instance of a JavaScript type.

NOTE   There's no need for all the intermediary variables (such as `owner`) that we've created for illustrative purposes in these code fragments. In a short while, we'll see more efficient and compact ways to declare objects and their properties.

Up to this point, we've referenced properties of an object by using the dot (period character) operator. But, as it turns out, that's a synonym for a more general operator for performing property referencing.

What if, for example, we have a property named `color.scheme`? Do you notice the period in the middle of the name? It throws a monkey wrench into the works because the JavaScript interpreter will try to look up `scheme` as a nested property of `color`.

"Well, just don't do that!" you say. But what about space characters? What about other characters that could be mistaken for delimiters rather than part of a name?

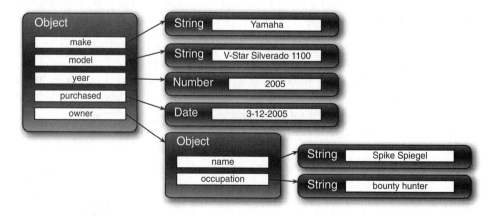

Figure A.1   Our object hierarchy shows that `Objects` are containers for named references to other `Objects` or JavaScript built-in types.

And most importantly, what if we don't even know what the property name is, but we have it as a value in another variable or as the result of an expression evaluation?

For all these cases, the dot operator is inadequate, and we must use the more general notation for accessing properties. The format of the general property reference operator is

```
object[propertyNameExpression]
```

where `propertyNameExpression` is a JavaScript expression whose evaluation as a string forms the name of the property to be referenced. For example, all three of the following references are equivalent:

```
ride.make
ride['make']
ride['m'+'a'+'k'+'e']
```

So is this reference:

```
var p = 'make';
ride[p];
```

Using the general reference operator is the only way to reference properties whose names don't form valid JavaScript identifiers, such as this,

```
ride["a property name that's rather odd!"]
```

which contains characters not legal for JavaScript identifiers, or whose names are the values of other variables.

Building up objects by creating new instances with the new operator and assigning each property using separate assignment statements can be a tedious affair. In the next section, we'll look at a more compact and easy-to-read notation for declaring objects and their properties.

A.1.3 *Object literals*

In the previous section, we created an object that modeled some of the properties of a motorcycle, assigning it to a variable named `ride`. To do so, we used two new operations, an intermediary variable named `owner`, and a bunch of assignment statements. This is tedious—as well as wordy and error-prone—and it is difficult for us to visually grasp the structure of the object during a quick inspection of the code.

Luckily, we can use a notation that's more compact and easier to visually scan. Consider the following statement:

```
var ride = {
  make: 'Yamaha',
  model: 'V-Star Silverado 1100',
  year: 2005,
  purchased: new Date(2005,3,12),
  owner: {
    name: 'Spike Spiegel',
    occupation: 'bounty hunter'
  }
};
```

Using an *object literal*, this fragment creates the same `ride` object that we built up with assignment statements in the previous section.

This notation, which has come to be termed JSON (JavaScript Object Notation[1]), is much preferred by most page authors over the multiple-assignment means of object building. Its structure is simple; an object is denoted by a matching pair of braces, within which properties are listed delimited by commas. Each property is denoted by listing its name and value separated by a colon character.

NOTE   Technically, JSON has no way to express date values, primarily because JavaScript itself lacks any kind of date literal. When used in script, the `Date` constructor is usually employed as shown in the previous example. When used as an interchange format, dates are frequently expressed either as a string containing the ISO 8601 format or a number expressing the date as the millisecond value returned by `Date.getTime()`.

Note also that when using JSON as an interchange format, there are some stricter rules that need to be followed, such as quoting property names. See http://www.json.org or RFC 4627 (http://www.ietf.org/rfc/rfc4627.txt) for more details.

As we can see by the declaration of the `owner` property, object declarations can be nested.

By the way, we can also express arrays in JSON by placing the comma-delimited list of elements within square brackets, as in the following:

```
var someValues = [2,3,5,7,11,13,17,19,23,29,31,37];
```

As we've seen in the examples presented in this section, object references are frequently stored in variables or in properties of other objects. Let's take a look at a special case of the latter scenario.

A.1.4   *Objects as window properties*

Up to this point, we've seen two ways to store a reference to a JavaScript object: variables and properties. These two means of storing references use differing notation, as shown in the following snippet:

```
var aVariable =
  'Before I teamed up with you, I led quite a normal life.';

someObject.aProperty =
  'You move that line as you see fit for yourself.';
```

These two statements each assign a `String` instance (created via literals) to something: a variable in the first statement, and an object property in the second. (Kudos to you if you can identify the source of the obscure quotes; no cheating with Google! There was a clue earlier in this appendix.)

---

[1] For more information, you can visit http://www.json.org/.

But are these statements *really* performing different operations? As it turns out, they're not!

When the `var` keyword is used at the top level, outside the body of any containing function, it's only a programmer-friendly notation for referencing a property of the predefined JavaScript `window` object. Any reference made in top-level scope is implicitly made on the `window` instance. This means that all of the following statements, if made at the top level (that is, outside the scope of a function), are equivalent:

```
var foo = bar;
```

and

```
window.foo = bar;
```

and

```
foo = bar;
```

Regardless of which notation is used, a `window` property named `foo` is created (if it's not already in existence) and assigned the value of `bar`. Also, note that because `bar` is unqualified, it's assumed to be a property on `window`.

It probably won't get us into conceptual trouble to think of top-level scope as *window* scope because any unqualified references *at the top level* are assumed to be `window` properties. The scoping rules get more complex when we delve deeper into the bodies of functions—much more complex, in fact—but we'll be addressing that soon enough.

That pretty much covers things for our overview of the JavaScript `Object`. These are the important concepts to take away from this discussion:

- A JavaScript object is an unordered collection of properties.
- Properties consist of a name and a value.
- Objects can be declared using object literals.
- Top-level *variables* are properties of `window`.

Now, let's discuss what we meant when we referred to JavaScript functions as *first-class objects*.

A.2 *Functions as first-class citizens*

In many traditional OO languages, objects can contain data and they can possess methods. In these languages, the data and methods are usually distinct concepts; JavaScript walks a different path.

Functions in JavaScript are considered objects like any of the other object types that are defined in JavaScript, such as `Strings`, `Numbers`, or `Dates`. Like other objects, functions are defined by a JavaScript constructor—in this case `Function`—and they can be

- Assigned to variables
- Assigned as a property of an object

- Passed as a parameter
- Returned as a function result
- Created using literals

Because functions are treated in the same way as other objects in the language, we say that functions are *first-class objects.*

But you might be thinking to yourself that functions are fundamentally different from other object types like `String` or `Number` because they possess not only a value (in the case of a `Function` instance, its body) but also a *name*.

Well, not so fast!

A.2.1 *What's in a name?*

A large percentage of JavaScript programmers operate under a false assumption that functions are named entities. Not so. If you're one of these programmers, you've been fooled by a Jedi mind trick. As with other instances of objects—be they `Strings`, `Dates`, or `Numbers`—functions are referenced *only* when they are assigned to variables, properties, or parameters.

Let's consider objects of type `Number`. We frequently express instances of `Number` by their literal notation, such as `213`. The statement

```
213;
```

is perfectly valid, but it is also perfectly useless. The `Number` instance isn't all that useful unless it has been assigned to a property or a variable, or bound to a parameter name. Otherwise, we have no way to reference the disembodied instance.

The same applies to instances of `Function` objects.

"But, but, but ...," you might be saying, "what about the following code?"

```
function doSomethingWonderful() {
  alert('does something wonderful');
}
```

"Doesn't that create a function *named* doSomethingWonderful?"

No, it doesn't. Although that notation may seem familiar and is ubiquitously used to create *top-level* functions, it's the same syntactic sugar used by `var` to create `window` properties. The `function` keyword automatically creates a `Function` instance and assigns it to a `window` property created using the function "name" (what we referred to earlier as a *Jedi mind trick*), as in the following:

```
doSomethingWonderful = function() {
  alert('does something wonderful');
}
```

If that looks weird to you, consider another statement using the exact same format, except this time using a `Number` literal:

```
aWonderfulNumber = 213;
```

There's nothing strange about that, and the statement assigning a function to a top-level variable (the `window` property) is no different; a function literal is used to create

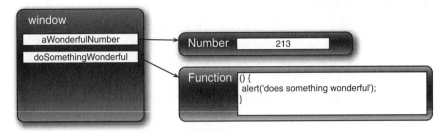

Figure A.2 A `Function` instance is a nameless object like the `Number` 213 or any other JavaScript value. It's named only by references that are made to it.

an instance of `Function` and then is assigned to the variable `doSomethingWonderful` in the same way that our `Number` literal 213 was used to assign a `Number` instance to the variable `aWonderfulNumber`.

If you've never seen the syntax for a *function literal*, it might seem odd. It's composed of the keyword `function`, followed by its parameter list enclosed in parentheses, then followed by the function body.

When we declare a top-level named function, a `Function` instance is created and *assigned* to a property of `window` that's automatically created using the so-called function name. The `Function` instance itself no more has a name than a `Number` literal or a `String` literal. Figure A.2 illustrates this concept.

Remember that when a top-level variable is created in an HTML page, the variable is created as a property of the `window` instance. Therefore, the following statements are all equivalent:

```
function hello(){ alert('Hi there!'); }
hello = function(){ alert('Hi there!'); }
window.hello = function(){ alert('Hi there!'); }
```

Although this may seem like syntactic juggling, it's important to understanding that `Function` instances are *values* that can be assigned to variables, properties, or parameters just like instances of other object types. And like those other object types, nameless disembodied instances aren't of any use unless they're assigned to a variable, property, or parameter through which they can be referenced.

We've seen examples of assigning functions to variables and properties, but what about passing functions as parameters? Let's take a look at why and how we do that.

Gecko browsers and function names

Browsers based on the Gecko layout engine, such as Firefox and Camino, store the name of functions defined using the top-level syntax in a nonstandard property of the function instance named `name`. Although this may not be of much use to the general development public, particularly considering its confinement to Gecko-based browsers, it's of great value to writers of browser plugins and debuggers.

A.2.2 Functions as callbacks

Top-level functions are all well and good when our code follows a nice and orderly synchronous flow, but the nature of HTML pages—once loaded—is far from synchronous. Whether we're handling events, instituting timers, or making Ajax requests, the nature of the code in a web page is asynchronous. And one of the most prevalent concepts in asynchronous programming is the notion of a *callback* function.

Let's take the example of a timer. We can cause a timer to fire—let's say in five seconds—by passing the appropriate duration value to the `window.setTimeout()` method. But how does that method let us know when the timer has expired so that we can do whatever it is that we're waiting around for? It does so by invoking a function that *we* supply.

Let's consider the following code:

```
function hello() { alert('Hi there!'); }

setTimeout(hello,5000);
```

We declare a function named `hello` and set a timer to fire in 5 seconds, expressed as 5000 milliseconds by the second parameter. In the first parameter to the `setTimeout()` method, we pass a function reference. Passing a function as a parameter is no different than passing any other value—just as we passed a `Number` in the second parameter.

When the timer expires, the `hello` function is called. Because the `setTimeout()` method makes a call *back* to a function in our own code, that function is termed a *callback* function.

This code example would be considered naive by most advanced JavaScript coders because the creation of the `hello` name is unnecessary. Unless the function is to be called elsewhere in the page, there's no need to create the `window` property `hello` to momentarily store the `Function` instance to pass it as the callback parameter.

The more elegant way to code this fragment is

```
setTimeout(function() { alert('Hi there!'); },5000);
```

in which we express the function literal directly in the parameter list, and no needless name is generated. This is an idiom that we'll often see used in jQuery code when there is no need for a function instance to be assigned to a top-level property.

The functions we've created in the examples so far are either top-level functions (which we know are top-level `window` properties) or assigned to parameters in a function call. We can also assign `Function` instances to properties of objects, and that's where things get really interesting. Read on ...

A.2.3 What's this all about?

OO languages automatically provide a means to reference the current instance of an object from within a method. In languages like Java and C++, a variable named `this` points to that current instance. In JavaScript, a similar concept exists and even uses the same `this` keyword, which also provides access to an object associated with a function. But OO programmers beware! The JavaScript implementation of this differs from its OO counterparts in subtle but significant ways.

In class-based OO languages, the this pointer generally references the instance of the class for which the method has been declared. In JavaScript, where functions are first-class objects that aren't declared as part of anything, the object referenced by this—termed the *function context*—is determined not by how the function is declared but by how it's *invoked*.

This means that the *same* function can have *different* contexts depending on how it's called. That may seem freaky at first, but it can be quite useful.

In the default case, the context (this) of an invocation of the function is the object whose property contains the reference used to invoke the function. Let's look back to our motorcycle example for a demonstration, amending the object creation as follows (additions highlighted in bold):

```
var ride = {
  make: 'Yamaha',
  model: 'V-Star Silverado 1100',
  year: 2005,
  purchased: new Date(2005,3,12),
  owner: {name: 'Spike Spiegel',occupation: 'bounty hunter'},
  whatAmI: function() {
    return this.year+' '+this.make+' '+this.model;
  }
};
```

To our original example code, we add a property named whatAmI that references a Function instance. Our new object hierarchy, with the Function instance assigned to the property named whatAmI, is shown in figure A.3.

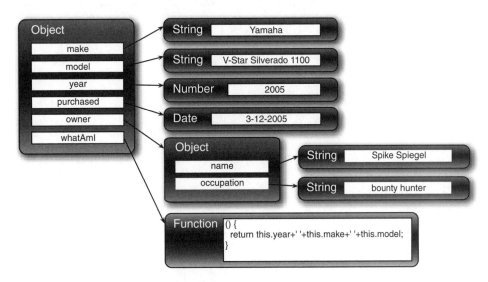

Figure A.3 This model clearly shows that the function isn't part of the Object but is only referenced from the Object property named whatAmI.

When the function is invoked through the property reference, like this,

```
var bike = ride.whatAmI();
```

the function context (the `this` reference) is set to the object instance pointed to by `ride`. As a result, the variable `bike` gets set to the string `2005 Yamaha V-Star Silverado 1100` because the function picks up the properties of the object through which it was invoked via `this`.

The same is true of top-level functions. Remember that top-level functions are properties of `window`, so their function context, when called *as* top-level functions, is the `window` object.

Although that may be the usual and implicit behavior, JavaScript gives us the means to explicitly control what's used as the function context. We can set the function context to whatever we want by invoking a function via the `Function` methods `call()` or `apply()`.

Yes, as first-class objects, even functions have methods as defined by the `Function` constructor.

The `call()` method invokes the function specifying, as its first parameter, the object to serve as the function context, while the remainder of the parameters become the parameters of the called function—the second parameter to `call()` becomes the first argument of the called function, and so on. The `apply()` method works in a similar fashion except that its second parameter is expected to be an array of objects that become the arguments to the called function.

Confused? It's time for a more comprehensive example. Consider the code of listing A.1 (found in the downloadable code as appendix/function.context.html).

Listing A.1 The function context value depends on how the function is invoked

```html
<html>
  <head>
    <title>Function Context Example</title>
    <script>
      var o1 = {handle:'o1'};
      var o2 = {handle:'o2'};                      ❶
      var o3 = {handle:'o3'};
      window.handle = 'window';

      function whoAmI() {
        return this.handle;                        ❷
      }

      o1.identifyMe = whoAmI;                    ◁—❸

      alert(whoAmI());                  ◁—❹
      alert(o1.identifyMe());              ◁—❺
      alert(whoAmI.call(o2));                ◁—❻
      alert(whoAmI.apply(o3));                  ◁—❼

    </script>
  </head>
```

```
<body>
</body>
</html>
```

In this example, we define three simple objects, each with a `handle` property that makes it easy to identify the object given a reference ❶. We also add a `handle` property to the `window` instance so that it's also readily identifiable.

We then define a top-level function that returns the value of the `handle` property for whatever object serves as its function context ❷ and assign the *same* function instance to a property of object `o1` named `identifyMe` ❸. We can say that this creates a method on `o1` named `identifyMe`, although it's important to note that the function is declared independently of the object.

Finally, we issue four alerts, each of which uses a different mechanism to invoke the same function instance. When loaded into a browser, the sequence of four alerts is as shown in figure A.4.

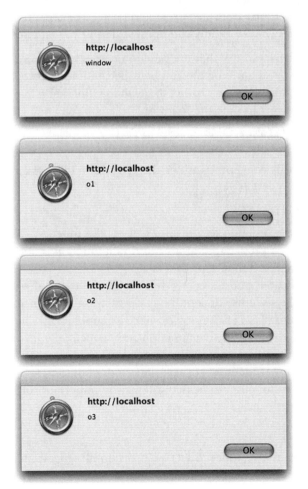

Figure A.4 The object serving as the function context changes with the manner in which the function is called.

This sequence of alerts illustrates the following:

- When the function is called directly as a top-level function, the function context is the `window` instance ❹.
- When called as a property of an object (o1 in this case), the object becomes the function context of the function invocation ❺. We could say that the function acts as a *method* for that object—as in OO languages. But take care not to get too blasé about this analogy. You can be led astray if you're not careful, as the remainder of this example's results will show.
- Employing the `call()` method of `Function` causes the function context to be set to whatever object is passed as the first parameter to `call()`—in this case, o2 ❻. In this example, the function acts like a method to o2, even though it has no association whatsoever—even as a property—with o2.
- As with `call()`, using the `apply()` method of `Function` sets the function context to whatever object is passed as the first parameter ❼. The difference between these two methods only becomes significant when parameters are passed to the function (which we didn't do in this example for simplicity).

This example page clearly demonstrates that the function context is determined on a per invocation basis and that a single function can be called with any object acting as its context. As a result, it's probably never correct to say that a function *is* a method of an object. It's much more correct to state the following:

> *A function* f *acts as a method of object* o *when* o *serves as the function context of the invocation of* f.

As a further illustration of this concept, consider the effect of adding the following statement to our example:

```
alert(o1.identifyMe.call(o3));
```

Even though we reference the function as a property of o1, the function context for this invocation is o3, further emphasizing that it's not how a function is declared but how it's invoked that determines its function context.

When using jQuery commands and functions that employ callbacks, this proves to be an important concept. We saw this concept in action early on (even if you didn't realize it at the time) in section 2.3.3 of chapter 2, where we supplied a callback function to the `filter()` method of `$` and that function was sequentially invoked with each element of the wrapped set serving as its function context in turn.

Now that we understand how functions can act as methods of objects, let's turn our attention to another advanced function topic that will play an important role in effective usage of jQuery: closures.

A.2.4   *Closures*

To page authors coming from a traditional OO or procedural programming background, *closures* are often an odd concept to grasp, whereas to those with a functional programming background, they're a familiar and cozy concept. For the uninitiated, let's answer the question: What are closures?

Stated as simply as possible, a *closure* is a Function instance coupled with the local variables from its environment that are necessary for its execution.

When a function is declared, it has the ability to reference any variables that are in its scope at the point of declaration. This is expected and should be no surprise to any developer from any background. But, with closures, these variables are carried along with the function *even after* the point of declaration has gone out of scope, *closing* the declaration.

The ability for callback functions to reference the local variables in effect when they were declared is an essential tool for writing effective JavaScript. Using a timer once again, let's look at the illustrative example in listing A.2 (the file appendixA/closure.html).

Listing A.2   Closures allow access to the scope of a function's declaration

```html
<html>
  <head>
    <title>Closure Example</title>
    <script type="text/javascript"
            src="../scripts/jquery-1.2.js"></script>
    <script>
      $(function(){
        var local = 1;                                    ←❶
        window.setInterval(function(){                    ←❷
          $('#display')
            .append('<div>At '+new Date()+' local='+local+'</div>');
          local++;                          ←
        },3000);                            ❸
      });
    </script>
  </head>
  <body>
    <div id="display"></div>                              ←❹
  </body>
</html>
```

In this example, we define a ready handler that fires after the DOM loads. In this handler, we declare a local variable named local ❶ and assign it a numeric value of 1. We then use the window.setInterval() method to establish a timer that will fire every 3 seconds ❷. As the callback for the timer, we specify an inline function that references the local variable and shows the current time and the value of local, by writing a <div> element into an element named display that's defined in the page body ❹. As part of the callback, the local variable's value is also incremented ❸.

Prior to running this example, if we were unfamiliar with closures, we might look at this code and see some problems. We might surmise that, because the callback will fire off three seconds after the page is loaded (long after the ready handler has finished executing), the value of local is undefined during the execution of the callback

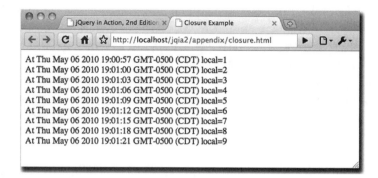

At Thu May 06 2010 19:00:57 GMT-0500 (CDT) local=1
At Thu May 06 2010 19:01:00 GMT-0500 (CDT) local=2
At Thu May 06 2010 19:01:03 GMT-0500 (CDT) local=3
At Thu May 06 2010 19:01:06 GMT-0500 (CDT) local=4
At Thu May 06 2010 19:01:09 GMT-0500 (CDT) local=5
At Thu May 06 2010 19:01:12 GMT-0500 (CDT) local=6
At Thu May 06 2010 19:01:15 GMT-0500 (CDT) local=7
At Thu May 06 2010 19:01:18 GMT-0500 (CDT) local=8
At Thu May 06 2010 19:01:21 GMT-0500 (CDT) local=9

Figure A.5   Closures allow callbacks to access their environment even if that environment has gone out of scope.

function. After all, the block in which `local` is declared goes out of scope when the ready handler finishes, right?

But on loading the page and letting it run for a short time, we see the display shown in figure A.5.

It works! But how?

Although it *is* true that the block in which `local` is declared goes out of scope when the ready handler exits, the closure created by the declaration of the function, which includes `local`, stays in scope for the lifetime of the function.

> **NOTE** You might have noted that the closure, as with all closures in JavaScript, was created implicitly without the need for explicit syntax as is required in some other languages that support closures. This is a double-edged sword that makes it easy to create closures (whether you intend to or not!) but it can make them difficult to spot in the code.
>
> Unintended closures can have unintended consequences. For example, circular references can lead to memory leaks. A classic example of this is the creation of DOM elements that refer back to closure variables, preventing those variables from being reclaimed.

Another important feature of closures is that a function context is never included as part of the closure. For example, the following code won't execute as we might expect:

```
...
this.id = 'someID';
$('*').each(function(){
   alert(this.id);
});
```

Remember that each function invocation has its own function context so that, in the preceding code, the function context within the callback function passed to `each()` is an element from the jQuery wrapped set, not the property of the outer function set to `'someID'`. Each invocation of the callback function displays an alert box showing the `id` of each element in the wrapped set in turn.

When access to the object serving as the function context in the outer function is needed, we can employ a common idiom to create a copy of the this reference in a local variable that *will* be included in the closure. Consider the following change to our example:

```
this.id = 'someID';
var outer = this;
$('*').each(function(){
    alert(outer.id);
});
```

The local variable outer, which is assigned a reference to the outer function's function context, becomes part of the closure and can be accessed in the callback function. The changed code now displays an alert showing the string 'someID' as many times as there are elements in the wrapped set.

We'll find closures indispensable when creating elegant code using jQuery commands that utilize asynchronous callbacks, which is particularly true in the areas of Ajax requests and event handling.

A.3 *Summary*

JavaScript is a language that's widely used across the web, but it's often not *deeply* used by many of the page authors writing it. In this appendix, we introduced some of the deeper aspects of the language that we must understand to use jQuery effectively on our pages.

We saw that a JavaScript Object primarily exists to be a *container* for other objects. If you have an OO background, thinking of an Object instance as an unordered collection of name/value pairs may be a far cry from what you think of as an *object*, but it's an important concept to grasp when writing JavaScript of even moderate complexity.

Functions in JavaScript are *first-class citizens* that can be declared and referenced in a manner similar to the other object types. We can declare them using literal notation, store them in variables and object properties, and even pass them to other functions as parameters to serve as callback functions.

The term *function context* describes the object that's referenced by the this pointer during the invocation of a function. Although a function can be made to act like a method of an object by setting the object as the function context, functions aren't declared as methods of any single object. The manner of invocation (possibly explicitly controlled by the caller) determines the function context of the invocation.

Finally, we saw how a function declaration and its environment form a *closure* allowing the function, when later invoked, to access those local variables that become part of the closure.

With these concepts firmly under our belts, we're ready to face the challenges that confront us when writing effective JavaScript using jQuery on our pages.

index

433

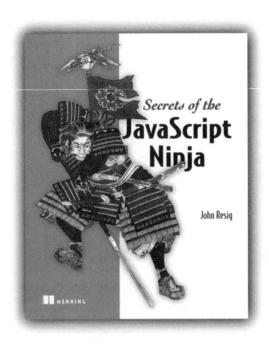

MORE TITLES FROM MANNING

Website Owner's Manual
The Secret to Successful Websites
by Paul Boag

ISBN: 978-1-933988-69-6
296 pages
$44.99
November 2009

The Quick Python Book
Revised edition of The Quick Python Book
by Daryl K. Harms
and Kenneth M. McDonald

by Vernon L. Ceder

ISBN: 978-1-935182-20-7
360 pages
$39.99
January 2010

For ordering information go to www.manning.com

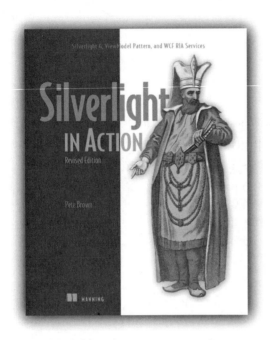

Silverlight in Action, Revised Edition

by Pete Brown

ISBN: 978-1-935182-37-5
425 pages
$44.99
July 2010

PHP in Action

by Dagfinn Reiersøl with Marcus Baker
and Chris Shiflett

ISBN: 978-1-932394-75-7
552 pages
$44.99
June 2007

For ordering information go to www.manning.com

MORE TITLES FROM MANNING

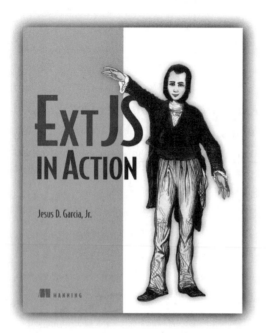

ExtJS in Action

by Jesus D. Garcia

ISBN: 978-1-935182-11-5
425 pages
$44.99
July 2010

Azure in Action

by Chris Hay and Brian H. Prince

ISBN: 978-1-935182-48-1
425 pages
$44.99
August 2010

For ordering information go to www.manning.com